CROATIA:

THE MAKING OF A NATION

VLADOVICH INTERNATIONAL PUBLISHING

P. O. BOX 75465, OKLAHOMA CITY, OK (USA) 73147-0465

Library of Congress Catalog Card Number: 96-60531

ISBN   0-9623753-2-2

CROATIA: THE MAKING OF A NATION

(Author: Vladovich, Simon)

PRINTED IN THE UNITED STATES OF AMERICA

i

CONTENTS

Acknowledgment iii

Preface iv

Chapter 1   History 1
              Pre-Croat History 1
              Early-Croat History 7

Chapter 2   Struggle For Freedom, 1900-1918 25
              First Balkan War, 1912-1913 28
              Second Balkan War, 1913 29
              First World War, 1914-1918 30
              Corfu Declaration 34

Chapter 3   Tragic Experiment, 1919-1940 40
              Map-Kingdom of Serbs, Croats and Slovenes, 1921. 43
              Map-Banovine of the Kingdom of Yugoslavia, 1929.. 49
              Map-Banovine of Croatia, 1939 72

Chapter 4   Second World War, 1941-1944 85
              Map-Independent State of Croatia, 1941-1945 102

Chapter 5   Communist Yugoslavia, 1945-1990 168
              Map-Socialist Republic of Croatia, 1945-1990 181
              Lijepa Naša Domovino 208
              Map-Republic of Croatia (Republika Hrvatska) 209

Chapter 6   Serbian War of Aggression, 1991-1995 210

Appendix: A. Basic Facts About Croatia 311

              B. Bosnia Peace Agreement. 315

              C. United Nations Security Council Resolutions 318

              D. UNPROFOR Troop Deployment by Country 321

              E. Abbreviations Used in this Book 322

Index 323

ACKNOWLEDGMENT

"CROATIA: THE MAKING OF A NATION" is the outgrowth of years of ceaseless diligent research on various topics pertinent to Croatia. Hence, the full measure of heartfelt gratitude goes to my wife, Delena, for her enduring patience, cheerfulness, cooperation, and encouragement that contributed in countless ways toward the successful collection of material essential to the completion of this valuable and unique publication.

Profound gratitude is extended to the U.S. Department of State, U.S. Department of Defense, and the Organization on Security and Cooperation in Europe, for providing suitable input documents to this important and up-to-date reference on all the concerns of Croatiia governance.

TO THE READERS:

We the people of Croatia, shall forever remember those barbarians who committed the most heinous crimes against humanity. Those despicable savages guilty of massacring our innocent people; wilful killing, mutilating, torturing, ill-treating, and humiliating our people; raping our women and young girls; assassinating our men and young boys; exterminating our children and elderly; wantonly destroying our cities, towns, and villages; systematically plundering and pillaging our private and public property; bombing hospitals, schools, libraries, civic centers, historical monuments, museums, churches, cemeteries, and our infrastructures.

LONG LIVE CROATIA (ŽIVILA HRVATSKA)

Vladovich International Publishing
P. O. Box 75465
Oklahoma City, OK (USA) 73147-0465

iii

PREFACE

This unique book has been published to coincide with the 50th anniversary of the end of the Second World War, the observance of the 50th anniversary of the United Nations, and a commemorative celebration on the 5th birthday of the sovereign and independent Republic of Croatia.

This publication is deemed advisable because heretofore no single volume existed which in any adequate way provided a wealth of documentary evidence concerning the history of Croatia in perspective to other nations. From the causative events of pre-war Europe through the war calamities and post-war aftermath, this monumental volume offers superb coverage of major aspects of Croatia and brings together an enormous amount of data never before considered for inclusion in an historical reference of this kind. This will prove to be an invaluable and authoritative reference tool for setting the facts straight. In addition, the presented data will provide the best enlightenment for ameliorating the understanding of Croatia. Among the material included and organized according to sequence of events are diplomatic communications, top secret telegrams, memoranda, and briefing papers issued by various governments that are unusually illuminating and succinct in the relevant testimony within subject matter.

Because of the broad coverage in the presentation, the material has been organized for the purpose of comprehension and concisiveness without altering the testimony or documentary evidence in any way, except for abridgment. The arrangement of materials are set in chronological date sequence in order to provide the necessary facts and depict what occurred concurrently in various places around the world, although occasional exceptions have been made where it seemed useful and appropriate to maintain clarity of purpose.

The holocaust stands alone as the most heinous crime against humanity, nevertheless, the genocidal war in Croatia waged by fanatic and habitual criminals against Croatians is not a religious war, nor is it an ethnic conflict, but an outrageous and despicable war of aggression inflicted by assassins and terrorists. It is not a religious war because the aggressors (Serbs and Montenegrins) are bigots and scoundrels. Nor is it an ethnic conflict between the peace loving Croats on one side and the schizophrenic četnici (Serbs and Montenegrins) on the other because the aggressors committed war crimes and crimes against humanity by wantonly destroying properties, plundering, and raping not only Croats, but people of other nations.

iv

CHAPTER 1

HISTORY

Pre-Croat History

As a matter of historical and cultural interest, the remains of Iguanodon dinosaur (the largest extinct land lizard, measuring 32 ft./10 m. in length and 14.8 ft./4.5 m. in height, living millions of years before Man), have been unearthed on the Brijuni Archipelago, Istria (NE Adriatic Sea). On the islands of Veliki Brijuni and Vanga were discovered fossilized bones (which testify to the existence of diluvial cattle) in the lower strata of petrified red soil.

Archeological discoveries reveal that the territory of Southeastern Europe has been inhabited since the Paleolithic Age (200,000-8000 BC), they were the ancestors of hunters and food gatherers. In the Mesolithic Age (8000-6000 BC), people implemented the use of bows and cutting tools, gathered wild vegetables, and fished and hunted large game. During the Neolithic Age (6000-2800 BC, later Stone Age) people introduced important changes; invented the making of stone implements, learned to practice agriculture, raised livestock, made pottery, weaved textiles, manufactured serviceable tools by hammering, grinding and polishing rocks, and built houses and settlements.

Prehistoric excavations and remains from the diluvial primitive man of the Neanderthal horde have been found at Črni Kal near Kopar, Istria, and also the so-called "Homo Crapiniensis" who lived one hundred and fifty thousand years ago, was uncovered in the Valley of Krapina, along the Krapinčica River (33 miles/53 km from the city of Zagreb, capital of Croatia). Through Neanderthal descendants, traces of the Paleolithic and Mesolithic periods were discovered, indicating a low level of cultural development. However, this primitive culture developed into a significant Neolithic culture from the fourth to the second millenium on the Adriatic seaboard, as well as in the Pannonian lowlands.

Other significant centers of Neolithic culture were discovered on the island of Veliki Brijuni in Istria, at Dalj near Osijek, Šandalj and Verudica near Pula, Ponikve near Varaždin, Veternica near Zagreb, Smilčić near Zadar, Danilo near Šibenik, and on the island of Brač (Kopačina, Škrip, Veliko i Malo Grašće, and the Illyrian ruins of Koštio). During the Bronze Age (2800-700 BC), settlements multiplied, and craftsmen began casting ornaments, tools, and weapons. After 1450 BC, people began working with locally mined gold and silver, used horses and chariots as mode of transportation. During the

Iron Age (beginning 700 BC), trade developed among various peoples.

The Illyrians, an Indo-European people, made their home in ancient Illyria beginning the 10th century BC, along eastern shores of the Adriatic coast and its hinterland of southeastern Europe. The inhabitants of ancient Illyria, collectively known as Illyrians were self-governed tribes organized under their tribal chieftain, usually associated into several larger tribal entities, and administratively joined into regional kingdoms.

One of the Illyrian tribes, called the "Dalmatae" is the original name for the territory of the eastern Adriatic coast of today's Dalmatia. Similarly, the "Histri" tribe were the habitants of Histria (Istria), a peninsula on the northeastern coast of the Adriatic Sea; the "Liburni" tribe, inventors of the Liburnian galley, were the inhabitants of Liburnia, the area along the northeastern Adriatic Sea, an inlet of the Kvarner and northern Dalmatia; and the Neretni tribe were the inhabitants of southern Dalmatia, between the rivers Cetina and Neretva. The kingdom of Illyria also comprised the Austrian territories of Carinthia, Carniola, and Kustenland. The Illyrians organized their settlements, minted their own currency, and developed trade with Mediterranean people. Generally, the people living north of the Epirus (Greek: Epeiros) and west of the Vardar river (ancient Axius, Greek: Vardares) were known as Illyrians, while those living east of the Vardar were referred to as Thracians (inhabitants of ancient Thrace or Thracia).

During the period between the seventh and fourth centuries BC the Greeks arrived from the south to establish colonies and trading posts. They founded the settlements of Issa (Vis), Pharos (Hvar), Corcyra (Korčula), Tragurium (Trogir), and Epethio (near Stobreč) along the Dalmatian coast and on the islands of the southeastern Adriatic Sea. The Greek colonies were the cultural and economic centers of the eastern Adriatic. The Celts, people of central and western Europe, migrated from the north and occupied most of Istria during the 4th century. They amalgamated culturally and ethnically with regional Illyrian tribes. In the fourth century BC significant events disrupted the peaceful development of the Illyrians. The various Illyrian tribes fought the invaders in order to maintain their territorial independence and unity. In doing so, they practiced tough piracy against foreign shipping. After a series of wars beginning the third century BC the Romans penetrated into southeastern Europe to establish their colony by waging war on the Illyrians. The Romans were interested in Dalmatia and Istria where they established their colonies: Umag (Humagum), Poreč (Parentium), Pula (Pola), Labin (Albona), Plomin (Flanona), Rijeka (Tarsatica), Krk (Curicum), Senj (Senia), Nin (Aenona), Zadar (Iadera), Solin (Salona), Omiš (Oneum), Vis (Issa), Hvar (Pharus), Korčula (Corcyra), Narona (Muicurum/Metković), Skradin (Scardona), Cavtat (Epidaurun), etc. There were some settlements built in

Pannonia: Sisak (Siscia), Osijek (Mursa), Vinkovci (Cibalae), etc., and near the thermal springs such as Aqua Viva, Aqua Iassae, and Aqua Balissae.

In 231 BC, King Agron, one of the oldest kingdoms of Illyria with its capital at Scodra (Shkoder, Albania) allied with Demitrius II (b. 276-d. 239 BC), King of Macedonia, to defeat the Aetolian League (tribes of ancient district in central Greece). Following the death of King Agron, his widow Queen Teuta defeated all Greek attempts to subjugate Illyria, and vigorously attacked the Greek settlements along the coast of Illyria (southern Dalmatia). These constant attacks provoked and antagonized the Romans who retaliated by launching repeated assaults causing Queen Teuta to yield her authority in 228 BC. Because the Kingdom of Illyria was not yet destroyed, the Romans launched renewed attacks and invaded Illyria in 219 BC. King Philip V of Macedonia unsuccessfully intervened in defense of their Illyrian neighbors, this interventionist policy magnified the conflict and brought about a protracted war that ended with Roman conquest of the Balkan peninsula.

In 178 BC the Romans established the colony of Pola (they named it "Julia Pollentia Herculanea") in southern Istria, became the administrative center of the whole of Roman Istrian Peninsula. In the first century AD, the Romans constructed an Amphitheater (arena/colosseum), elliptical in form, is 435 ft./132 meters long and 335 ft./102 meters wide with three tiers of arches up to 90 ft./27 meters high. The two best-preserved sites of the Roman period are the town of Pula (Pola), and the ancient colonial capital of Salona (Solin) near the city of Split in central Dalmatia.

In 168 BC, one of the last Illyrian kings, Genthius, was decisively defeated; and the last Macedonian King, Perseus, was defeated by the Romans under Aemilius Paulus at Pydna (ancient town in Macedonia) on the west shore of the Gulf of Salonika, Greece. After the surrender of the last Illyrian king Genthius, Dalmatia and Macedonia became Roman provinces. The Istrian rivers of Rizan and Raša became a Roman frontier in 42 BC, and later the frontier was extended to the Liburnian settlement of Tarsatica (Trsat), the present day city of Rijeka. Most of the coast of Dalmatia was conquered by Romans in 34 BC. At first the Romans confined their conquests along the coastal area, then additional conquests and the integration of Illyria under the Emperor Augustus Caesar Octavianus (27 BC-14 AD), this territory was used as an outpost for Roman legionaires to launch their campaign of conquest in southeastern Europe and the region of Pannonian Valley.

Emperor Tiberius (Tiberius Claudius Nero Caesar) conducted campaigns in Germany, Pannonia, and Dalmatia; created the Roman perfecture of Illyricum thus bringing under a central administration the territory of contemporary Croatia. Tiberius succeeded Augustus as emperor in 14 AD and reigned until 37 AD. It was during the reign of Tiberius that Jesus Christ was crucified. The Roman empire ruled for five centuries, exposing the native population to its civilization. Military installations became the main centers of Roman influence. Illyricum became urbanized, and the western and central lands were known for their mineral wealth and the Pannonian Plains for their agricultural products.

The Illyrian natives of Dalmatia and Pannonia, accepted the culture and economy of the Romans but continued to protect their language and customs, joined the Roman legions and rose through the ranks to become military and political leaders. The following eight emperors were native Illyrians:

- Claudius II (Marcus Aurelius Claudius, nicknamed Gothicus), Roman emperor (268-270), as a soldier rose to the highest post in the army, designated by emperor Claudius to become his successor; victorius by defeating the Goths, Vandals, and Alemanni; captured Zenobia, queen of Palmyra in Syria; in 271 built the famous Aurelian Wall, a fortification surrounding the capital city of Rome.

- Probus (Marcus Aurelius Probus), Roman emperor (276-282), distinguished himself as a leader, rose to the highest post in the army, served under Aurelian, Lucius Domitus Aurelianus (270-275), repulsed the invasion by Alamannic. During the reign of Marcus Claudius Tacitus (275-276), Probus became the commander of the Roman Empire in Syria and Egypt. In 276, Probus was proclaimed emperor and became known as the "Restorer of Illyria." As emperor, defeated the Franks, and waged successful wars against the Vandals that overran Gaul (France) and Spain. In 281, Probus returned to the Eternal City of Rome to celebrate the many triumphs.

- Diocletian (Gaius Aurelius Valerius Diocletianus), commander of the bodyguard of Emperor Numerian Marcus Aurelius (283-284), during his twenty years as Roman emperor from 284 until he voluntary abdicated from the throne in 305, launched a persecution of Christianity and established the Roman prefecture which included a large area of southeastern Europe. Emperor Diocletian (born in Dalmatia in 245 and died in 316) like another compatriot from Dalmatia, such as Pope St. Caius (who reigned as Pope from 283 to 296), took a personal interest concerning their native land of Dalmatia. Diocletian erected (295-305) a huge and luxurious, well fortified villa, the famous "Diocletian palace" in the city of Spalatum (Asphalathos, now Split) at the shores of Dalmatia.

- Maximian (Marcus Aurelius Valerius Maximianus), Roman emperor (286-305), rose to the highest post in the army; was first designated Caesar by Diocletian in 285, and then was given the title of Augustus in 286, ruling in the West.

• Constantine I (Flavius Valerius Aurelius Constantinus), Roman emperor (306-337), the son of Caesar Constantius who became Augustus Constantius I (305-306) of the west after the abdication of Diocletian on May 1, 305; reunited the Roman Empire after years of turmoil; subsequent his victory in 312 AD at the Battle of the Milvian Bridge (Saxa Rubra) near Rome, gained control of the Roman Empire in the west; Constantine I had a dream that led to his conversion to Christianity in 313, issued an edict legalizing Christianity throughout the empire; and in 330, transferred his imperial residence from Rome to Byzantium (ancient Greek city of Konstantinoupolis renamed Constantinople), chosen for its geographic location between eastern and western halves of the vast Roman Empire. However, the city of Rome continued to remain the official capital of the entire Roman Empire.

• Valentinian I (Flavius Valentinianus), Roman Emperor (364-375), older brother of Valens, served as soldier under Julian the Apostate (Flavius Claudius Julianus, 361-363), and Jovian (Flavius Jovianus, 363-364). After Jovian's death, Valentinian was proclaimed Roman emperor (reigned from 364-375). In 364, Valentinian and his brother Valens became co-emperors of the Roman Empire, Valentinian ruled the west and Valens ruled the east.

• Valens (Flavius Valens, 328-378), at the invitation of his older brother Valentinian I, became co-emperor of the Roman Empire (reigned from 364 to 378). Valens ruled the east and Valentinian I ruled the west. In 376, permitted the Visigoths to settle south of the Danubian valley, inside the territory of the Roman Empire. Signed a truce treaty in 377 with Persia. A year later, the Visigoths under Frithigern revolted against the Romans, and in 378 defeated and killed Valens at Adrianople. Southeastern Europe became an open territory for Visigothic raids.

• Justinian I (Flavius Anicius Justinianus, a.k.a. Justinian the Great), born in 483 reigned as Byzantine Emperor from 527 to 565; victorious against Vandal kingdom in Africa and the Ostrogothic kingdom in Italy. The biggest achievement was the codification of Roman law (Justinian code), a valuable compilation and annotation of legislative records and legal opinions, the whole forming the Corpus Juris Civilis (Body of Civil Law), considered the most historic documents of jurisprudence published in 529 AD, became the basic Roman law used in numerous European countries.

In 374, Flavius Theodosius commanded the Roman legionnaires in Moesia, southeastern Europe; because of his braveries was appointed co-emperor by Emperor Gratian (375-383), reigned from 379 to 395 under the name of

Theodosius I (a.k.a. "Theodosius the Great"); defeated the Goths, and after 382 incorporated the Goths in the Roman Empire. In 395, when the Roman Empire was divided into the Eastern and Western Empires, Emperor Theodosius I established his two sons as his coregents. Honorius I (395-423) received the Western Roman Empire with Rome as its capital, and Arcadius (395-408) received the Eastern Roman Empire with Byzantium (Constantinople) as its capital. The approximate frontier between the two Empires encompassed areas from today's Hungary on the Danube river and along the Drina river down south of Skutari (now Shkoder in Albania) in the Adriatic Sea. The Illyricum prefecture became part of the Western Roman Empire. At the beginning of the Christian era, southeastern Europe was under the Roman Empire. Much of this territory was incorporated into the Roman province of Illyricum, with an administrative center at Salona (Solin), northeast of the present-day city of Split in Dalmatia.

After the destruction of Aquileia and Padua in 452 AD, thousands of civilian refugees who fled oppression and persecution from the barbaric Huns (Asiatic nomads led by Attila, king of the Huns from 434 to 453 who invaded and ravaged Europe), established a settlement among the islands in the Lagoon of Venice in northeast Italy.

After the Western Roman Empire collapse, Dalmatia was conquered by Odoacer (434-493) and later by Theodoric the Great, also known as Theodoric the Ostrogoth or Dietric von Bern (454-526), born in Pannonia. Theodoric invaded Italy in 488, defeated the Gepidae and Odoacer in 489, conquered and ruled Italy and founded the East-Gothic power (Germanic) state with its capital at Ravenna, Italy. The process of Romanization took place mostly in the towns and along the coast; inland, especially in the mountain areas, various indigenous groups preserved their primitive traditions. Following the fall of the Western Roman empire in 476 under Flavius Romulus Augustulus (475-476), the Visigoths, Huns, Ostrogoths, Lombards and Avars overran the entire Southeastern Europe.

The Eastern Roman empire, with its capital in Constantinople (formerly Byzantium, now Istanbul) reached its peak under emperor Justinian I (527-565), who defeated the Ostrogoths, annexed Dalmatia to the Byzantine Empire, and withstood attacks of Persians, Arabs, and Bulgars. During the Ostrogoths - Byzantium war (535-555), Istria returned to the Roman Empire in 538, and the Lombards' migration from the Pannonian Plains into Italy vacated a large territory making it ready for settlement. When the Romans arrived in Illyria, at first they engaged in commercial activities with native Illyrians, then later, under emperor Augustus the Roman legions succeeded in penetrating the hinterland, laying roads, and setting up their strongholds. Roman settlements developed around the military installations.

During the period of 565-570 the Avars invaded lower Austria and Hungary and proceeded south toward their conquest of the Balkan peninsula by defeating the Lombards (Germanic people). In 568 the Lombards invaded northern Italy and established their kingdom along the river Po Valley. But, the Byzantines maintained the exarchate of Ravenna. The fundamental ethnic change occured after the sixth century AD with the arrival of the Slavs, including Croat tribes from northeastern Europe establishing permanent settlements throughout the region, and gradually assimiliating the remnants of the Illyrians and Thracians, except for small Illyrian groups that retreated into the mountainous regions along the southern Adriatic coast - the ancestors of the present-day Albanians. For twelve years (599-611) the Lombards ravaged over the Istrian peninsula. After the looting was over, the Slavs arrived and settled on the sparsely populated areas of Istria.

Early-Croat History

Despite vague theories seeking to explain the origin of the Croatian people, most sources agree that the Croat tribes lived northeast of the Carpathian (anc. Carpates/Karpati) Mountains, between the rivers Dnieper and Dniester. They journeyed to northcentral Europe and settled on the banks of the upper Vistula River near present-day Krakow in southern Poland, where they created the state of White Croatia (Bijela Hrvatska). They gradually mingled with other civilized people, adopted their own language, and assumed the cultural tribal identity of "Croats" (Hrvati). Thereafter, the Croat tribes migrated southward to the land between the Sava and Drava rivers (Slavonia), and land south of the Slovene area (Croatia), and into the northern Adriatic coastal region (Dalmatia) where they formed their own small independent principalities or counties (županije) and developed their own distinct way of life in a territory located at that time between the Eastern and Western empires.

In 558 the Avars (nomads of Asiatic origin) and their eastern Slavic opportunists appeared in Europe as allies of Byzantium emperor Justinian I (527-565); however in 568 invaded Southcentral Europe and the Balkan Peninsula, during which time, they defeated and routed the Lombards out of the Pannonian Plain and in 597 conquered and demolished the ancient Roman city of Sirmium (Sremska Mitrovica).

During the years of 622-626, the city of Constantinople, the capital of the Byzantine empire, was beseiged from the east by Persians and from the west by Avars. Thereafter, the Avars descended south toward Greece; they killed, plundered, and destroyed everything in their path including the settlements of the Roman colony of Salona (Solin) in 614, Scardona (Skradin), Epidaurum (Cavtat), Narona (Metković), but they never achieved destroying the two fortified cities of Jadera or ladera (Zadar) and Tragurium (Trogir) along the Dalmatian coast.

Byzantine Emperor Heraclius (610-641), in an effort to save his collapsing empire, invited the Croat tribes from east central Europe to help him defeat and expel the Avars and their Slavic stooges. As promised, in 626, after the Croat's victory over the barbaric Avars and their conspirators, Emperor Heraclius awarded to the Croats their right to permanently settle in the liberated territories of Pannonia and Illyria (west of the rivers Drina and Kilubara to the Adriatic Sea), and from Vlore (ancient Aulon) located on the southwest coast of Albania to Trieste, on the northwest coast of the Istrian peninsula. Consequently, Croatia was founded by immigrants.

In 640, the Dalmatian born Pope John IV (who reigned as Pope from 640 to 642) sent Abbot Martin as his personal emissary to Dalmatia in order to advance the cause of Christianity among tribes of southeastern Europe. During the years from 640 to 678, the majority of Croats were converted to Christianity by Roman and Frankish missionaries. In 679, having embraced the Catholic faith, the Croats signed an agreement (the first international nonaggression treaty) with Pope Agatho (678-681) denouncing all wars.

The influence of the Byzantine empire became weaker when, in 751, the Lombards succeeded in deposing the exarchate of Ravenna, thereby destroying the Byzantine authority in Italy. Two large principal settlements developed, Dalmatia (southern Croatia) along the Adriatic, and Pannonia (northern Croatia), centered in the valley of the Sava River. In 788 Charlemagne, known as "Charles the Great," also "Charles I" (742-814), Emperor of the Holy Roman Empire (800-814), King of the Franks (768-814), conquered Istria and Slovenia, succeeded in the campaign against the Avars in the Danubian plains, and destroyed the Avar state in 796.

In 800, Charlemagne was crowned emperor of the Romans, this action displeased the Byzantium regime at Constantinople which considered this action a direct affront to their sphere of influence; thus precipitating a military confrontation between the two. By Peace Treaty of Aix-la-Chapelle of 802, Croatia and Slavonia were awarded to the Franks, and the Dalmatian towns of Zadar, Trogir, Split, Dubrovnik (Ragusa) and Kotor, including the islands of Krk, Cres, Rab and Osor were retained under Byzantine rule.

In 803, Frankish missionaries from Aquileia extended their activity in Dalmatia. Early in the ninth century the two Croatian principalities of Pannonia and Dalmatia were kept separate and independent, under the same Frankish suzerainty but each governed by their own native Duke (prince). Pannonia was governed by Duke Ljudevit Posavski (800-823) whose residence was the capital city of Sisak; and Dalmatia was governed by Duke Višeslav (800-810) whose residence was the capital city of Nin, near Zadar. Višeslav's successor was Borna (810-821).

Croatia's adherence to the Roman Catholic religion has been a continuing influence in its relations with certain slavic neighbors who nurture their upbringing full of prejudiced view and extreme hatred toward those who dare be different. Consequently, the area came to be divided not only between the two Roman empires, but also between rival branches of the Christian church. The religious estrangement between Rome and Constantinople began in the fifth century, but the schism dividing the Roman Catholic and Eastern Orthodox faiths came in the eleventh century. Generally, the boundary separating the Eastern and Western churches coincided with that which divided the political empires and contested control over the various Slavs. During the next thousand years, the varying Slavs were introduced to such diverse influences that they fostered even greater dissimilarity among them in language, culture, political assimilation and the way of life.

In 819, Duke Ljudevit Posavski of Pannonia made an unsuccessful attempt to unite his Pannonian state with the other two Croatian states of Istria and Dalmatia. Ljudevit defeated Borna and also repelled Frankish assaults in 820 and 821. However, a serious attack by Frankish forces in 822, ended in Ljudevit's defeat and self imposed exile. Mislav, Borna's nephew, governed Dalmatia (835-845), introduced the western civilization and maintained a pro-Frankish policy. In 843, the Frankish empire was divided in two territorial entities; Istria and Dalmatia became suzerain of the Frankish Italy, while Pannonia became suzerain of the Frankish Germany.

As nations maneuvered for supremacy, the Neretljani pirates (operating from the eastern Adriatic coast between the rivers Cetina and Neretva) dominated the navigational route along the Adriatic Sea. The Republic of Saint Mark (Venice) in the 9th century developed as an independent maritime power, sought to expand its commercial trade around the world. In 839 AD the Venetians launched a major successful attack against the Neretljani who no longer became the threat to the Venetian merchant marine in the Adriatic.

Trpimir governed Dalmatia (845-864), founder of the Croatian dynasty of Trpimirović, moved his residence from Nin to Klis. Trpimir recognized the Frankish authority, reinforced the culture of western civilization, established the Benedictine monastery at Solin, and donated property rights of Dalmatian lands to the diocese of Split.

Domagoj, a nobleman from Knin and successor of Trpimir, governed Dalmatia (864-876) fought against the Saracens (Islamic nomadis of the

Syrian-Arabian region) who raided and plundered the southern Adriatic coast, and looted Dubrovnik. In 875, after years of indifference, the Franks attempted to reassert their authority in Dalmatia. Domagoj succeeded in destroying Frankish rule in Dalmatia. However, Pannonia continued to remain a Frankish suzerainty. Domagoj's successor was his son who governed less than one year.

Zdeslav governed Dalmatia (878-879), during his time recognized the authority of the Byzantine emperor and the Patriarch of Constantinople for which act Zdeslav was overthrown.

Branimir, governed from 879 to 892, became the first independent Duke of Croatia. Promptly repudiated Zdeslav's Byzantine policy and, therefore, ended the ecclesiastical subjugation under Constantinople. In 882, the Croats of Pannonia and Dalmatia freed themselves from Frankish and Byzantine control. The Croats remained in the sphere of western civilization.

In 887, during a Venetian expedition, Doge Candian, again defeated the Neretljani. However, the Croats defeated Venice in a sea battle, and forced Venice to pay a continued revenue that lasted 150 years, for the privilege to navigate on the Adriatic Sea.

Mutimir governed from 892 to 910 with residence at Bianci (Bijance) near Trogir in central Dalmatia. To demostrate that legal order and respect for the laws must prevail, Mutimir ordered that ecclesiastical properties expropriated from the diocese of Split by the Patriarch of Constantinople be returned.

The kings of Croatia (Hrvatski Kraljevi) were: Tomislav (925-928), Trpimir II (928-935), Krešimir I (935-945), Miroslav (945-949), Mihajlo Krešimir II (949-969), Stjepan Držislav (969-997), Svetoslav (997-1000), Krešimir III (1000-1030), Stjepan I (1030-1058), Petar Krešimir IV (1058-1074), Stjepan-Petar Slavić (1074-1075), Dmitar Zvonimir (1075-1089), Stjepan II (1089-1091), and Petar Svačić (1091-1097).

In 893-901, the Magyars (Hungarian ethnic group) occupied the valley along the rivers of Danube and Tisza, and in 955 they advanced westward by defeating the German emperor Otto I, called "Otto the Great" (912-973).

Tomislav, native of Nin, Dalmatia, a powerful tribal leader (Župan), became Governor (Banus) Tomislav (910-914), helped the Croats of Pannonia fight against the Magyars. Tomislav defeated the Magyars (Hungarians) in several battles, repulsed the Magyars invasion into Croatian territory and established a lasting border along the river Drava as the northern frontier between Croatia and Hungary. In 924, Tomislav succeeded in unifying the two

Croatian principalities of Dalmatia (southern Croatia) and Pannonia (northern Croatia), and extended the borders to include part of Bosnia. In 925, at Duvno Polje in Bosnia, Tomislav proclaimed himself King of Croatia. Under King Tomislav (925-928), Croatia was administratively divided into three major regions: (a) Slavonia, the northern territory, extended from Drava-Sava-Kupa rivers; (b) Central, the territory of Gacka, Krbava, and Lika; and (c) Adriatic, the territory of Dalmatia and northwestern Bosnia. The kingdom lasted about 177 years, until 1102 when Croatia entered into a personal union with Hungary, which continued until the end of the First World War in 1918. Tomislav, responded with compassion for the suffering of homeless and stateless Serbs when, under their leader Zacharia (Zaharije) a pro-Byzantine ruler of Serbia, they were forced to flee their native land of Serbia from invading forces of Emperor Simeon of Bulgaria. Tomislav prevented the destruction of the Serbian people by allowing Serbian refugees and Zacharia safe haven in Croatian land. As a result of asylum offered to the Serbs by the generous Croatian people. Emperor Simeon of Bulgaria in 926, invaded the territory of Croatia. King Tomislav soundly defeated the invading Bulgarian army in northeastern Bosnia.

In 926, Pope John X (reigned during 914-928) who discouraged the Old-Slavonic "Glagolitic" liturgy, convened a church council at Split, to establish a hierarchy for Dalmatia and eliminate the overlapping jurisdictions between Split and Nin. With Tomislav's support, the archbishop of Split became the central authority. Because Bishop Grgur of Nin protested against the council's decision, a second council convened in 928 at Split, abolished the office of Nin, and placed the archbishop of Split over the whole Croatia, which included the bishop of Pannonia at Sisak. At the Church of St. Lucia (Sveta Lucija) in the village of Jurandvor near Bačka (Island of Krk) was found a stone tablet "Bašćanska ploća" dated 1080 inscribed with Glagolitic text representing the first written document in the Croatian language.

In 955 Holy Roman emperor Otto I (912-973) defeated the intruding Magyars (Hungarians) on the battle field of Lechfeld (near Augsburg, a former Roman colony founded by Augustus in 14 BC) in Bavaria, Germany.

The tribal structure of Croatian society was gradually replaced by feudalism, a class system based on landholdings. The leader of the powerful clans assumed the status of a hereditary nobility; the royal family and institutions of authority accumulated extensive properties, and the peasants were reduced to serfdom. As a result of major differences in the political and religious philosophy between the Eastern and Western Roman empires, the schism destined to split Christendom into the Eastern (Constantinople) and Western (Rome) churches began in 1054.

Croatia was united under King Petar Krešimir IV (1058-1074). In the late eleventh century the increasing strength of the nobility limited the authority of the king, and his power began to wane. During the reign of King Dmitar Zvonimir the capital of Croatia was moved from Biograd na Moru (Biograd on the Sea) to Knin, in the interior of northern Dalmatia. Following the death of Stjepan II in 1091, the last descendant of the Trpimirović dynasty, the throne of Croatia became vacant, a long struggle ensued between rival claimants. In 1095 Ladislas I (László I) of Hungary who was Helen's brother, the widow of King Zvonimir, ended the war. Ladislas's successor, Kálmán made peace with the Croats. In 1102 the Croatian nobles offered the crown to Hungary's King Kálmán (1095-1116). Henceforth, the recognition of the Croatian constitutional law "Državno Pravo," and subsequent agreement with Hungary "Personal Union" (Pacta Conventa), lasted for eight centuries. Although the Croats enjoyed a special status, Croatia remained tied to the House of Arpad, the Hungarian dynasty that reintroduced the feudal system. During the union with Hungary, Croatia retained its own Assembly (Sabor), and was legally an independent state. The Hungarian King was represented in Croatia by a "Herceg" (from German "Duke"), nobleman who ruled the dukedom same as "Governor". Following the death of Andrew II, the last descendant of the Arpad dynasty, the Croatian Governor Pavle Subić in 1301 offered to Karl Robert of the Anjou royal dynasty the throne of Croatia.

Marco Polo (1254-1324) native of Korčula, Dalmatia, was a Venetian traveler and trader. In 1271, Marco (Marko) joined his father Niccolo (Nikola) and uncle Matteo (Mate), departed from Acre a seaport in Galilee, traveled through Central Asia, arrived in China in 1275 where they met Kublai Khan. After studying Chinese culture, in 1292 Marco departed by sea to Persia and in 1295 returned to Venice (Venezia). In 1298, a naval battle off the island of Korčula (Curzola) between Venetian and Genoese fleets, Marco joined the Venetian fleet commanded by Andrea Dondolo. The Venetians were defeated by the Genoese commanded by Doria. Consequently, both Marco and Dondolo were captured and imprisoned in Genoa. After his release from prison in 1299, Marco published two books concerning his adventures, "Description Of The World" and "Million Wonders Of The World."

The first public schools, financed by the local city authorities, were founded at Zadar in 1282, Dubrovnik in 1333, and Zagreb in 1362. The first Croatian grammar school was founded by the Paulist Missionary Society of Saint Paul the Apostle in Lepoglava.

In 1376, Bosnian Stjepan Tvrtko I (1376-1391) proclaimed himself "King of Bosnia and Serbia," and in 1390 assumed the title of "King of Croatia and Dalmatia," thus controlling parts of western Serbia and most of the eastern Adriatic coast except the cities of Zadar and the Republic of Ragusa

(Dubrovacka Republika) which was established February 18, 1358. The Ottoman Turks under the command of Sultan Murad I (ruled from 1359 to 1389), on June 28 ("June 20" under the old style calendar), 1389, defeated the Serbian armies under Czar Lazar, at Kosova Polje (Blackbirds' Plain), as a result Serbia became vassal of the Ottoman empire. In 1396 the combined forces of Hungary and Croatia under the command of the Hungarian King Sigismund (1387-1437) of the House of Luxemburg, were defeated at Nicopolis (Nikopol) in Bulgaria, by the Turkish army led by Sultan Bayazet I, (ruled from 1389 to 1402). After the second defeat of the Serbs in 1459, at their stronghold of Smederevo (capital of the Serbian principality), Sultan Mohammed II, who succeeded his father Murad II (ruled from 1451 to 1484), placed the Serbian lands under Turkish occupation and it so remained for more than 350 years. Sultan Mohammed II invaded Bosnia in 1463, captured and executed King Tomašević, and incorporated Bosnia into the Turkish empire. After that, a large number of the population embraced the Muslim faith, the Bosnian nobility kept their farm holdings, and adopted the Turkish feudal system.

As the Ottoman army occupied additional territories, they lacked the necessary personnel to maintain adequate military and administrative controls. Thereby, they implemented a mobiliztion system whereby foreign citizens (called: "Jemissaries") from occupied territories were hired for military service. The Jemissaries were drawn mostly from "slave" elements and became the backbone of the Ottoman tyranny. Subsequently, the Ottoman empire began its incursions into the northern regions of the Balkan Peninsula, and after Bosnia fell to Turkish Sultan Mohammed II forces in 1463 and Herzegovina in 1483, the Sultan's armies pushed into Croatian lands. For sixty years the Croats and Hungarians sought to resist the periodic raiding of the Turks, but on the field of Mohács in 1526 the Hungarian King Ludovik II army was defeated in a disastrous encounter with the Turkish forces; the king was killed, and Hungarian resistance collapsed.

Croatian writer Marko Marulić (1450-1524), native of Split (a.k.a. "The father of Croatian literature") wrote in Croatian and Latin. In 1501 his famous poem "Judita" was published in Venice. Another literary writer was Hanibal Lučić (1485-1553) from Hvar, he wrote the drama "The Slave Girl" (Robinja) published in Venice. Also, Petar Hektorović (1487-1571), a Croatian poet and collector of Croatian folk poems, wrote in the Croatian ča-dialect (čakavci/čakavian) and in Latin. His best play entitled "Fishing and Fisherman's Conversation" (Ribanje i ribarska prigovaranje). Hektorović built a castle in Tvrdalj on the island of Hvar.

Among the thousands of refugees from Europe were people from Dalmatia. Pope Sixtus V (a.k.a. Felice Peretti) born on December 13, 1521, at

Grottomare near Montalto, Italy, was a son of poor parents (original family name: Peretić) who immigrated from Kruščica, Dalmatia (Croatia). In 1534 young Peretti entered the convent of Minorite at Montalto as a novice, and was ordained as Franciscan Friar in 1547 at Siena, Italy. As an eloquent communicator with impressionable theologian knowledge he gained fast recognition among the church's hierarchy; became Procurator-general of the Franciscans, bishop, cardinal, and elected pope on April 24, 1585, reigning until his death in 1590. Pope Sixtus V, completed various public works, constructed a 20 mi / 32 km long acqueduct which supplied water to the city of Rome. He built and restored edifices, churches, monasteries, schools, including the construction of the cupola of St. Peter's basilica in Rome.

The Ottoman Turks gained an appetite for more territorial domination, continued to press northward and by the end of the sixteenth century had absorbed much of Croatia and almost all of Slavonia. On January 1, 1527, the Croatian nobility at Cetingrad (Cetin, Croatia) offered the Croatian Crown to Austrian Archduke Ferdinand I (b. 1503), Emperor of Habsburg (1558-1564), who that same year became ruler of Hungary. The territories of Croatia and Slavonia were divided between the Austrian empire and the Turkish Ottoman empire. However, Istria and Dalmatia was ruled at different times mostly by the Republic of Venice, Austria, and France.The Ottoman Turks dominated southeastern Europe and became arrogant with their assumption of superiority, implemented a forced Islamization. Muslims received special privileges and the rights of citizenship. Christians were considered inferior and, therefore, subjects to discrimination. Having no compassion, the Ottomans kidnapped Christian children and brainwashed them to villify and persecute their own slavic people. Hundreds of thousands of Croatian Christians were killed for their religion, or forced into captivity and sold as slaves in the markets of Asia Minor. Following the Battle of Lepanto (the strait between the Gulf of Corinth and the Ionian Sea), five years after the death of Suleiman The Magnificent (1520-1566), the Ottoman Turks launched their attacks in northern Dalmatia, captured Zemunik, but failed to conquer Novigrad. Although the Turkish forces were located in the vicinity of Zadar, they were never successful in capturing the fortified city of Zadar.

During the winter of 1572-1573, the peasants of Croatian Zagorje registered their strong grievances to the Governor to intercede in their behalf to the Emperor of Austria, demanded that the cruel landlord of Susjedgrad-Donja Subica, Franjo Tahi, a feudal master who mistreated the peasants be punished for his wrongs. Because their reasonable appeals for justice had been deliberately ignored, in January 1573 the peasants decided to fight for their cause against serfdom. Matija Gubec, a peasant from Stubica, was chosen to lead the insurgency which spread in the neighboring territories. The peasant's uprising (Seljacka Buna) was short lived; the last battle was fought at Donja Subica on February 9, 1573. The peasants failed in their struggle because they were poorly armed and unable to match the competence of the regular army. On February 15, 1573, Matija Gubec was taken prisoner and executed in Zagreb (Agram). Although the peasants movement against tyranny was quelled, the struggle for freedom continues to remain a vivid symbol of the consciousness of the brave Croatian people to establish dignity, respect for human rights, and equal justice for all. To memorialize the peasants' insurrection, at Saint Mark Church square and the corner of Čirilometodska ulica (street) at Gornji Grad in Zagreb where Gubec ("king of the peasants") was executed, there is a stone sculpture of a bust representing Matija Gubec's head.

The Croatian language had a genesis much older than other slavic people. Bartul Kašić, a Jesuit missionary, born in 1575 on the island of Pag, northern Dalmatia (Croatia), was the founder and first pryor of the Jesuit monastery in Dubrovnik. He wrote a number of works; in 1622 translated the Holy Bible, and in 1604 published the first grammar of the Croatian language. Kašić died in Rome (Italy) in 1650. Author Ivan Franjo Gundulić (1589-1638) from Dubrovnik wrote "Suze sina razmetnoga" (Tears of the Prodigal Son) and "Dubravka" which portrayed Dubrovnik enjoying the gift of freedom.

In 1578, Maximilian's successor, King Rudolf II (b. 1552), Emperor of Holy Roman Empire (1576-1612), commissioned his brother Charles of Styria, to establish a Vojna Krajina (Military Frontier or in German "Militärgrenze") to be built between Austria and the Turkish Empire. In 1630, Ferdinand II (b. 1578), Emperor of Habsburg (1619-1637) ordered the expropriation of territory from Croatian nobles and removed their lands from the authority of the Croatian Banus (Governor). Concurrently, the Emperor redistributed these lands to soldier-peasants, free from taxable obligations in return for their volunteer military servitude.

In 1645, the Republic of Venice renewed the war against the Ottoman Turks. The war of the Sea of Candian (also known as the Creatan war, named for the seaport of Crete in Greece), lasted until 1669. During the Creatan War of 1645-1669, Venice defeated the Ottoman Turks, and gained control of the territory of Dalmatia, which ran from Starigrad - over Mount Velebit and the source of the river Zrmanja - to Knin, Vrlika, Sinj, Vrgorac, to Metković on the Neretva river. The entire area was under Venice and the Dalmatia boundary remained unaltered until the fall of the Republic of Venice in 1797.

The Academy of Science (School of Theology), at Zagreb, was established by the Jesuit Order in 1632. The School of Philosophy was opened in 1664, and a full university developed. The Paulist Missionary Society of Saint Paul the Apostle in 1656 established the first University (Sveučiliste) of Croatia, and operated the school until the abrogation of the monastic order in 1786 by Joseph II (1741-1790). However, the University (Sveučiliste) of Zagreb was established on September 23, 1669 by Leopold I (1640-1705) Emperor of Habsburg-Lorraine (1658-1705) and operated by the Jesuit Order founded in 1534 by Saint Ignatius Loyola. On April 30, 1671, Petar Zrinski (1621-1671) and his brother-in-law, Franjo Krsto Frankopan (1643-1671), were beheaded at Wiener Neustadt in Austria by order of Emperor Leopold I, for their unsuccessful revolt to liberate Croatia from the Austrian monarchy. After the collapse of Austro-Hungary in 1918, the bones of Zrinski and Frankopan were transferred and buried in the underground sanctuary behind the main altar of Sveti Stefan's Church in Zagreb

In 1683, hampered by overextended lines of communications and logistics the Ottoman Turk army that besieged Vienna was defeated by the Austrian army and forced to retreat southward. This outcome marked the beginning of the end of the Turks from southcentral Europe. Subsequently, the Republic of Venice in 1693 succeeded in defeating and expelling the Ottoman Turks from the Dalmatian coastal area. Leopold I, Emperor of Austria, in 1690 urged the Christian people of the Austrian empire to rise against the Ottoman Turkish oppressor. After Leopold's death he was succeeded by his son Josef I (b. 1678), Emperor (1705-1711).

By Treaty of Karlowitz (Srijemski Karlovci) signed on January 26, 1699, the Habsburgs recovered most of Croatia and Slavonia territories from the Ottoman Turks, the Military Frontier Province was extended to include the southern half of Croatia, Slavonia, and the Vojvodina - the southern part of the Hungarian Danubian Plain directly east of Slavonia. The land was settled by Croats, Germans, and a large number of Serbs who migrated into the area to escape Ottoman Turks oppression and persecution. The Croat nobility opposed the Austro-Hungarian emperor's efforts to retain the frontier lands under his direct control, but the imposed system continued until the late nineteenth century. The frontier soldier-peasants became subjects of the emperor; as late as the First World War these frontier people resisted Croatian sentiment in favor of the Austro-Hungarian monarchy.

The Dalmatian coastal area of the medieval Croatian state was the object of 300 years of conflict between Austria-Hungary dual monarchy versus the growing power of the Republic of Venice. Jurisdiction of some Dalmatian cities changed repeatedly. From the fifteenth century to the end of the eighteenth most of the eastern Adriatic coastal area was subordinate to Venice, shared in its art, commerce, and wealth. The Republic of Dubrovnik (Ragusa) remained independent of foreign control throughout most of the period, and developed its own economic prosperity.

After the death of Josef I, the throne of Austria passed to Charles VI (1685-1740), Emperor (1711-1740), who lived in the Netherlands, Portugal, and Spain hoping to win the Spanish crown, instead he received the German imperial crown and the Croatian-Hungarian kingdom. Charles VI developed the Croatian infrastructure by constructing the road from Karlovac (Ger. Karlstadt) to the Adriatic coast, the ports of Bakar, Senj, and Karlobag, and the shipyard of Kraljevica. The Croatian Parliament (Sabor) signed the Pragmatic Sanction on March 15, 1712, and sent the document to Emperor Charles VI in Vienna, declaring that "the Croatian people are free, sovereign, and possess their State-right." The Republic of Venice began to compete with Austria for supremacy and maritime power in the Adriatic. In 1717, Charles VI proclaimed the Adriatic sea as free-navigation, and named the two Austrian cities of Triest (Italian, Trieste; Croatian, Trst), and Sank Veit am Flaum (Italian, Fiume; Croatian, Rijeka) as free-ports.

In 1729 the archbishop of Zadar, Vinko Zmajević (1713-1745), with the approval of Pope Benedict XIII (who reigned as Pope from 1724 to 1730), restored the Old-Slavonic "Glagolitic" liturgy and reorganized the educational system for Catholic priests. Ruđjer Josip Bošković (1711-1787) native of Dubrovnik, was a member of the Jesuit Order; mathematician, physicist, astronomer, and philosopher. His most important works are De Maculis Solaribus (1736), Element Universae Matheseos (1754), and Theoria Philosophiae Naturalis (1758).

The Treaty of Passarowitz (Požarevac) signed on July 21, 1718, ended the Austro-Turkish war of 1716-1718, and Austria extended its control in the Balkans when Turkey acquiesced the territories of Banat and Sumađa; and Croatia received the territory of Srijem. The region of Međumurje became part of Hungary, but was returned to Croatia in 1848. However, in 1861, Emperor Franz Josef returned Međumurje to Hungary where it remained until 1918. Upon the death of Charles VI of Austria on December 1, 1740, Croatia recognized the king's daughter Maria Theresa (1717-1780) as Queen (1740-1780) and her husband Francis Duke of Lorraine (b. 1706) as co-ruler, who became Emperor Franz I (1745-1765). The military frontier of Vojna Krajina was established in 1746 and divided into seven districts. The Austrian monarchy imposed increased taxation in 1755, which prompted the peasants around Mount Kalnik, already fed up with serfdom, to rise up and fight against additional taxes. The rebellion prompted Queen Maria Theresa to proclaim new laws improving the relationship between the serfs and their landlords. Emperor Franz I, husband of Queen Maria Theresa died on August 18, 1765. Their son, Josef II (b. 1741) was designated by the Queen to become co-ruler and Emperor (1765-1790) of the House of Habsburg-Lorraine. In 1767, Queen Maria Theresa formed a royal council headed by a Governor (Ban) and five counselors for the territory of Dalmatia, Croatia, and Slavonia. In

1776, Queen Maria Theresa united Rijeka with Croatia under the Austrian monarchy. However, in 1779 Rijeka, Karlovac, and Gorski Kotari became parts of Hungary of the Austro-Hungarian monarchy. Thus, the port of Rijeka became the only Hungarian outlet to the Adriatic sea. In 1779, the Queen abolished the Royal Council and transferred the authority to the Hungarian vice-regent.

To promote the German language throughout the Habsburg empire, on March 6, 1784, it was declared the official language of Hungary, to be implemented and mastered by November 1, 1786. The Austrian government on November 1, 1789 implemented and revised the tax structure, thus compelling peasants to surrender 30% of their earnings (allocated as follows: 12.2% to the state and 17.8 to their landlords). Emperor Josef II declared on January 28, 1790, a decree by which he annulled all his decrees about religious toleration and the emancipation of the peasants. When Josef II died on February 20, 1790, Hungary was restive and Belgium was in open rebellion. Josef's successor, Leopold II (1790-1792), the governor of Tuscany (central Italy), abandoned centralization and Germanization. To promote Magyrization, on June 10, 1790, the Hungarians demanded that parliamentary records be written in the Magyar language.

On August 4, 1791, the Austrian empire and the Ottoman Turks signed a Treaty of Sistova (Svištov, Bulgaria), which defined the boundary between the two belligerent countries. Austria ceded Belgrade to the Turks and retained northern Bosnia. The Ottoman Turks ceded Kordun, Cetin (Cetingrad), and Drežnik to Croatia.

With the collapse of the Venetian Republic on July 2, 1797, under the provisions of the Peace Treaty of Campo Formio (now Campoformido, village in Udine province of Italy) dated October 17, 1797, between Austria and France, Austria ceded Belgium and Lombardy to France and obtained Istria, Dalmatia, and Venice. By Peace Treaty of Požum dated November 26, 1805, the city of Zadar was transferred to France. On December 2, 1805, at the battle of Austerlitz (Slavkov) in Brno, Czechoslovakia, Napoleon Bonaparte (1769-1821), Emperor of France (1804-1815) defeated the combined Austrian and Russian forces. With the signing of the Treaty of Pressburg (Bratislava) on December 26, 1805, Austria recognized Napoleon as King of Italy, ceded Istria, the city of Trieste, and Dalmatia to France. On January 31, 1808, France incorporated the independent Republic of Dubrovnik (Ragusa) with territories of Dalmatia, Istria, and western Croatia, Slovenia, and created the Illyrian Provinces with Ljubljana (anc. Emona, or Ger. Laibach), as its capital. French Gen. Molitor defeated and expelled the Russians from the town of Kotor in the Gulf of Kotar, (Boka Kotorska). During the seven years of French control (1805 to 1813) much progress was made in education, public health, economic conditions, roads constructed, and public buildings erected, etc. The Croatian newspaper "Dalmatin," appeared from 1806 to 1810. Vinko Dandolo organized an administrative and judiciary system based on the Napoleon code, and established the University of Zadar with seven faculties - law, medicine, economics, mathematics, architecture, etc. New schools for higher education were opened in preparation for courses at university level.

In late 1806, the French and Russian navies waged a battle off the western shore of the island of Brač (Brazza). In May 1807, the Russians occupied Brač. The short lived Russian occupation in the Adriatic ended with the Peace of Tilsit (formerly in East Prussia, now Sovetsk in Russia) signed on July 8, 1807 between France on one side and Prussia and Russia on the other. In 1808, after a naval battle between France and Austria the island of Brač passed to Austria. On July 5-6, 1809, Napoleon defeated the Austrian Archduke Charles Louis at the village of Wagram near Vienna. The Peace Treaty of Schönbrunn (royal palace in Vienna) was concluded October 14, 1809 between Napoleon I of France and Emperor Francis I (1804-1835) of Austria. Napoleon received the territories of upper Carinthia, Kranj, Gorica, Istria, Dalmatia, and Croatia (south of river Sava), creating the "Province of Illyria," with Ljubljana (Laibach) as its capital. In Karlovac (Karlstadt), Napoleon established a military academy for Croatians to pursue higher military learning. On March 10, 1810, Emperor Napoleon of France married Marie Louise (1791-1847), the daughter of Emperor Francis I of Austria.

Throughout the French occupation, the Adriatic sea was blockaded by British navy, and in 1811 and 1812 the British attacked the islands of Vis and Brač. With the defeat of Napoleon in 1813, Austria-Hungary regained control of the Illyrian Province, the military border and the Dalmatia region were reincorporated to Austria, and Hungary received Croatia proper and Slavonia. From 1813, the Illyrian lands were again under Austria, and by the Congress of Vienna in 1815, Austria received Lombardy, Venice, Tyrol, Galicia, and Salzburg. On July 7, 1814, Dalmatia was occupied by Austria and it remained under the Habsburg rule until the end of the First World War in 1918. To neutralize and contain the Republic of France, Count Klemens von Metternich (1773-1859), chief henchman of the Austrian monarchy, at the Congress of Vienna in 1815 produced the Quadruple Alliance comprised of Austria, Russia, Prussia, and Britain in the hope of maintaining international stability. In 1823, Britain broke away from the alliance.

Following Napoleon Bonaparte's retreat from the Russian campaign, and his final crushing defeat at Waterloo, Belgium, on June 18, 1815, by agreement of the Congress of Vienna in 1815 the territories of Slovenia, Dalmatia, part of the Military Frontier, and the southern part of Croatia were retained by

Austria; the northern part of Croatia and Slavonia went to Hungary within the Habsburg empire. Feudalism was formally ended by the Habsburg emperor, thereby Slovene and Croat peasants were permitted to buy land from their feudal landlords. In 1822, Austria occupied the islands of Krk (Veglia), Cres (Cherso), and Lošinj (Lussino), and made them part of Istria.

In 1832, Vuk Stefanović Karadžić (1787-1864), pretended to be a reformer of the Serbian language, when in reality he was a lunatic Serb who made his commitment to distort the truth and disseminate falsehoods about Croatia and Croatian people. Karadžić published a package of lies and mystification comprised of typical Serbian propaganda, unequivocally the most ridiculous and outrageous fabrications under the moonstruck slogan of "Serbs all and everywhere" (Serbi svi i svuda). Throughout the years, Serbian fanatic and extremist organizations -religious, political, military and similar cliques - blindly accepted Karadžić's assertion to promote their expansionist goal and achieve homogeneous greater Serbia (Serboslavia) at the expense of others.

The poem "Horvatska Domovina" (Croatia Homeland) written by Antun Mihanović (1796-1861) native of Zagreb, was first published on March (Szusheza) 14, 1835 in the magazine "Danicza Horvatzka, Slavonzka y Dalmatinzka" by Ljudevit Gaj, editor and publisher. In 1891, the title of the poem was changed to "Lijepa Naša Domovina" (Our Beautiful Homeland) and became officially the national anthem of Croatia. In the Zelenjak valley along the Sutla river near the town of Klanjec, north of Zagreb, there is an obelisk to commemorate the "place" where the national anthem of Croatia was composed.

The Croat patriot Ljudevit Gaj (1809-1872), journalist and linguist, reformed the Croatian language, in 1835 founded a newspaper, "Novine Hrvatske" (Croatian News) and a magazine, "Danica" (Morning Star) both published in Zagreb. He joined the "Illyrian movement" of the 1830's to promote literary and cultural fusion for the people of Croatia; promoted a distinct literary language, devised a Latin alphabet based on script with diacritical marks taken from the Czech orthography - language of phonetic spelling. In the 19th century, the što-dialect (Štokavian), one of three Croatian dialects, was promoted to be established as the standard "literary" language of Croatia.

In 1836, the Hungarian authority deliberately introduced the "Magyar" language into Croatian schools. The Croats strongly objected and declared their readiness to prevent implementation of the new law, calling it an infringement of their autonomy, and saturated Vienna with petitions for immediate separation from Hungary. Henceforth, the Hungarian-Croatian Commonwealth became a shaken alliance.

In 1841, Bishop Josip Juraj Strossmayer (1815-1905) founded the National Party. Strossmayer was an advocate of Slav Unity including the unification of Dalmatia with Croatia, within the framework of the Habsburg Empire. After the death of Strossmayer (of German father and Croatian mother), the National Party which he founded split into different political groups representing Croats and other nationalists living in Croatia.

In 1842 the Matrix Illyrian (Matica Ilirska) the literary and cultural society, was founded in Zagreb whose name was changed in 1874 to Matica Hrvatska (Matrix Croatica). The first issue of the literary magazine "Zora Dalmatinska" (Dawn of Dalmatia) was published at Zadar in 1844. This created a movement in 1847 for the consolidation of Dalmatia and Croatia. The Croatian Parliament (Sabor) introduced the Croatian language as the official language in Croatian schools, business, and public affairs.

In 1844 Ilija Garašanin (1812-1874), a Serb, the minister of internal affairs of the principality of Serbia, wrote the "Načertanije" (the "Blueprint") based on "suggestions" passed along and submitted by Adam Juraj Czartoryski (1770-1861), a Polish émigré living in Paris, France, and his agent Franjo Zach who promoted a union of South Slavs state. However, Garašanin's "Blueprint" contrived a policy of deceit to achieve territorial aggrandizement within the Serbian Eastern Orthodox sphere of influence, hence establish a homogeneous Serboslavia. This dogma of enslavement is the ever present policy of subjugation by Serbian extremism.

Ferdinand I (1793-1875), Emperor of Austria (1835-1848), by imperial proclamation on January 11, 1848, forbade the use of the name "Illyrian Movement" and all vestiges of that name and emblems. Consequently, the Illyrian Movement reluctantly adopted the change of its name to "Popular Movement." Meantime, the Croatian Parliament (Sabor) in 1848 restored the Triune Kingdom of Croatia and under the Croatian Governor (Banus) Josip Jelačić (1801-1859) on April 25, 1848 abolished serfdom. On September 9 Governor Jelačić rejected the Hungarian laws which radically affected Croatia's autonomous aspiration, thereby helping Austria to put down the Hungarian revolution of 1848-1849 and as a result, Croatia and Slavonia became Austrian crownlands. On September 7, while the Croatia army under the command of General Jelačić occupied Fiume (Rijeka), Jelačić's larger expedition army arrived at Drina River on September 28, engaged in battle against the Hungarian forces; captured the territory of Međumurje and rejoined it to Croatia.

The virus of nationalism came alive. Revolutions broke out throughout Central Europe, in Austria, Poland, Hungary, and France. A revolt erupted in Vienna which forced Emperor Ferdinand I to leave the capital city. General

Jelačić organized a pro-Ferdinand force and attacked the renegade forces in Vienna. The rebellious Austrian assisted by Hungarian troops capitulated. On December 2, 1848, Ferdinand abdicated in favor of 18 year-old Franz Josef (b. 1830), who became Emperor of Austria (1848-1916). General Jelačić, was rewarded for saving the Habsburg and was appointed Governor of Rijeka and Dalmatia.

On April 14, 1849, Emperor Franz Josef banned free press and abolished the Croatian Parliament. On December 31, 1850, Franz Josef introduced absolutism and insisted on a centrally organized state with German as the official language. The Croatian people did not succumb. The monarch realized that absolutism was the cause of all evils. In 1859, Franz Josef reorganized the imperial parliament in Vienna. The people of Croatia were represented in the imperial parliament by Bishop Strossmayer and Baron Ambrose Vraniczany. In October 1860, Franz Josef renounced his absolutistic government and returned the Constitution to Croatia and Hungary, but postponed the question of an independent Dalmatia. The Austrian Constitution of February 22, 1861, established a centralized government. The monarchy possessed a Lower House (Central Parliament), represented by members of all regions which included Croatia and Hungary, and the Upper House which included noblemen, princes, governors, higher clergy, trusted and loyal individuals appointed by the emperor. Hungary conducted Parliamentary election on April 12, 1861 without Croatian participation, which provoked unrest throughout Croatia. Franz Josef became bitter about the Hungarian hypocrisy, and revoked the Hungarian Parliament.

The short lived Austro-Prussian War which commenced on June 15, 1866, ended with the Treaty of Prague, signed on August 23, 1866. Austria was defeated by Prussia at Sadova (Sadowa or Königgrä), a village in southern Bohemia northwest of Hradec Kralove, and Italy as the ally of Prussia, was defeated by Austria at Custozza (near Verona, Italy) on June 24, 1866. At sea, near the island of Vis (Lissa, or anc. Issa), the Austrian navy under Admiral Tegetthoff defeated the Italians under Admiral Persano on July 20, 1866. The war enmities ended by Peace Treaty of Prague signed October 3, 1866; nevertheless Austria ceded Venice to Italy. The Prussian defeat of Austria brought the Habsburg empire to the brink of collapse, which gave rise to the dual monarchy of Austro-Hungary. The two nations were united under a single crown after signing the Ausgleich (Compromise) on July 28, 1867. Franz Josef of Austria was crowned King of Hungary on June 8, 1867. The Austrian constitution adopted on December 31, 1867, provided for equality of nationalities, preservation of national languages, and a "bill of rights." Croatia, Slavonia, and Srem remained under Hungary; while Dalmatia and its islands, Istria, the Kvarner islands, and Rijeka (Fiume) were incorporated under Austria.

During the intensive debates on how best to serve the aspirations of the Croatian people, two major factions came into prominence. One group headed by Josip Juraj Strossmayer advocated closer union with Austria and closer ties with Hungary. The other group under the leadership of Ante Starčević, the man from the village of Žitnik, (located in Ličko Polje near the southern edge of Jezero/Lake Krušćičko, north of Gospić, southwest of Lički Osik, and west of Smiljan), who became known as "the father of the country" (otac domovine), represented patriotic Croatians who wanted an independent and free Croatia, "friendship with all nations, servant to none." The Party of Rights, (Hrvatska Stranka Prava)), founded in 1861 by Starčević (1823-1896) who said, "people without a country are not a people" (narod bez države nije narod). Starčević and Eugen Kvaternik (1825-1871) became ardent, defenders of Croatian nationalism. They opposed both Austrian and Hungarian dominance and were in favor of an independent Croatia. Their vision of Croatia included the historical territories of Dalmatia, the military frontier territory, Slavonia, and Istria. Kvaternik organized an unsuccessful revolt against the oppressor, was killed in Rakovica in 1871 and later buried inside the Basilica of Sveti Stjepan in Zagreb. Due to reorganization, in 1895 Starčević founded the Croatian Party of Rights - Frankovci or Frankists.

On July 28, 1867, Bishop Strossmayer of Đakovo founded the Academy of Science and Arts at Zagreb, with Franjo Rački as President. In 1870 Strossmayer promoted the unification of the Croatian Catholic and the Serbian Orthodox churches; he also proposed on January 5, 1874 that the Croatian Sabor establish the first University of Zagreb. The Croatian-Hungarian "Compromise" (Nagodba) of 1868 regulated the relations between the kingdom of Dalmatia, Croatia, Slavonia and the kingdom of Hungary, on the basis of the legal traditions of both states and the Pragmatic Sanction of 1712. The "Nagodba" permitted the establishment of the Croatian Parliament (Croatian Sabor), with a governor-to-be appointed by Hungary, but Croatia would retain the administration of the education, justice, and internal affairs.

On September 20, 1873, Ivan Mažuranić (1814-1890), was the Governor of Croatia (1873-1880), the first Governor not belonging to nobility. Mažuranić reorganized the government by making the judiciary and the executive branches independant to ensure the separation of power. He elevated the Croatian nation to a higher moral, cultural, and intellectual level by establishing freedom of the press and assembly.

Rivalry between Serbs, Bulgars, Russians, Greeks, and Turks increased in the late nineteenth century. Russian troops invaded Turkey in 1877 and dictated a peace treaty signed on July 13, 1878 at San Stefano (now Yesilkoy, a village near Istanbul, Turkey), ending the Russo-Turkish War

(1877-1878) which provided for an enlarged Bulgaria that was to include most of Macedonia, and recognized the autonomy of Bosnia-Herzegovina. However, on August 14, 1878, the Congress of Berlin annulled the decision of San Stefano of 1878 and mandated that Austria-Hungary occupy Bosnia-Herzegovina, which was formally annexed in 1908 in conformity to the Treaty. In 1881 the military frontier (Vojna Krajina) was reincorporated into Croatia, thus increasing the number of ethnic Serbs living in Croatia. At the Congress of Berlin in 1878, Serbia was made free from Turkey and recognized as an independent principality. In 1882, the Serbian (Skupština) Assembly proclaimed Serbia a kingdom under King Milan Obrenović (1868-1889) of the Serbian dynasty. Montenegro was de facto an independent state. It received de jure recognition at the Congress of Berlin in 1878. Prince Nikolas in 1910, proclaimed himself King of Montenegro (Crno Gora).

The newly appointed Governor of Croatia (1883-1903), Count Dragutin Khuen Hedervary refused to allow Croatia to completely manage their internal affairs. Instead, Hedervary with his slogan "Law and Order" ruled by exercising his authority in a harsh and cruel manner; insidiously contrived schemes to create a climate of hatred, fear, and antagonism between Croats and Serbs living in Croatia, exploited their religious affiliation in order to divide and conquer, and discriminated against Croats by favoring Serbs who supported the Hungarian policies detrimental to Croatian people. After years of barbaric rule, an arrogant and domineering Governor Hedervary decided to make an extravagant presentation of his own "show and tell" to stage and glorify his great leadership quality to give the appearance that Magyarization in Croatia was successful. Thus, Hedervary invited Emperor Franz Josif of Austro-Hungary to visit Agram (Zagreb) and attest for himself the great Hungarian city outside Hungary. The "show and tell" did not sell because the Croatian people on October 16, 1895, surprised the visiting dignataries by parading and displaying their patriotism and by burning the Hungarian flags, revealing that Croatian patriotism was there to stay. Hedervary by preponderance of evidence failed to tell the truth, ended his personal tyranny, and resigned.

Thanks to the Croatians' connection and their unique contribution, the world is a better and richer place to live. The three best known facts in the list are the least identified with their place of origin: (a) The 17th century Croatian "cravat" (in Croatian language "kravata"), a necktie/scarf made of silk, cotton, or worsted yarn is a popular and fashionable apparel; (b) The 14th century "Dalmatic garment," an ecclesiastical loose-fitting knee length vestment with short wide-sleeves is still worn during ceremonial occasions by clergy hierarchy and (c) The well-known "Dalmatian dog," a short-haired, smooth white coat with black or brown spots is appropriately named for the islands along the Dalmatian coast of the Adriatic sea in Croatia.

CHAPTER 2

STRUGGLE FOR FREEDOM, 1900 - 1918

At the beginning of the twentieth century, three wars were fought in the territory of Southeastern Europe, geographically known as the Balkans. Located in a strategic geopolitical region, the Balkans became a tempting object for international rivalry among warmongering nations.

In 1900 Stjepan Radić (1871-1928) and his older brother Ante Radić (1868-1919), unified and harmonized their resources, founded and published the Croatian newspaper "Dom" (Home).

On September 1-2, 1902, anti-Serbian demonstrations and riots erupted in Zagreb after Nikola Stojanović (1880-1964), a Serb, published an article entitled "Its you [Croats] or us [Serbs]" in the August 1902 issue of the Serbian periodical "Defender of Serbs" (Serbobran) based in Zagreb. This article contained most defamatory and callous insults against Croatian people by asserting that Croatia as a nation, language, and culture does not exist, therefore, the Croats cannot have their own sovereign nation. It concluded by stating that "the struggle must continue until Croatia is exterminated." These preposterous, inflamatory, and malicious statements were expressions of evil intentions by people belonging to a primitive society, hypocritical, arrogant, unscrupulous, extremist, and low esteemed Serbs. This demagoguery by despicable Serbs who unjustifiably criticize Croatia deserve only one answer, that is: "Every civilized and knowledgeable individual with common sense and a healthy mind knows for a fact that Croatia exists as a nation with its own unique language and its own colorful culture - always better than that of Serbia with its uncivilized culture which encourages bigotry, promotes paranoia, cultivates hate, and causes devisiveness. After all, not much can be expected from a nation like Serbia that was built on lies, cheats, and deceits." Perhaps, not all Serbs are ominous but, a majority allowed themselves to be indoctrinated and brainwashed, thus becoming dependant on their selfish barbaric leaders.

During the night of April 6-7 (March 24-25 of the old calendar), 1903, King Aleksandar I Obrenović of Serbia, abolished the Serbian constitution of 1901, long enough to decree the annulment of the Serbian National Representatives (Srpsko narodno pretstavništvo), the State Council (Državni savez), reorganized the Serbian Supreme Court, and prohibited the publications of anti-monarchy press, and crush worker's organizations.

25

A group of Serbian army officers, headed by Dragutin T. Dimitrijević (alias "Apis"), on May 29, 1903 founded a terrorist movement, the Serbian "National Defense" (Narodna odbrana), nicknamed "četnici" (singular, četnik), meaning detachment(s). The četnici were established to pursue terrorist activities against organizations and individuals who impeded the progress and development toward Greater Serbia.

During the night of June 10-11 (May 28-29 of the old calendar), 1903, a group of Serb conspirators led by Dimitrijević-Apis, invaded the royal court, and assassinated King Aleksandar I (1889-1903) of the Obrenović Serbian dynasty, the son of abdicated King Milan (1868-1889); his wife, Queen Draga Mašin (nee: Lunjević); Draga's two brothers, Nikola and Nikodije Lunjević; the Minister of War, Col. Milovan Pavlović; the king's adjutant, Gen. Laza Petrović; and others, which ended the Obrenović dynasty. On June 15, 1903, the Serbian Assembly (Skupština) in Belgrade, elected Petar I (1844-1921) of the Karađorđević dynasty to the throne of Serbia monarchy (1903-1921).

In Macedonia, the Internal Macedonian Revolutionary Organization (IMRO) was established to promote an autonomous Macedonia. On August 2, 1903 (St. Elijah's Day - Ilinden), an uprising broke out at Kruševo, and Macedonia declared itself independent from the Ottoman Turkish Empire. However, the Turks crushed the Macedonian uprising.

On August 24, 1903, Theodore Pajacević was appointed Governor of Croatia. Although most Croatians supported a separate state, others began sharing a false belief that a national union of South Slavs was possible and could improve their overall chances of freedom and economic development. Because Pajacević refused to enforce the use of the Magyar language on the state railways operation in Croatia, because it violated Article 57 of the Nagodba of 1868, he was dismissed from his post on June 26, 1907. During the restless years from 1902 and 1904 many political parties emerged in Croatia. However, the dominant parties remained the Croatian Party of Rights, or "Frankovci" named for its founder Josip Frank (1844-1911), a Croatian Jew, established on January 15, 1902; and the Croatian People's Peasant Party founded in 1904 by the two brothers, Ante and Stjepan Radić. In 1905, representatives of the province of Dalmatia in the parliament of Reichsrath at Vienna, demanded the unification of Dalmatia with Croatia-Slavonia and the granting of political freedom within the Austrian empire. Following the resolutions of Zadar in 1905 and that of Rijeka in 1906, misguided Croats and distrustful Serbs formed the Croat-Serb Coalition (Hrvatsko-srpska koalicija) purportedly to promote the unification of South Slavs based on equality and justice for all. Although most Serbs acted on instructions from deceitful Serbs in Belgrade, many Croatian politicians were very gullible in believing those hypocritical and disgraceful Serbs.

In January 1904, Russia and Japan conducted negotiation regarding the future of Manchuria and Korea territories. Japan claimed Korea, but Russia claimed both Manchuria and Korea. On February 6, Japan severed diplomatic relations with Russia. On February 8, Nikolas II, czar of Russia, launched a naval attack against Japanese ships north of latitude 39 north, then all-out war became a reality. The Russo-Japanese War (1904-1905) contained an element of surprise when the Japanese navy attacked the Russian fleet in Port Arthur (Lushan), Manchuria, where on April 13 the Russian fleet met with disaster. On January 22, 1905, the Russian revolution broke out when striking Russian workers in St. Petersburg (Leningrad) demanded better pay and economic reforms. The Treaty of Portsmouth, NH (USA) mediated by U.S. President Theodore Roosevelt on September 5, 1905, ended the Russo-Japanese war. Results, Russia lost the war, Japan received the Liaotung Peninsula of Manchuria, and Korea became a protectorate of Japan on July 25, 1907.

By maintaining a secluded lifestyle, the Austrian monarchy failed to give appropriate consideration to the plight of the diverse ethnic, cultural, and religious desires of the people in its empire. The Habsburg dual-monarchy of Austria-Hungary annexed the territory of Bosnia-Herzegovina in 1908, thus implementing the mandate of the Berlin Congress of August 14, 1878 which revised the Treaty of San Stefano (July 13, 1878) that ended the Russo-Turkish war. The annexation of Bosnia-Herzegovina was objected by the Ottoman Turks, also caused Serbia to see its dream for a greater Serbia (Serboslavia) impeded. The region became a property sought by Austria-Hungary, Britain, France, Russia, Serbia and Turkey.

On October 5, 1908, Ferdinand I (b. 1887) declared himself King of the independent and sovereign kingdom of Bulgaria (1908-1918). After the Turkish National Assembly in Ankara ratified the Peace Treaty imposed by the Balkan League, the combined group of citizens lead by Talaat Bay, member of the Committee of Union and Progress (Young Turks), and military officers lead by Mahmud Shefket Pasha, on February 24, 1909 overthrew the Turkish government. At the beginning of the twentieth century, the Ottoman Empire ruled the territories of Iran, Israel, Jordan, Lebanon, Saudi Arabia, Syria, Yemen, and most islands in the Aegean Sea.

The ultra-extremist Serbians conducted sporadic waves of terrorist operations throughout Bosnia-Herzegovina during the years prior to the First World War, targeting the Croatian people and Austro-Hungarian officials. To maintain a belligerent attitude, Serbia kept arming itself and demanding that Austro-Hungary deannex Bosnia-Herzegovina in favor of Serbia. Also, Serbia made it known that there will never be peace until the ultimate goal of a Pan-Slavic empire under greater Serbia (Serboslavia) is fully achieved.

By international agreements with Germany and Austria-Hungary in 1887, Britain in 1890, France in 1900, and Russia in 1909, Italy obtained approval to acquire Tripoli, Libya (under Turkish administration since 1835). An ultimatum by Italy on September 18, 1911, was rejected by the Turkish Ottoman empire. Consequently, on September 19, 1911, Italy declared war on Turkey. On October 5, 1911, Italian forces landed in Tripoli and proceeded with the conquest of other towns along the coast. The Italian dreams and aspirations became a reality when on November 5, 1911, Italy proclaimed the annexation of occupied territory that ended the Tripolitan War (1911-1912). At the Peace Treaty of Ouchy (Switzerland), signed on October 18, 1912, the Ottoman Turks ceded Libya to Italy.

In Belgrade on May 9, 1911, a group of Serb-extremists, popularly known as members of the "Black Hand" (Crna ruka), headed by Dimitrijević-Apis, created another ultra-secret terrorist organization called "United or Death" (Ujedinje ili smrt), different from the "White Hand" (Bela ruka) who were led by Gen. Petar Živković. The Black Hand group terrorized anyone who would not adhere to Serbian imperialistic ideas. In summary the "United or Death" constitution was as follows: The coat-of-arms was a skull with crossed bones [similar to the symbol used by Nazi Schutzstaffel-SS]. The purpose of the organization was to realize the ultimate ideals of Greater Serbia. The Supreme Central Directorate with its headquarters in Belgrade was the supreme authority; exert influence over all Serbian activities; conduct revolutionary actions in all territories where Serbs reside; and use all means to fight the enemies of Serbia. The interest of the organization was above all other interests; members were known only by their assigned secret number. Membership was irrevocable, those joining the organization gave up their own individuality, and had to unconditionally obey the order of the Directorate. The Directorate had the authority to collect financial contributions. Disobedience was tantamount to treason, and the penalty for treason was death. Members who exploited the organization for personal gains or unauthorized reasons would be punished by death.

Notwithstanding the uneasy attitude toward one another and their long conflicting territorial claims, Bulgaria, Greece, Montenegro, and Serbia concluded a Balkan League Treaty of 1912 to force the Ottoman Turks out of Europe. After years of dialogue and less than a good faith negotiation between Turkey and neighboring Balkan states concerning the Christians living under the Ottoman empire, Austria and Russia unsuccessfully pressed the Young Turk government to implement the promised reforms.

First Balkan War, 1912-1913

On October 8, 1912, Montenegro declared war on Turkey, thus precipitating the First Balkan War waged by the Balkan League (the alliance of Bulgaria, Greece, Montenegro, and Serbia), which ended in the defeat of Turkey. A strong Albanian resistance and uprising against the Ottoman Turks in 1912, ultimately created an independent Albania with Ismail Qemal as its leader. Threatened with military occupation and partition by bellicose Greece, Serbia, and Montenegro, on November 28, 1912, the Albanian National Assembly at Valona (Vlorë) declared its independence. Promptly, the European Powers recognized the independence and sovereignty of Albania. The Treaty of London signed on May 30, 1913, ended the First Balkan War between Turkey and the Balkan League, which reduced Turkey's possession in the Balkans within a small confined area of eastern Thrace.

Second Balkan War, 1913

The quarrelsome Balkan League, concluded their agreement for the equitable partition and annexation of Macedonia, and the distribution of goods and property seized from Turkey during the previous war. The Second Balkan War errupted on June 30, 1913, within the pugnacious Balkan League when Bulgaria launched an attack against Greek and Serbian forces stationed in Macedonia. Thus, Montenegro, Romania, and Turkey joined Greece and Serbia to defeat Bulgaria on August 30, 1913. A separate Peace Treaty of Bucharest was signed with Bulgaria on September 29, 1913; Greece, November 14, 1913; and Serbia, March 14, 1914. Greece obtained Salonika, Kavala, the island of Crete and most of the Aegean islands. The province of Edirne (formerly Adrianople) taken by Bulgaria in 1913, was returned to Turkey whose frontiers were moved to the Maritsa (Evros) river. Serbia obtained substantial territories including northern and central Macedonia, but returned the southern part of Macedonia to Greece. Bulgaria retained a small territory of eastern Macedonia.

Even though the uncompromising and warlike Greeks, Montenegrins, and Serbs considered their newly incorporated territories somewhat temporarily acceptable, they never renounced future expansionist aspirations. Likewise, Bulgarians never abandoned their claims to the territory of Macedonia. According to the Carnegie Commission set up to investigate atrocities committed by Serbia, in 1913 the commission reported that Serbian Army and četnici groups committed crimes against humanity by raping females and killing the population of ethnic Albanians and Macedonians. After two Balkan wars and respective peace treaties, tension between the two major protagonist empires, Russia and Austro-Hungary, both continued to claim the Balkans as their sphere of interest. The Austrians and Hungarians alike perceived the emergence of an irrational and troublesome Serbia to be the real threat to European security and peace. The Russians supported Serbia and Montenegro not because of their prevalent Eastern Orthodox religion, but for their common contemptuous defiance for freedom and democracy. The Serbs infatuated with their military conquests, became insatiated and anxious to implement their imperialist and expansionist conquest. This perilous Serbian adventure, aroused deep concern and uneasiness in Germany, Italy, and Austria for they may have to contend with a Serbian hostile presence.

On November 29, 1913, Baron Ivo Skrlec the royal commissary in Croatia was appointed Ban (Governor) of Croatia. His immediate official actions were the removal of Hungarian inscriptions from all public places, declared the Hungarian laws in Croatia "null and void", and announced elections for the Croatian Sabor. For approximately six-hundred years Croats and Slovenes were dominated by various western nations. The Eastern Orthodox Slavs and Islamized Slavs were subjugated to the Ottoman Turkish empire for much of the time between the fourteenth and nineteenth centuries. Prior to the outbreak of the First World War in 1914, Croatia, Slavonia, Slovenia, Istria, Rijeka (Fiume), Dalmatia, and Bosnia-Herzegovina were integral parts of the Austro-Hungarian empire. The territory of Macedonia was partitioned among the three independent states, Greece, Serbia, and Bulgaria. Despite the intrigue, Montenegro was still an independent monarchy.

Austro-Hungary Monarchy (Osterreichisch-Ungarische Monarchie) was a constitutional hereditary monarchy (1867-1918), and as "dual monarchy" in a personal union, the Emperor of Austria was also the king of Hungary. Geopolitically, Austria-Hungary was divided into two geopolitical territories. The Cisleithan (the area west of Leitha river, in eastern Austria) consisted of 14 provinces including Istria and Dalmatia represented in the Reichsrath at Vienna, composed of a bicameral parliament of 516 members; and the Transleithan consisted of Hungary, Croatia-Slavonia, and Rijeka (Fiume), represented in the Diet at Budapest, composed of a bicameral parliament of 453 members. The Austro-Hungary legislative powers was vested in the "120 delegates" comprised of 60 members from each of the two parliaments. During the Austro-Hungarian empire the national consciousness among the ethnic minority striving for autonomy by Croats, Czechs, Poles, Slovaks, Slovenes, etc. created a strong desire for the rights to use their own language which ultimately led to the dissintegration of the Habsburg empire at the end of the First World War in 1918.

First World War, 1914-1918

The First World War was unleased due to distrustfulness, lack of freedom and justice, and unwillingness of nations to preserve the peace. Some nations wavered between neutrality and partisanship, others were opposed to prevent war because, for one reason or other, they were eager to "settle accounts" and achieve territorial conquest and destroy their enemies.

The ever growing Serbian fanaticism advocated by Serb politicians lead to the road of infamy. This became evident when Archduke Franz Ferdinand (b. December 18, 1863) of the Habsburg dynasty, heir to the Austro-Hungarian throne, and his consort the Countess-Sofie Chotek, Duchess of Hohenburg, married in 1890 were both assassinated on Sunday June 28, 1914, at Sarajevo, Bosnia-Herzegovina, by 19 year old Gavrilo Princip (1894-1918) in association with the notorious group of terrorists, members of Serbian ultra extremist organization, the "Black Hand" (Crna Ruka) under the assassin Dimitrijević-Apis.

Following the assassination of the Austrian crown prince and his wife, it appeared that no military confrontations were thereupon contemplated, and that a possible international crisis had been averted. However, an infuriated Count Leopold von Berchtold (1863-1942), the Austrian Foreign Minister, rightfully believed that the Serbian government and the clique of conspirators residing in Belgrade were the actual culpable force beyond the political conspiracy in the assassination at Sarajevo, the Austro-Hungary government decided to make use of the infamous act by extinguishing the dangerous Serbian political and military aspirations.

Austro-Hungary presented Serbia with an ultimatum on July 23, 1914, demanding a reply within forty-eight hours. Serbia replied to the ultimatum on July 25, 1914, accepted most demands but rejected Austro-Hungary participation in a full investigation, inquiries, judicial proceedings and trial of accusers involved in the Sarajevo plot and murders. Since Serbia's reply was actually evasive and insufficient because the crucial point did not meet Berchtold's demand, Austro-Hungary promptly rejected the inept excuse and broke diplomatic relations with Serbia.

Hatred, exploitation, territorial expansionism, and underlying economic rivalries converged at Sarajevo where a spark triggered and ignited a major war (beginning July 28, 1914 and ending November 11, 1918), between the Central Powers (Austria-Hungary, Germany, Bulgaria, and Turkey) versus the Allied Powers (France, Belgium, Britain, Greece, Serbia, Montenegro, Russia, Romania, Portugal, Italy, Japan, and later the United States). Because the conflict proliferated throughout the world, the Third Balkan War became appropriately known as the First World War (1914-1918).

Preceding the First World War, Croatians of every political persuasion overwhelmingly expressed a strong desire to create their own independent and sovereign state. Outrightly, Croatians rejected the idea of any union with the untrustworthy and pugnacious Serbs. The union of South Slavs became an idea acceptable among the few gullible intellectuals and politicians in exile, who sponsored and supported the concept for the multi-national union;

provided, the government become a federal democracy with equal rights for all political, civic, and religious establishments. This democratic system was imperative in order to prevent Serb extremists from gaining complete power, and imposing their own undemocratic self serving scheme of government, thus contributing to the establishment of greater Serbia (Serboslavia).

After the outbreak of the First World War hostilities, Italy, a member of the Triple Alliance of Italy,Germany and Austria-Hungary since 1882 declared on August 3, 1914, that Austria agree to cede the Trentino, south Tyrol, Gorizia, Trieste, Istria, and most of Dalmatia to Italy in exchange for Italy's neutrality.

Under the Treaty of London dated April 26, 1915, signed by Edward Grey, Minister of Foreign Affairs of Britain; Pierre Paul Cambon, Ambassador of France; Graf Benckendorf, Ambassador of Russia; and Marchese Imperiali, Ambassador of Italy, it was agreed to reward Italy with territorial concessions for Italy's participation in the war on the side of the Allied Powers against Germany and Austria-Hungary. Based on the agreement: Italy will receive the province of Trentino; southern Tyrol; the city of Trieste; the counties of Gorizia and Gradisca; all of Istria including the islands of Cres (Cherso), Lošinj (Lussino), Unije (Unie), Palacol (Palazzuoli); Ilovik (Asinello), and Grujica (Gruica) with the neighboring islets. Italy will also receive the province of Dalmatia and the islands of Premuda, Silba (Selve), Olib (Ulbo), Škrda (Scherda), Maun (Maon), Pag (Pago), Mljet (Meleda), Sv. Andrija (St. Andrew), Biševo (Busi), Vis (Lissa), Hvar, (Lessina), Korčula (Curzola), Sušac (Cazza), Lastovo (Lagosta), and Pelagruža (Pelagosa) with all the islets and rocks lying near them; but exclusive of the islands of Drvenik (Zirona), Čiovo (Bua), Šolta (Solta), and Brač (Brazza).

Following the Treaty of London, a group of Croats, Slovenes, and Serbs in exile from the territory controlled by the Austro-Hungarian empire gathered in Paris on May 1, 1915, to contrive the South Slav Committee (Jugo-slovenski odbor) under the leadership of Ante Trumbić (1864-1938).

On May 3, 1915, Italy renounced her membership in the Triple Alliance and joined the Allied Powers; declared war against Austria-Hungary on May 22, 1915, and against Germany on August 28, 1916. Bulgaria, concluded an alliance with Germany and Austria-Hungary on September 6, 1915, thus joining the Central Powers in war against the Allied Powers.

With prior approval of Constantine I (1868-1923), King of Greece (1913-1917 and 1920-1922), French and British troops landed on October 7, 1915, at Salonika, Greece. Premier Eleutherios Venizelos of Greece and the members of his Cabinet resigned in protest and disapproval of the Monarch's pro-Allied Powers action

Serbia and Montenegro shared the same destiny, they were overrun by the Central Powers occupation armies. The Serbian government under King Petar of the Karađorđević dynasty found itself in total bewilderment and moved from Belgrade to various locations to escape the advancing invaders, Following Serbian military retreats and mortifying defeats inflicted by forces of the Central Powers, a combined German-Austrian-Bulgarian attack compelled King Petar I of Serbia, his government, and the majority of the Serbian army to retreat and make their escape into exile. However, most of the defeated Montenegrin troops were captured and interned in various POW camps. King Nikolas I of Montenegro and members of his government officials also made their escape into exile.

The Serbian army embarked on an unscheduled winter journey southward to Montenegro whence across the Albanian mountains where, under the auspicious undertaking by the Italian navy, the Serbian troops were successfully transported to the Greek island of Corfu. French troops occupied the Greek island of Corfu on January 11, 1916, and prepared the island as a staging facility for the defeated Serbian royal army. The Serbian government of King Petar I was established in-exile on the Island of Corfu, Greece, where Col. Dragutin Dimitrijević-Apis together with a group of his collaborators, were brought to trial for treason, sentenced to death by a Serbian military court and executed. On June 2-13, 1953, Dimitrijević-Apis and his co-defendants were retried in Belgrade by the Supreme Court of the People's Republic of Serbia. In a typical communist staged tribunal which exonerated Dimitrijević-Apis and his collaborators, all the defendants were found not guilty and acquitted.

Under the authority of French military officers, the beaten, despaired, and leaderless Serbian army regrouped, and received the much needed military training and equipment. Subsequently, the Serbs were transported by the Italian navy from Corfu to Salonika, Greece, where they joined the Allied forces on April 1, 1916. Later, Italian troop reinforcements arrived on August 22, 1916, to bolster the Serb, French, and British forces at Salonika.

After 68 years on the throne of the Habsburg dynasty, Franz Josef (b. 1830) Emperor of Austria-Hungary (1848-1916) died on November 21, 1916. His successor to the throne, Charles I (1887-1922) reigned as Emperor of Austria-Hungary (1916-1918). The new Emperor was the younger brother of Archduke Franz Ferdinand, whose assassination on June 28, 1914, by Serbian extremists precipitated the First World War. At the coronation on December 28, 1916, Emperor Charles I pledged to establish an independent Croatia. But, confronted with the collapse of the Habsburg Monarchy, formal recognition and ratification of the constitution failed to be implemented.

In the United States, President Woodrow Wilson had been reelected in 1916 on the slogan "Wilson will keep us [USA] out of war." On March 18, 1917, German "U-boat" submarine sank three U.S. merchant vessels. President Wilson called Congress into extraordiary session. On April 2, 1917, President Wilson in his message delivered to the Joint Session of Congress requested approval for a declaration of war. On April 6, 1917, the U.S. declared war on Germany; and on December 7, 1917 on Austria-Hungary.

In the Austrian parliament at Vienna, on May 30, 1917, representatives Ante Laganja, Croat leader; and Anton Korošec, Slovene leader demanded: "self-determination for Croatia-Slavonia, Dalmatia, and Slovenia as democratic and independent state within the Habsburg dynasty."

In the meantime, under British instigation a group of self-appointed political troublemakers created an unauthorized Committee (Jugo-slovenski odbor), purporting to represent the oppressed South Slav people under Austria-Hungary, with their seat in London, England, decided at the end of May 1917 to accept an invitation from the untrustworthy and deceitful Serbian Karađorđević government in exile to participate in a conference. The unofficial committee nominated the following delegates: the President of South Slavs Committee, Ante Trumbić (Attorney, Leader of the Croatian National Party in the Dalmatian Parliament at Zadar, former Mayor of Split, Representative for the District of Dalmatia in the Austrian Parliament), Hinko Hinković (Croatia), Dusan Vasiljević (Bosnia), and Bogumil Vosnjak (Slovenia). The Serbian government nominated the following delegates: Nikola P. Pašić (Premier and Minister for Foreign Affairs of the Kingdom of Serbia), Stojan Protić, Momčilo Ninčić, Vojislav Marinković, Marko Đuričić, and Milorad Drasković. The conflict between Pašić's "greater Serbia" (Serboslavia), and Trumbić's "confederation of nations," a compromise was reached for a monarchy based on the principle of self-determination.

The Declaration of Corfu (Kérkyra), an Ionian Island of Greece, initiated by the exiled Serbian government and the South Slav Committee, which proclaimed that Serbians, Croatians and Slovenes ought to join in a loose federation within one State with full liberty, equality and justice for all.

*****

~ CORFU DECLARATION ~

July 20, 1917

The members of the Serbian Coalition Cabinet in exile, and representatives of the South Slav Committee in London, England, all of whom have hitherto been working on parallel lines, views have been exchanged in a collaboration with the President of the Skupstina, on all questions concerning the life of the Serbs, Croats and Slovenes in their joint future state.

The idea of its national unity has never suffered extinction, although all the intellectual forces of its enemy were directed against its unification, its liberty, and its national existence. Divided between several states, our nation is in Austria-Hungary alone split up into 11 provincial administrations coming under 13 legislative bodies. The feeling of national unity, together with the spirit of liberty and independence, have supported it in the never-ending struggles of centuries against the Turks and against the Magyars.

The moment has come when our people are no longer isolated. The war imposed by German militarism upon Russia, upon France, and upon England for the defense of their honor as well as for the liberty and independence of small nations, has developed into a struggle for the liberty of the world and the triumph of right over might. All nations which love liberty and independence have allied themselves together for their common defense, to save civilization and liberty at the cost of every sacrifice, to establish a new international order based upon justice and upon the right of every nation to dispose of itself and so organize its independent life; finally to establish a durable peace consecrated to the progress and development of humanity and to secure the world against a catastrophe similar to that which the conquering lust of German imperialism had provoked.

To noble France, who has proclaimed the liberty of nations, and to England, the hearth of liberty. the United States of America and the new, free and democratic Russia have joined themselves in proclaiming as their principal war aim the triumph of liberty and democracy and as basis of the new international order the right of free self-determination for every nation.

Our nation of the three names, which has been the greatest sufferer under brute force and injustice and which has made the greatest sacrifices to preserve its right of self-determination, has with enthusiasm accepted this sublime principle put forward as the chief aim of this atrocious war, provoked by the violation of this very principle.

The representatives of the Serbs, Croats and Slovenes, declaring that the desire of their people to free themselves from every foreign yoke and to constitute themselves a free, Independent National State, a desire based on the principle that every nation has the right to decide its own destiny, agree in declaring that this state must be founded on the following democratic principles:

1. The State of the Serbs, Croats and Slovenes, also known as the Southern Slavs, shall be a free and independent kingdom, with indivisible territory and unity of allegiance. It shall be a constitutional, democratic and parliamentary monarchy under the Karađorđevic dynasty.

2. This State shall be named the Kingdom of the Serbs, Croats and Slovenes, and the title of the sovereign shall be "King of the Serbs, Croats and Slovenes."

3. The State shall have a single coat-of-arms, a single flag and a single crown with all emblems composed from those present existing.

4. The individual Serb, Croat and Slovene flags and coats-of-arms may be freely hoisted on all occasions and used with equal freedom.

5. The three national names-Serbs, Croats and Slovenes-shall be equal before the law throughout the territory of the kingdom, and everyone may use them freely on all public occasions.

6. The two alphabets, the Cyrillic and the Latin, shall rank equally, and everyone may use them freely throughout the territory of the kingdom. The royal authority and the local self-governing authorities shall have the right to employ both alphabets in accordance with the wishes of the people.

7. All recognized religions shall be freely and publicly exercised. The Orthodox, Roman Catholic and Muslims creeds which are chiefly professed by our people, shall rank equally and enjoy the same rights in relation to the State. In consideration of these principles the legislature shall take special care to safeguard religious concord in conformity with the spirit and tradition of our whole nation.

8. The calendar shall be unified as soon as possible.

9. The territory of the kingdom of the Serbs, Croats and Slovenes shall include all territories inhabited compactly by our people and shall not be mutilated without detriment to the vital interests of the whole. Our nation demands nothing that belongs to others but only that which is its own. It desires freedom and unity. Therefore, it consciously and firmly refuses every partial solution of the problem of their deliverance from Austro-Hungarian domination and their union with Serbia and Montenegro in one State forming an indivisible whole. In accordance with the right of self-determination no part of this territorial totality may without infringement of justice be detached and incorporated with some other state without the consent of the nation itself.

10. In the interests of freedom and equal rights of all nations, the Adriatic Sea shall be free and open to all.

11. All citizens throughout the territory of the kingdom shall be equal and enjoy the same rights in relation to the State and before the law.

12. Members of the National Representative body shall be elected by universal suffrage, with equal, direct and secret ballot. The same shall apply to the elections in the communes and other administrative assemblies.

13. The Constitution, to be established after the conclusion of peace, by a Constituent Assembly elected by universal suffrage and direct secret ballot, shall be the basis of the entire life of the nation.

The Constitution shall provide the nation with the opportunity of exercising its special energies in local autonomies delimited by natural, social, and economic conditions. The Constitution must be passed in its entirety by a numerically defined majority of three-fifths in the Constituent Assembly. The Constitution, like all other laws passed by the Constituent Assembly, shall be effective after receiving the Royal sanction. The nation thus unified shall form a State of twelve million inhabitants which shall be the guaranty for their independence and national development and a powerful bulwark against German aggression and the inseparable ally of all those civilized nations which have proclaimed the principle of right, liberty and international justice. It shall be a worthy member of the community of nations.

Signed: Ante Trumbić (1864-1938)
                    Chairman, South Slav Committee in exile

                    Nikola P. Pašić (1845-1926)
                    Prime Minister and Minister of Foreign
                    of the Kingdom of Serbia in exile

* * * * *

The Russian revolution-actually two revolutions: (a) the "February revolution," on March 8 (February 23 old style calendar), 1917; strikers in St. Petersburg (Petrograd), resulted in outbreaks of rioting; and (b) the "October revolution," on November 7 (October 25 old style calendar), 1917 under the leadership of Vladimir Ilych Uljanov, nickname: Lenin (1870-1924) started an armed revolt against the provisional government, thus began the Russian civil war (1917-1922) which brought the Bolsheviks to power in Russia.

Arthur James Balfour (1848-1930), during his tenure as British foreign secretary (1916-1919), framed "The Balfour Declaration" which has been submitted to and approved by the Cabinet on November 2, 1917: "The government of Britain views with favor the establishment in Palestine of a national home for the Jewish people, and will use their best endeavors to facilitate the achievement of this object, it being clearly understood that nothing shall be done which may prejudice the civil and religious rights of existing non-Jewish communities in Palestine, or the rights and political status enjoyed by Jews in any other country."

On January 8, 1918, U.S. President Woodrow Wilson in his speech to the U.S. Congress, proclaimed the "Fourteen Points" program for peace in Europe. The most important point was the right of self-determination for the peoples of the former Austria-Hungary monarchy. During the peace negotiations, world leaders proposed various reforms in order to reduce international tensions among nations and ensure that another world-wide conflict could never happen again. A decision based on ignorance and lack of understanding in international affairs, became obvious at the end of the First World War, when the Allied Powers (France, Britain, and United States of America) agreed to the most disgraceful idea to create a South Slav State from the former territories of Austria-Hungarian empire to be united with those of Serbia, Montenegro, and northern Macedonia.

A group of sailors on the Austrian battleship "Sankt Georg" enchored at the Gulf of Kotor (Boka Kotorska) on southeastern Adriatic coast, on February 1, 1918, mutinied against the Austrian authority. The mutineers arrested and captured their naval officers, including the Austrian admiral, and replaced the Austrian black and yellow banner with that of the Revolutionary Marxist red flag. The mutiny was crushed and four revolutionary sailors were sentenced to death and executed.

The Central Powers (Germany, Austria-Hungary, Bulgaria, and Turkey) as the victor, concluded two separate treaties of Brest-Litovsk, one with Ukraine on Febryary 9, 1918, and the other with Soviet Russia on March 3, 1918 which ended Russian participation (as member of the Allied Powers). The treaty provided for Russia to recognize the sovereignty of Ukraine and also the Russian evacuation from Poland, Finland, Estonia, Livonia, and Kurland.

In 1918, before the imposed creation of the so-called Kingdom of Serbs, Croats, and Slovenes under the Karađeorđević Dynasty of Serbia, the despicable Serbian foreign minister Stojan Protić, a devoted Serb-Orthodox, explained how to solve the ethnic "Muslim problem," by expelling one-third to Turkey, converting the other third to the Eastern Serbian Orthodox religion, and liquidating the remaining uncooperative elements.

On April 8-10, 1918, the Congress of Oppressed Nationalities, comprised of representatives from Croatia, Czechoslovakia, Italy, Poland, Romania, and Slovenia meeting at Rome, Italy, unanimously recognized the national rights and independence of every nation.

In a last desperate move to save the Habsburg dynasty, on October 1, 1918, Emperor Charles of Austria-Hungary, offered to create a multi-nationalist federation within the Habsburg empire, but the offer was useless. The Croatian National Parliament convened at Zagreb on October 2 declared, "all previous state relationship and ties, between Croatia, Slavonia, Rijeka, and Dalmatia from one side, and the Austria-Hungary empire from the other side are hereby dissolved." The national constitutional parliament will decide with a qualified majority about the form of government and the internal system of the new state based on the complete equality among nations.

A self-appointed and unelected body, the Council of Slovenes, Croats, and Serbs (Narodno vijeće - SHS) was organized in Zagreb on October 5, 1918 by pro-South Slav elements. Its president was Anton Korošec, a Slovene, and the Council was dominated by Svetozar Pribičević, a Serb from Croatia, who wanted a union of Croatia and Serbia at any price. The Croatian Party of Rights did not recognize the union of Croatia with other nationalities under the Serbian monarchy.

Meanwhile in Montenegro, the Serbian ethnic minority with help from Serb-četnici, in October 1918 conspired against their longtime friend, wartime comrade and a member nation of the victorious Allied Powers, set up a fraudulent national assembly of Montenegro at Podgorica and by coup d' état deposed the non-Serbian King Nikolas I (1910-1918) of Montenegro - Petrović Dynasty, and declared a permanent union of Montenegro with the Serbian Karađorđević monarchy.

The proclamation of the Croatian National Parliament (Sabor) on October 29, 1918, announced the severance of all ties between Croatia and Austria-Hungary, and by signing the Geneva Declaration on November 9, 1918, the Habsburg monarchy was dissolved. The conclusion of the First World War on November 11, 1918, ended the Habsburg dynasty and marked the fragmentation of Austro-Hungarian "dual monarchy" formed July 28, 1867.

Following the end of the First World War and the collapse of Austro-Hungarian Empire, the Croatian faction, led by a Croat, Stjepan Radić (1871-1928) President of the Croatian Peasant Party, demanded a degree of autonomy for all constituent members within the union of federal states. The Serbian faction, headed by Serb Premier Nikola Pašić (1815-1926), ignored the right of self-determination, liberty, equality, and justice for all. Instead, the arrogant Pašić advocated a strong centralized state under complete control and supremacy of Serbia. Nevertheless, the Croatian people demanded the right of self-determination and the holding of a plebiscite under international supervision for the Republic of Croatia.

As the people everywhere contemplated about the future of their nation following the post-war era, in November 1918 the despicable Serbian army invaded Croatia, Slovenia, Macedonia, Bosnia-Herzegovina, etc., and imposed their ruthless military authority. As the Croatian soldiers and sailors were returning to their homes, unarmed, and ready to rebuild a new nation, free and independent, they were mystified and shocked to find that Croatia was occupied by the imperialistic and barbaric Serbian military force.

On November 24, 1918, the National Council in Zagreb purporting to represent Croatia and Slovenia, decided to join Serbia in a democratic federation of "equal" nations in compliance with the Corfu Declaration of July 20, 1917. The catastrophic union of South-Slavs was announced in Belgrade on December 1, 1918, without the approbation of the Croatian National Parliament (Sabor). Prince Aleksandar Karađorđević of Serbia accepted the Regency of the new state. On December 4, 1918, the Kingdom of the Serbs, Croats, and Slovenes (Kraljevsto Serba, Hrvata i Slovenaca) was formally proclaimed in Belgrade, Serbia.

The people of Croatia, Slovenia, and Bosnia-Herzegovina, etc, had no voice or access to the Peace Conference in Geneva whereas the government of the Serbian Karađorđević dynasty had representatives defending their own special interest. The politicians promoting the unitarian kingdom of Serbia saw in the unification of South-Slavs their opportunity for the aggrandizement of Serbia and the creation of a new state of Serboslavia with Serbs having the supreme or, at least, preponderant influence.

Henceforth, the Croatian people for the first time witnessed the unmasked Serbian political and military circles in action as they revealed their true identity and unmistakable personality as being untrustworthy, unmerciful, morally degenerated, corrupt, and dangerous.

CHAPTER 3

TRAGIC EXPERIMENT, 1919 - 1940

Europe emerged from the devastation of the First World War (1914-1918) lacking in security and stability as attested by numerous bankruptcies, worthless currencies, damaged trade, destroyed infrastructure; millions of people suffered and died from sickness, despair, and starvation; this chaotic situation created a major political discontent, and gave rise to communist conspiracy and totalitarian takeover.

The armistice declared at the eleventh hour of November 11, 1918, that ended the First World War, was based on the Fourteen Points proclaimed on January 8, 1918, by Woodrow Thomas Wilson (1856-1924), U.S. President (1913-1921),which imposed the imperfections of the Versailles Treaty signed on November 19, 1919, disregarding self-determination, justice, and human rights. The victorious Allies ignored the national rights of Croats, Slovenes, and other ethnic minorities when they arbitrarily created the most unscrupulous union of South Slavs under the Serbian regime of the Karađorđević Dynasty. In September 1919, Wilson suffered a stroke that left him paralized; he kept his disability away from the media and politicians until the end of his term in 1921; retired in Washington, D.C.; died on February 3, 1924. President Wilson was awarded the Nobel Peace Prize on December 10, 1920, for his "peace initiative" which, in reality and contrary to international opinion, contributed to the greatest instability of Europe and ultimately produced the Second World War. Wilson was naive because he lacked perception, analytical insight, and intuitive judgment that are the basis of sound behavior in a practical world. Moreover, Wilson was a failure because the condition he imposed upon millions of innocent people in Europe have not achieved the desired peaceful results.

On April 28, 1919 the Covenant of the League of Nations (consisting of 26 Articles) received unanimous acceptance by the planetary assembly of the Versailles Peace Conference. Under Treaty of Saint Germain on September 10, 1919, Austria ceded: Dalmatia, Trieste, Istria, south Trentino, Bosnia-Herzegovina, Bohemia, Moravia, and Galicia; and by Treaty of Trianon on June 4, 1920, Hungary ceded: Croatia, Slavonia, Fiume (Rijeka), Banat, Transylvania, and western Hungary. The city of Rijeka held by Hungary until the collapse of the Austro-Hungarian empire was rewarded to Italy by the secret Treaty of London dated April 26, 1915, when Britain, France, and Russia agreed to cede Rijeka to Italy. It became an issue at the International Peace Conference and was seized on September 20, 1919 by an expeditionary force under the command of Gabriele D'Annunzio (1863-1938), prince of Monte Nevoso. On November 12, 1920, by Treaty of Rapallo between Italy and Yugoslavia, Fiume (Rijeka) became a free seaport city, formally incorporated by Italy in 1924.

The kingdom of Serbs, Croats, and Slovenes was contrived from parts of the defeated Austro-Hungarian and Ottoman Turkish empires, after they were dissolved by the Treaty of Versailles. Included in the new state were the former kingdoms of Serbia and Montenegro; Bosnia-Herzegovina, previously administered jointly by the dual monarchy of Austria and Hungary; Croatia, Slavonia and Vojvodina, the semi-autonomous regions of Hungary; Dalmatia and Slovenia (part of Styria), formerly administered provinces of Austria (Österreich) meaning "the eastern kingdom".

The South Slav regime was burdened by numerous conflicts and difficulties immediately upon its creation, which was rapidly exacerbated due to the hegemony of the Serbian netted social system, the monarchy, and the nationalistic policy of the Serbian government. The regime afflicted with national antagonisms throughout its existence, refused to tackle the exceedingly important national ethnic question that remained unsolved. The Serbian monarchy erroneously claimed that the Serbs, Croats, and Slovenes were one and the same people, and that the Macedonian and Montenegrin peoples did not even exist as ethnic groups. The coerced creation of the kingdom of South Slavs fulfilled the contrived scheme of many intellectuals who arrogantly disregarded the fundamental differences among the various slavic and non-slavic people. The primary form of government, such as centralization favored by Serb monarchists versus a federation and decentralization demanded by Croat and Slovene republicans, caused deep resentment, became a major political disagreement, and remained the main obstacle to any future union of nations. In addition to the Croats, Slovenes, and Serbs conflicting political and cultural traditions, the kingdom of South Slavs under the Karađorđević monarchy ignored the existence and importance of sizeable minorities; Germans, Italians, Hungarians, Romanians, Bulgarians, Greeks, Czechs, Slovaks, Poles, Ukrainians, Russians, Albanians, Turks, Sephardic and Ashkenazic Jews, and Gypsies. Furthermore, the linguistic unlikeness and divergence kept the Croats, Slovenes, Serbs, and Macedonians disunited.

The Eastern Orthodox Christian, Catholic, Islamic (Muslim), Jewish, Uniat, and Protestant faiths all were well established across ethnic and regional areas. The kingdom of South Slavs encompassed Slovenia, Croatia, Slavonia, Dalmatia, Bosnia-Herzegovina, Montenegro, Serbia, Vojvodina, Kosova, and parts of Macedonia. The people of Croatia, Slovenia, and others persevered the kingdom of South Slavs for what it represented, a tyrannical government. Clear demands by Croatians, Slovenes, and other non-Serbian ethnic groups for equal rights, job opportunities, and justice was not only stubbornly resisted by the Serbian monarchy, but also counteracted by Serbian obstinate policy.

On January 10, 1920, the League of Nations was established, and on April 19, 1946 was dissolved. For the record, on March 15, 1920, the U.S. Senate, by a vote of 57 to 39 (a margin of seven votes short of the 64 votes required for two-thirds majority), refused to ratify the Treaty of Versailles.

French troops occupied the Ruhr Basin on April 7, 1920. German civilians in Frankfurt taunted the French occupation forces. French armored cars and soldiers patrolled the streets and responded with gunfire against local demonstrations. Six civilians were killed and numerous wounded.

By Treaty of Trianon signed June 4, 1920, Hungary lost 67% of its pre-war territory and 58% of its population. Following an ultimatum to Germany, on March 8, 1921, French troops occupied the industrial cities and river ports of Dusseldorf, Duisburg, and Ruhrort. In accordance with the Treaty of Versailles, a plebiscite was held on March 20, 1921 in the region of Upper Silesia (Oberschlesien). Voting results were: 717,000 in favor of reuniting the territory with Germany, and 483,000 to remain with Poland. An armed rebellion on May 3, 1921, under the Polish commissioner Adalbert Korfanty prevented the normal transfer of Upper Silesia to Germany.

After deliberate delay, the kingdom of South Slavs scheduled election for the Constituent Assembly were held on November 28, 1920. The Croatian Republican Peasant Party (Hrvatska republikanska saljačka stranka) under the leadership of Stjepan Radić won a landslide victory in Croatia. On January 1, 1921, the Constituent Assembly in Belgrade approved the Constitution by a simple majority (of the 419 eligible deputies, 223 voted in favor, 35 against, and 161 abstained). Premier Nikola Pašić received a simple majority of votes by promising concessions to Bosnian Muslims, that is, the cancellation of announced agrarian reform in Bosnia. This reneged previous agreements requiring the necessary three-fifths (252) votes for approval. Nevertheless, the political procedure legalized the national inequality and created a centralized system of government with absolute power under the Serbian royal dynasty to which the Croats and Slovenes continued to register their unyielding opposition. On June 28, 1921 the Constitution of the Kingdom of Serbs, Croats, and Slovenes (Ustava Kraljevine Srba, Hrvata i Slovenaca) a.k.a. the Vidovdan Constitution (Vidovdanski Ustav) was ratified. The constitution provided for threefold government functions (branches) - legislative, executive, and judicial - and vested the monarchy with dictatorial power.

CROATIA

THE KINGDOM OF SERBS, CROATS AND SLOVENES, 1921

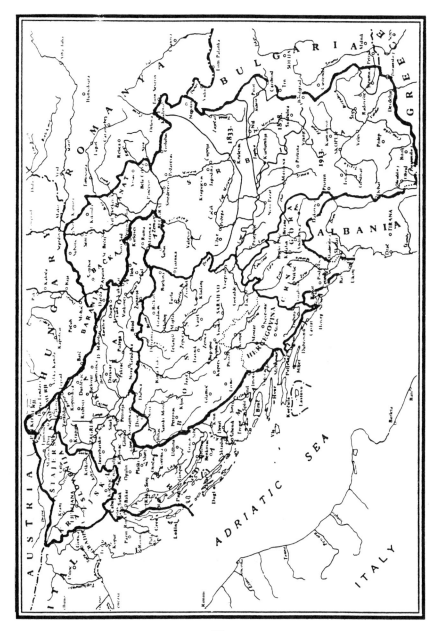

A political struggle ensued between Serbs on one side, versus Croats and Slovenes who wanted a federal structure with certain regional and ethnic autonomy. Croat and Slovene representatives withdrew from the Constituent Assembly, declaring the Vidovdan Constitution null and void. Nevertheless, on August 16, 1921, the arrogant and hypocritical Aleksandar I (1888-1934) became king.

French and Belgium troops on January 11, 1923, invaded the Valley of the Ruhr (Ruhrgebiet) and occupied it until July 1925 when they agreed to evacuate the territory and normalize relations with Germany.

The political situation caused by the king's dictatorial power did not please Croatian republicans and federalists, neither did it please the Slovenes. Consequently, the Croats and Slovenes continued to boycott the National Assembly in Belgrade even after the election of March 18, 1923.

By Treaty of Friendship signed in Rome, Italy, on January 27, 1924 between the Kingdom of Serbs, Croats, and Slovenes (under the Serbian Karađorđević monarchy) a settlement was concluded whereby the Adriatic seaport city of Fiume (Rijeka) was awarded to Italy. This five-year treaty was never renewed.

In the meantime, the Croatian Republican Peasant Party - CRPP under the leadership of Stjepan Radić (1871-1928) became the largest opposition political party in the country. By deceit and political brutality the Serbian monarchy remained in power. On December 24, 1924, the Serbian Karađorđević monarchy with recommendation of Premier Nikola Pašić, an arrogant Serb, implemented the so-called law of state's protection, dissolved and outlawed the CRPP, thus suppressing the Croatian democratic opposition. Most of the CRPP's leadership were under house arrest. On January 6, 1925 Stjepan Radić, leader of the CRPP, was imprisoned for demanding political and economic reforms, freedom of the press and speech. Radić was released from prison on July 18, 1925, and soon resumed his political crusade for reforms, freedom, justice, and human rights. The Kingdom of Serbs, Croats, and Slovenes, overwhelmingly dominated by Serbs, repulsed all Croat and Slovene demands seeking a greater share in government participation.

Pavle Radić, cousin of Stjepan Radić, on March 27, 1925, made a personal declaration to join the government in Belgrade. The CRPP dropped the word "republican" from its name, and assumed the new name of Croatian Peasant Party - CPP (Hrvatska seljačka stranka - HSS). Subsequently, Croatian representatives entered the government on July 18, 1925, and reluctantly agreed to remain in the government until February 1, 1927, in order to campaign in the preparation for the next election. During the election campaign the legitimate rights of the Croatian people were to be settled peacefully and by paramilitary and democratic procedures.

The Serbian authoritarian climate continued to prevail, human rights, political and civil liberties were conveniently circumscribed in varying degrees. Arrests for "hostile propaganda" were common throughout Croatia, where ethnic Croats accused of separatism and nationalism were the primary victims of Serbian continuous persecution. Increasing unrest within the Serbian kingdom, culminated in demonstrations and strikes. The Karađorđević monarchy authorized the Serb-četnici to maintain continuous repressive action against Croats and others, including Serbs who happened to disagree with the monarch's insensitivity for human rights. The pacifist attitude used by Croats and other ethnic groups, encouraged the Serb-četnici to become more aggressive and ruthless in their goal to maintain the totalitarian government of Serbia (Serboslavia). Even peaceful protest against the barbaric Serbian government resulted in personal incarceration and also the possibility of punishment for family members. The ever increasing Serbian repressive policies, which made Croatians second class citizens, contributed to the justifiable anti-Serb opinion and Croatian increasing opposition.

Throughout the country, controversies continued in every aspect of public life. The ever present disputes between Serb-officials and supporters of the Serb monarchy on one side and those who critized the government's insensitivity to ethnic minority like Croatians on the other side, was not about to be extinct. The Serb monarchy used the national police "gendarmes," paramilitary units, to enforce their tyrannical laws enacted by the National Assembly in Belgrade. The Serb gendarmes were vicious and unruly. They created fear and terror with their unlimited authority, and maintained police surveillance on individuals and groups. Serb gendarmes and Serb-četnici collaborated to solidify a police-state; they acted as judge, jury, and executioners in the name of Serbia (Serboslavia).

After the election of September 11, 1927, Stjepan Radić for the Croatian Peasant Party - CPP (HSS), and Svetozar Pribičević for the Independent Democratic Party - IDP (Samostalna demokratska stranka - SDS), formed the Peasant Democratic Coalition -PDC (Seljačka demokratska koalicija - SDK) to oppose King Aleksandar's dictatorship and to expose the Serbian monarchy for its wide-spread corruption and human rights violations.

In a system of international alliances, King Aleksandar I of Serbia signed the Treaty of Friendship on November 11, 1927, with Romania and Czeckoslovakia, which led to the creation of the Little Entente in 1933. France and Yugoslavia signed a Treaty of Friendship on November 11, 1927.

This treaty was similar to the treaties France had previously concluded with two other states, Czechoslovakia (January 25, 1924) and Romania (June 10, 1925). The treaty provided for mutual support in case of attack, but, except for the one concluded with Czechoslavakia, the treaties were not implemented by any military agreement. The Franco-Yugoslav Treaty was renewed on October 12, 1937, for another five years.

As a result of domestic political crises and conflict, between Croats and Serbs, the internal situation continued to show widespread unrest. Inside the National Assembly (Narodna Skupstina) in Belgrade, on June 20, 1928, five deputies of the Assembly and members of the Croatian Peasant Party (CPP) were shot by Paniša Račić (a Serb deputy from Montenegro). Two Croatian deputies, Pavle Radić and Đuro Basariček were killed on the spot; three other Croatian deputies Stjepan Radić, Ivan Grandja, and Ivan Pernar were seriously wounded. Croatian reaction was particularly sad and bitter. In protest, on August 1, 1928, Croatian deputies withdrew from the bloodstained parliament in Belgrade, the capital city of hatred. On August 8, 1928, Stjepan Radić died in Zagreb from wounds received on the June 20, 1928 attack. Peace will never be achieved as long as the Serb-četnici insist in their hegemony over other nationalities. In a typical unremorseful style attributed exclusively to Serb politicians and Serbian elite, they congratulated the assassin for his outrageous crime against humanity. Although Serbian people are like any other people in the world, history attests that the Serbian military and political leadership are basically dirty, rotten, no good, and must never be trusted. Those who take chances and trust the Serbs, deserve all the unpleasant consequences.

During the dual alliance proposals to establish a French-USA non-aggression pact, French Foreign Minister Aristide Briand (1862-1932) and U.S. Secretary of State, Frank Billing Kellogg (1856-1937), agreed to invite other nations to join in outlawing warmongering. On August 27, 1928, Australia, Belgium, Britain, Canada, Czechoslovakia, France, Germany, India, Irish Free State, Italy, Japan, New Zealand, Poland, South Africa, and United States of America signed at Paris, the "Kellogg-Briand Peace Treaty" renouncing the use of war as an instrument to settle conflicts and international disputes. By the end of 1929 another 54 nations joined by signing the treaty banning war. The U.S. Senate ratified the Kellogg-Briand anti-war covenant on January 15, 1929. Although the treaty lacked the mechanism to enforce its provisions and became powerless in preventing aggression, it was used to punish persons guilty of war crimes.

To convey dissatisfaction and disapproval with the Serbian monarchy, the Croatian representatives established and convoked their own Parliament in Zagreb on October 1, 1928. All the efforts or lack of efforts by the Serbian

King Aleksandar to achieve a Serbian compromise with Croats ended in failure. The Croats became displeased and discouraged with the Serbian insensible and arrogant attitude. Complicated election laws were established on January 6, 1929, by the Serbian monarchy to ensure the election of a maximum number of Serbs. The electorial formula was very arbitrary and unjust because it was designed to steal the election and rob the people from having a free election. The disgraceful law allowed Serbian candidates to receive only 8,000 votes in order to get elected. Conversely, Croatian candidates were required to receive at least 11,500 votes to get elected. Obviously, the disparity of this undemocratic election process favored a political system in which the Serbian ruler controlled the power of government.

The Serb monarchy made every effort to persuade the Croatian people to forget their desire for freedom, equality, and human rights, and adopt the ideas of Serbia. Hereupon, arose the irreconcilable strife between Serbs and Croats. Wide spread poverty, social underclass, ethnic oppression, flagrant disregard for human life, economic and cultural backwardness were all salient features of the Karađorđević Serbian regime. The dictatorial policy of King Aleksandar succeeded in exacerbating the existing social and political antagonisms, which lead to the establishment of a strong anti-Serb movement. King Aleksandar I and his Serb collaborators were frustrated by the inability to govern due to ever increasing Croatian demand for a democratic federal state, but remained unyielding and unwilling to share authority with Croats and other ethnic groups. By a coup d'etat on January 6, 1929, King Aleksandar I issued the "Law On Royal Power and Supreme State Administration" (Zakon o kraljevskoj vlasti i vrhovnoj državno upravi) dissolving the National Assembly (Narodna Skupstina) in Belgrade, abolishing the stinking Vidovdan Constitution of 1921.

After numerous anti-democratic decrees annunciated by the Serbian government, the non-Serbian political and social organizations were forced to operate clandestinely. Croats and other opponents of Serbian hegemony were ruthlessly mistreated, vigorously and systematically persecuted, imprisoned, tortured, and assassinated. To fight the Serbs and to counteract against their vicious atrocities, repressive methods, savage and destructive behavior, the inevitable became a reality. Enough was enough, on January 10, 1929, a former deputy parliamentarian in the Serb monarchy at Belgrade, and member of the Croatian Party of Rights, Ante Pavelić (1889-1959), announced the formation of the "Ustaše" (singular, Ustaša), from the Croatian word "Ustanak" meaning "insurgent". This movement was organized for the common struggle in defense of Croatia and the Croatian people in opposition to Serbian brutality and autocracy. Understandably, the Ustaše movement gained popularity, especially among those Croatians who were victimized by the Serb-četnici and Serb-gendarmes under the Karađorđević tyranny.

On January 21, 1929, non-Serbian political parties and social organizations were dissolved, and a legislative council as an advisory board was established on February 17, 1929, to replace the National Assembly in Belgrade. The Serb monarch issued a series of degrees restricting individual rights and strengthening the Serbian police powers in order to harass, persecute, enforce long-term prison sentences, and carry out death penalties for all anti-Serb and anti-monarchy political activities.

By royal Proclamation, on October 3, 1929, King Aleksandar I of Serbia officially renamed his state the "Kingdom of Yugoslavia" (literally: the land of South Slavs). Subsequently, King Aleksandar I named his new government and appointed a General of the Karađorđević royal guard, Petar Živković as Premier. Unsurprisingly, in 1903, the same Živković, as a young military officer and a member of the Black Hand (Crna ruka), participated in the assassination of Serbia's King Milan Obrenović, his wife Draga Mašin and others.

The territory of the kingdom of Yugoslavia was officially gerrymandered and divided into nine administrative provinces called "Banovine" (Governorships) designated by identifiable names of respective rivers without regard for historic and ethnic boundary. Each Banovina was headed by a Governor (Ban). In six of the nine administrative provinces, after being gerrymandered to suit the Serb's own advantage, the ethnic Serbian population became an instant statistical majority. The capital city of Belgrade, including Zemun and Pancevo, became a separate entity:

Banovina	Capital	Territories
Dravska	Ljubljana	Slovenia
Drinska	Sarajevo	Western Bosnia
Dunarska	Novi Sad	Vojvodina, Serbia
Moravska	Niš	Western Serbia
Primorska	Split	Dalmatia, Southern Bosnia
Savska	Zagreb	Croatia, Slavonia, Kvarner
Vardarska	Skoplje	Kosova
Vrbaska	Banja Luka	Eastern Bosnia
Zetska	Cetinje	Herzegovina, Montenegro

BANOVINE OF THE KINGDOM OF YUGOSLAVIA, 1929

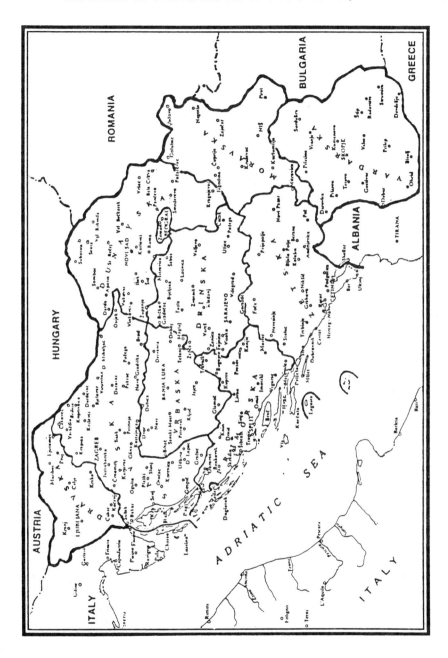

Henceforth, the despotic dictatorship of Serbian Karađorđević monarchy ruled by military decree based on the following:

(a) All municipal and departmental councils, outside Serbia proper, were abolished;

(b) The use of the name "Croatia" (Hrvatska) was strictly forbidden;

(c) Freedom of the press, speech, and assembly was abolished;

(d) National emblems and national flags of non-Serb nationalities were illegal and forbidden;

(e) Only the flag of the Serbian Monarchy was authorized and permitted to be displayed;

(f) The Serbian flag was permitted to be the standard emblem of the Serbian Orthodox Church;

(g) Non-Serb Orthodox religious practices were vigorously controlled and curtailed;

(h) Established the "Yugoslav Falcon" a political youth organization to promote Serbian nationalism;

(I) Outlawed all non-Serb organizations with ethnic and religious affiliation, as the "Croatian Eagle" (Hrvatski orao) which promoted patriotic and family values, freedom, and human rights;

Vladko Maček (1879-1964), leader of the Croatian Peasant Party was arrested on May 27, 1929, by Serbian gendarmes and subsequently released. Again on December 22, 1929, Vladko Maček was arrested and imprisoned until June 14, 1930. Moreover, King Aleksandar I of Yugoslavia outlawed the "ustaše" movement. Ante Pavelić (1869-1959), native of Bradina, Herzegovina, appealed to the League of Nations on July 17, 1929, and supplicated that the Croatian people be given their human rights and the necessary protection from Serbian tyrannical monarchy.

In a major effort to indoctrinate the Yugoslav youth to accept the Serbian doctrine, the Serbian monarchy introduced the "Yugoslav Falcon" in December 1929. Also, the Serbian monarchy outlawed all non-Serb organizations based on "ethnic-political-cultural" affiliations.

The change of the official name to Yugoslavia did not change the Serbian desire to preclude Croatia from becoming a democratic and free nation. However, Serbs continued to intimidate, persecute, torture, and maintain a reign of terror against those who opposed the tyranny of Serbian monarchy. In 1931, two outstanding and world's most renown citizens interceded on behalf of the League for Defense of Human Rights, and protested against the Serbian terror in Croatia. Physicist, Albert Einstein (1879-1955) and novelist, Heinrich Mann (1871-1950) appealed to all freedom loving peoples to protect and defend the Croatians by stating: "All countries are duty bound to shield the small, peaceful, and civilized nation of Croatia."

The commander of the Serbian army in Zagreb, Gen. Belimarković (a Serb) organized atrocities, harrassment, and terrorist activities against Croatian people. Milan Šufflay was assassinated on February 18, 1931, by members of Gen. Belimarković's Serbian terrorist group. Šufflay, editor of the Croatian Rights (Hrvatsko pravo), was a spokesman for an independent and democratic Croatia, and staunch defender of human rights. Due to increased Serbian police terror, thousands of Croatians and other ethnic non-Serbs were forced to emigrate. Because of incompetence, ignorance, and egocentric interests, the kingdom of Yugoslavia slowly but surely, excavated its own grave for their self-imposed final internment, and succeeded to deliver the Karađorđević Serbian monarchy to it's deserved extinction. Continuous antagonism and territorial disputes impeded friendly progress with its neighboring countries.

On September 3, 1931, King Aleksandar I of the Karađorđević Serbian monarchy superseded the Law of January 6, 1929, and promulgated a new Constitution of the Kingdom of Yugoslavia (Ustav kraljevine Jugoslavije). Although a pseudo-parliamentary system of National Representation (Narodno predstavništo) was established, the Croats and Slovenes viewed the document as another disgraceful Serbian instrument. The Constitution was a mischievous action that provided for a parliamentary manipulation to ensure political victory for the Serbian monarchy and their cronies. Discrimination became the way of life in the kingdom of Yugoslavia. The fact remained that the Serbs, who accounted for less than 38 percent of the total population in Yugoslavia, held the disproportional 80 percent of the positions in the national and local administration. The monarchy of King Aleksandar I of Serbia devised a rigged election law whereby democratic political opposition was virtually impossible. The election law required the political party be represented in all electoral districts of the country. A realistic nationwide electoral representation became impossible to achieve because a Croatian political party was not allowed to open an office in Serbia, and Slovenian political party was not allowed to open an office in Montenegro, etc. Only the Serb political parties were allowed to open an office in all electoral districts of the country, regardless of the numerical representation.

The electoral law entitled Law On Voters Lists (Zakon o biračkim spiskovina) revealed the deep arrogance and hypocrisy of the inhumane monarchy. The devised formula provided the electoral winner receive two-thirds of the mandates, the remaining one-third was divided among all participants, including the winner. The voting was public and oral, one-half of senators were elected and one-half appointed by the king. The legislative, executive, and judicial powers was vested in the king. Opposition to the dictatorship of King Aleksandar was not confined to the non-Serbian population.

In the Far East, Manchuria became a territorial rivalry between two imperialist countries which contributed to the Russo-Japanese War of 1904-1905. After the Mukden (Shenyang) incident on September 18, 1931, Japanese troops invaded all of Manchuria (Manchukuo), set up in 1932 as independent state, and in 1934 established as Japanese puppet regime. In 1933 and 1935, Japan extended its frontiers to include an area of NE China. In July 1937, a confrontation at the Marco Polo bridge near Peking, between Japanese and Chinese troops brought the two Asian countries to war.

In the German national elections for the Reichstag held on July 31, 1932, the Nazis won 230 seats, Socialists 133, Center party 97, and Communists 89. Paul von Hindenburg (1847-1934), Germany's president (1925-1934), on August 31, 1932 offered the vice-chancellorship to Hitler under chancellor Franz von Papen (1879-1969), but Hitler declined. On September 12, 1932 the Reichstag was dissolved, new elections were held on November 6, but failed to break the deadlock. Therefore, von Papen resigned on November 17 and von Hindenburg on January 30, 1933, named Hitler as chancellor.

On February 12, 1933, Albert Dufour, German minister in Yugoslavia had a conversation with King Aleksandar of Yugoslavia, at which time Aleksandar spoke of his past efforts to reach a political settlement with Italy. Aleksandar stated that his negotiations with Mussolini, after having lasted almost a year, were about to be concluded when the Italian government suddenly changed its attitude and the negotiations were broken off for the reason that Yugoslavia no longer appeared sufficiently stable for the conclusion of such political agreements. The king regretted that as a result of these developments he had been forced against his will last fall to renew the offensive and defensive alliance with France. Aleksandar stated that there is no doubt that the continuation of tension between Italy and Yugoslavia contributes substantially to the disturbed internal situation of Yugoslavia and thereby seriously increase the possibilities of a disintegration of Yugoslavia; that is, a secession of Croatia and Slovenia. Nothing could give legitimism in Austria a stronger impetus than the political rapprochement of an independent Croatia and Slovenia.

On February 16, 1933, Czechoslovakia, Romania, and Yugoslavia signed a "Pact of Organization of the Little Entente" designed to strengthen the alliance by the establishment of common organs such as the Permanent Council and the Economic Council of the Little Entente.

Heinrich Himmler (1900-1945) chief of Hitler's SS (Schutzstaffeln), black-shirted Nazis, on July 9, 1934 was named director of detention camps in Germany; the first known camp had been created as a Nazi institution in March 1933 at Dachau, Bavaria, to keep in custody the undesirable communists or alleged anti-Nazi elements.

* * * * *

~ Conversation With King Aleksandar ~

Belgrade, June 1, 1933

To: German Foreign Minister

From: German Minister in Yugoslavia

Record of conversation with the King of Yugoslavia at Dedinje. After the usual words of introduction, King Aleksandar asked why Germany attached so much importance to the Four Powers Pact. I replied, that if my [German] government decided to sign the pact, the chief reason was to assure to Europe a 10-year peace, all so urgently in need, so that after the perpetual disturbances we might finally have tranquillity for rebuilding our countries.

The king thereupon stated that he would prefer a customs union of Germany and Austria. To have Germany as a neighbor would suit him quite well, for an understanding between Germany and Austria would solve the Austrian question. Whereupon, I told the king that in 1931, the German-Austrian plan for a customs union failed because of the opposition of France. The Republic of France was at that time at the peak of her power, and most of the delegates at Geneva had bowed to this power; Vojslav Marinković, Yugoslav foreign minister, had at a meeting of the committee for European Union expressed himself in the sharpest form against the customs union. "Yes," said King Aleksandar, "but Marinković's statement does not in any way reflect my personal wishes."

The king asked me to tell him about the new Germany. This I did in detail. He was particularly interested in the method by which the German states had been unified, an action that the king considered very fortunate. He also openly expressed his satisfaction at the suppression of communism, which always collapsed when opposed by a really strong will. He personally had much experience in this field. (In fact, communism in Yugoslavia has been suppressed by truly draconian, party quite medieval, means). He went on to say that he had a certain understanding for the manner in which the Jewish question had been handled, but he feared that some difficulties of one kind or another might yet arise from it for Germany. There were, in his opinion, quite excellent Jews; for example, the Jews in Yugoslavia, that is, in Zagreb, Sarajevo, and Skopje, were very patriotic, while in Romania they were actually a curse for the morals of the country.

Germany was now exposed to sharp attacks from abroad, and the king therefore had a certain sympathy for Germany, for he, too, for other reasons, to be sure, in recent years had to endure numerous and vehement reproaches. But every government had to try to put through vigorously what it considered right, and if no danger resulted from this for the outside world, the

53

other countries that employed different, possibly democratic methods would gradually calm down. The king then asked me whether I had made the acquaintance of the Chancellor Adolf Hitler and whether I thought he still had the National Socialist Movement (Nazi) firmly in hand. I was able to answer both questions in the affirmative, the latter decidedly so. Since the king seemed to be afraid that the national awakening of Germany might perhaps lead to armed conflict, I told him that, National Socialism, as the Chancellor himself has publicly stated, had arisen from a burning patriotism; that its aim was to free Germany from the shackles laid upon her and obtain for her equality in all spheres; that National Socialism was not harboring aggressive designs, but was on the defensive, in order to liberate Germany from an excessive alien influence and externally from foreign interference. The king showed full understanding for this, but since, in the matter of foreign policy, Italy, particularly Mussolini, was for him the alpha and omega of almost all his thoughts and cares, he wondered whether I could tell him what the meaning was of the numerous visits of German ministers to Rome.

I replied that in many respects a community of ideas existed between Mussolini and Hitler, and that also in many respects the situation of Italy and Germany was similar. It was therefore entirely comprehensible that German ministers should be seeking opportunities for an exchange of opinion with Mussolini, which, of this the King Aleksandar could rest assured - in no way affected the interests of Yugoslavia or threatened to disturb the peace of Europe. The king replied that he was glad to believe that the German ministers did not intend to do anything to the disadvantage of Yugoslavia, but he was afraid that a closer collaboration between Germany and Italy would strengthen the latter country and might possible induce Italy to take a more aggressive attitude toward Yugoslavia - an opinion which I tried to refute.

We then spoke about the meeting of the foreign ministers (Permanent Council of the Little Entente) on May 30 - June 1, 1933 in Prague. The king seemed to be well satisfied with the development of closer solidarity among the Little Entente states and considered a hoax the newspaper report that Italy was attempting to bring about cooperation of Albania, Bulgaria, Greece, and Turkey as a counterpoise to the Little Entente, in the hope of finally winning over Romania also to his association. The king replied in the negative to my question whether it was the intention of Yugoslavia, as reported in a Prague newspaper, to alter her attitude toward the Soviet government and to recognize it.

Signed: Albert Dufour

* * * * *

On May 27, 1933, on behalf of their Legations in Budapest and Sofia, the German ministry requested the Legation in Belgrade whether Yugoslavia would accept peaceful revisions of the territorial clauses of the dictated peace treaties. On June 30, 1933, Albert Dufour, German minister in Yugoslavia, replied that Yugoslavia's willingness to return territories she was awarded by the dictated peace treaties is quite simple. The answer would be "No." There was no willingness to enter negotiations about a possible cession of territory in the interest of justice. On the contrary, it was being stated that in case the Great Powers should attempt to force Yugoslavia to cede part of her territory to Hungary or Bulgaria, the government of Yugoslavia would respond to such pressure by military action.

The Italians and Hungarians were nourishing the hope that parts of Yugoslavia, e.g., Croatia and Slovenia, would detach themselves from the existing Yugoslav regime. There was dissatisfaction among Croats and Slovenes, as well as among the minorities and those Serbs who were born not in Serbia, but in Austria-Hungary and became Yugoslav citizens only under the dictated peace treaties. The Hungarians harbored hopes that a plebiscite in the territories ceded to Yugoslavia would slow a majority in favor of Hungary, and also the community of German majority in the Vojvodina would decide to revert to less evil status. As far as Bulgaria was concerned, the Yugoslav government simply did not recognize the existence of a Bulgarian minority in Yugoslavia and curtly and without discussion rejected the very idea of any territorial cessions to Bulgaria.

At Dugo Selo, Serbian terrorists on July 14, 1933, assassinated Josip Predavec, Vice President of the Croatian Peasant Party. On September 21, 1933, Stipe Devčić a Croatian political activist, was murdered at Velebit by Serbian assassins.

The Danzig (Gdańsk) Free city (an area of 730^2 mi. / $1,891^2$ km) was established by the Treaty of Versailles in 1919 under the administration of the League of Nations. However, the plebiscite in 1933 resulted in an absolute majority in favor of returning the city to Germany. On October 14, 1933 Nazi Germany withdrew from membership of the League of Nations and began to establish a strong economic and military establishment.

A secret memorandum of November 3, 1933, issued by the Department for German Internal Affairs, D-II, the status of two Croatian émigré newspapers which appear in Berlin and their publisher, Branimir Jelić had been the subject of several exchanges between the German Foreign Ministry and the German Interior Ministry and representatives of the Yugoslav Legation in Berlin. The friendly treatment by German authorities of the Croatian émigrés was desirable because the Croatians were useful in the procurement of intelligence, and because of their ties with their organizations abroad. The German Government proceeded from the assumption that in the event of a possible warlike involvement in Europe, Yugoslavia would be on the side of German opponents and that the organized Croatian émigrés who were hostile to Yugoslavia would be welcomed to Germany as allies. The number of Croatian émigrés that could be considered for use against Yugoslavia in case of war was estimated at 8,000 men. The German Foreign Ministry steered clear of Croatian matters, and tried to maintain smooth relations with Yugoslavia. Through the existence in Germany of the two Croatian newspapers, the Independent Croatian State (Nezavisna Hrvatska Država), and the "Croatia-Press," these relations were being injured.

The petition dated November 16, 1933 addressed to the German Chancellor by the Yugoslav national, Branimir Jelić, who lived in Berlin and classified himself as a stateless person, was one of the leaders of the Croatian opposition and the publisher of the two Croatian émigré newspapers in Berlin. The memorandum attached to the petition describes the history of the Croatian people, especially the events of 1918 at the creation of the Yugoslav regime, the present sufferings of the Croats under Serbian rule, and appeals to the League of Nations, the governments of the United States and of Canada, as well as of all other civilized nations, furthermore, to the press and the individual statesmen and political leaders of the world. to demand of the Serbian king and the government of Yugoslavia that they withdraw the Serbian troops and the Serbian administration from the territory of Croatia, so that then the Croatian nation could exercise its right of self-determination. Otherwise the Croatian people would have no choice left but to resort to the kind of self-help which also comprises open rebellion. The two named émigré newspapers placed a more perceptible and entirely unnecessary burden on German relations with Yugoslavia. The Prussian Interior Ministry took steps to suppress the two political broadsheets. At first the ban was issued, but then, it was rescinded. The publisher was admonished by the Prussian authorities to refrain in the future from any attack against the Yugoslav regime. In view of the political situation, and report from the Prussian Gestapo to the German Foreign Ministry on November 3, 1933, prompt suppression of the two Croatian papers was urgently recommended.

The United States of America (USA) on November 16, 1933, formally recognized the Union of Soviet Socialist Republics (USSR) under the dictatorship of Iosif [Josip] Vissarionovich Dzhugashvili, nicknamed "Stalin" (1879-1953); General Secretary of the Communist Party of the Soviet Union (1922-1953); Premier of USSR (1941-1953).

* * * * *

~ Order of Reich Chancellor ~

Berlin, November 30, 1933

Bernhard von Bülow:
State Secretary, German Foreign Ministry

"By order of the Reich Chancellor I transmit to you herewith the copy of a letter I sent to the Head of the Aussenpolitisches Amt of the NSDAP (Foreign Affairs Office of the National Socialist Party), which letter was occasioned by your letter of November 16, 1933." As you requested, I am herewith returning the enclosures of your first-mentioned letter."

Signed: Hans Heinrich Lammers
State Secretary and Head of the Reich Chancellery

Enclosure:

The November 30, 1933 letter from Lammers to von Bülow reads as follows:

"I have been informed by State Secretary von Bülow of the conflict concerning the former Croatian national, Branimir Jelić, which has arisen between the Aussenpolitisches AMT headed by you and the Foreign Ministry. On instructions of the Reich Chancellor I have the honor to communicate to you the following:

"The policy of the Reich Government, especially as it applies to the Balkans, aims at the maintenance of normal and amicable relations with the existing states, insofar and as long as Germany's own interest demands this, and not to undertake or encourage anything that could be interpreted as active intervention in the domestic policy of these states. The activity of the Croatian émigré, Branimir Jelić, is directed against the existence of the Yugoslav regime. With respect to foreign policy we have no interest whatever in tolerating or indeed encouraging activity in any way. The Reich Chancellor is also for ideological reasons opposed to overrating the political influence of émigrés."

Signed: Hans Heinrich Lammers
               State Secretary and Head of the Reich Chancellery

* * * * *

On February 9, 1934, the governments of Greece, Romania, Turkey, and Yugoslavia signed "the Balkan Entente" agreement that mutually guaranteed the security of their Balkan frontiers; aimed specifically at Bulgaria, which had lost territory following the First World War.

During the official visit to France on October 9, 1934, Aleksandar I (b. 1888), King of Yugoslavia (1921-1934) was assassinated at Marseilles, France, by Dimitro "Vlatko" Gheorghieff, a Bulgarian citizen and body guard of Ivan Mihailoff, a Macedonian leader, both were members of the Internal Macedonian Revolutionary Organization (IMRO). Gheorghieff died that same day from wounds inflicted by a saber-wielding French officer. During the shooting melee, the French Foreign Minister, Jean Louis Barthou (1862-1934) was slain by the French police who were assigned to escort and protect the accompanying convoy of dignitaries. The heir apparent, Petar Karađorđević, eldest son of Aleksandar I, although he was only eleven years old on October 11, 1934, became King Petar II of Yugoslavia (1934-1945). The royal power was assumed by a three-man Regent Council. In accordance with Aleksandar's will, Prince Pavle Karađorđević, a cousin of defunct King Aleksandar I, became Chief Regent; Radenko Stanković (a Serb), professor of the Facility of Medicine in Belgrade and former Minister of Education; and Ivo Perović (a Croat), Governor of Savska Banovina.

The assassination of King Aleksandar I touched off a chain of incidents and created acts of cruelties instigated by Serb gendarmes and Serb-četnici who indiscriminately committed brutal acts against innocent Croatian people. The Serb gendarmes and Serb-četnici killed anyone who hoisted the Croatian National flag. Using ruthless police methods, the Serbs provoked bloodshed throughout Croatia, beating, imprisoning, and killing peoples without due process. This situation within the Yugoslav monarchy became dangerously explosive and the Serbs found comfort in keeping Croatians under fear and insecurity. In a verbal note of October 10, 1934, the Yugoslav Legation had released the names of five Croat émigrés suspected of activities directed against the life of King Aleksandar I and against the government of Yugoslavia; the names were Mile Budak, Slavko Kvaternik, Josip Milković, Mladen Lorković, and Branimir Jelić who later resided in the USA.

In a subsequent verbal note dated October 15, 1934 the Yugoslav Legation asked for inquiries to be made by the Prussian secret police as to the whereabouts of Slavko Kvaternik between September 25 and October 10; and in a further verbal note dated October 15, the Legation asked that inquiries should also be made as to the whereabouts of Stjepo Perić and Josip Milković between September 26 and October 10. The German Foreign Ministry replied to these verbal notes on October 22 in the terms stated in the document of October 25, 1934 printed below.

* * * * *

~ Circular of the Reich Foreign Ministry ~

Urgent   Berlin, October 25, 1934

This circular was addressed to German Missions in Bucharest, Budapest, Lisbon, London, Moscow, Paris, Prague, Rome, Sofia, and Vienna. A copy was sent to the Legation in Belgrade on November 1, 1934.

Some sections of the press abroad have, in connection with the assassination in Marseilles, the instigators of which are being sought for amongst Croat émigré circles, also made accusations against Germany. These accusations are to the effect that a center for Croat émigrés had been tolerated in Berlin, and that it had been frequented particulary by Croats whose names have come up most frequently in the Marseilles investigations, such as Ante Pavelić and Slavko Kvaternik, as well as Branimir Jelić. It is being asserted that Germany tolerated and even promoted for political purposes the activities of these émigrés against the Yugoslav state.

Such utterly tendentious assertions are nothing but transparent maneuvers to create a diversion and attempts to cause bad blood. The real facts of the matter are as follows:

The Croats have never received any financial support whatever from German circles. On the contrary, the German government has always complied to the greatest possible extent with all the Yugoslav government's wishes in respect of the Croats.

1. As early as the beginning of 1934, at the request of the Yugoslav government, the two émigré papers published here by Jelić and Pavelić, Croatia-Press and Nezavisna Hrvatska Država (The Independent Croat State), which constantly printed articles and comments hostile to Yugoslavia, were banned by instructions issued by the German State Police on January 25, 1934. The papers then transferred publication to Danzig. Thereupon the Foreign Ministry drew the attention of the Danzig authorities to these papers and, acting through the German authorities, prevented both papers from being admitted into Germany. In Danzig both papers ceased publication owing to financial difficulties as early as April or May. Since then the Croatia-Press has not appeared anywhere but the Nezavisna Hrvatska Država continues to appear in the United States. Jelić is also there.

2. When in the early months of this year the Yugoslav Legation asked for an inquiry to be made in connection with the attempt, already planned in December 1933, on the life of king Aleksandar and also in connection with some bomb outrages in Yugoslavia, a full police investigation was conducted forthwith. But no connection could be established between the Croats here in Germany and the plots in question.

3. The Yugoslav government has never made any applications for the extradition or expulsion of Croat émigrés. Not until after the assassination had occurred did the Yugoslav Legation draw our attention to certain Croats and ask for inquiries to be made by the police, especially regarding the whereabouts of these persons at certain times.

These requests were met in the most comprehensive way. The Secret State Police who, in constant consultation with the Foreign Ministry, followed up all the clues indicated, were only able to ascertain, however, that Pavelić had on several occasions stayed in Berlin for brief periods, that Jelić and Kvaternik - who, incidentally, has a sister here, married to a former naval officer - had already left Germany in May 1934, and that, on the other hand, Mile Budak and his wife did not leave Germany until October 5 or 6, the husband supposedly bound for England and the wife on her way to Hungary. Stjepo Perić, who has been arrested in Belgium, was also here on a visit.

There have been no results from the inquiries regarding the unknown woman mentioned in newspaper reports, with whom Kvaternik was supposed to have been seen in the South of France a few days before the assassination and about whom the Yugoslav Legation thought they could give more detailed information. The only others found to be in Berlin were a student by the name of Mladen Lorković, who had not apparently been engaged in politics, and a certain Slavko Cihlar. The latter was kept under arrest for the duration of the funeral ceremonies, for security reasons, but was afterwards released as there were no charges against him. Police inquiries regarding the origin of the weapons found on the murderer and on one of his accomplices have proved that these weapons were products of a German arms factory, but that they had been delivered to a firm in Trieste as far back as August 1932; it was possible to establish this clearly from the serial numbers on the firearms.

On the strength of this information you are requested to oppose in an appropriate manner any attacks that may be made at your end on Germany's attitude over the Croat émigrés.

By order: Gerhard Kopke
Ministerialdirektor, Dept. II, Reich Foreign Ministry

* * * * *

References concerning names identified in the above circular dated October 25, 1934, are described below. Ante Pavelić was a leader of the Ustaše (Croatia Militia) and émigré living in Berlin, Germany, was a co-editor, with Branimir Jelić, of the Croatia-Press and the Nezavisna Hrvatska Država published in Berlin. Slavko Kvaternik was a member of the Ustaše. Pavelić and Kvaternik were both arrested on October 17, 1934 at Turin, Italy, on suspicion of complicity in organizing the assassination, but it was subsequently announced that the French's unsubstantiated request based on absurd allegations for their extradition was denied.

To calm down the political situation in Yugoslavia, on December 19, 1934, Vladko Maček was pardoned and released from prison. However, only one political party was permitted in Yugoslavia and that was the Yugoslav (Serbian) National Party. Premier Bogoljub Jeftić, authorized general elections to be held May 5, 1935. The results of the general election were, as follows: the Yugoslav Government received 1,738,390 votes (303 seats); and the Croatian Peasant Party received 1,076,345 votes (67 seats).

On January 13, 1935, the industrial territory of Saarland (Saar) which by Treaty of Versailles in 1919 was arbitrarily assigned to France and placed under the administration of the League of Nations, by overwheliming majority of 90% of the voters in a plebiscite favored reunion with Germany.

A resolution dated June 3, 1935 issued by the Peasant Democratic Coalition, comprised of Croat and Serb representatives from Croatia, reiterated the right of Croatia to national sovereignty and independence. On June 20, 1935, a new Yugoslav government was formed under Premier Milan Stojadinović, a Serb, who embarked on a foreign policy of closer relations with Germany, Italy, and other Western nations. The relations between the Yugoslav monarchy and Hitler's Germany became friendlier, after the powerful Nazi Air Force Commander of the Reich Marshal, Hermann W. Göring (1893-1946), visited Belgrade on June 6-7, 1935.

Under the Nüremberg Laws of September 15, 1935 the Jews in Germany were disfranchised of their equal rights. Italy invaded Ethiopia (a.k.a. Abyssinia) on October 3, 1935 and forced Emperor Haile Selassie, also known as Ras Taffari (1892-1975), into exile in England. The League of Nations on November 18, 1935, voted to implement sanctions against Italy. The Italians were not impeded in their conquest because of French and British reluctance to enforce sanctions. The Ethiopians were defeated and the war ended on May 9, 1936, thus international sanctions were lifted. In retrospect, sanctions without harsh penalties for non-compliance became a big joke. Undisturbed by interferences, Italy combined Ethiopia with Eritrea and Italian Somaliland to a new colony of Italian East Africa (1936-1941).

There was an increase in dictatorships in Europe from 1922 to 1936: October 1922 Italy, June 1923 Bulgaria, September 1923 Spain, October 1923 Turkey, January 1925 Albania, May 1926 Poland, May 1926 Portugal, December 1926 Lithuania, January 1929 Serbia (Yugoslavia), February 1930 Romania, July 1932 Portugal, December 1932 Lithuania, January 1933 Germany, March 1933 Austria, March 1934 Estonia, May 1934 Latvia, August 1936 Greece, and September 1936 Spain. On August 31, 1935 the U.S. approved the Neutrality Act which prohibited the shipment or the use of U.S. vessels to transport war materials to belligerents. On February 29, 1936 the Neutrality Act of 1935 was amended to forbid granting loans or credit to nations at war.

On January 15, 1936, the Japanese delegation walked out from the London Naval Conference after their nation was denied naval parity with Britain and the USA. Likewise the Italian delegation also abandoned the conference.

Early in 1936, Yugoslav Premier Milan Stojadinović was confronted with numerous national and international problems. Inside the National Parliament in Belgrade, Serbia, he managed to maintain a strong balance between his Yugoslav Radical Union against the opposition of his Serbian brothers of the Yugoslav National party, headed by former Premier Bogoljub Jeftić. Outside those bloody walls of Serbian controlled Parliament, Milan Stojadinović was confronted with the increasingly active Croatian demand for immediate and complete autonomy. During February of 1936, Croatian demonstrations assumed more active forms. Anti-Serb rioting broke out in Zagreb and less serious clashes occurred from time to time in various parts of the Karađođević Serbian kingdom.

On March 6, 1936 during a Parliamentary session, a group of Serbian terrorists headed by Damian Arnautović, a Serbian Deputy and member of the Yugoslav National party, failed in their attempt to assassinate Premier Stojadinović. Following the conspiracy, Premier Stojadinović presented his resignation to Prince Pavle, who accepted it and instructed him to form a new government. The new cabinet excluded the troublemaker former minister of war, Gen. Pero Živković, who opposed conciliatory policy toward the Croats and other ethnic minorities.

In defiance of the Treaty of Versailles of 1919, on May 7, 1936 Germany annexed the Rhineland (a territory on the left bank of the Rhine river). Since Britain and France to the greatest extent accepted this German annexation, Hitler was encouraged to procced with his ambitious military goal. In France, the Popular Front (Front Populaire) formed a coalition government (composed of socialists, radical socialists, and communists) under the socialist Leon Blum (1872-1950), premier of France (1936-1937) and (1946-1947). Leon Blum who was the first Jew to serve as Premier of France, on June 30, 1946 outlawed the Nazis and Fascists organizations.

The ongoing bitter conflict within the Russian Communist party between two major Russian revoluntionary elements, orthodox factions of Josip Stalin, (1879-1953), General Secretary of the Communist Party of the Soviet Union (1922-1953), Premier (1941-1953); versus the adherents of Leon Trotski, original name Lev Davidovich Bronstein (1879-1940), caused worldwide divisiveness among communist leaders and fanatics, at the same time awakened the formation of anti-Communist alliance.

Scene of civil war in Spain from July 18, 1936 to April 1, 1939, resulted in defeat of the communist Popular Front government headed by president Manuel Azana, supported by the USSR, France, and Mexico. The victorius anti-communist "Insurgents" under Francisco Franco Bahamonde (1892-1975), who became the leader ("Caudillo") of the Falange Party, were openly supported militarily by Nazi Germany and Fascist Italy. Several thousand communists from many countries fought in Spain on the side of the Popular Front government, including hundreds of Yugoslav communists recruited by Josip Brozović (a.k.a. Tito), and hundreds of U.S. citizens who volunteered to serve in the Abraham Lincoln red-brigade. The Falangist government was recognized by Germany and Italy in 1936; and by Britain, France, and USA in 1939. Although Spain joined the Anti-Comintern Pact in April 1939, Spain remained neutral during the Second World War.

The Great Purge in the Soviet Union under Stalin commenced on August 16, 1936, first high-ranking military and political officials, and then with rank and file communists, until the elimination of all known anti-Stalinist elements. During Stalin's reign of terror, approximately 8,000,000 people were arrested, sent to various labor camps of northern Russia and Siberia, or summarily executed by firing squads.

Meanwhile, Nazi Germany and Fascist Italy signed the Berlin-Rome Axis (Achse Berlin-Rom) on October 25, 1936. One month later, on November 25, 1936, Germany and Japan signed the Anti-Comintern Pact to oppose communist expansionism and fight the communist internationals. On November 11, 1937 Italy joined Germany and Japan by signing the Anti-Comintern Pact.

In 1937 the Yugoslav Parliament consisted of a Higher Chamber comprised of 92 members (46 elected and 46 appointed by the Karađeorđević monarchy - guaranteeing the king control of any final outcome), and a Lower Chamber comprised of 317 members. The Serbian regime was charged with repression of political opposition, corruption, and exploitation of poverty-stricken peasants by government officials and bankers. Despite growing opposition to its national and international policies, Stojadinović remained in power. Croats under the leadership of Vladko Maček, continued their demand for free elections. Premier Stojadinović and Maček met for the first time at Zagreb in January 1937, but Maček reportedly rejected the Serbian superficial concessions offered to Croats as ridiculous and shameful.

Yugoslavia signed on January 24, 1937, the pact of friendship and "perpetual peace" with Bulgaria, thus ending for the time being the deep hostility between the two countries over the Macedonian territory.

Pope Pius XI (1857-1939) on March 5, 1937 issued a papal letter, an encyclical (encyclicus) on a specific subject, "The Catholic Church in the German Reich." The pope openly condemned Hitler's Nazi regime for its theories and its actions.

On March 7, 1937, Vaso Čubrilović, member of the Serbian Cultural Club in Belgrade, proposed a Serbian plan of action to "discipline" the Kosovar Albanians. Čubrilović demanded that maximum pressure be imposed by the Serbian government so as to make life as difficult as possible for the ethnic Albanians. The same method that Serbia used after 1878 when Albanians were killed, women raped, and their villages destroyed and burned. At Maček's birthday celebration on July 18, 1937 in Zagreb, he declared that Yugoslavia is self-destructing like the Austro-Hungarian Empire if Milan Stojadinović remained in power much longer. The Croatian Peasants organized their self-defense corps against the Serb dictatorial regime.

At the Marco Polo bridge on July 7, 1937 fighting started between Chinese and Japanese forces, the incident precipitated the Second Sino-Japanese War of 1937-1945. The Japanese conquered Nanking (Nanjing), capital of China, on December 12, 1937. After the Japanese entered the capital they massacred more than 200,000 civilians, sexually assaulted chinese women and girls, and devastated the city. For these horrible and contemptuous crimes, the city became known as "the Rape of Nanking."

Premier Stojadinović recommended the Serbian Parliament (Skupstina) ratify the Concordat agreement between the Vatican and the Yugoslav government negotiated by the late King Aleksandar. The Serbian Orthodox church opposed ratification on the ground that the Concordat granted Roman Catholics in Yugoslavia certain privileges concerning education, marriage, and property rights reserved exclusively for the Serbian Orthodox religion. After continuous demonstrations organized by Serb Orthodox and street riotings in Belgrade, the Concordat was ratified by the Chamber of Deputies on July 23, 1937. Hours after the Parliament's action, Patriarch Varnara, head of the Serbian Orthodox church, committed suicide in protest of the Concordat. On July 25 the Serb Orthodox bishops voted to excommunicate all members of the Serb Orthodox religion who favored ratification of the Concordat. Vicious and malicious campaigns organized by Serb Orthodox clergy, succeeded in gathering political strength, compelling Stojadinović's government to reconsider his agenda. Therefore, on September 8, 1937 Premier Stojadinović announced the Concordat would not be submitted to the Yugoslav Senate for ratification, and the agreement was allowed to lapse.

Disenchanted with the government of Belgrade, an agreement signed at Zagreb on October 6 by the following organizations - Croatian Peasant Party (Vladko Maček), Independent Democrat Party (Adam Pribicević), Yugoslav

Democratic Party (Ljubomir Davidović), Agrarian Party (Ivan Jovanović and Dragoljub Jovanović), and Yugoslav Popular Movement (Dimitrije Ljotić), sought the resignation of Premier Milan Stojadinović and the abrogation of the existing 1931 Constitution. They also demanded an election for a new Parliament to draft a new Constitution embodying the principles of sovereignty and granting autonomy to each ethnic group.

On September 28, 1937, Viktor von Heeren, Reich Minister in Yugoslavia, reported to Reich Foreign Minister, Freiherr von Neurath that Yugoslav Premier and Foreign Minister Milan Stojadinović would be in position at any time after 60 days to accept an invitation to pay an official visit to Berlin, returning Neurath's visit of last June 7 thru 9 to Belgrade. Stojadinović believed that it was in the interest of both countries (Germany and Yugoslavia) to give the visit the character of an official state visit and dispense with such camouflage as a hunting exhibit, a hunting invitation, etc., a view with which von Heeren stated his personal agreement. Stojadinović intends to go to Paris during the first half of October for the purpose of extending the Franco-Yugoslav Treaty of Friendship. Perhaps he will also accept a British invitation and visit London afterwards. The visit to London could only be very short, to be sure, since he has to return to Belgrade by October 18 for the convening of the Serbian Parliament (Skupstina). Stojadinović wishes to go to Rome at the beginning of November to return Galeazzo Ciano's visit.

* * * * *

~ **Memorandum of Situation in Yugoslavia** ~

Berlin, January 3, 1938

1. The internal political situation.

The Stojadinović government, which has been in office since May 1935, has to contend with strong opposition. This consists of the so-called Leftist opposition, of groups around former prime minister Boguljub Jević, as well as the Croatian Peasant Party led by Vladko Maček. These two groups joined forces in October 1937 in order combat Stojadinović. This in turn injured Maček with his own followers, however, since most of the Croatians want nothing to do with pacts with any Serbian groups whatsoever. On the other hand, owing to the position which the government was forced to take because the Serbian Leftist opposition supported the Croatian desire for autonomy, it has received renewed support among the Serbs and the wind has been taken out of the sails of the Rightist opposition.

The position of the Stojadinović government seemed particularly endangered in the late summer of 1937, when it submitted to the parliament for ratification the Concordat concluded by Boguljub Jeftić. Led by the Serbian Orthodox Church, which felt slighted, a considerable number of Serbs rose in opposition against the Concordat and against Stojadinović; there were even bloody clashes. Although parliament finally accepted the Concordat, Stojadinović refrained for the time being from submitting it to the Skupstina (National Assembly), and the situation gradually calmed down. The Croatian question, too, could not be brought any closer to a solution by Stojadinović, in spite of his apparent good intentions. The Croatians are maintaining their demands: first, abolition of the Yugoslav Constitution, and then general free elections for a National Assembly. In this way Croatians, especially those living in foreign countries, are relentlessly keeping up the fight for an Independent State of Croatia.

2. The foreign policy situation.

Since assuming the office of Premier and Foreign Minister, Stojadinović has given evidence of an endeavor for free Yugoslavia from the previously dominating influence of France and to pursue his own political plans. Of course, Stojadinović cannot and does not wish to abandon the friendship with France, especially since this is deeply rooted in extensive circles of the Yugoslav people. Thus last October he renewed the Treaty of Friendship with France which was signed in 1927. This should not be interpreted as a strengthening of ties with Paris. From the very beginning Yugoslavia has successfully resisted the repeated urging of France and Czechoslovakia to conclude a treaty of alliance and to develop the Little Entente into a general mutual assistance system. The independence and the new interpretation of Yugoslav foreign policy have become apparent in particular: (a) by the conclusion of the Treaty of Friendship with Bulgaria in January 1937 without the assistance of any Great Power, by means of which Yugoslav foreign policy has freed itself from the continuous tensions in the Balkans and a real pacification has been introduced there; and (b) further, by the conclusion with Italy in March 1937 of the pact for mutual recognition of boundaries and for consultation, by which Yugoslavia has been relieved of the Italian danger, which was felt constantly in every aspect of policy before that time.

By his independent foreign policy Stojadinović is continuing to pursue the aim of keeping Yugoslavia out of the game played by the Great Powers and of protecting it from being drawn into a possible conflict between other powers. Yugoslavia does not want to be in the position some day of having to choose between Italy and France or between England and Italy. Thus, Yugoslavia likewise maintains good relations with England - which are further promoted by the fact that the two royal houses are related - but here too, Yugoslavia avoids any commitments to England at the expense of Italy.

Within the Little Entente Yugoslavia is the country that has conducted her relations with Hungary in the most acceptable fashion, and is consequently the least interested in maintaining the Little Entente, even though she does not wish to withdraw from the alliance. Yugoslav membership in the Balkan Pact, signed at Athens on February 9, 1934 by Greece, Romania, Turkey, and Yugoslavia, now has in effect merely formal significance, in view of the Treaty of Friendship with Bulgaria.

Yugoslavia under Milan Stojadinović has exceedingly friendly relations with Germany, which not only are based on the highly developed exchange of goods but also have an ideological foundation. The settlement between Yugoslavia and Italy, which was emphasized and strengthened by Stojadinović's visit to Rome and Milan in December 1937, is also advantageous for Germany's own relations with Yugoslavia. The fact that Yugoslavia has not recognized Soviet Russia in the past, and obviously does not intend to do so.

* * * * *

In defiance of the Treaties of Saint Germain and Versailles, the Union "Anschluss" of Germany (Deutschland) and Austria (Österreich) was consummated on March 13, 1938 and affirmed by a Plebiscite of April 10, 1938 by 99 percent favorable vote; Hitler declared the unification of the two German speaking nations. Austria was incorporated into the German Reich (1938-1945) under the official name of Ostmark.

During May 3-9, 1938, Hitler visited Mussolini in Rome, Italy, whereby they planned their strategy on how to implement "law and order" in Europe. Arthur Neville Chamberlain (1869-1940), Britain's Premier (1937-1940) and Adolf Hitler (1889-1945) met at Berchtesgaden resort in the Bavarian Alps and later at Bad Godesberg, a city in north Rhine-Westphalia, on September 15, and 22, 1938 respectively. An international conference was held at Munich on September 29, 1938 with representatives of Britain, France, Germany, and Italy, which concluded a peace agreement. When Chamberlain returned to Britain, he stated that the Munich agreement meant "peace in our time." The agreement was an appeasement that lead to additional concessions without peace. Consequently, Czechoslovakia was dismembered for the benefit of Germany, Hungary, and Poland. On October 2, 1938, Teschen former territory of Silesia, Austria, in dispute after the First World War was divided between two claimants: Cieszyn was occupied by Poland and Český Těšín by Czechoslovakia. In 1938, Slovakia and Ruthania were granted autonomy, declared their independence on March 14, 1939, but on March 16, 1939 together with Sudetenland (Bohemia and Moravia) they became German protectorates.

After the Japanese captured the Chinese seaport of Canton on October 21, 1938, Japan declared that the "New Order in Asia" had been accomplished, meaning, the Japanese are now the super power. On October 25, 1938, Libya became an integral part of Italy. Under General Italo Balbo (1896-1940), governor general (1933-1940), 60,000 pioneer-settlers, mostly poor and unemployed Italians, were transported from Italy to Libya under the fascist government auspices. New housings, schools, hospitals, and office buildings were constructed to promote colonialism.

In Paris, France, on November 7, 1938 a German embassy official had been shot by a Polish Jew. Consequently, during the night of November 9-10 occurred the "Crystal Night" (Kristallnacht) which marked the systematic persecution of the Jews in Germany by the Nazis.

In Croatia a large but peaceful demonstration, on December 1, 1938, turned into a bloody riot that resulted in Croatian casualties, two killed and eleven wounded by Serb gendarmes. During the new national elections held on December 11, 1938 a total of 3,038,729 votes were cast. Premier Stojadinović's regime, which was represented by the Yugoslav Radical Union (Jugoslovenska radikalna zajednica) received 1,643,783 votes or 54.09 percent; the United Opposition Party headed by Vladko Maček received 1,364,244 votes or 44.90 percent; while the other opposition groups combined received 30,702 votes or 1.01 percent. The United Opposition party established on October 8, 1937 was comprised of the Croatian Peasant Party - Vladko Maček; Independent Democratic Party - Adam Pribićević; Anti-

Stojadinović Radicals - Aca Stanojević; Democratic Party - Ljubo Davidović; and the Serbian Agrarian Party - J.M. Jovanović. The United Opposition platform demanded a democracy and popular sovereignty of each state.

The opposition political parties charged the Yugoslav government with election fraud and using fear, terror, and misrepresentation by allowing oral voting, and falsifying the election results. When the new Parliament elected on December 11, 1938 convened on January 16, 1939 in Belgrade, the 47 elected Croat members again boycotted the session. Consequently, five members of the Stojadinović cabinet resigned stating that an agreement with Croats was imperative if a democracy had to survive. As a result, Premier, Stojadinović was forced to resign on February 4, 1939, and replaced on March 9, 1939 by Dragiša Cvetković (a Serb) and member of the Stojadinović cabinet. Because of the perilous international situation that beset Yugoslavia it convinced Prince Pavle Karađorđević and a few other Serb leaders that a prompt settlement of Croat grievances became imperative for the preservation of the Karađorđević dynasty. This program was bitterly opposed by most Serbians because they were unwilling to share power with non-Serbs and extend equal rights to other ethnic groups.

Attesting to the good relations between the Yugoslav Karađorđević monarchy and the German Third Reich, on January 16, 1939, Prince Pavle Karađorđević of Serbia presented the highest decoration, "the Grand Cross of the Star of Karađorđević of Serbia" to Heinrich Himmler, Reichsfuhrer-SS (Schutzstaffeln) and Chief of the Nazi Police.

* * * * *

~ Political Report from Yugoslavia ~

Belgrade, March 7, 1939

To: Reich Foreign Ministry

From: Reich Minister in Yugoslavia

This report addresses the new direction of domestic policy in Yugoslavia and its effect on our further treatment of the Croatian question.

Until the fall of the Stojadinović government, I supported in my reports the view that the Croatian demands might, indeed, be entirely justifiable on moral grounds, but their fulfillment seemed hardly possible without detriment to the functioning of Yugoslavia. Therefore, a strong Yugoslavia would have to realize that only an authoritarian regime based on Serbian supremacy, such as the Stojadinović regime was trying to achieve, offered the necessary guarantee for it. It would therefore not be in the German interest to support Croatian ambitions that were opposed to such a regime.

Meanwhile the prince regent has withdrawn his confidence from Stojadinović and thus removed the only personality who is capable at present of carrying on a strong authoritarian regime.

67

He decided to do this precisely in order to propitiate those circles in the country which, under the leadership of the Croats, were in fundamental opposition to the authoritarian methods of the Stojadinović government. The change of government quite evidently means, therefore, the conscious abandonment of authoritarian government in favor of a policy whose goal is to resolve internal differences by "democratic" methods through compromise. A policy that hopes to win the goodwill of Croatian federalism and Serbian circles of the Left would inevitably be pursued at the cost of weakening the authority of the state; the prince regent can have no illusions on this score. In the face of anxiety over a further deterioration in the internal situation, however, he actually seems to have regarded this as the lesser evil.

The shift in Yugoslav internal policy away from authoritarian governnment has created a situation which makes it seem to me expedient to revise our attitude on the Croatian question. The fear that by siding with the Croats we should endanger the authoritarian regime which we welcome in Yugoslavia has become meaningless. On the other hand, the friendship of the Croats has grown in value by reason of the fact that the change of course which has taken place will increasingly strengthen the influence of the Croats in the government. The further fact that, besides the Croats, the Serbian Leftist opposition aligned with them will receive new impetus and greater influence as a result of the change of course makes it all the more to our interest to offset this influence in circles already ideologically hostile to us by winning the friendship of the Croats.

There is no doubt that the conditions for attempting to strengthen German-Croatian friendship are entirely favorable. The close ties between the Croats and the world of German culture and the geopolitical danger threatening them from Italy, which will always make it seem to them necessary to align themselves with Germany, create a very good basis for this. All the moral support that we are able to give them in their battle for equality in the state will, under these circumstances, bear abundant fruit. The new situation which has arisen through the fall of the Stojadinović government restores our freedom of action fully to exploit all these favorable conditions for winning the friendship of the Croats.

I would therefore recommend that the restraint thus far exercised by our press in its attitude toward the Croatian problem be gradually relaxed and that our basic position as to the right of self-determination of nations now be given stronger expression in the treatment of this question also.

Signed: Viktor von Heeren

* * * * *

The dismemberment of Czechoslovakia was completed as Bohemia and Moravia on March 16, 1939, were proclaimed territories under German protectorates. Slovakia was annexed next. And, Hungary occupied Ruthenia (Carpatho-Ukraine). Britain's Premier A. N. Chamberlain on March 17, 1939 proclaimed the end of political appeasement. On March 23, 1939 German troops occupied the Lithuanian city of Memel (Memelgebiet of Klaipeda); and on October 10, 1939, Soviet troops occupied the province and the capital city of Vilnius, Lithuania. Britain and France on March 31, 1939, signed an agreement to assume the responsibility to intervene on behalf of Poland in the event of aggression, and on April 6, 1939 the agreement was extended into a mutual pact of military and economic assistance. Italian troops on April 7, 1939 invaded Albania, a sovereign state under Ahmed Bey Zog I (1895-

1961) King of Albania (1928-1939) and annexed it on April 12, 1939 to the Italian Crown of Emperor Vittorio Emmanuele III.

The British legislative body (made up of the House of Lords and the House of Commons) on May 17, 1939 issued the "white paper" establishing a new policy for the British mandated territory of Palestine (Canaan), located between the Mediterranean sea and the Jordan river. This action, reversed the Balfour Declaration of November 2, 1917 which promulgated Jewish homeland in Palestine. With respect to the new British policy, Jewish immigration would be limited to 15,000 settlers annually for the next five years, after which time the Arabs would dictate the policy.

On May 22, 1939, a military alliance "Pact of Steel" between Germany and Italy was signed in Berlin by Hitler and Mussolini. It united Germany and Italy by pledging to support each other in case of war. In another event, on June 1, 1939, the Yugoslav Karađorđević monarchy presented the highest decoration the "Grand Cross of the Star of Karađorđević of Serbia" to Reich Marshal Hermann Wilhelm Göring, a Nazi leader who formed the Gestapo (Geheime Staatspolizei), and organized the Nazi Air Force (Luftwaffe).

At the suggestion of other scientists, Albert Einstein (1879-1955) on August 2, 1939 wrote to U.S. President Franklin D. Roosevelt divulging that nuclear energy could be used to produce atomic bombs (A-bombs), an explosive weapon of great destructive power.

As the old adage goes, politics makes strange bedfellows. Germany and the Soviet Union, on August 19, 1939 signed their first economic agreement. Later, the two supposedly ideological enemies, Hitler (representing the rightwingers) and Stalin (representing the leftwingers), used deception to conceal their military intentions, signed in Moscow on August 23, 1939 the temporizing German-Soviet Nonaggression Pact. In a secret protocol of this pact, Poland would be partitioned; the western one-third of Poland would be annexed by Germany and the eastern two-thirds of Poland would be annexed by the USSR. Also, Germany would annex Lithuania, while the Soviet Union would annex Estonia, Latvia, Finland, and Besserabia.

* * * * *

~ **German-Soviet Nonaggression Pact** ~

Moscow, August 23, 1939

Guided by the desire to strengthen the cause of peace between German Reich and the Union of Socialist Soviet Republics, and basing themselves on the fundamental stipulations of the Neutrality Agreement concluded between Germany and the Union of Socialist Soviet Republics in April, 1926, the German Government and the Government of the Union of Socialist Soviet Republics have come to the following agreement:

1. The two contracting parties undertake to refrain from any act of force, any aggressive act, and any attacks against each other undertaken either singly or in conjunction with any other Powers.

2. If one of the contracting parties should become the object of war-like action on the part of a third Power, the other contracting party will in no way support the third Power.

3. The Governments of the two contracting parties will in future remain in consultation with one another in order to inform each other about questions which touch their common interests.

4. Neither of the two contracting parties will join any group of Powers which is directed, mediately or immediately, against the other party.

5. In case disputes or conflicts on questions of any kind should arise between the two contracting parties, the two partners will solve these disputes or conflicts exclusively by friendly exchange of views or if necessary by arbitration commissions.

6. The present agreement is concluded for the duration of ten years with the stipulation that unless one of the contracting partners denounces it one year before its expiration, it will automatically be prolonged by five years.

7. The present agreement shall be ratified in the shortest possible time. The instruments of ratification are to be exchanged in Berlin. The treaty comes into force immediately it has been signed.

Signed: Joachim von Ribbentrop, Reich Foreign Minister

Vyacheslav Mikhailovich Molotov, USSR Foreign Minister

* * * * *

Although the nations of Britain, France, and Poland combined were competent in industrial resources and military manpower, the mechanized German Army (Wehrmacht) was more efficient and qualitative superior force. The German "lightning war" (blitzkrieg) of the Panzer divisions constituted formidable power. The German Air Force (Luftwaffe) was the best at the outbreak of conflict in 1939. The German Navy perhaps had less fire-power, but was aggressive enough to be the main hindrance to British and French shipping. German submarine U-Boats (abbreviation for Unterseeboot "undersea boat") caused enormous difficulties for Allied navigation, and especially to merchant shipping.

Growing international tension preceding the Second World War compelled the government of Yugoslavia to alleviate the internal political situation toward Croatia. Following extensive consultations, a compromise was reached. Dragiša Cvetković and Deputy Premier Vladko Maček (a Croat) signed an Agreement (Sporazum) on August 26, 1939, commencing the reorganization of the government of Yugoslavia; the membership in the Cabinet comprised of ten Serbs, six Croats, one Slovene, and one Bosnian Muslim. The Agreement reinstated the historic name of "Croatia" (Hrvatska) and created the Province of Croatia (Banovina Hrvatska), with Zagreb as its capital. The authorities of the Province of Croatia acquired the control of most activities except national defense, foreign affairs, foreign trade, and communications. On August 29, 1939, a separate Croatian Legislative Assembly (Sabor) was established and Ivan Šubašić (1892-1955), member of the Croatian Peasant Party, was appointed Governor (Ban) of Croatia. The Province of Croatia on August 26, 1939 comprised a population of 4,400,000 out of a total of 14,000,000 in the kingdom of Yugoslavia; of these 866,000 were Eastern Orthodox Serbs, and 164,000 were Muslims.

The franchise obtained by Croats was also contemplated to be extended to the Slovenes. While some Serbs accepted the Cvetković-Maček covenant, Serb extremists opposed the mutual accommodation. The federalization and decentralization was not accepted by Serbs because the proposed streamlined government organization would cut deeply into the roots of Serb-četnici and Serb gendarmes extravagant expensive living, fat retirement, bonuses, and special benefits. Also the Serbian civic, cultural, and religious organizations would no longer receive unrepayable financial support from the government. Moreover, the Serbian military circles rejected the arrangement due to fear for their hitherto unchallenged domination.

On August 25, 1939, Britain and Poland signed a treaty of mutual assistance. After extensive diplomatic negotiations, Germany failed to obtain Polish agreement whereby Danzig would be returned to Germany and that a corridor (construction of highway and railway) be authorized across the territory of northern Poland connecting Germany proper with East Prussia (Ostpreussen); Hitler ordered military operation "Case White" to commence against Poland. The Wehrmacht and the Luftwaffe crossed the Polish frontier from the west early morning of September 1, 1939. Because Britain and France had guaranteed to protect Poland, first Britain and then France declared war against Germany on September 3, 1939. Australia and New Zealand joined the Anglo-French declaration of war. Following the German occupation in 1939 of Bohemia-Moravia (two western territories of Czechoslovakia) and Slovakia, the western and southern frontiers of Poland became part of open invasion. The German forces had made progress by swift maneuvering and encircling the Polish forces. The Polish forces could not react fast enough, became detached from a whole, moved uncoordinated by retreating and making meaningless attempts of disjointed attack on the fast advancing German forces.

BANOVINA OF CROATIA, 1939

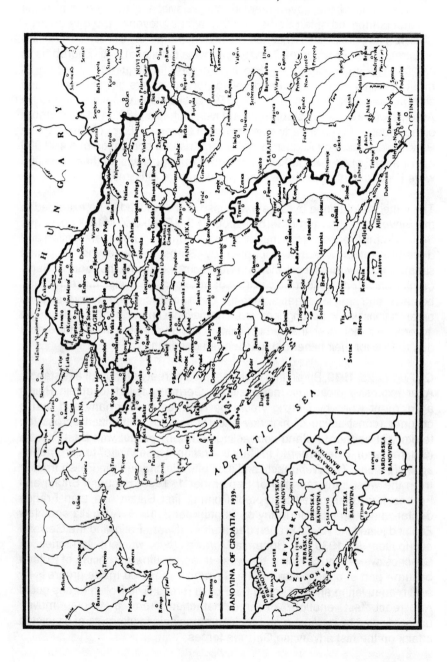

U.S. President Roosevelt on September 5, 1939, declared the United States neutrality in the European war. However, Canada declared war on Germany on September 10, 1939; they did this before receiving the customary approval of the King of England.

On September 17, 1939 the Red Army of the Soviet Union attacked and invaded Poland from the east. The capital city of Warsaw held under siege, collapsed on September 26, 1939 to the German army. After the Polish government and the military high command crossed the Romanian border on their way into exile, the defeated Polish Army surrendered on October 5, 1939. Germany and the Soviet Union on September 28, 1939, modified their previous treaty dated August 23, 1939; whereby, Lithuania came under the Soviet sphere of influence, and the dividing "border-line" in Poland was changed and moved eastward to the Bug river, rearranged in favor of Germany. The city and port of Danzig and the Suwalki region of NE Poland was annexed by Germany.

On October 6, 1939, Hitler delivered an address before a special session of the Reichstag in Berlin. Text excerpts of the speech are as follows:

"If Europe is really sincere in her desire for peace, it is necessary that the aims in the foreign policy of the European nations should be made perfectly clear. The demand for a real revival of international economic life coupled with an extension of trade and commerce presupposes a reorganization of the internal economic system, in other words, of production in the individual states. In order to facilitate the exchange of the goods thus produced, markets must be organized and a final currency regulation arrived at so that the obstacles in the way of unrestricted trade can be gradually removed...The most important condition for a real revival of economic life in and outside of Europe is the establishment of an unconditionally guaranteed peace and of a sense of security on the part of the individual nations...The Geneva Convention once succeeded in prohibiting, in civilized countries at least, the killing of wounded, the ill-treatment of prisoners, war against non-combatants, etc., and just as it was possible gradually to achieve the universal observance of this statute, a way must surely be found to regulate aerial warfare, the use of poison gas, of submarines, etc., and also so to define contraband that war will lose its terrible character of a conflict waged against women and children and against non-combatants in general...I do not believe that there is any responsible statesman in Europe who does not in his heart desire prosperity for his people. But such a desire can only be realized if all the nations inhabiting this continent decide to work together. To achieve this great end, the leading nations of this continent will one day have to come together in order to draw up, accept, and guarantee a statute on a comprehensive basis which will ensure from them a sense of security, of calm - in short, of peace. As Führer of the German people and Chancellor of the Reich, I can only thank God at this moment that He has so wonderfully blessed us in our hard struggle for what is our Right, and beg Him that we and all the other nations may find the right way, so that not only the German people but all Europe may once more be granted the blessing of peace."

Taking advantage of noncommittal stance by the international community, and the increasing desire to expand northwest toward the Baltic Sea, the USSR on October 10, 1939, threatened to use force unless the three sovereign states of Estonia, Latvia, and Lithuania consent the Soviet troops onto their territories. To show his barbaric characteristics and superior military strength, the bully dictator of the USSR, Josip Stalin ordered the Soviet troops to occupy the defenseless Lithuanian city of Vilnius.

A German-Yugoslav trade pact signed October 16, 1939 provided for increased shipments of minerals and timber to Germany in return for German armaments to Yugoslavia. By a telegram dated October 22, 1939, Reich minister in Yugoslavia, Viktor von Heeren asked the Reich ministry in Berlin the possibility that the principles concerning repatriation of German splinter groups, expressed in Adolf Hitler's speech, might be applied to the Volksdeutsch groups in Yugoslavia begin to arouse serious concern among Volksdeutsche and Yugoslavs. Viktor von Heeren requested instruction to reply to inquiries and for publication in the Volksdeutsch press concerning the repatriation of German groups in Yugoslavia. The Reich State Secretary, Freiherr Ernst von Weizsacker, on October 28, 1939, replied to Heeren's inquiry: "The Reich government is interested in limiting discussion of this problem for the present time. Any discussions in the press are therefore undesirable and to the extent that we can influence it, should be prevented as much as possible. The idea underlying the repatriation is an important contribution by Germany to the pacification of Europe by eliminating causes of serious friction between countries. If at the proper time a resettlement of the Germans in the southeast should appear desirable, such an action would naturally be undertaken only with the agreement of the government and the concerned German community."

The United States Neutrality Act (dated August 31, 1935 and February 29, 1936) were amended on November 4, 1939 to authorize foreign nations at war to buy weapons in the USA if they "pay cash and carry" the war material in their own transports.

To provide Germany with maximum supplies of copper, lead, and zinc produced by French and British-owned mines in Yugoslavia, the Serbian Karađorđević monarchy on November 12, 1939 nationalized the production and controlled the export of all materials. Strong protests from France and

Britain and the threat of retaliatory action, prompted the Yugoslav government to postpone implementation of the program. To reduce the available supplies to Germany, the French and British began purchasing large quantities of agricultural products from Yugoslavia and negotiated for a large armament credit to Yugoslavia.

On November 26, 1939, the Soviets threatened Finland but Finland rejected the Soviet demands. On November 30, 1939, Soviet forces attacked Finland and on March 12, 1940, Finland signed a peace treaty, ceded the Karelian Isthumus and Viipuri, northern Rybachi peninsula, the port of Hango, and islands in the gulf of Finland to USSR. Because of Soviet Union invasion of Finland on December 14, 1939, the Soviet Union was expelled from the League of Nations. In June 1941, Finland joined Germany in war against the Soviet Union and temporarily regained its lost territory.

In accordance with secret Greco-British agreement of February 21, 1940, a British expeditionary force landed in Greece on March 7, 1940. While Britain's prime minister Neville Chamberlain and the French Premier Paul Reynaud, decided to postpone the mining of Norwegian waters before landing their invasion troops, German intelligence reports confirmed the Anglo-French impending military landing at Norway. Hitler responded by ordering the implementation of operation "Weser;" therefore, German troops (including a parachute battalion - the first ever employed in warfare) invaded Norway on April 9, 1940. King Haakon VII (1905-1957) of Norway, together with his family and his government entourage fled to London, England, where they established a government in exile on May 5, 1940. A Norwegian army officer, diplomat, and political leader of the Nasjonal Samling Party, Vidkun Abraham Lauritz Quisling (1887-1945), became the Head of the Norwegian pro-Nazi government. To ensure the safety of military enterprise in Norway, on April 9, 1940 German forces occupied the Kingdom of Denmark, which surrendered without struggle. The Danish government which continued in office as a Plenipotentiary of the German Reich, resigned on August 25, 1943, but Denmark remained under Germany until May 1945.

Upon military occupation and defeat of Denmark by Germany on April 9, 1940, the status of the Island of Greenland (area: 842,799 mi^2/2,182,852 km^2) located off northeastern Canada, a colonial possession of Denmark since 1380, became a concern of possible German invasion. After brief consultations with representatives of Denmark, Britain, and Canada, on April 10, 1940, President Roosevelt announced that Greenland (Danish: Grønland) was part of the Western Hemisphere security zone, thus covered by the Monroe Doctrine of 1823. Because Greenland was a strategically important area, the U.S. established meteorological observations, naval stations, and air bases on the island. The "Monroe Doctrine" was promulgated by James Monroe (1758-1831), the 5th President of the USA (1816-1824), in his message to U.S. Congress on December 2, 1823; proclaimed that as a principle, the U.S. would not permit European nations to interfere in the intenal affairs of the Western Hemisphere.

Anglo-French troops landed in Norway on April 14, 1940, attacked the German forces from the north and south. The Germans delivered a well coordinated counterattack by five seaborne landings of reinforcement troops in the rear of Anglo-French military positions who were surprised to find themselves surrounded by German forces. The Anglo-French troops were compelled to retreat and evacuate the Scandinavian peninsula. Neville Chamberlain, British Premier resigned on May 10, 1940 following criticism for the defeat in Norway. On May 13, 1940, Winston Leonard Spencer Churchill (1874-1965) formed a coalition cabinet, became British Premier (1940-1945), and again (1951-1955), addressed his nation, declaring: "I have nothing to offer you but blood, toil, tears, and sweat." Chamberlain remained in the Cabinet as Lord President of the Council until his death. On May 10, 1940 British forces occupied the Faeroe Islands and Iceland in order to prevent the Germans from using the strategic territories for U-boat activities. Therefore, the territories were placed under British military occupation as part of the Atlantic Security System to prevent a German invasion.

The German strategy using the element of surprise, overrun the Low Countries and then turned south to invade France along its unfortified and unprotected northern frontier. Opeartion "Yellow" was implemented on May 10, 1940, consequently,the German forces invaded Luxembourg, the Netherlands, and Belgium. The Dutch army gave up on May 15, and established a government-in-exile in London, with Wilhelmina the queen of the Netherlands at its head. Gauleiter Simon on August 2, 1940, became head of the civilian administration in Luxembourg. Arthur Seyss-Inquart became Reichkommissar for the Netherlands, supported by Anton Andrian Mussert (1894-1946), leader of the Dutch National Socialists. Leopold III (1934-1951), King of Belgium, surrendered on May 28, 1940 and Leopold was held prisoner and interned by the Germans. The Belgian Neo-Nazi "Rexists" under Leon Degrelle supported the Germans.

Soviet newspapers, Pravda and Izvestija, announced on May 11, 1940 that a Treaty of Commerce and Navigation was signed between the Soviet Union and Yugoslav monarchy with an attached protocol concerning the trade representation. These instruments were signed on behalf of the Soviet Union by Anastas Ivanović Mikoyan, People's Commissar for foreign trade of the Soviet Union, and on behalf of the Karađorđević Yugoslav government by Milorad Đorđević, Assistant Minister of Trade and Industry.

Following a terrible military defeat inflicted by the advancing German armies, during the Battle of Dunkerque (Dunkirk), France, from May 28 to June 4, 1940, approximately 350,000 soldiers (British, French, and Belgian) retreating from Vlaanderen (Flanders) were rescued and evacuated to England. In their retreat, they abandoned tons of war usable equipment.

German forces on June 5, 1940 struck against France from the north, and after the breakthrough of the "Weygand Line," advanced almost unchecked, while to the east the French troops entrenched along the fortified Maginot Line were attacked from behind by the Germans. The "Maginot Line," named for Andre Maginot (1877-1932), comprised of fortifications 200 mi. / 322 km long from the Swiss border in the east to the Belgian border to the north west, was constructed to prevent Germany from ever again invading France. On June 10, 1940, Italy declared war on France and Britain. The city of Paris was occupied by the Germans on June 14, without struggle and on June 19 they reached the Atlantic coast. France signed an armistice with Nazi Germany in the forest of Compiegne on June 22, in the same railroad car in which Germany recognized their defeat in the First World War with France; and on June 24, 1940, France concluded an armistice with Italy. The French territory was partitioned into two zones; one under the Germans, and the other "unoccupied" zone under the Vichy French Government.

The Yugoslav foreign office announced on June 24, 1940, that diplomatic relations between the Soviet Union and Yugoslavia have been established and that respective ministers to Belgrade and Moscow have been named. Milan Gavrilović, Chief of the Serbian Agrarian Party, and Journalist, was appointed Yugoslav minister to the Soviet Union, and Viktor A. Plotnikov was transferred from Norway to become the Soviet Union minister to Yugoslavia.

* * * * *

~ Memorandum by Reich State Secretary ~

Berlin, June 24, 1940

At the direction of Joachim von Ribbentrop, Reich Foreign Minister, I told Viktor von Heeren, German Minister in Yugoslavia, by telephone at 1:45 p.m. that:

We had reports that the life of Milan Stojadinović, former Yugoslav Premier (June 1935 - February 1939), was seriously threatened and that there were plans to assassinate him. Herr von Heeren was hereby instructed to call on the Yugoslav government, as well as the Prince Regent Pavle, and by direction of the Reich Foreign Minister to tell them both the following:

Because of the well-known pro-Axis activities of Stojadinović in recent years, the report, would be received very offensively as an extremely injurious effect and cause extreme astonishment, particularly at the present moment.

Herr von Heeren might, moreover, get in touch with his Italian colleague, who is making a similar démarche. Herr von Heeren was requested to report here by telephone as soon as possible the carrying out of these instructions, the time of his démarche, and the success it achieved.

Signed: Freiherr Ernst von Weizsäcker

* * * * *

Counselor Siegfried of the Reich State Secretary's secretariat recorded in a supplement of the above memorandum of June 24, 1940 that at 7:20 p.m. and again at 7:35 p.m. he urgently requested by telephone that Viktor von Heeren, who so far had been unable to see Aleksandar Cincar-Marković, Yugoslav foreign minister, carry out the démarche. Later that day Ernst von Weizsäcker, State Secretary of the Reich Foreign Ministry, informed Joachim von Ribbentrop, Reich Foreign Minister, that Herr von Heeren had reported at 9:30 p.m. he had seen Cincar-Marković who had promised to take all the necessary measures to comply with the German demand. Finally, on June 25, 1940, Herr von Heeren reported that he had made similar representation with the prince regent Pavle, who denied emphatically that Milan Stojadinović had been in any danger of being assassinated.

The Soviet Union demanded that Romania relinquish Bessarabia and northern Bukovina to the USSR. On June 27, 1940, the USSR seized Bessarabia (an area of 17,151 mi^2/44,419 km^2) and northern Bukovina (an area of 3,396 mi^2/8,795 km^2) from Romania. The Baltic states of Estonia, Latvia, and Lithuania were occupied by Soviet troops on June 5, 1940, and incorporated in the USSR on August 3, 1940, with German connivance.

The British government on June 28, 1940, officially announced the recognition of Charles Andre Joseph Marie de Gaulle (1890-1970), French General, as head of the Free French government in exile and resistance movement. In France, a military court martial of the Vichy regime, sentenced General de Gaulle to death in absentia.

On June 28, 1940, the Alien Registration Act became law in the USA, requiring aliens to register and be fingerprinted. The same law made it a crime to belong to any organization advocating overthrow of the government.

After the defeat of France, the Germans invaded the archipelago of Channel Islands (a.k.a. Norman Isles), the only British territory occupied by Nazi Germany from June 30, 1940 until May 9, 1943. The archipelago comprises the island of Jersey (45 mi^2/116 km^2); Guernsey (24 mi^2/62 km^2); Alderney (3 mi^2/7.8 km^2); Sark (2 mi^2/5.2 km^2); also Brechou, Herm, Jethou, and several uninhabited islets.

Henri Philippe Petain (1856-1951), Marshal of France, on July 10, 1940 was appointed as nominal head of the "French State" by the French National Assembly in session at the capital city of Vichy, a spa and health resort of central France. The constitution of France's Third Republic was abolished on July 10, 1940, a new French constitution adopted and a new state created. French resistance (France Forces of the Interior - FFI) the "Maquis," kept up their guerrilla activities by constant harassment of the Axis occupation troops. With France conquered, Hitler turned his focus on Britain. Therefore, on July 16, 1940, Hitler issued a directive, operation "Sea Lion" ordering the preparation of a military plan for the invasion of Britain. To this goal, the German air attacks began first on ports and airfields along the English Channel, then inland over the interior. Under Petain's regime, the citizenship of naturalized Jews was automatically revoked as of July 16, 1940; subsequently, on July 18, 1940, Jews were barred from being employed in the government and management posts in business and industry. After the war, Petain was arrested and tried for high treason, sentenced to death, but pardoned by Gen. Charles de Gaulle, President of France (1945-1946; 1959-1969), was imprisoned in August 1945 on the island of Yeu, off the coast of Brittany, France. Prior to the Second World War, Pierre Laval (1883-1945) favored collaboration with the Axis Powers. In December 1940, Lavall was ousted as Foreign Minister and placed under arrest by Petain. Following German demands, in April 1942 Laval returned as Chief of Staff in the Vichy government. At the end of the Second World War, Laval escaped to Spain and was returned to France for trial on charges of treason. Found guilty, he was executed by a firing squad at the Fresnes prison in Paris.

* * * * *

~ Yugoslavia and the USSR ~

Belgrade, July 23, 1940

To: Reich Foreign Ministry

From: Reich Minister in Yugoslavia

The arrival of Viktor A. Plotnikov, first USSR representative in Yugoslavia since the World War, gave a strong impetus not only to the Communist, but, above all, to the Russophile tendencies of the country. These Russophile tendencies are to be found not only in Serbia, but also in other regions, and in both cases go back to the times when these people saw in Russia their protector in the struggle for their freedom and independence. These circles realize that the USSR is something other than Czarist Russia, but they do not at the bottom of their hearts regard it as decisive. This Russophile tendency, which is rather widespread, particularly among the peasantry, recently received a not inconsiderable addition in strength from Francophile circles, which are now seeking to substitute for the collapse of their hopes of a French victory the hope that alignment with the USSR might offer protection, however slight, against the Italian-German danger. In political circles that are to be taken more seriously, although here, too, few illusions are entertained on this score, and even in important circles in the government and the Ministry of Forign Affairs, the USSR represents a certain hope. For just recently, the view is being circulated

79

in these same circles that after the present war is terminated, a German-Russian conflict sooner or later is inevitable. If Germany triumphs, she will attack Russia; if Germany succumbs, she will be attacked by Russia. It is believed in these former Francophile circles that in either case only an easing of the political situation could result from this for the Balkans and in particular for Yugoslavia.

Whether and to what extent these ideas are promoted by officials close to the Russian Legation is at present not yet evident. I have thus far not yet made the acquaintance of my Russian colleague, Plotnikov, and have therefore formed no impression of his personality. For the present it can only be stated that he is obviously trying to make friendly gestures toward Yugoslavia.Thus he has not neglected to adapt himself scrupulously to the usages here by not only visiting the grave of the Unknown Soldier, but also the grave of king Aleksandar in the mausoleum of Oplenac, 50 mi. / 80 km distant from Belgrade, and depositing wreaths there.

Poletayev, the representative of Tass, who arrived here with minister Plotnikov, has, however, in the short time that he has been here, by his uncouth behavior and his heavy drinking, alienated many of the sympathies which persons in certain circles were very enthusiastically prepared to bestow on him.

Signed: Viktor von Heeren

* * * * *

Italian military forces on August 4, 1940 invaded British Somaliland (area of 67,936 mi.² / 175,953 km²) located on the south shore of the Gulf of Aden and the Indian Ocean, East Africa and occupied it until March 16, 1941.

According to the "Schwarze Korps" (Black Corps), organ of the Nazi Elite Guard, published on August 7, 1940, approximately 3,800,000 Jews were under the Axis spheres of influence. This estimate included the established population and refugees in occupied Europe and in North Africa.

On August 21, 1940, Romania ceded Dobruja (an area of 8,979 mi²/23,247 km²) to Bulgaria, and the territory of northern Transylvania (an area of 17,000 mi²/44,013 km²) was ceded to Hungary. King Carol of Romania was forced on September 6, 1940 to abdicate, and was succeeded by his son Michael I. Ion Antonescu (1882-1946) became Premier of Romania.

In September 1940, the British RAF retaliated against German air attacks over England by bombing the capital city of Berlin. This unexpected bombing raid so infuriated the Führer that he ordered the German Luftwaffe to concentrate its attacks on London and other major cities.

The Berlin-Rome Axis formed on October 25, 1936, was formalized on May 22, 1939, now called the Pact of Steel. Japan joined on September 27, 1940 to create the Berlin-Rome-Tokyo Axis (a.k.a. Tripartite Pact), ten years mutual military and economic treaty.

* * * * *

~ Berlin-Rome-Tokyo Axis (Tripartite Pact) ~

Berlin, September 27, 1940

The governments of Germany, Italy, and Japan, considering it as a condition precedent of any lasting peace that all nations of the world be given each its proper place, have decided to stand by and cooperate with one another in regard to their efforts in Greater East Asia and regions of Europe respectively wherein it is their prime purpose to establish and maintain a new order of things calculated to promote the mutual prosperity and welfare of the peoples concerned. Furthermore, it is the desire of the three governments to extend cooperation to such nations in other spheres of the world as may be included to put forth endeavors along lines similar to their own, in order that their ultimate aspirations for world peace may thus be realized. Accordingly, the governments of Germany, Italy and Japan have agreed as follows:

1. Japan recognizes and respects the leadership of Germany and Italy in establishment of a new order in Europe.

2. Germany and Italy recognize and respect the leadership of Japan in the establishment of a new order in Greater East Asia.

3. Germany, Italy and Japan agree to cooperate in their efforts on aforesaid lines. They further undertake to assist one another with all political, economic and military means when one of the three contracting powers is attacked by a power at present not involved in the European war or in the Chinese-Japanese conflict.

4. With the view of implementing the present pact, joint technical commissions, members of which are to be appointed by the respective governments of Germany, Italy and Japan, will meet without delay.

5. Germany, Italy and Japan affirm that the aforesaid terms do not in any way affect the political status which exists at present as between each of the three contracting parties and Soviet Russia.

6. The present pact shall come into effect immediately upon signature and shall remain in force ten years from the date on which it became effective. At the proper time before expiration of said term the high contracting parties shall at the request of any of them enter into negotiations for its renewal.

In recognition whereof, the undersigned, duly authorized by their respective governments, have signed this pact and have affixed hereto their signatures.

Signed: Joachim von Ribbentrop, Foreign Minister
For the German Government

Galeazzo Ciano, Foreign Minister
For the Italian Government

Saburo Kurusu, Ambassador to German
For the Japanese Government

* * * * *

Since September 27, 1940 when the Tripartite Pact was signed, and following the adherence of Hungary on November 20, 1940; Romania on November 23, 1940; Bulgaria on March 1, 1941; with the exclusion of Greece, all the states bordering Yugoslavia were members of the Axis Powers. The newly created state of Slovakia adhered on November 24, 1940; and Croatia joined on June 15, 1941. German troops entered Romania on October 8, 1940, to protect the important oil fields against possible British commandos and air raids. Operation "Felix" designed to invade British Gibraltar was cancelled after a meeting on October 23, 1940 at Hendaye, France, between Hitler and Francisco Franco (1892-1975), Chief of the Spanish state (1939-1975).

The Fifth Conference of the Communist Party of Yugoslavia (CPY), attended by 105 delegates was held in Dubrava, a northeastern suburb of Zagreb, on October 19-23, 1940. The delegates elected a Central Committee of 21 members and a Politbureau of seven members (Josip Broz as Secretary General, Edvard Kardelj, Milovan Djilas, Aleksandar Ranković, Ivan Milutinović, Franc Leskošek, and Rade Končar). The CPY was able to reorganize and to see that Party cadres, especially the cadres of intellectuals, were well-indoctrinated, and that the commanding personnel for future revolutionary action was thoroughly trained.

Mussolini was fully aware that Hitler and his military strategists would be opposed to an adventurous campaign in the Balkans; nevertheless, without consulting or least informing Hitler, decided to invade Greece confident of a successful execution of military operations without the help of Germany. The Italian army launched an attack against Greece on October 28, 1940 from occupied Albania. Initially, the Italian forces consisting of 10 divisions, commanded by Gen. Sebastino Visconti Prasca, were able to advance inside Greece. The time and terrain chosen for the campaign were unsuited for mechanized warfare. The weather (heavy rains turned to snow) introduced disadvantages and enormous difficulties to the Italian units unable to maintain communications and receive aerial support. Greek troops utilizing the mountain height, allowed the Italian mechanized columns to advance inside Greek territory along the valleys where the Italian troops became vulnerable to artillery and small weapon fire. There was no opportunity for the Italian mechanized force to operate effectively. On November 14, 1940, Greek Gen. Papagos took advantage of the Italian ill-prepared campaign, launched a counter-offensive which succeeded not only halting the Italian forces, but repelling the invasion and compelling the Italian troops to retreat deep into Albanian territory. Meanwhile, British troops landed October 30, 1940, on the Greek islands of Crete (Kriti) and Lemnos (Limnos) to reinforce the British combat units in Greece since March 7, 1940, thus improving their strategic position in the eastern Mediterranean. Later on, British troops arrived in Piraeus and Volos. The British possession of the islands endangered the Italian lines of communication to North Africa and assured Greece a flow of continuous supplies from Egypt. Moreover, the British bombers were now within range of Romanian oil fields under German control. On November 4, 1940, Hitler ordered the German Army General Staff (Generalstab des Heeres) to prepare plans for the invasion of Greece from Romania via Bulgaria.

Due to Italian military failures in Greece, on November 9, 1940 the Italian commander Gen. Prasca was replaced by Gen. Ubaldo Soddu. Meanwhile, the town of Korçë in Albania was occupied on November 22, 1940 by Greek forces. Before year end, one-fifth of Albanian territory was in Greek hands. On November 12, 1940, Hitler signed the Weisung (Directive) No. 18 which reads in part as follows: "The Commander-in-Chief of the Army, Field Marshal Walther von Brauchitsh shall make preparation to take possession of the Greek mainland north of the Aegean Sea with troops from Bulgaria, and to establish bases for the use of German Luftwaffe units against the aims in the eastern Mediterranean, especially against those British Air Force bases which threaten Romanian petroleum fields."

In a letter dated November 20, Hitler wrote to Mussolini, enumerating the psychological and military consequences of the Italian failure. The Germans disapproved the Italian plan of operations for the reason that any campaign in the Balkans would have to be executed in a manner similiar to the "blitzkrieg" applied by the Germans in the campaign in Norway. Mussolini replied to Hitler on November 22, and expressed his regret. In a telegram of November 24, 1940, Viktor von Heeren, Reich Minister in Yugoslavia reported to Ribbentrop, Reich Foreign Minister, that the Yugoslav foreign minister had complained about Bulgarian propaganda efforts regarding Macedonia, in particular to a statement made in Bulgaria which amounted to a claim of southern Serbian territory of Bulgaria.

* * * * *

~ Political Position of Yugoslavia ~

Urgent   Belgrade, November 25, 1940

To: Reich Foreign Ministry

From: Reich Minister in Yugoslavia

The present political position of Yugoslavia can be summarized as follows:

1. Very large sections of the population including the Army are completely under the impact of both the Italian defeat in Albania, which is considered a confirmation of the small regard here for Italian fighting power, and of the provocative debate in the Sobranje which

is causing the old, deep mistrust of Bulgaria to flare up once more. Under the impact of these two [events] the determination to resist, if necessary by force of arms, any threat from Italy and Bulgaria to vital Yugoslav interests has increased to an extraordinary degree, particularly among the Serbian people and in the Army. Through this development the feeling with regard to Germany is also being unfavorably affected.

2. Within the government the attitude toward Italy and Bulgaria has also stiffened, though out of consideration for Germany it retains a purely defensive character. The attitude toward Germany is unchanged. As in the past it is determined by unqualified recognition of Germany's military supremacy on the Continent, growing realization of the senselessness of Russophile tendencies, not of least importance, by the hope that for economic reasons Germany is really interested in an unimpaired and pacified Yugoslavia. To be sure, the resulting wish for a closer alignment with Germany is still today being weakened by doubts as to the outcome of the war and the suspicion that Germany has promised her Axis partner a preferred position in settling Yugoslav questions.

3. Yugoslavia's foreign policy, in which the decisive influence continues to be exercised by the prince regent and which, because of the weakness of the government, must take account of the mood among the Serbian people and in the Army, will therefore try to adhere in the future, too, to a formal neutrality in the present pattern. A voluntary, clear choice in favor of the German camp would at the most, be desired if, as a quid pro quo, a guarantee of Yugoslav integrity in the newly ordered Europe could be given or perhaps of a prospect of an outlet to the Aegean were offered.

Signed: Viktor von Heeren

* * * * *

Mussolini was so humiliated by the Italian military failures in Yugoslavia, Albania, Greece, and north Africa that he ordered a shakeup in the Italian top military establishment. On December 5, 1940, Marshal Pietro Badoglio, Military Chief of Staff (formerly famed commander of the Italian conquest of Ethiopia in 1936), was replaced by Gen. Ugo Cavallero; Adm. Domenico Cavagnari was replaced by Adm. Arturo Ricardi; and Gen. Cesare de Vecchi, Governor-General of the Dodecanese (Greek: Dhodhekánisos), a group of islands in the southeastern area of the Aegean Sea, was replaced by Gen. Ettore Bastico. Because of the unsuccessful Italian campaign, and fearing a British landing in Greece, on December 13, 1940 Hitler issued Directive (Weisung) No. 20, code name "Marita" enterprise. On December 18, 1940, Hitler issued Directive No. 21 "Barbarossa" (Redbeard), named for Frederick I (1121-1190) of Germany, Emperor of the Holy Roman Empire (1152-1190). The planned German invasion of the USSR commenced on July 22, 1941, under the command of Field Marshal Walther von Brauchitsch, Commander-in-Chief of the German Army. The military operation was implemented as a three pronged attack, one toward the second largest Russian city of Leningrad (St. Petersburg/Petrograd) in the east via Lithuania, Latvia, and Estonia; one toward the Soviet capital city of Moscow in the center via Bialystok (Belostok), Minsk, Katyn, and Smolensk; and one toward Kiev in the south via Lemberg (Lvov), Vinnitsa and Zhitomir.

CHAPTER 4

SECOND WORLD WAR, 1941 - 1944

Psychological propaganda disseminated after the First World War by the victorious nations, asserting that the last conflict ended all wars, was untrue and completely inconsistent with the facts. The undue burden imposed by the Treaty of Versailles, not only resuscitated the recollections of ethnic assimilation, but also introduced new problems which contributed to the appeasement of few and dissatisfaction of most. Equal rights, freedom, democracy, justice, tension, turmoil, and territorial disputes remained ever present and contributed to uneasy peace and international instability.

On February 6, 1941, Joachim von Ribbentrop, Reich Foreign Minister, received a visit from Danilo Gregorić (a Serb), Yugoslav journalist and political editor of the Belgrade based publication "Vreme" (Times), who stated that it was the wish of Dragiša Cvetković (a Serb), Yugoslav Premier to be invited to Germany together with Aleksandar Cincar-Marković (a Serb), Yugoslav Foreign Minister, in order to discuss political problems of mutual concern, such as Yugoslavia's accession to the Tripartite Pact (Axis Powers). By memorandum of February 12, 1941, the German government informed Giuseppe Cosmelli, Italian Chargé de'Affairs in the Italian Embassy in Germany, concerning the German-Yugoslav discussion and the impending visit of the Yugoslav delegation.

The conversation between Adolph Hitler and Cvetković, in the presence of Ribbentrop, and Cincar-Marković, took place February 14, 1941 at the Berghof in Fuschl. On February 25, 1941, Viktor von Heeren, German Minister in Yugoslavia, in his telegram to Ribbentrop stated: "The Prince Regent of Yugoslavia accepts the Führer's suggestion regarding a meeting at the Berghof for the purpose of an oral discussion."

King Boris III of Bulgaria (1918-1943), fearing the reaction of the Union of Soviet Socialist Republics (USSR) on the one hand, and Turkey, on the other, delayed until March 1, 1941 the signing of the Tripartite Pact allowing German troops to enter into Bulgaria. On March 2, 1941, the German army crossed the Danube river from Romania into Bulgaria.

On March 5, 1941, Ribbentrop sent a telegram to the German Minister in Italy, to tell Filippo Anfuso, Chief de Cabinet to Ciano, to inform Mussolini (Il Duce) that March 4th, Hitler received Prince Pavle of Yugoslavia at the Berghof. In the conversation, Hitler stated that the time had come for all

European countries to adopt themselves to the coming "new order" in Europe. Yugoslavia was being offered the unique opportunity which would not recur, to establish and secure her position in the reorganized Europe, aligning herself with the Axis Powers by way of accession to the Tripartite Pact, thus Yugoslavia could assure for herself Germany's definite guarantee of her territorial integrity. Prince Pavle was visibly impressed by Hitler's remarks, but Pavle explained how difficult it was for him to make a decision based on advice presented by Hitler, and as far as he personally was concerned, the Greek descent of his wife, his personal sympathies for England (the circle of Prince Pavle who had close relations with the British Royal House), and his attitude toward Italy as well were opposed to it. Hitler stressed that he did not expect of Yugoslavia more than accession to the Tripartite Pact; particularly no participation in the war. Germany would see to it that when the war ended, Salonika would go to Yugoslavia. When Prince Regent Pavle took his leave, he reserved his decision.

On March 6, 1941 Mussolini visited the city of Tirana (Tiranë), Albania, for a conference with Gen. Ugo Cavallero (1880-1943), Italian Commander in Albania, regarding Italian counter-offensive against Greece. Cavallero pointed out there were three things that must be considered before reaching the decision to launch a counter-offensive against Greece: (a) Italian artillery consisting chiefly of old guns are not equal to that of Greece; (b) Italian Air Force has not been able to gain air superiority; and (c) Italian Army is staging "passive revolt" and are unwilling to fight.

The Yugoslav Crown Council met on March 6, 1941, in the presence of both Regents (Radenko Stanković and Ivo Perović); Premier Dragiša Cvetković; Croat leader Vladko Maček; Slovene leader, Antun Kulovec; Foreign Minister Cincar-Marković; War Minister Gen. Petar Pešić; and the Court Minister, Milan Antić. The Yugoslav Prince Regent Pavle reported on his talk with Hitler and on Germany's wish that Yugoslavia accede to the Tripartite Pact. The result of deliberation was that before a decision is taken, the Yugoslav Foreign Minister should clarify through Viktor von Heeren, the following three questions. In the event of Yugoslavia accession to the Tripartite Pact, would Yugoslavia be able to receive a written declaration from Germany and Italy stating that: (a) The sovereignty and territorial integrity of Yugoslavia will be respected; (b) No military assistance will be requested of Yugoslavia and also no passage or transportation of troops through Yugoslavia during the war; and (c) Yugoslavia's interests in free outlet to the Aegean Sea through Salonika will be taken into account in the reorganization of Europe This confirmed that the Serb Karađorđević Monarchy believed in the supremacy of Axis Powers and their final victory.

Joachim von Ribbentrop, on March 10, 1941, instructed Viktor von Heeren that the questions posed by the Yugoslav Crown Council are answered affirmatively in all three points. The Tripartite Pact was a unified structure with fundamentally equal obligations for all members. It was therefore impossible to grant an individual member a special privilege. Consequently, the assumption of the obligations under Article 3 of the Tripartite Pact was inseparably linked to the protection of Yugoslavia's future resulting from accession to the Tripartite Pact.

The present situation with respect to public feeling, numerous reports about an alleged German ultimatum in the matter of Yugoslavia's accession to the Tripartite Pact have, in conjunction with extensive mobilization measures, occasioned great agitation among the population and have further increased the pressure of the circle inside the Yugoslav government. At the same time everything was being done on the part of the USA and England to strengthen the Royal Yugoslav government's resistance to the German pressure. On the other side, Germany was doing everything it could in every possible way to hasten the accession of Yugoslavia. Concerned about possible secret agreement between Germany and Yugoslavia the Hungarian Premier Dome Sztójay, speaking for his government on March 17, 1941, informed the German government that if and when Yugoslavia accedes to the Tripartite Pact care be taken to ensure Hungary's wishes for territorial revision with respect to Yugoslavia will not be obstructed.

On March 18, 1941, Yugoslav Prince Regent Pavle of the Karađorđević Serbian Dynasty, and his Premier Dragiša Cvetković and Foreign Minister Aleksandar Cincar-Marković all agreed to Yugoslavia's adhesion to the Axis Powers. Following exchange of communications between Yugoslavia and Germany and between Germany and Italy to coordinate and clarify the fine points dealing with the Tripartite Pact, the road to ultimate agreement appears to have been achieved. However, on March 21, 1941, the resignation of three Yugoslav ministers: Minister of Justice, Konstantinović; Minister of Agriculture, Cubrilović; and the Minister of Social Welfare, Budislavljević; supposedly delayed the signing of the agreement. Premier Cvetković welcomed the resignation of these three ministers who had always made difficulties for implementation of government policies.

Due to the awkward situation in which the Yugoslav Premier Cvetković had been placed as a result of the resignation of the three ministers from the Cabinet , Hitler on March 22, 1941, considered it urgently necessary that the Yugoslav internal political difficulty be resolved at once in one way or another. The situation was such that Germany was ready, at the most until March 25th to conclude the Tripartite Pact agreement. On March 25, 1941, at the Belvedere Palace in Vienna, the accession of Yugoslavia was concluded. The instrument was identical with those signed by previous adherents.

~ Yugoslavia Adhesion to the Tripartite Pact ~

Vienna, March 25, 1941

The Governments of Germany, Italy, and Japan on the one hand and the Government of Yugoslavia on the other hand, through their plenipotentiaries, acknowledge the following:

Article 1. Yugoslavia adheres to the Tripartite Pact, signed at Berlin, September 27, 1940, between Germany, Italy, and Japan.

Article 2. Representatives of Yugoslavia will be present at Conferences of Commissions for common technical questions created under the Article 4 of the Tripartite Pact so far as the Commission deals with matters touching Yugoslavia's interests.

Article 3. The text of the Tripartite Pact is added as an annex to this protocol. This protocol is drawn up in the German, Italian, Japanese and Yugoslav languages, each of which is authentic. The present protocol is effective on the day of signing.

Signed: Joachim von Ribbentrop, Foreign Minister
For the German Government

Galeazzo Ciano, Foreign Minister
For the Italian Government

Dragiša Cvetković, Minister President
For the Royal Yugoslav Government

* * * * *

The Yugoslav government had hardly prepared the people in advance concerning the negotiations and up to March 26, 1941 had declared itself in favor of neutrality. Meanwhile, agents of the British government persuaded the military elite of the Serbian monarchy to depose the Karađorđević government. During the night of March 26-27, 1941, the Yugoslav government residences and buildings in Belgrade were occupied by Yugoslav troops. At 2:30 a.m. on March 27, a group of Serbian military, led by Air Force General Dušan Šimović (a Serb), executed a successful military coup d'état by overthrowing the Regency of Serbian Prince Pavle Karađorđević (1893-1976) in favor of the seventeen year-old Serbian King Petar II Karađorđević who promptly assumed the throne. A proclamation by King Petar II was read over the radio early morning of March 27, stating that King Petar II has ascended to the Yugoslav throne of the Serb Karađorđević Dynasty and has appointed Gen. Šimović as Premier. The royal Yugoslav government was sending deceitful and ambiguous signals to assure the Axis Powers that Yugoslavia would stand by and honor its commitment to the Tripartite Pact; but Hitler and Mussolini refused to believe the wishy-washy, untrustworthy, and lunatic Serb leaders. The coup d'etat in Belgrade was a typically Serbian military Putsch. It was backed by two-dozen conspirators - mostly Air Force officers - that engineered the Putsch. The motive was, aside from the ordinary spirit of adventure, the violent aversion to Prince Pavle and Cvetković, whom fanatical Serbs claimed had betrayed them in Vienna. Serbian propaganda had circulated reports that secret clauses had been signed in Vienna, in which the Yugoslav government had to prostrate and humble herself before Nazi Germany and Fascist Italy. The excesses that occurred in Belgrade on the first day following the rebellion were organized and supported by many unusual and unscrupulous bedfellows, such as monarchists, communists, anarchists, troublemakers, and opportunists.

On March 27, 1941, Hitler called his top political and military leaders to a conference regarding the situation in Yugoslavia. Hitler began by describing the Yugoslav situation, emphasizing his resolve to make all necessary preparations in order to smash Yugoslavia militarily and as a state.

The gravity of the situation left no doubt about the consequences which would result from a change in Yugoslav foreign policy or even from serious incidents involving Reich Germany or Volksdeutsche. There were reports that an assistant to the German military attaché had been attacked and injured on the street of Belgrade, that the windows in the German Travel Agency had been smashed, and the interior office destroyed. The upheaval resulted from the violent and savage reaction of extremist and irrational Serb-četnici. Therefore, operation "Marita" was to commence as early as possible, but implementation of operation "Barbarossa" was postponed for a few months. In this connection, Hitler issued the overall written orders for the execution of the operation against Yugoslavia. These written orders to be applied vigorously were put forth in Directive No. 25.

* * * * *

~ Hitler's Directive No. 25 ~

Top Secret   Berlin, March 27, 1941

1. The military Putsch in Yugoslavia has changed the political situation in the Balkans. Even if Yugoslavia should give declarations of loyalty, she must be considered as a foe and therefore must be destroyed as quickly as possible.

2. It is my intention to break into Yugoslavia in the general direction of Belgrade and southward by a concentric operation from the area of Fiume [Rijeka] - Graz on the one side and from the area around Sofia on the other and to give the Yugoslav armed forces an annihilating blow. In addition I intend to cut off the extreme southern part of Yugoslavia from the rest of the country and seize it as a base for the continuance of the German-Italian offensive against Greece. The early opening up of the Danube traffic and occupation of the copper mines of Bor are important for reasons of military economy. The attempt will be made to win over Hungary and

Bulgaria for participation in the operations through the prospect of winning back the Banat and Macedonia. The domestic political tension in Yugoslavia will be sharpened by political assurances to the Croats.

3. In detail I order the following: (a) as soon as sufficient forces stand ready and the weather situation permits, the ground organization of the Yugoslav Air Force and Belgrade are to be destroyed by continuous day and night attacks of the Luftwaffe; (b) operation "Marita" is to begin as closely at the same time as possible but in no case earlier. For the time being it is to have the limited aim of occupying the basin of Salonika in order to get a foothold on the high ground of Edessa. For this purpose the Eighteenth Army Corps can jump off from Yugoslav territory. Favorable opportunities are to be exploited for preventing the systematic formation of a front between Olympus and the high ground of Edessa; (c) all the forces still available in Bulgaria and Romania may be enlisted in the attacks which are to be conducted from the area around Sofia in a northwesterly direction and from the area Kyustendil - Gorna Džumaja in a westerly direction, with the stipulation that forces in the strength of about one division along with air defense forces must remain in the Romanian oil region for the protection of the latter. The protection along the Turkish frontier is provisionally to be left to the Bulgarians. A German formation, an armored division if possible, is to be newly assembled in back of them for support; (d) the thrust from the general direction of Graz aiming toward the southeast is to be conducted as soon as the forces necessary for it are assembled. It is left to the Army whether or not they should lunge across Hungarian territory in order to open up the Frontier. The guard along the Yugoslav frontier is to be reinforced immediately. Just as on the Bulgarian border important objects can be occupied simultaneously with the aerial attack on Belgrade, even before the general attack; and (e) the Luftwaffe with two attack groups is to support the operations of the Twelfth Army and those of the new assault group to be formed in the area around Graz. It will make the main effort in this connection, depending on the time needed for the progress of the operations of the Army. The Hungarian ground organization can be used for the concentration and commitment. It is to be examined whether the Tenth Air Corps is to be drawn in for commitment from Italian territory. Nevertheless the convoy protection of the transport to Africa must remain assured. The preparations for the seizure of the island of Lemnos, Greece, are to be continued, but I reserve to myself the decisions as to the execution. Provision is to be made for sufficient anti-aircraft protection of Graz, Klagenfurt, Villach, and Leoben, and also for Vienna.

4. The basic agreements with Italy will first of all be made by the Oberkommando der Wehrmacht-OKW (High Command of the Armed Forces). Liaison staffs with the Italian Second Army and with the Hungarians are to be provided by the Army. As regards the delimitation of aerial operational areas respecting the Italian and Hungarian flying personnel the Luftwaffe is authorized to reach agreements even at this time with the High Commands of the states concerned. The supplying of the Hungarian ground organization can begin immediately.

5. The Commanders in Chief are to report to me through the OKW regarding the intended conduct of the operations and the related questions.

Signed: Adolf Hitler
                    Führer and Chancellor
                    Supreme Commander of the Wehrmacht

* * * * *

Upon accepting the assignment to establish a royal government of Yugoslavia, Gen. Šimović directed his deceptive political compromise to include Croat representation as a symbol of appeasement. Premier Šimović on March 28, 1941, stated that the Karađorđević government will avoid discussion of the Tripartite Pact. Furthermore, Šimović does not wish to denounce the Tripartite Pact nor will the Yugoslav government ratify it, since the Karađorđević government is not obligated to observe the terms which have not been ratified. Apparently the Šimović administration displayed a diplomatic incoherentness by falsely disseminating information alleging that the Tripartite Pact signed on March 25, 1941, was not yet official because it was never duly ratified. In reality, the Tripartite Pact stipulated as follows: "the treaty shall come into effect immediately upon signature and shall remain in force ten years from the date on which it became effective." Therefore, assertions by Šimović were not only completely erroneous but confirmed his ignorance. After all, generals and admirals in Yugoslavia, with rare exceptions, were men of limited integrity and military competence because promotions had been awarded on the basis of subservience rather than military leadership ability, character, and high moral principle.

Following the coup d' état Franklin Delano Roosevelt (1882-1945), President of the United States (1933-1945), sent a congratulatory message on March 28, 1941 to the teenage King Petar II (1934-1945) of Yugoslavia: "At this moment when Your Majesty has assumed the full exercise of Your Royal Rights and Powers and the leadership of a brave and independent people, I wish to share with the people of the United States of America in the expression of our sincere and genuine wishes for the health and well-being of Your Majesty and for the freedom and independence of Yugoslavia. Furthermore, I extend the hope that the relations between your Government and the Government of the USA may be mutually beneficial in the support of those principles of liberty and tolerance so cherished by our two peoples."

In compliance with Führer's Directive No. 25, on March 29, 1941, Gen. Friedrich Paulus, Deputy Chief of Staff for Operations, presided over the German military commanders meeting in Vienna, Austria, finalized the operational timetable for the imminent planned military campaigns. At the end of March 1941, the Luftwaffe had readily available for combat 135 fighter and reconnaissance aircraft in Romania, and 355 bombers and dive-bombers in Bulgaria. Early in April 1941, about 600 various types of aircraft were brought to the Balkans from France, Africa, and Sicily.

Joachim von Ribbentrop on March 31, 1941, sent a telegram to Alfred Freundt, German Consul General at Zagreb: "The German government urgently advised Maček and the other Croatian leaders against cooperating in any manner with the present royal Yugoslav government in Belgrade. It goes without saying that when we give such advice, it must be kept in strictest secrecy. Should Maček follow our advice, we would wish to maintain contact with him." On the same day Freiherr Ernst von Weizsäcker, State Secretary of the Foreign Ministry, dispatched a circular to all German Missions, except those with closed circuit teletype systems, as follows: "Excesses against Reich Germany and Volksdeutsche in Yugoslavia continue. The German colony, and their wives and children of the German Legation have been instructed to make their departure."

The Yugoslav Armed Forces comprised of a fully mobilized strength of approximately 1,000,000 men, divided into three Army Groups, one Independent Command, and one Coastal Defense Command:

1. First Army Group, subdivided: (a) the Seventh Army, responsible for the northwestern area along the Italian and German frontiers; and (b) the Fourth Army, responsible for the northeastern area along the Hungarian frontier; deployed behind the Drava River from Varaždin to Slatina, with one Cavalry Division in reserve stationed in the Zagreb area and three Infantry Divisions in reserve stationed south of Zagreb.

2. Second Army Group, subdivided: (a) the Second Army, responsible for the area adjacent to the Fourth Army (First Army Group) up to the Danube River; with one Infantry Division in reserve stationed south of Brod; and (b) the First Army, responsible for the northwest corner of the area between the Danube and Tisza (Tisa) Rivers.

3. Third Army Group, subdivided: (a) Fifth Army, responsible for the eastern area along the Romanian frontier from the Iron Gate to the Kriva Palanka, and adjacent area to the south, extending to the Greek frontier; and (b) Third Army, responsible for the southeastern area along the Albanian frontier from Lake Ohrid (Ohiridsko Jezero) to Lake Skadar (Skadarsko Jezero), with one reserve Infantry Division stationed near Skopje.

4. The Sixth Army, an independent command not subordinated to an army group; deployed around Belgrade and in the Banat area east of River Tisza (Tisa), with two Infantry Divisions in reserve stationed along the banks of the lower Morava Valley.

5. Coastal Defense Command, responsible for the defense of the Adriatic coast from Gospić in the northwest to the Gulf of Kotor (Boka Kotorska) in the southwest.

The Yugoslav defensive military plan proved to be outrageous, ridiculous, and completely laughable. This plan comprised mainly of unconnected lines of defense with major military forces stationed around designated areas of interest or importance. The troops were committed primarily to the defense of those specific isolated areas. The frontier defenses, although built around favorable terrain features, lacked the necessary depth, consequently were considered totally incapable to defend against organized attack. Because of the obvious inadequate transportation and communication networks, poor military organizational structure, and lack of leadership, the Yugoslav military strategy was inefficient. Considering the various defensive strategies, the Yugoslav High Command planned to take advantage of the mountainous area and reinforce its garrisons throughout Macedonia, hoping to maintain direct connection with Greek and British troops stationed in Greece.

In the meantime, the Šimović Yugoslav government became known as an administration of procrastinating bureaucrats and chicken outfit. This was due to their selfishness and absence of sound judgment. They deliberately obfuscated the issue by continuous flip-flop foreign policy; on one hand making pretense of friendly relations with Axis Powers and on the other reaffirming their neutrality. Hitler became fed-up and exasperated by the vexatious and repulsive Yugoslavs, was determined to vindicate the treaty, punish the wishy-washy and nilly-willy Yugoslavs, and settled the issue by strong military action. Under an extremely short deadline, the German Military High Command originated a coalescent plan for the simultaneous campaigns against Yugoslavia and Greece. This plan, after receiving Hitler's approval, was promptly incorporated into Directive No. 25.

Alfred Freundt, on April 1, 1941, communicated to the German Foreign Ministry in Berlin that Vladko Maček was informed by the Reich Consulate General concerning the instructions received from Ribbentrop, Reich Foreign Minister. Maček reported that, through August Košutić, Vice President of the Croatian Peasant Party, who had been sent to Belgrade, had laid down the following four conditions to the Yugoslav government in Belgrade: (a) recognition of the Tripartite Pact and implementation in the spirit of the Treaty; (b) the appointment of two co-Regents for the King, one of whom is to be a Croat; (c) the resignation of Gen. Bogoljub Ilić, Minister of War; and (d) the withdrawal of the military from all political activities.

As follow-up to the developments in Yugoslavia, on April 1, 1941, Emil von Rintelen, Directorate in the Political Dept. in Berlin, transmitted a telegram to Alfred Freundt: "Foreign Minister Ribbentrop asks that he be kept informed about developments in Yugoslavia. Walter Malletke, Office of Reichsleiter Rosenberg, as well as Veesenmayer, SS-Standartenfuhrer, are leaving today for the purpose of establishing contact with influential Croatians and will call on you [Freundt]. Also, the Foreign Minister asks that you inform the Croatian leaders that Veesenmayer is to be regarded as a trusted representative of the Foreign Minister."

On April 1, 1941, Milan Gavrilović, Yugoslav Minister and Envoy in Moscow, who was at the same time Minister Without Portfolio, had received instructions to stay in Moscow a few more days. Various statements made by the Yugoslav Military Attaché, Colonel Popović in a conversation with the German Naval Attaché, Capt. Norbert Baumbach, told a plain Serbian falsehood in order to start an "evil intrigue." Popović was quoted as saying that the Soviet authorities "had summoned him and offered to deliver war material to Yugoslavia; however he had turned this offer down emphatically."

Alfred Freundt, on April 2, 1941, corresponded with the Reich Foreign Ministry, to inform that August Košutić, Vice President of the Croatian Peasant Party, arrived in Belgrade and hoped to obtain a guarantee for the acceptance of the conditions to join the Šimović government. Also, Freundt reported having been informed by Vladko Maček through an intermediary that Maček may decide to go to Belgrade. Gerhard Feine, Counselor of the German Legation in Yugoslavia, on April 2, 1941, reported to the Reich Foreign Ministry that morale among the Yugoslav population was low. Conciliatory statements made by Bogoljub Jeftić, former Premier and now Minister of Transportation in the Šimović Cabinet, alleged during a conversation with an informant of the German Legation, that the Yugoslav government could guarantee a domestic and foreign policy satisfactory to the German Reich and observance of the Tripartite Pact. On April 2, 1941, Ribbentrop ordered that in the course of April 3, the staff of the German Legation in Yugoslavia be reduced to four or five men. Secret material, all coding and radio instructions, must be destroyed. The consequences of the tension existing between the Axis Powers and the present Yugoslav government cannot yet be foreseen. Therefore, the Wehrmacht Operations Staff, on April 2, 1941, requested the Chief of the Wehrmacht Mission in Bucharest to suggest to Gen. Ion Antonescu, President of Romania, increase preparation for defense on the Russian border. One cannot be serious enough in drawing attention to the need for carefully organizing the protection of the oil region around Ploesti both against air raids and against the landing of demolition teams with parachutes operating clandestinely by day or night.

On April 3, 1941, Freundt reported to Ribbentrop, that Veesenmayer had arrived in Zagreb. Considering the present situation in Yugoslavia and the impossibility of enlightening the Croatian people make it appear that a timely leaflet propaganda campaign be dropped over towns and rural areas, and especially over troops with Croatian units, such as the Fifth Army headquarters at Niš.

The Italian government on April 3, 1941, informed Momčilo Ninčić, Yugoslav Foreign Minister that the visit to Rome, Italy, by Slobodan Jovanović, Yugoslav Second Vice President, would make sense only if an adequate basis for negotiations were assured beforehand.

~ Hitler's Directive No. 26 ~

Top Secret Military   Headquarters, April 3, 1941

Cooperation with our allies in the Balkans.

1. The military tasks intended for the Southeastern European states in the campaign against Yugoslavia result from the political objectives:

Hungary, to whom the Banat will fall, will mainly have to occupy that area, but has declared herself in addition ready to cooperate in the destruction of the enemy.

Bulgaria should get back Macedonia and is therefore principally to be interested in an attack in this direction, but without particular pressure being exerted from the German side. Furthermore the Bulgarians, supported by a German armored unit, will provide the rear cover against Turkey. For that purpose Bulgaria will also employ the three divisions stationed on the Greek border.

Romania, in her own as well as in the German interest will have to limit her mission to protecting the frontier against Yugoslavia and Russia. Through the Chief of the Wehrmacht Mission we should seek to achieve an increase in Romania's defensive preparedness against Russia. At the very least two-way communications across the Romanian-Hungarian boundary must proceed between Hungarian and German Liaison Headquarters without hindrance.

2. The following guiding principles will apply for the military cooperation and the organization of command in the coming operations: I reserve to myself the unified command of this campaign, in so far as the operational objectives of the Italian and Hungarian forces within the framework of the whole operation are concerned. It must be carried on in a way that takes into account the sensibilities of our allies and leaves to the Chiefs of State of Italy and Hungary the possibility of appearing to their peoples and armed forces as sovereign military leaders. I shall therefore pass on the military demands for the coordination of operations, which are to be transmitted to me by the Commander in Chief of the Army and the Commander in Chief of the Luftwaffe as proposals and wishes, in the form of personal letters to the Duce and Regent Horthy. The same procedure is to be followed by the Commander in Chief of the Twelfth Army toward the Bulgarian governmental and military authorities. If single Bulgarian divisions participate in the operations against Yugoslavia, they must be subordinate to the German Commanding Officers of the given areas.

3. In Hungary a Headquarters named "The German General with the High Command of the Hungarian Armed Forces" shall be set up, to whose Staff a Liaison Staff of the Luftwaffe shall also be attached. This Headquarters will serve both my Liaison with the Regent, as well as the Liaison of the Wehrmacht branches with the Hungarian High Command. All details of the cooperation with the Italian and Hungarian forces are to be settled by the Wehrmacht Branches and by Liaison Staffs to be exchanged between adjoining armies and air fleets.

4. The air defense forces of Romania and Bulgaria remain integrated in the German air defense of these countries, in so far as they are not employed in the areas of their own armies. Hungary will defend her territory herself, provided that German units operating there, and the buildings essential to them, are protected by the German Wehrmacht.

5. Apart from the new arrangement regarding the unified command, the agreements with Hungary remain in effect. The Second Italian Army will gain freedom of movement only after the

attack of the German Second Army and the motorized group of the Forty-Sixth Army Corps begin to take effect. To this end it may become necessary that at first it be made more in a southern than southeastern direction. Limiting the Italian Air Force to protection of the flank and the rear of the front in Albania, to attacks on the Mostar airfield and coastal airports, and to cooperation along the front of the Second Italian Army as soon as it advances to the attack, will be arranged by the OKW.

6. I shall later regulate the tasks in the occupation devolving upon the various countries after the campaign. In the manner of the cooperation with the allies even during the opeartions the brotherhood in arms for the achievement of a common political goal must be stressed in every possible way.

Signed: Adolph Hitler
                               Führer and Chancellor
                               Supreme Commander of the Wehrmacht

* * * * *

On April 3, 1941, Veesenmayer, SS-Standartenfuhrer, and Freundt, German Consul General at Zagreb, reported that it seemed hopeless to try to persuade Vladko Maček from going to Belgrade because Maček had already committed himself through the press. According to Gerhard Feine, Counselor of Legation in Yugoslavia, Maček had accepted the post of Deputy Premier in the Yugoslav government. As the last effort, on April 4, 1941, Walter Malletke had a conversation with Maček. The latter was entirely negative with respect to all of Malletke's objections and attempts at influencing him. Maček believed in his mission for preservation of peace. Maček is obviously in a dreamland and is carried along by the supposedly imaginative success of his policy. However, Maček could not make any convincing statement concerning practical possibilities of carrying it out in Belgrade. The substance of Maček's press statement reads as follows: " I am a Christian and mindful of the words of Christ: Blessed are they who build, for they shall be called sons of God. The sense of responsibility toward the people, who have already given me their trust for more than 9 years, impels me to try everything to save the peace, the highest good of mankind. I am deeply convinced that the present leaders of Serbia, too, are just as sincere as I myself [Maček]. I am aware that in spite of all the difficulties of recent times we will preserve the peace through joint cooperation and will bear the difficulties that arise more easily. Furthermore assurance has been gained that through this cooperation the rights which Croatia has gained will not only be preserved and consolidated, but also strengthened. "

Bewildering the international situation, on April 3, 1941, the Yugoslav government sent a Serbian delegation, (comprised of Božin Šimić and Colonel Savić), to Moscow to conclude a Treaty of Alliance with the USSR. Instead, on April 5, 1941, Vyacheslav Mikhailovich Molotov, Soviet Foreign Minister, and Milan Gavrilović, Yugoslav Minister and Envoy in Moscow, signed a Pact of Friendship and Non-Aggression.

Despite the strong opposition from various military and political circles, on April 4, 1941, Vladko Maček joined the Šimović Royal Government in Belgrade.

On April 5, 1941, Field Marshal Walther von Braushitsch, Commander-in-Chief of the German Army, moved to Wiener Neustadt (35 miles/56 km south of Vienna) to assume command of the German Second and Twelfth Armies which were designated to conduct the campaigns against Yugoslavia and Greece. Joachim von Ribbentrop, on April 5, 1941, transmitted a most urgent top secret communication to the German Minister in Greece, to convey without delay the following statement to the Greek Foreign Minister: "At this very moment [on Sunday, April 6, at 5:20 a.m.] the Greek Minister in Berlin is being handed by the German Foreign Minister a note with an enclosed memorandum. These documents point out that the Greek Government - concerning whose unneutral conduct since the beginning of the war numerous documentary proofs are in the hands of the German Government as a result of discovery of the files of the French General Staff in La Charité - by permitting strong British forces to enter Greece has itself brought the situation toward which Germany can no longer remain inactive. The German Government has ordered its troops to expel the British forces from Greek soil. Any resistance offered to the Wehrmacht will be ruthlessly crushed. It is emphasized that the German troops do not come as enemies of the Greek people and that the German people have no intention of fighting or destroying the Greek people as such. Rather the blow which Germany is compelled to strike on Greek territory is aimed at England."

* * * * *

~ Imminent Action in the Balkans ~

Top Secret - Most Urgent   Berlin, April 5, 1941

To: For the Italian Ambassador Personally

From: German Foreign Minister

Please inform Filippo Anfuso, Chef de Cabinet to Count Ciano, Italian Foreign Minister, at once in strict confidence the following:

Simultaneously with the start of the action against Yugoslavia and Greece, which is imminent, the Reich Government will publish an official statement which will explain to world opinion the reasons for the action against Yugoslavia. The content of this statement in broad outline is as follows:

The Balkans are the objective of the latest British attempt to establish a front against Germany. After Greece has already fallen victim to this policy, Britain now sees in Yugoslavia a willing tool for her objective. On the other hand it has always been Germany's aim to spare the Balkan countries from the war. Since his assumption of power the Führer has worked for a policy of friendship and cooperation with Yugoslavia, while at the same time the Duce [Mussolini], too, placed the Italo-Yugoslav relationship on a new basis of friendship. But as early as after the fall of Milan Stojadinović, Yugoslav Premier it was evident that forces were at work in Yugoslavia aiming at abandoning the path of compromise and friendship. The documents found in La Charite prove since the summer of 1939 Yugoslavia carried on a policy unequivocally directed against Germany. [Large amounts of French diplomatic and military documents had been found by German troops advancing in France at the railroad station of La Charite]. They clearly show the constantly closer contacts between the General Staffs of Yugoslavia and the Allies.

Despite her knowledge of these things, Germany continued the policy of understanding with Yugoslavia, and in this went as far as the Vienna Agreements of March 25, 1941 which promised Yugoslavia recognition of her sovereignty and integrity, exemption from the transit or transshipment of troops, and other military assistance as well as the future acquisition of the city and harbor of Salonika, in return for which Yugoslavia had to assume merely the obligation of loyal cooperation in the new organization of the Continent. In this matter, Germany and Italy were exclusively guided by the wish to win Yugoslavia over to loyal cooperation and to secure for her a definitive position in Europe.

To this historically unique chance the clique of conspirators in Belgrade has now given an answer that is as stupid as it is criminal; the same clique is involved here which in the past did not shrink from regicide, and by the Sarajevo murder unleashed the First World War. With this Belgrade has let drop the mask once and for all. Ministers who had signed the Tripartite Pact were arrested; all over Yugoslavia outrageous acts of terror against members of the Axis Powers were unleashed; General Šimović threatened the Italian Minister with war; mobilization was ordered; contact was established with the British and Greek General Staffs; and an appeal for assistance was made to Britain and the United States of America. Thus Yugoslavia has finally decided to make common cause with Germany's enemies and to make herself available to Britain as an assembly area against Germany. The Reich government does not intend to watch these activities any longer and to permit Yugoslavia to become, like Greece, the battleground for British mercenaries alien to the Continent. It has given orders to German troops to restore peace and security in this part of Europe, too, by every possible military means.

End of the content of the official statement. No diplomatic steps with the Yugoslav government will be taken at the start of the action.

We propose to the Italian government that it proceed in the same manner and likewise make public an official statement along the lines of ours.

As far as our action against Greece is concerned, the Greek Minister here will be handed a note which in the first place puts on record Greece's unneutral conduct since the outbreak of the war (likewise with reference made to the documents found at La Charite) and then states that in spite of all warnings Greece nevertheless let herself be used for the establishment of a new British front against Germany. The Reich Government has now ordered its troops to expel the British forces from Greek soil and to break ruthlessly any resistance offered to the German Wehrmacht. At the same time as this note is handed over in Berlin a démarche will be made by our Minister in Athens.

Please inform Anfuso of this, too, in confidence. You will yet be notified of the time of the start of the operation; however, it is so imminent that we would be grateful to the Italian Government if it would begin at once to prepare the statement.

Signed: Joachim von Ribbentrop

* * * * *

As the customary law of war applies to cases of international armed conflict and to the forcible occupation of territory as well as to declared war in its strict sense, a declaration of war is not an essential condition of the applicable international law. Similarly, treaties relating to war may become operative notwithstanding the absence of a formal declaration of war. Subsequent follow-up, the official statement of the German Government, together with a supplementary memorandum, was published in the German press on April 6, 1941. In a telegram, April 6, 1941, 4:00 a.m., Ribbentrop informed the Embassy in Rome that the operation would start that morning. Identical telegrams were sent to Budapest, Bucharest, and Sofia. According to the Hague Convention, the contracting powers recognize that hostilities between themselves must not commence without previous and explicit warning, in the form either of a reasoned declaration of war or of an ultimatum with conditional declaration of war. Nothing in the foregoing rule requires that any particular length of time shall elapse between a declaration of war and the commencement of hostilities.

Since Karađorđević's Yugoslavia was a member of the Axis Powers, Hitler decided that once the Yugoslav Embassy in Berlin was informed of the imminent military action, a formal declaration of war was unnecessary. Therefore, in the early morning hours on Palm Sunday, April 6, 1941, without breaking off diplomatic relations, Germany implemented operation "Punishment" as waves of Luftwaffe bombers attacked Yugoslavia by bombing Belgrade, Serbia. Following the Luftwaffe assailment, the Royal Yugoslav Air Force was severely paralyzed, thus allowing the German Air Force to devote its maximum effort to such targets as Yugoslav military airfields, supply depots, routes of communications, troop concentrations, and to provide close support to the German ground operations. The Wehrmacht were given effective Luftwaffe support by the German Fourth Air Force. The actual air operations were carried out by the German Eighth Air Corps under the command of Gen. Wolfram von Richthofen. Concurrently, Britain landed over 60,000 troops in Greece. The German military operations were conducted by German blitzkrieg fashion. German troops stationed in Styria, SE Austria, crossed the northern frontier of Yugoslav at Mureck and Radkersburg, NE of Maribor, along the Mur river. Early in the morning of April 8, 1941, the German army under Field Marshal Wilhelm List launched their attack from Bulgaria and converged on Yugoslavia. The First Panzer Group from its assembly area northwest of Sophia, Bulgaria, crossed the Yugoslav frontier near Pirot on the Nišava River. German armies drove westward from Austria and southward from Hungary, they advanced through Skopje to the Albania border, cutting communications between Yugoslavia and Greece. On April 9, 1941 the city of Niš surrendered to Gen. Ewald von Kleist. After the breakthrough of the Metaxas Line, on April 9, 1941, the German forces captured the port city of Salonika (Thessaloniki), Greece.

Early morning hours of April 10, 1941, the Germans occupied Maribor, and continued southwards in pursuance of the retreating Royal Yugoslav forces, with dive-bombers clearing the route of advance, the Fourteenth Panzer Division broke out of the Drava River bridgehead and advanced southwestward toward Zagreb. Cold weather and snow-covered roads hampered progress of the German forces, nevertheless, by the evening of the same day, the lead tanks of the Fourteenth Panzer Division of the XLVI Panzer Corps (Second Army, commanded by Gen. Maximilian von Weichs) reached the outskirts of Zagreb. When the German troops triumphantly entered the city of Zagreb, they were enthusiastically greeted and welcomed as the liberators by an excited, emotional, and naturally exuberant anti-Yugoslav populace, cheering "we are free again!"

Just before the German troops entered Zagreb, Col. Slavko Kvaternik (1878-1947), a former member of the General Staff in the Austrian Imperial Army, on April 10, 1941 proclaimed the " Independent State of Croatia " (Nezavisna Država Hrvatska-NDH). Notwithstanding the independence, Italian troops remained in parts of Croatian territory and German troops occupied important Croatian towns outside the Italian zone. Ante Pavelić, leader of the ustaše movement, returned from exile to Croatia in the wake of the German occupation with hundreds of his ustaše militia. On April 16, 1941, Pavelić established the Croatian government, naming himself Chief of State "Poglavnik" and appointed Kvaternik Deputy Chief of State and Commander of the Armed Forces. Later, an army of 10 battalions, a ustaše guard of one infantry regiment, and a cavalry squadron were organized. The Croatian government began the conscription of a national military force, which did not progress beyond eight mountain and light infantry brigades and a railroad security brigade which was not activated until late in the war, when these brigades were joined with the expanded ustaše forces to function as divisions. Croatian-German "Legion" units which were recruited in Croatia by the Germans drained off much of the manpower that might have gone to the Croatian forces.

Accompanied by his entourage, on April 11, 1941, Hitler arrived aboard his special train and stationed nearby a tunnel along a railway route between Wiener Neustadt and Fuerstenburg (50 mi/80 km east of Graz), located near the Styrian (Steiermark) Alps, in order to monitor the Balkan campaigns until April 25, 1941. To provide better coordination, Reichs Marshal Hermann Wilhelm Göring, Commander-in-Chief of the Luftwaffe (German Air Force), established his field headquarters at Semmering Pass, southwest of Wiener Neustadt, Austria. On the same date, the German High Command was informed by the commander of the Italian Second Army that the Italian Fifth, Sixth, and Eleventh Corps were ready to launch their attack against Yugoslavia. In preparation of the Italian attack, the German Fourth Air Force attacked the columns and troop concentrations in the Ljubljana region in Slovenia to consummate the encirclement of the Yugoslav Seventh Army who were attempting to withdraw southeastward. A great number of prisoners and much booty were captured as entire Yugoslav divisions surrendered. About 30,000 Yugoslav troops concentrated near Delnice were captured by the Italians who were advancing southward from Istria in the direction of the Dalmatian coast.

On April 11, the Hungarian Third Army crossed the Yugoslav frontier north of Osijek and near Subotica. The next day the Hungarian forces pursued the retreating Yugoslav First Army and occupied the area between the Danube and Tisza (Tisa) rivers. German forces from bases in Romania, occupied Belgrade on April 12, 1941. The remnant of the crumbled and ineffective Yugoslav Army was encircled and unable to fight.

Elements of the German forces linked up with the Italian forces at Vrboska in northwest Croatia on April 12, 1941. The demarcation line of Novo Mesto-Slunj-Bihać-Livno south of the Sava River was designated as the boundary between the German and Italian sphere of influence. The German Second Army moved its command post to Zagreb on April 13, 1941. That evening, the main body of the German forces reached the Kupa River, the temporarily designated border line between Slovenia in the north and Croatia in the south. After the fall of Belgrade on April 13, 1941, Gen. Weichs, Commander of the German Second Army, launched a vigorous pursuit of the Yugoslav forces withdrawing toward Sarajevo. Coincidently, on April 13, 1941, the Soviet Union and Japan concluded a five-year neutrality treaty.

On April 14, 1941, the German troops reached Jajce in central Yugoslavia, approximately 50 mi/80 km NW of Sarajevo. On the same day, the Yugoslav Second and Fifth Armies asked for separate cease-fire agreements. The Germans turned down the request because only the unconditional surrender of the entire Yugoslav Armed Forces could be considered as a basis for negotiations. Late that evening, a representative of the Royal Yugoslav Government asked Gen. Kleist for an immediate cease-fire. The German High Command, advised of the latest turn of events, designated Gen. von Weichs to conduct the negotiations in Belgrade. Gen. Edmund Glaise von Horstenau was appointed on April 14, 1941, as Liaison Officer between the German occupation troops and the Croatian government at Zagreb. On April 17, 1941, Siegfried Kasche replaced von Horstenau as German Minister in Croatia. As the German Second Army closed in on Sarajevo from east and west, entered the city on April 15, 1941, the Yugoslav Second Army whose headquarters was in Sarajevo capitulated.

INDEPENDENT STATE OF CROATIA, 1941-1945

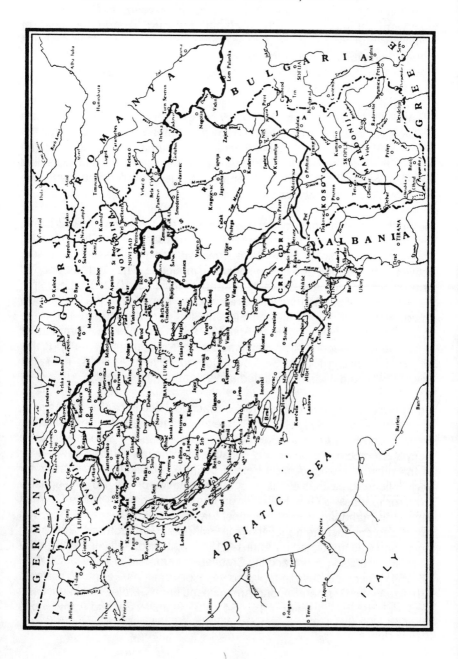

The ineffective and disgruntled Yugoslav military establishment, 6,000 Royal Yugoslav officers, and 337,000 NCO's and enlisted men became prisoners of war (POWs). The weakness and defeatist attitude of government politicians and military commanders were revealed within the first days of the April War. Collectively, the armed forces top brass, for the most part corrupt and incompetent, capitulated like a house built on sinking sand.

Two weeks after assuming the throne of Yugoslavia, King Petar II Karađorđević (1923-1970) evacuated from Kotor in an Royal Air Force Sunderland flying-boat to London, England, via North Africa. Upon the arrival of the second governmental entourage, including Premier Dušan Šimović, the Yugoslav government-in-exile was established. Šimović remained the Premier until his resignation in 1942.

The Protocol of Surrender was concluded and signed on April 17, 1941. Aleksandar Cincar-Marković, Foreign Minister, and Gen. Milojko Janković, Deputy Chief of Staff, signed for the Royal Yugoslav Government. Gen. Weichs signed for the German government, and Col. Bonfatti, Italian Military Attaché in Belgrade signed on behalf of his country. The Hungarians were represented by a liaison officer who, however, did not sign the "Instrument of Surrender" since Hungary was technically "not at war with Yugoslavia". The armistice became effective at noon April 18, 1941, just twelve days after the initial German attack was launched.

After the collapse of Yugoslavia, the Germans and Italians were emotionally overwhelmed by the Axis speedy victory. In their jubilation, the Axis occupation forces came to realize that during the war of April 1941, hundreds of thousands of prisoners of war (POW) were in custody at various POW detention centers. To comply with the applicable International Laws a solution had to be found to provide safe quarters, necessary food, medical care, and adequate clothing for detainees. With limited manpower the Axis decided to free the POWs and accord them a full amnesty. First, all enlisted men and non-commissioned officers were released without the usual interrogation procedures and documentation processing. However, some junior and senior officers were retained for their safety and released a few days later. Ironically, most of the released POWs, voluntarily or involuntarily became members of the various anti-Axis powers resistance movements.

Meanwhile, the British army comprised of 65,000 troops lead by General Henry Maitland Wilson was assigned to defend the mountain approaches along the Greece and Bulgaria frontier. As the German forces broke the Metaxas Line and captured the city-port of Salonika, the British were in a speedy desperate retreat from the mainland of Greece.

The Hague Regulations Respecting the Laws and Customs of War on Land, provide that: "Territory is considered occupied when it is actually placed under the authority of the hostile army." There are substantial evidences that the resistance movements failed to comply with the rules of war entitling them to be accorded the right of a lawful belligerent. Evidence clearly shows that once the governments of Yugoslavia, Greece, and Albania capitulated, the Axis Powers maintained control of the occupied countries. Although the resistance movements were able to control sections of territories at various times, the Germans and Italians could at any time assume physical control of the defeated countries. The partial control of the resistance movements was considered temporary only, therefore, didn't deprive the military occupation forces the status of an occupant.

Furthermore, the Geneva Convention Relative to the Treatment of Prisoners of War, prescribes that prisoners of war are persons belonging to one of the following categories, who have fallen into the power of the enemy: (1.) Members of the armed forces of a Party to the Conflict, as well as members of militias or volunteer corps forming part of such armed forces; and (2.) Members of other militias and members of other volunteer corps, including those of organized resistance movements belonging to a Party to the Conflict and operating in or outside their own territory, even if this territory is occupied, provided that such militias or volunteer corps, including such organized resistance movements, fulfill the following conditions: (a) being commanded by a person responsible for his subordinates; (b) having a fixed distinctive sign recognized at a distance; (c) carrying arms openly; and (d) conducting their operations in accordance with the laws and customs of war.

Incidentally, the United States and Prussia (a former German state in north-central Germany) in 1785 signed the world's first treaty concerning the treatment for prisoners of war. The Hague Conventions of 1899 and 1907 and the Geneva Conventions of 1929 and 1949 established international rules concerning the POW. In spite of the Hague and Geneva regulations, mistreatment of POWs has occurred. During the Second World War (1939-1945), Germany, Japan, USSR, etc., treated their POWs harshly and inhumanely. Millions of POWs died of cold, starvation, and mistreatment.

Resistance bands, roamed Yugoslavia and actively participated in terrorist activities, destroyed and disrupted transportation and communication lines, captured and executed anyone who was not on their side, demolished properties and burned entire villages because the local residents refused to cooperate. Elements of the German, Italian, and Croatian military and civilian authorities were often targets of assassination and constantly became victims of surprise attacks, captured Axis personnel were always tortured and often killed. Resistance movements usually, after consummating their terroristic activity, would hastily retreat or conceal their weapons and mingle with the local population pretending to be innocent and harmless members of the community.

Occasionally the resistance movements were designated as units common to military organization. They had no common uniform. Their uniform consisted of civilian clothes or mixed parts of German, Italian, and any other easily available uniforms. The most common insignia, the communist-red star worn by Tito's communist partisans, and the skull and crossbones (similar to the symbol of Nazi SS-Schutzstaffeln) worn by Serb-četnici was of such size that it could not be seen at a distance. They didn't carry their arms openly except when it was to their advantage to do so. Generally, resistance movements seldom met the requirements prescribed by the Hague Regulations. This means that the majority of captured members of these unlawful bands were not entitled to be accorded the protection and treatment of prisoners of war (POWs).

* * * * *

~ Meetings between Ribbentrop and Ciano ~

April 21-22, 1941

At the Hotel Imperial in Vienna, meetings were held between Joachim von Ribbentrop, German Foreign Minister, and Galeazzo Ciano, Italian Foreign Minister, regarding the reorganization of the areas of former Yugoslavia and Greece, resulting in the following:

Croatia - The boundary between Croatia and Germany has already been determined by Hitler and will be definitively fixed with the Croatian government when the occasion presents itself. During the time that Serbia is occupied by German troops, Germany will, keep under occupation a strip of territory extending from the northwest to the southeast, fixed as Zagreb - Banja Luka -Sarajevo, to be agreed upon between German and Italian military authorities, in order to safeguard the lines of communication to Serbia. Italy intends to link Croatia closely to Italy possibly through a personal union. The Italians intend to annex the territory of Dalmatia; it is to be given the status of an Italian Government of Dalmatia, "Governatorato Italiano della Dalmazia," which included the littoral of the Adriatic coast from Fiume [Rijeka] in Istria, to Kotor [Cattaro] bordering Montenegro. In principle, Germany is politically disinterested in the Croatian questions. Hence Hitler has no reason to take any position concerning Croatia. Hitler will leave it entirely to Italy to make whatever political decision is suitable and deal with the Croatians directly. Croatia's frontier with Hungary will follow the Drava River. Croatian wishes on the eastern frontier between the rivers Danube and Sava (Syrmia) are to be satisfied. The rest of Croatia's eastern boundary will follow the previous eastern boundary of Bosnia-Herzegovina, in which connection Italy wants the frontiers of Montenegro advanced westward.

Slovenia - to the extent that it does not fall to the Reich, will be annexed by Italy and given administrative autonomy.

Montenegro - will be restored as an independent state but will be linked to Italy by personal union under the Italian Royal Dynasty. This would be all the more understandable due to the generally known fact that Queen Elena of Italy was a Montenegrin princess.

Albania - will receive additional territory at the expense of Greece, Macedonia, and Serbia. However, the Bulgarian national shrine Ohrid and the chromium mine of Ljuboten in Macedonia, to be operated as a kind of German enterprise, will go to Bulgaria, and the lead deposits of Trepca in Mitrovica, likewise to be used by Germany under German management, will go to Serbia. Considerable additions to Albanian territory at the expense of Greece, from the former Yugoslav-Greek frontier northeast of Florina to Arta.

Serbia - will be given the boundary drawn by the Germans; but will remain under German military occupation for the time being. Serbia is to remain as small and weak as possible, and all measures will be taken to make impossible for all time a repetition of the recent betrayal by the clique of Serbian conspirators.

Bačka and Banat - will go to Hungary, likewise Medjumurje and Prekmurje, unless separate arrangements for these two areas are made between Hungary on the one hand and Germany and Croatia on the other. The Banat will for the time being remain occupied by German troops in order to prevent clashes between Hungarians and Romanians.

Macedonia - as well as smaller areas ceded to former Yugoslavia after World War II will go to Bulgaria, with a broad western strip including Struga, Gostivar, and Tetovo going to Albania. Bulgarian wishes with respect to Salonika, which Hitler noted with sympathy, will, like the question of the final fate of Greece, be reserved until the end of the war for agreements between Mussolini and Hitler.

Greece - The Ionian Islands will be annexed immediately by Italy. For the rest, Italy's intentions with respect to Greece are apparently extensive.

Note: In view of Germany's special economic interests in the former Yugoslav state it is agreed that the German economic interests will be given special consideration in the areas falling to Italy. Germany is primarily interested in the development of the production of the Dalmatian bauxite mines. The production of these mines will be developed as far as possible, and the satisfaction of German requirements will be given preferential consideration in connection with exports. The procedure by which the new boundaries to be established between Serbia, Montenegro, Albania, and Bulgaria are to be formally determined will be the subject of a proposal by the Reich foreign minister and the Italian foreign minister.

* * * * *

Puppet regimes were installed throughout occupied German and Italian territories to lighten the administrative burden of the sponsored and controlled forces and exploited the difference between the various ethnic, religious, and political factions in occupied areas. Local police, security forces, and national armies were organized to reduce the number of occupation troops required to keep law and order and protect the various newly established governments.

German troops continued advancing across the Pindus Mountains (Pindhos Óros) in NW Greece and on April 21, 1941, made it possible for the breakthrough at the Thermopylae Pass, between Mt. Oeta and the Gulf of Maliakos. Also on April 21, German Field Marshal Wilhelm List, Commander of the Twelfth Army, informed the Italian High Command that the Germans had entered into armistice negotiations with the Greek Army in Epirus and, therefore, requested the Italian Army stop its advance in order not to hamper the negotiations. Mussolini replied that Italy was prepared to stop its advance and enter into armistice negotiations only if the Greeks would also ask the Italian troops for an armistice. The Führer agreed with the Duce, in that, an armistice was to be concluded with the Greeks only by the German and Italian military jointly and that, military operations were to continue until the armistice was signed. The Duce was not about to let the Greek military get off easy. The Italian troops had for six months been fighting against the Greeks; 500,000 military personnel had been committed, and 63,000 had been killed. Now the Italian Army demanded the satisfaction of victory. While the Germans advanced toward the capital city of Athens, on April 22 the Greek government entourage comprised of King George II, Premier Emmanuel Tsouderos and other elite officials fled by ship to Candia, Island of Crete, and on the night of May 23 they escaped by a British warship to Cairo, Egypt, where the Greek government-in-exile was established and on September 22, 1941, transferred to London, England. The retreating British forces embarked on April 30, thus the Germans succeeded in safeguarding the important Romanian oil fields. The puppet regime in Greece was organized under Gen. George Tsolakoglou, Commander of the Greek forces in Epirus and Macedonia, who had surrendered the Army of Epirus and Macedonia to the Germans and Italians on April 23. Six days later, Gen. Tsolakoglou became the titular head of the Axis sponsored Greek government in Athens, April 29, 1941. Premier Tsolakoglou resigned on November 23, 1942, and was succeeded by George Logothetopulos formerly the Minister of Social Welfare, Culture, and Education.

The German Legation in Zagreb received a telegram dated May 3, 1941 from Ernst Woermann, Director, Political Department, German Foreign Ministry, stating: "On the basis of the line laid down by the Führer a state treaty concerning the German-Croatian frontier is to be concluded as soon as possible. A short draft is being prepared in Berlin. The new frontier corresponds to the former administrative boundary between Austria (southern Styria) and Croatia. The draft with a map will be transmitted very soon by Senior Counselor von Kamphoevener who will be authorized to sign jointly with the Chief of the German Legation. After signing of the state treaty it is intended that there should be negotiations by mixed delegations on the spot for the purpose of concluding the usual frontier treaty. The Croatian government should be informed that the state treaty could be signed not later than next week, if possible. At such time, please get quarters for Kamphoevener, who will probably be accompanied by Oberregierungsrat [a grade in the German Civil Service] Essen and Fraulein [Miss] Schone."

* * * * *

~ Resettlement of Slovenes ~

Telegram   Belgrade, May 6, 1941

To: German Foreign Ministry

From: German Plenipotentiary Minister in Serbia

At the conference on the resettlement of the Slovenes held today in Maribor under the chairmanship of Siegfried Uiberreither, Reichsstatthalter and Gauleiter of Styria, the military commander in Serbia promised that, to carry out the directive issued by the Führer [Hitler] that southern Styria should be made a German land, he would accommodate in Old Serbia as many as possible of the estimated 220,000-260,000 Slovenes to be evacuated from southern Styria and Carinthia; this, in spite of great misgivings about feeding and lodging them, and also about the danger to security in the territory under his authority.

According to information from the chief of transportation the resettlement cannot start before the beginning of July for technical reasons (for example, dynamited bridges, oil transports for Italy), although domestic Reich authorities attach the greatest importance to quick action.

Furthermore, thorough preparation is necessary; regarding this, the military commander has requested data from the Gauleiter.

The plans are for resettlement in three waves; first, the Slovene intelligentsia, 6,.000 persons; second, the 30,000 Slovenes who immigrated from the littoral; and third, the remainder.

The Führer has rejected the proposal to remove part of the Slovenes to Croatia. However, the military commander wants to induce Italy and Bulgaria to take a part of the evacuees. He requests the cooperation of the Foreign Ministry in inducing the Italians to take 60,000-70,000. Reasons for this are: the littoral where many of the Slovenes come from will be Italian. Furthermore, 18,000 German nationals (Volksdeutsche) from Kočevje [Gottschee], likewise falling to Italy, are being brought to Lower Styria, which will make room for the Slovenes.

Furthermore the military commander requests that Bulgaria be persuaded to take 40,000-50,000 Slovenes in southern Serbia, which has become Bulgarian. Since finding shelter for the bulk of 120,000-150,000 Slovenes in the reduced area of Old Serbia encounters even now the most serious difficulties, I very emphatically support the military commanders' request.

                              Signed: Felix Benzler

* * * * *

108

In response to Ribbentrop's request regarding the evacuation of Slovenes to Bulgaria, the German Minister in Bulgaria, Herbert von Richthofen, on May 6, 1941 stated that new areas falling to Bulgaria confront the government of Bulgaria with very difficult tasks. The area of Thrace presents them with a large Greek minority because of the compulsory removal of Bulgarian elements after the First World War and the settlement of Greeks from Asia Minor. Macedonia contains, besides a large Bulgarian population, not inconsiderable portions of Walachians and Albanians. New settlements of Slovenes in Macedonia would perhaps render permanently impossible any chance of a pacification and economic development of Macedonia.

On May 7, 1941, Benito Mussolini (Il Duce) and Ante Pavelić (Poglavnik) met at Monfalcone, northwest of Trieste (Italy), for a conference to determine their countries new frontiers and sign a "Treaty of Alliance, Guarantee and Cooperation" between Italy and Croatia. Subsequently, Pavelić arrived in Rome on May 18, 1941, with a special delegation in order to offer the royal crown of Croatia to the King of Italy. At the Palazzo Venezia in Rome, Mussolini and Pavelić signed the proclamation. The King of Italy accepted this offer and promptly transferred the Kingship to Duke of Spoleto (Aimone di Savoia - Aosta) who presumably became "King Tomislav II of Croatia," without ever setting foot in Croatia. The Poglavnik Ante Pavelić would remain a titular head of the Croatian government. Siegfried Kasche, German Minister in Croatia reported on May 12, 1941, that the German delegation had arrived in Zagreb on May 10, 1941, and that the subsequent negotiations with the Croats had resulted in full agreement on the text of a treaty (German-Croatian Frontier) which would be signed on May 16, 1941 at Zagreb.

A Top Secret memorandum dated May 13, 1941, signed by Karl Ritter, Ambassador on special assignment in the German Foreign Ministry, stated that Gen. Alfred Jodl (Chief, Wehrmacht Operations Staff of the OKW) had given Gen. Walter Warlimont (Chief, Department of National Defense, Abt.L, Wehrmacht Operations Staff) instructions from the Führer concerning the military occupation and administration of Greece. The Führer decided as follows: "Germany's efforts must be directed toward evacuating Greece as soon as possible and toward withdrawing as many forces as possible and leaving the protection of the entire area of Italy. It is out of the question for Germany to play the part of arbiter between Greece and Italy, and for the Greek government to turn to the German Commander in Chief in all of these questions. Twelfth Army Headquarters is therefore to be transferred back to Salonika (Thessaloniki) as soon as the situation permits. It is none of Germany's business whether the Italian occupation troops can cope with the Greek government or not. After the elimination of the Greek Army and its weapons there no longer exists any military danger which could result in the renewed employment of German troops.

In a telegram dated May 14, 1941, Fritz von Twardowski, Director of the Cultural Policy Department, German Foreign Ministry, asked the German Embassy in Rome, Italy, to take a position regarding the suggestion by the German military commander in Serbia that Italy accept part of the Slovenes to be evacuated. On May 16, 1941, Otto Christian von Bismarck, Minister in the German Embassy in Italy, advised Twardowski against approaching the Italian government with the proposal of settling 60,000-70,000 Slovenes from southern Styria in those parts of Slovenia which had fallen to Italy. At the most, Otto von Bismarck urged, Germany might ask the Italians to take a number of Slovenes equivalent to the number of German nationals (Volksdeutsche) that would leave the Italian portion of Slovenia. Initially, on October 26, 1939 and expanded on August 1, 1941, Nazi Germany created the General Government (Generalgouvernement) in occupied Poland to be used as reception center for abducted or displaced forced labor.

* * * * *

~ Reich Foreign Minister for the Führer ~

Fuschl, May 16, 1941

According to a telegram from Minister Kasche in Zagreb on May 13, 1941, the Croatian government would if necessary be willing to receive in Croatia the 220,000 to 260,000 Slovenes to be evacuated from Lower Styria, or part of them, if it could deport the same number of Serbs to Old Serbia.

According to a directive of the Führer's there actually should be no deportation of Slovenes to Croatia. However, since the Croatian government apparently is anxious to be able to reduce the exceedingly strong Serbian minority in Croatia, and seems to be ready to receive a corresponding number of Slovenes in order to achieve this goal, the question arises whether this idea should not be given some consideration after all. The transportation difficulties which so far have stood in the way of carrying through the evacuation of the Slovenes from Lower Styria could thereby be considerably eased.

Furthermore it is doubtless correct that acceptance of these Slovenes represents a lesser danger for the Croatian State internally than the continued existence of the undiminished strong Serbian minority.

I should like to ask for a decision by the Führer as to whether this idea should be pursued and the Croatian Government be approached accordingly.

Signed: Joachim von Ribbentrop

* * * * *

On May 16, 1941, a Confidential Protocol signed in Zagreb by Mladen Lorković, Foreign Minister and Lovro Sušić for the government of Croatia, and by Siegfried Kasche, German Minister in Croatia, and Carl Clodius. Deputy Director of Economic Policy, for the government of Germany, agreed as follows: the two governments will each establish a governmental committee for the regulation of German-Croatian economic relations, the chairman of each to be appointed by the government concerned. It shall be the task of these committees to settle all questions concerning the economic relations between the two states. The work of these committees shall be carried out according to the following principles: (a) In view of Germany's special economic interests in the former Yugoslav State it is agreed that the German economic interests in Croatia are to have special consideration. The two governments will see that the trade between the two countries remains at least at the same level as in the past; (b) Germany may continue unrestricted exploitation of industrial raw materials, in particular minerals, which she has instituted. In granting additional new concessions the Croatian State will give special consideration to the German interests. The same applies to the export of raw materials, and in particular of minerals, to Germany. The oil concessions belonging to German companies may be exploited under the same conditions as in the past. In cases where binding promises regarding concessions had already been made but where the contracts for concessions had not yet been drawn up this will be done, under the same conditions as were intended for this and in accordance with the conditions applying to the other concessions. In the export of the petroleum extracted in these areas the German requirements will be given preferential treatment; (c) It is agreed that the financial questions resulting from the presence of German troops in Croatia must be settled quickly; in this connection it must in any case be made certain that these troops in Croatia can dispose of the currency necessary for their needs. The expenses arising within the country itself, will be borne for the duration of the war by Croatia; (d) It is agreed that the states which have received areas of the former Yugoslavia will be liable proportionately to Germany and her citizens for all the obligations of former Yugoslavia and the former Yugoslav National Bank.

* * * * *

~ Reich Foreign Minister Circular ~

Berlin, May 17, 1941

The collapse of the Yugoslav government and the defeat of the Greek government resulted in a political reorganization of the occupied countries. The most important thing was the newly established Independent State of Croatia. Further the neighbors and opponents in war with former Yugoslavia, Greece, and Albania, have drawn the natural conclusions by re-establishing old historic frontiers or by translating into reality old claims recognized as being justified.

Thus the German Reich has proceeded to reincorporate the northern half of Carniola, a border strip of Carinthia and of southern Styria. Hungary will also cede to the Reich four German communities belonging to the compact Volksdeutsche area of settlement of the so-called Prekmurje (Ubermurgebiet) which will now become Hungarian.

Italy has already incorporated by decree the southern corner of Slovenia as the province of Ljubljana, and has also obtained from Croatia the cession of the areas and islands around Fiume (Rijeka), Zara (Zadar), Sibenico (Šibenik), Spalato (Split), and Cattaro (Kotor). In southern Serbia, Italy has occupied the area bordering on Albania, mainly inhabited by Albanians, whereas Bulgarian troops have moved into the area to the east which is settled by Macedonian-Bulgarian population. It can be expected that this military occupation will lead to the political incorporation of the strips of territory in question in Albania and Bulgaria.

At the northern edge of the former Yugoslav territory, Hungary has taken possession of so-called Medjumurje (Murinsel), the Prekmurje as well as of the triangle further east between the Drava and the Danube (Baranja) and between the Danube and the Tisza (Bačka) so as to reincorporate them. The western Banat (east of the Tisza), which formerly belonged to Hungary and to which Hungary and Rumania lay claim simultaneously, is for the moment occupied by German troops in order to avoid complications.

As a result of the foregoing Croatia has as her frontier in the west the Adriatic Sea and the aforementioned areas along her border claimed by Italy, in the north the province of Ljubljana; with respect to Germany in the old historic frontier between the Austrian crown land Styria and the former Kingdom of Croatia (which has already been determined in the treaty of May 16, 1941); in the northeast with respect to Hungary in general the historic frontier which follows the course of the Drava and the Danube up to the mouth of the Sava. The negotiations on determination of the frontier between Croatia and Serbia have not yet been concluded. In the main this frontier is marked by the course of the Drina up to the Sava, and by the course of the Sava up to where it flows into the Danube. In the south, Croatia will border on the kingdom of Montenegro, which will probably be re-established within approximately its old historic frontiers. Thus, Croatia comprises the area formerly known under the designations of Croatia, Slavonia, Syrmia, Dalmatia, Bosnia, and Herzegovina.

The area not affected by the reorganization, the extent of which corresponds to the earlier Old Serbia, is to be regarded as the area of the Serbian residual state; at the present time it is under a German Military Commander.

As far as Greece is concerned, Italy has expressed the intention to incorporate Epirus to an extent not yet known. Bulgaria is occupying western Thrace, aside from a strip along the Turkish border, up to and including the Strymon valley. As in Macedonia, Bulgaria considers this occupation of Thrace to be a preliminary state in its reincorporation in the mother country.

Since Italy has not yet made public the extent of her acquisitions along the Adriatic, please do not, for the time being, make any disclosure to the outsiders regarding information derived from the above statement until the control of subject territories are put in final form and concurred.

By order: Werner von Schmieden

* * * * *

Following the capitulation of the royal government of Yugoslavia, Colonel Dragoljub Mihajlović (1893-1946), during the summer of 1941, organized his Serbian resistance movement "četnici" (singular, četnik) in the wooded mountains of Ravna Gora between Čačak and Valjevo in western Serbia. Mihajlović established liaison with the government-in-exile of King Petar II of Yugoslavia in London, England. A short time later Mihajlović was named commander of the resistance forces within Yugoslavia, and then minister of defense of the royal government-in-exile. The Serb-četnici operations were generally restricted to small-scale actions and sabotage. This did not prevent the Serb-četnici from perpetrating bloody massacre by killing Croat and Muslim people and burning their houses within unprotected villages throughout Croatia and Bosnia-Herzegovina. Mihajlović and his četnici collaborated with the Axis occupation forces and committed large-scale slaughter of the Muslim populations in Bosnia-Herzegovina, Sandžak, Kosova, and Montenegro, as well as of Croatian Catholics in Croatia and Bosnia-Herzegovina, all in line with their criminal project of building a Serbian empire by "cleaning" the territories of non-Serbians.

It was the communists who adopted the name of partisan and made it synonymous with guerrilla under the leadership of Josip Broz, full name Brozović (nicknamed "Tito"), a Croat, former noncommissioned officer in the Austrian army during the First World War, who was brainwashed and converted to communist ideals while a prisoner of war of the Russians at the time of the Bolsheviks Revolution (November 7, 1917 or October 25, 1917 under the old style calendar), became the Secretary General of the communist party of Yugoslavia in 1937, and in May 1941, established a network of military-political committees under the communist party leadership in Belgrade. German references to partisans did not necessarily mean the specific resistance movement, but rather the resistance forces in general, regardless of political sympathies. Although the Axis Powers came to know the different resistance forces, it could not always distinguish one group from the other, therefore they came to use the word partisans or guerrillas in its broadest sense. It was Mihajlović that first came to the attention of the Allies, at the time when German domination of the European continent was almost complete and the Soviet forces were retreating from western Russia. Whereas, the Serb-četnici comprised mostly of local units to be called up as needed, the communist partisans had a great number of large and active mobile units capable of moving about the country and not tied down to any particular locality. The anti-monarchist policy of the partisans and anti-communist attitude of the Serb-četnici soon led to a fratricidal conflict between the two diametrically opposed underground organizations, a cleavage the Germans were to turn to their own advantage.

A conflict within a conflict soon developed, with one underground force attacking the other while both forces were already engaged against the Axis occupation troops. The uštase of Pavelić and the Serb-četnici of Milan Nedić and others were also engaged in fighting each other, as well as the communist partisans of Tito and the Serb-četnici of Mihajlović. The use of systematic propagation of allegations reflecting self-serving views or interests became normal during the belligerent actions. In numerous cases the partisans were given credit for Serb-četnici attacks against the occupation forces and their auxiliaries; on the other hand, the Serb-četnici were credited with successful partisan forays, etc. Although no one was sure who perpetrated the attrocities, each group accused the other for the crimes.

Following the defeat of Greece, the British and Greek troops withdrew to the island of Crete (Kriti). On April 25, 1941, Hitler issued Directive No. 28 under the code "Merkur" and named General Löhr, Commander of the Fourth Air Force, in charge of executing the operation. Early morning of May 20 the Luftwaffe, waves of dive bombers and lowflying fighter planes, bombarded the areas of Maleme, Canea, and Suda Bay. The first German JU-52 aircraft, each carrying twelve men, landed near the airfield and on the beaches near Canea. At the same time, 2,000 German parachutists jumped in waves of 200 each at fifteen-minute intervals. At Maleme, the parachute troops jumped into strong British and Greek resistance emplaced in positions built into the hills south of the airfield. Many of the German paratroopers were killed during the descent or shortly after landing.

During this first major military operation executed by airborne forces acting independently of regular ground forces, the Commander of the Seventh Airborne Division, Gen. Wilhelm Suessmann was killed during the approach flight at Canea; while Gen. Eugen Meindl, the Commander of the Maleme group, was critically wounded. King George II of Greece (1922-1924; 1935-1947) evacuated from the Crete island to Egypt on May 22 established a Greek government-in-exile in London. While the struggle for western Crete was raging, British planes returned to Heraklion airfield on May 23. The Germans reinforced their troops in Heraklion by dropping four companies of Parachute units to take possession of the airfield on May 28 and, until relieved by ground forces, prevent the landing of British planes. Immediately after landing, the parachute units contacted the embattled pocket force and launched a concerted attack against the British positions, eliminating several British strongholds with the support of dive bombers. German troops outflanked the British positions east of Maleme, and on the next day they occupied Canea, the capital of Crete, and entered Suda Bay after a forced march across the mountains. The British made use of the terrain and delayed the German advance by sniper and machine gun fire but, British resistance had crumbled everywhere. German supplies and equipment arrived at Suda Bay without interference from British naval and air units. On May 28 following the German capture of Heraklion, and Italian forces landing at Sitia Bay, Gen. Freyberg had ordered his British ground forces to withdraw and fight their way back toward the south coast of Crete ready to be evacuated to Egypt. After repeated encounters with British rear guards, the German forces reached the south coast of the island on June 1, 1941. The seizure of Crete by the Germans was thereby completed.

~ Discussions on Resettlement ~

Telegram - Most Urgent   Zagreb, June 4, 1941

To: German Foreign Ministry, Joachim von Ribbentrop

From: German Minister in Croatia

Today there were discussions here regarding resettlement of the Slovenes and Serbs on the one hand and the Zemun border area (in the Syrmia district) on the other. Participants in the discussion of the resettlement question were: Minister Kasche as Chairman; Minister Benzler, State Councilor Turner, and Gruppenfuhrer Neuhausen for the Military Commander in Serbia; Chief of the Civil Administration of Lower Styria, Gauleiter Uiberreither; Marshal Kvarternik, Corporation Minister Dumandzić; State Secretary of Foreign Affairs Lorković for Croatia; General Glaise von Horstenau and the experts of those mentioned above. Agreement was reached that 5,000 politically tainted persons and intellectuals are to be resettled by July 5, 1941; 25,000 Slovenes who immigrated after 1914 by August 30, 1941; and about 145,000 Slovene farmers on the frontier by October 1941. The bulk of the 5,000 politically tainted persons and intellectuals are to go directly to Serbia, the bulk of the others to Croatia, while a corresponding number of Serbs are to be transferred from Croatia to Serbia. A record regarding this was drawn up. In the following discussion of experts led by Herbert von Troll, Counselor of Legation at Zagreb, details regarding the implementation were established. The minutes of the first conference and a general draft for agreements between the German Reich and Croatia and between Croatia and the military commander in Serbia will be brought along to Salzburg. General agreement was reached and cooperation for the execution was assured.

In the discussion of the Zemun frontier questions the following participated: Minister Kasche as Chairman; Minister Benzler, State Councilor Turner, and Gruppenfuhrer Neuhausen for the military commander, Serbia; Marshal Kvaternik; State Secretary Lorković and District Chief Elicker for Croatia. Minutes of this were drawn up. They recorded the decision reached that the line Drava-Danube-Sava-Drina was the boundary, thus making Zemun and its environs Croatian national territory. In order to secure the necessary military requirements, Zemun and its vicinity are at first to remain to a limited extent under the military commander in Serbia and to be included in the Serbian currency area. Cultural and judicial administration is to be under Croatia. The general and internal administration, railroad, post office, telegraph under Croatian direction, but subject to the military commander in Serbia. A draft treaty concerning taxation, remuneration of officials, and other financial questions, and also regarding the general contractual settlement of conditions is being drawn up by Benzler, Turner, Neuhausen, and a representative of the Croatian government; it is to be handed to me so that I may consult with the government here and then submit it to the foreign ministry for a decision. Elicker being the responsible district chief will himself and through special deputies establish and maintain continuous cooperation. There was general agreement at the close of the discussion. The proposal is the best possible compromise, not an ideal solution. The office of the military commander is still in Zemun; because of lack of space in Belgrade, this solution could unfortunately not be avoided. In this connection a certain amount of disagreement between Turner and Neuhausen became evident. Moreover, today Military Commander General von Forster was relieved by General von Schroder.

I believe that the proposed solution is quite acceptable. The minutes will be passed on to Salzburg.

Signed: Siegfried Kasche, SA-Obergruppenfuhrer

* * * * *

British and Free French forces in joint operation, on June 8, 1941, invaded Syria and Lebanon to prevent the occupation of the territory by Axis troops. On June 22, 1941, operation "Barbarossa" went into effect, German armies under Field Marshal Walther von Brauchitsch, Commander in Chief of the German Army, attacked the Soviet Union.

The Communist Party of Yugoslavia (CPY) remained basically inactive until Germany attacked the Soviet Union. Through the Comintern (Communist International) the CPY received orders from Moscow, USSR. With the departure of the bulk of German combat troops in preparation for the forthcoming attack on the Soviet Union (Operation code "Barbarossa"), the German Military Intelligence reported an increasing number of sabotage incidents. Road and railroad bridges were blown; telephone and telegraph lines were cut; trains derailed; German military vehicles were fired on or destroyed; and isolated detachments guarding industrial and military installations attacked. Standing crops were burned, banks robbed, and a general state of uncertainty and unrest was created.

On June 23, 1941, Emil von Rintelen, Diregent in the Political Department of the German Foreign Ministry, informed the Legation in Zagreb that on the occasion of Croatia's accession to the Tripartite Pact signed at Venice on June 15, 1941, Reich Foreign Minister Ribbentrop had invited Marshal Slavko Kvaternik of Croatia to a visit in Germany. In a letter to Hitler, dated June 23, 1941, Ante Pavelić requested that Croatia be permitted to participate in the struggle against the Soviet Union by supplying a contingent of Croatian Volunteers. In a personal letter of July 1, 1941, Hitler informed Pavelić that Croatian Volunteers would be organized within each of the three branches of the German Armed Forces. On June 26, 1941, Poglavnik Pavelić had issued an "Extraordinary Decree and Order" for the prevention of arbitrary excesses by Croatian ustaše. This decree provided for trials by court martial with the death penalty against perpetrators of arbitrary acts. The decree was published in the Croatian Press on June 27, 1941. Gen. Edmund Glaise von Horstenau (Liaison of German occupation forces in Croatia) expressed to Ante Pavelić his concern over the excesses of the ustaše. Gen. von Horstenau and Pavelić agreed that in the future reported cases would be subjected to a thorough investigation. Moreover, the German occupation forces were much understrength to take over police surveillance to the extent necessary, however intervention in individual cases would involve the Wehrmacht much more than heretofore in a share of the responsibility.

During the period of June 27 - July 4, 1941, the Central Committee of the CPY met in Belgrade to develop the basic organization of the communist revolutionary army. It was decided at the meeting that acts of sabotage and subversion should give way to a general uprising. Also, that the communist partisans' method of warfare should be the principal form of armed struggle, with partisan detachments being the initial form of military organization, which in considering the conditions of occupation and an unfavorable ratio of forces was the most suitable solution. By the end of July and early August, the communist uprising had begun throughout most of the territory of former Yugoslavia, except in the region of Macedonia where it started in 1943. Hereafter, the communist detachments grew into larger guerrilla units with a strength of several hundred and, in some cases, even several thousand men and women fighting side-by-side. From remote farms and mountain areas, to the small villages, the fighting spread to towns and cities causing severe problems for the Axis forces and Serb-četnici resistance. The communist partisans engaged in active guerrilla warfare by using the element of surprise, the Axis forces and the Serb-četnici were kept wondering what was coming next, when, where, and how the partisans would attack. Herewith, the hit, hide, and run of isolated terrorist campaign, developed into a full scale war.

Small-scale operations by German Infantry Divisions, dispersed over Serbia and the German zone of interest in Croatia, resulted in a large number of resistance casualties and arrests, but accomplished little in effectively curbing the guerrilla movement. Nor did the shooting of hostages or burning of homes viewed with suspicion, and whole communities distrusted or suspected of sheltering the partisans, achieve the desired results.

* * * * *

~ United States Forces in Iceland ~

Washington, July 7, 1941

To: The Congress of the United States

From: U.S. President

"I am transmitting herewith for the information of the Congress a message I received from the Premier of Iceland on July 1, 1941 and the reply I addressed on the same day to the Premier of Iceland in response to this message.

In accordance with the understanding so reached, forces of the U.S. Navy have today arrived in Iceland in order to supplement, and eventually to replace, the British forces which have until now been stationed in Iceland in order to insure the adequate defense of that country.

As I stated in my message to the Congress of September 3 last regarding the acquisition of certain naval and air bases from Great Britain in exchange for certain over-age destroyers, considerations of safety from overseas attack are fundamental.

The United States cannot permit the occupation by Germany of strategic outposts in the Atlantic to be used as air or naval bases for eventual attack against the Western Hemisphere.

117

We have no desire to see any change in the present sovereignty of those regions. Assurance that such outposts in our defense frontier remain in friendly hands is the very foundation of our national security and of the national security of every one of the independent nations of the New World."

Signed: Franklin Delano Roosevelt

* * * * *

An agreement signed in Berlin on July 8, 1941, established the definitive line of the German-Italian frontier following the collapse of the royal Yugoslav state. Edmund Weizsäcker, SS-Standartenfuhrer, signed for Germany; and Dino Alfieri, Italian Ambassador in Germany signed for Italy.

The most important guerrilla operation took place against the Italians in Montenegro. The Montenegrins on July 13, 1941, swarmed down in well-coordinated revolt and attacked the Italian garrisons scattered throughout their mountain state. Taken by surprise, the Italian occupation forces were destroyed or compelled to retreat back to their major garrison town and communications centers. Returning with strong ground, naval, and air forces, the Italians required almost a year to put down the uprising, and managed to accomplish it only by enlisting the aid of the Serb-četnici. This insurrection cost the Montenegrins dearly, approximately 15,000 dead and wounded and an additional 10,000 of the population shipped off to forced labor. The arrangement with the Serb-četnici also set the pattern for the Italian occupation-troops seldom moving out of the garrison towns, and then only along the main roads and in strength, accompanied by armored vehicles and often under air cover.

The incongrous relationship between Italy and Montenegro was never fully understood, especially when considering that King Vittorio Emmanuele III of Italy (1900-1948) was always kind and gentle toward the citizens of Montenegro. King Emmanuele III was married to Princess Elena (1900-1946) of Montenegro, the daughter of Queen Milena Vukotić and King Nikola of Montenegro (1910-1918), descendant of the Petrović-Njegoš Dynasty.

On July 22, 1941, Marshal Slavko Kvaternik, head of the Croatian Armed Forces, visited Adolf Hitler at his field headquarters. In a memorandum signed by Minister Martin Luther, Director of the Department for German Internal Affairs, dated July 24, 1941, sent to Joachim von Ribbentrop, it became known confidentially that Hitler supposedly made a decision about the future of the German nationals (Volksdeutsche) from Southeastern Europe. Eventually, the German nationals were to be resettled in the Reich. It was said that Martin Bormann, Reichsleiter, and Heinrich Himmler, SS-Reichsfuhrer, were fully informed of Hitler's decision. Questions regarding ethnic policy in Southeastern Europe were of decisive importance to the future of the national groups. Therefore, the Department for German Internal Affairs requested Joachim von Ribbentrop, to ask the Führer about the policy matter for appropriate action.

On July 23, 1941, Japan occupied French Indochina, after the invasion that began on September 22, 1940. Meanwhile, the USA implemented an economic and financial policy on July 26, by freezing Japanese assets in the United States, and by placing on August 1, 1941 an oil embargo on Japan.

* * * * *

~ Confiscation of Ecclesiastical Property ~

Secret - Personal   July 30, 1941

To: Herr Gauleiter [Nazi official, head of a political district]
        Honored Party Comrade

The Fuhrer has ordered:

        The confiscations of church and monastic property shall be halted immediately until further notice. Independent measures may not be taken by the Gauleiters in any circumstances even if special circumstances in individual cases urgently require the utilization of church or monastic property on the basis of the legal regulations. If in a special case a Gauleiter considers these conditions to obtain, a report must first be made through me to the Führer.

                        Signed: Martin Bormann
                                             Reichsleiter of the NSDAP
                                             Head of the Party Chancellery

* * * * *

* * * * *

~ Guidelines in Religious Activities ~

                                                                August 6, 1941

To: The High Command of the Wehrmacht

        The Führer [Hitler] has issued the following guidelines for the conduct in religious questions of the Wehrmacht toward the civilian population in the newly occupied eastern areas:

        1. Religious or church activity of the civilian population is to be neither promoted nor prevented. Members of the Wehrmacht are unconditionally to keep away from such activities of the local inhabitants.

        2. The chaplain services of the Wehrmacht are intended exclusively for the members of the German Armed Forces. The military chaplains are to be explicitly forbidden to

undertake any sort of official church activity or religious propaganda as regards the civilian population.

3. It is likewise forbidden to admit or to summon civilian clergymen from the Reich or from abroad into the occupied eastern areas.

4. These regulations do not apply to the Bessarabian area occupied by Romanian troops nor to the Finnish front.

Signed: Field Marshall Wilhelm Keitel
Chief of the OKW

* * * * *

Memorandum signed by Georg Wilhelm Grosskoff, Senior Counselor, Dept. German Internal Affairs, dated August 7, 1941, regarding the postponement of the resettlement of the German nationals (Volksdeutsche) from Southeastern Europe until after the Second World War, stated according to Creutz, SS-Standartenfuhrer, and Greifelt, Deputy SS-Brigadefuhrer, the resettlement of the Volksdeutsche from Kočevje, Slovenia, was scheduled to start September 1941. Creutz stated that he had an opportunity of putting this question before Heinrich Himmler, SS-Reichsfuhrer, who said that he was present when Hitler gave the Reich foreign minister his instructions in this matter. Hitler apparently had in mind resettlement in Southeastern Europe but did not include Kočevje, i.e., Italian territory.

Kasche, German Minister in Croatia, reported to Ribbentrop on August 10, 1941, that the situation in the insurrectionary areas in Bosnia were no longer dangerous. Terrorist groups operating northeast of Sarajevo had been broken up by the German military forces. German losses were one dead and three wounded. There were reports which blamed these terrorist activities on Serb-četnici, others claimed that the communist partisans created the actual trouble, yet another report claimed that the Croatian ustaše bore part of the responsibility for these actions. Ante Pavelić took account of this situation and ordered the immediate disbanding of the so-called irregular ustaše units, excepting only the regular ustaše organizations. A drastic action to be noted in connection with criminal actions of an ustaše official, who on August 8, 1941, was sentenced to death by court-martial at Zagreb, and executed by firing squad.

The Atlantic Charter, declaring the common aims of the United States of America and Britain after the Second World War, was issued by Franklin Delano Roosevelt and Winston Spencer Churchill after they conferred during August 9-12, 1941 aboard a warship anchored in Placenta Bay, in southeastern Newfoundland.

* * * * *

~ Atlantic Charter ~

August 12, 1941

The Declaration of Principles, known as the Atlantic Charter:

"Joint declaration of the President of the United States of America and the Prime Minister, Churchill, representing His Majesty's Government of the United Kingdom, being met together, deem it right to make known certain common principles in the national policies of their respective countries on which they base their hopes for a better future for the world.

First, their countries seek no aggrandizement, territorial or other;

Second, they desire to see no territorial changes that do not accord with the freely expressed wishes of the peoples concerned;

Third, they respect the right of all peoples to choose the form of government under which they will live; and they wish to see sovereign rights and self-government restored to those who have been forcibly deprived of them;

Fourth, they will endeavor, with due respect for their existing obligations, to further the enjoyment by all States, great or small, victor or vanquished, of access, on equal terms, to the trade and to the raw materials of the world which are needed for their economic prosperity;

Fifth, they desire to bring about the fullest collaboration between all nations in the economic field with the object of securing, for all, improved labor standards, economic advancement and social security;

Sixth, after the final destruction of the Nazi tyranny, they hope to see established a peace which will afford to all nations the means of dwelling in safety within their own boundaries, and which will afford assurance that all the men in all the lands may live out their lives in freedom from fear and want;

Seventh, such a peace should enable all men to traverse the high seas and oceans without hindrance;

Eighth, they believe that all of the nations of the world, for realistic as well as spiritual reasons must come to the abandonment of the use of force. Since no future peace can be maintained if land, sea or air armaments continue to be employed by nations which threaten, or may threaten, aggression outside of their frontiers, they believe, pending the establishment of a wider and permanent system of general security, that the disarmament of such nations is essential. They will likewise aid and encourage all other practicable measures which will lighten for peace-loving peoples the crushing burden of armaments."

Signed: Franklin Delano Roosevelt
President of the United States of America

Winston Leonard Spencer Churchill
Prime Minister of the United Kingdom

* * * * *

121

On August 16, 1941, the Italian government demanded that Croatia relinquish executive authority in the entire eastern Adriatic littoral to the Italian military authorities in order to guarantee peace and security in this area. Because this demand caused strong reaction in Zagreb, Pavelić asked Kasche, German Minister in Zagreb, for German intervention and mediation. The Croatian Legation in Berlin asked for German help in solving the dispute between Croatia and Italy. In the matter of the demands addressed to the Croatian government by the Italian government, the German attitude according to Ribbentrop, the boundary between Croatia and Italy must remain the same as previously determined. Nothing else can be considered by Germany at this time than to advise the Croatian government to reach an agreement on these questions directly with Italy.

In dealing with this whole matter of controversy between Croatia and Italy, Croatians were asked never lose sight of the fact that the alpha and omega of German foreign policy in the entire Mediterranean area is the preservation of German cordial alliance with Italy, and that in comparison the Croatian question can only have lesser importance. Accordingly, the civil administration in the disputed territory remains with Croatia who will appoint a commissioner to ensure cooperation with the Italian government. In case the Croatian troops are employed in the eastern Adriatic littoral, they will be placed under Italian command. The details for carrying out this proposal will be settled between the Croatian governemt and Gen. Vittorio Ambrosio, Italian Commander-in-Chief of the Italian troops in Croatia.

The Serbian provisional government was in the process of dissolution. The finance minister resigned because he could not raise the 6.5 million Reichsmarks to pay the German monthly occupation costs. The installment due on August 15, 1941 was not paid. Furthermore, three ministers of the Ljotić group (Dimitrije Ljotić, leader of the right-wing Zbor Movement in Serbia) namely the Minister of Labor, the Minister of Economics, and the Minister for Social Welfare asked to be relieved of their offices.

A puppet Serbian government (mimic of Henry P. Petain, and Pierre Laval) sponsored by Nazi Germany was established in the person of Gen. Milan Nedić (a Serb), former royal Yugoslav minister of war 1938-1940. The German Military Commander in Serbia decided to entrust Gen. Nedić with the formation of a puppet Serbian government. Nevertheless, Joachim von Ribbentrop requested Felix Benzler, German Minister with the Military Commander in Serbia, to assure that the installation of the Serbian government must be in strict compliance with the Führer's policy. Gen. Nedić published his pro-Nazi list of collaborators. Accordingly, Ačimović retained the ministry of the interior (Serbian police authority). The Dimitrije Ljotić group was represented by three ministers. Otherwise, the list comprises mostly of colorless personalities, with the exception of Gen. Josip Kostec, the Minister of Posts and Transportation. The Nedić pro-nazi Serbian government was announced August 29, 1941. Gen. Nedić would bear the title of Premier of Serbia and his collaborators would be designated as ministers. The de facto new Serbian government, with Belgrade as its capital, had no substantive powers exceeding those previously given to the old Serbian provisional government.

Within Serbia's puppet regime, the state police and several militarized security forces were formed to keep order and lighten the German occupation task. The first of these Serbian units were approximately 6,000 border guards. Their primary mission was to control traffic across the Serbian frontier and to support the local and rural police should the need arise. In addition, the Serbian state guard comprising five battalions with an authorized total strength of about 4,000 men was organized.

Confronted with increasing terrorist activities and to deal with the various resistance movements in Yugoslavia, the Axis forces implemented countermeasures by declaring that everyone in arms against the Axis occupation forces was considered a threat to public order, consequently, those committing terrorist activities were regarded as enemies, whether they wore the hammer and sickle, the Serbian Crest of the royal government-in-exile, or any unauthorized insignia.

On August 25, 1941 following a pro-Nazi stand by Riza Shah Pahlevi, Shah of Iran, British forces invaded Iran from the south while the Soviet Union forces occupied Iran from the north. Subsequently, Riza Shah abdicated in favor of his son Mohammad Riza Pahlevi, who adopted a pro-Allied policy.

* * * * *

~ Conversation Between Hitler and Mussolini ~

Berlin, August 24-25, 1941

In Hitler's first conversation with Mussolini immediately after the latter's arrival at Führer's Headquarters on August 24, 1941, the Führer gave the Duce a general outline of the situation, together with a detailed account of the military developments. Hitler began by acknowledging to Mussolini that it had been a wise decision to liquidate Yugoslavia along with Greece before launching the Russian campaign. Yugoslavia and Greece were two enemies of the Axis, and eliminating them proved a great advantage when it became necessary to take action against the Soviet Union in order to eliminate the grave Bolshevik menace and to achieve effective control of Europe.

Hitler made a point of acknowledging that for the first time since the beginning of the conflict, the German Military Intelligence Service had failed. It had in fact not reported that the Soviet Union had a very well armed and equipped army composed for the most part of men imbued with a veritable fanaticism who, despite their racial heterogeneity, were fighting with blind fury.

123

Regarding military plans for the future, Hitler told Mussolini that after completion of the Russian campaign he intended to deal England the final blow by invading the island. Concerning other territories of importance, the conversation proceeded as follows:

France: Hitler held that there would be no point in dealing with that problem while the battle was still in progress in USSR. Hitler had found justification for his feeling of distrust of the French, whom he was watching carefully and with respect to whom he intended to maintain a negative attitude.

In the second conversation which Mussolini had with Hitler on the evening of August 25, 1941, Mussolini set forth his views on certain questions of major importance.

Turkey: Mussolini noted that Turkey was continuing to pursue a wavering policy between the Axis and England. It might be profitable to make some new efforts to win Turkey over to the Axis side by offering some compensation and by using as a lever Turkey's sensitiveness about her military position. Hitler agreed with Mussolini's thought.

Crete: Hitler expressed to Mussolini his desire to have an Italian division transferred to the island of Crete to take the place of the German Alpine Corps, which he wished to send to the Russian front. Mussolini gave his assent.

Spain: Hitler spoke in bitter terms about Spain, expressing his genuine and profound disappointment with that country. If Francisco Franco could have made up his mind in January or February, the German big special 620 mm heavy mortars (Thor and Odin) would have been extremely effective against Gibraltar, thanks to the crushing power of their 4,410 lb/2,000 kg projectiles. Mussolini, while concurring with Hitler's thought, observed that for all practical purpose and given Spain's particular situation and special circumstances, it was pointless to bring further pressure to bear to induce Spain to take an active part.

France: With respect to France, Mussolini outlined to Hitler the anomaly of the situation which had developed in the relations with that country. These were governed at present by the Armistice Agreement, canceled by the development of events. Profiting from the fact that marshal Petain was in deep water as a result of the unending domestic and external difficulties with which Petain had to contend. Hitler repeated to Mussolini that the feeling he entertained toward the French were those of antipathy and distrust, and that he was fully aware concerning the anomaly of the relations between France and the Axis Powers.

Sweden: Hitler expressed himself in rather harsh terms about the Swedes, calling them cowards. Sweden maintained a treacherously hostile attitude toward Germany and raised endless difficulties to German requests for troop transit.

Switzerland: Hitler spoke in adverse terms about Switzerland, which, while moving with great circumspection, entertained feelings of unadulterated aversion toward the Axis Powers.

Japan: Mussolini observed that Japan had a complex and difficult domestic political situation which was at the bottom of the uncertainty in Japanese foreign policy. Japan was strongly animated by a nationalistic dynamism that caused her to gravitate toward the Axis Powers.

United States: Mussolini pointed out that the "Potomoc meeting" [reference to the Roosevelt-Churchill meeting at Argentia, Newfoundland, August 9-12, 1941, which produced the Atlantic Charter. To get to Argentia, President Roosevelt had embarked on the U.S.S. Potomac at New London on August 3, 1941], in the last analysis, had not caused Roosevelt's political stock to rise. Hitler gave a detailed analysis of the clique surrounding Roosevelt and exploiting the United States people.

The Mediteranean: Hitler stated that he was satisfied with the situation in the Mediterranean. Mussolini agreed, noting that the new front opened up against England in Iran had relieved England pressure in the Mediterranean.

Italy: Mussolini expressed to Hitler his ardent desire for the Italian Armed Forces to participate in the operations against the USSR. Hitler replied that he greatly appreciated that offer and thanked the Duce heartily. Hitler added, however, that the great distance of Russia from Italy and the logistical difficulties would cause a serious problem with respect to transportation and the proper functioning of large masses of military forces. Mussolini affirmed that Italy could render a major contribution to the war effort against the USSR, and suggested that further contingents of Italian troops be used to take the place of German troops sent on leave. Hitler took note of Mussolini's proposal, which would be given further consideration. Hitler reiterated the point he had already made in his preceding conversation, namely, that he did not intend to wage a war of destruction or of prestige; but a war of annihilation of the enemy armed forces in order to liberate Germany and Europe from the recurrent threat of conflict and create the necessary basis for constructing the new European order.

Hitler concluded by expressing his very keen desire, once the war was ended, to visit Italy and spend some time in Florence (Firenze), the city he preferred above all others for the harmony of its art and the beauty of its natural surroundings. This project was enthusiastically received by the Duce, who immediately invited the Führer to come to Florence, once the war was over and assured him of the affection and friendship with which the Italian people would welcome him as their most honored guest.

* * * * *

* * * * *

~ Resettlement of Serbs from Croatia ~

Telegram   Berlin, August 30, 1941

To: Plenipotentiary of the Foreign Minister
          With the Military Commander in Serbia

From: Director, Department for German Internal Affairs

The German Legation in Zagreb wires as follows:

"The Military Commander in Serbia had State Councilor Friedrich Turner make the communication that Serb resettlement in Serbia from Croatia was no longer supportable. Turner's statements that the resettlement quota for Serbs from Croatia is already exhausted are by no means accurate. Turner's earlier statement to Veesenmayer proves that some arbitrary calculation is being made there."

Please report by wire especially concerning how many Serbs have so far been deported from Croatia to Serbia.

                    Signed: Martin Luther

* * * * *

Adolf Eichmann (1906-1962), Sturmbannfuhrer of the Reich Security Main Office stated upon inquiry that at the suggestion of Minister Todt last week the current resettlement transports of Slovenes were halted by order of Heinrich Himmler, Reichsfuhrer-SS, for strategic reasons. Since no directive had been issued by Heinrich Himmler to halt the preparations for admitting the German nationals (Volksdeutsche) from the Val Canale, the Val di Gardena, Ljubljana, and Kočevje, who are to be settled in the areas of Lower Styria and Southern Carinthia evacuated by Slovenes, the Reich Security Main Office and the Reich Commissariat for the consolidation of the German National Community had submitted a proposal to Heinrich Himmler that the evacuation of Slovenes in Lower Styria should be continued to the extent necessary for accommodating the Volksdeutsche mentioned. Eichmann supplied data regarding the evacuation of Slovenes from Lower Styria and Southern Carinthia thus far: about 7,000 Slovenes have been deported to Serbia from these two areas. Approximately 7,000 to 8,000 Slovenes have been deported to Croatia from Lower Styria (those who had moved in after 1914). A total of about 15,000 Slovenes, have so far been moved out of these two areas. Because the number of Volksdeutsche mentioned amount to more than 20,000, in the opinion of the Reich Security Main Office at least 40,000 to 50,000 Slovenes must be evacuated and deported so as to take the Volksdeutsche into the Reich. In the Zagreb agreements of August 27, 1941 the transfer of 170,000 Slovenes had been envisaged. Regarding the deportation of Serbs from Croatia to Serbia, Eichmann stated that according to his information about 12,000 Serbs had been deported in the regular way. The number of Serbs deported illegally, which was far higher, was not known to him at the moment.

The German Office of the Plenipotentiary in Serbia on September 8, 1941 dispatched a top secret telegram to the German Foreign Minister which reads as follows: "It is evident that Jews have participated in numerous acts of sabotage and rebellion. It is therefore most necessary that steps be taken speedily for the seizure and removal of at least all male Jews. The figure under consideration in this connection probably amounts to about 8,000. A concentration camp is being built at the moment, but it appears advisable in view of future developments to get these Jews out of the country as quickly as possibly, i.e., on empty freight barges down the Danube in order to unload them on an island in the Danube delta on Romanian territory."

As a follow-up to the previous telegram dated September 8, 1941, the German Minister in Serbia, Felix Benzler, sent a secret telegram to the German Foreign Minister on September 10, 1941 stating: "A quick and Draconian settlement of the question of the Serbian Jews is the most urgent and expedient requirement. I request an appropriate instruction from the Foreign Minister in order to take up the matter most vigorously with the military commander in Serbia. No resistance of any sort is to be expected on the part of the Serbian government and population, all the less so since the partial measures thus far have proved to be very effective."

In an internal memorandum dated September 11, 1941, Franz Sonnleithner, Counselor, Secretariat of the German Foreign Minister, recorded that Joachim von Ribbentrop had commented with regard to Veesenmayer and Benzler suggestion that "this measure could not be carried out without the approval of the Romanian government and that presumably another way would have to be found." In a telegram of September 11, 1941, Martin Luther, Director of the Department for German Internal Affairs, informed the German Minister with the military commander in Serbia, that "a removal of Jews to the territory of a foreign state could not be approved."

U.S. President Roosevelt's fireside chat, broadcast from the White House on September 11, 1941, referred to the attack on the United States destroyer "Greer" as an act of piracy which had followed similar attacks such as the sinkings of the Robin Moor, the Panamanian merchant ship Sessa near Greenland on August 17, and of the U.S. Merchant ship "Steel Seafarer" in the Red Sea on September 5, 1941. Referring to German submarines as "rattle snakes of the Atlantic" the president then announced the new U.S. policy in the following terms: "In the waters which we deem necessary for our defense, U.S. naval vessels and U.S. planes will no longer wait until Axis submarines lurking under the water, or Axis raiders on the surface of the sea, strike their deadly blow-first."

On September 12, 1941, Felix Benzler transmitted a telegram to the German Foreign Ministry stating that it was impossible to put Jews into labor camps under present conditions and requested that the Serbian Jews be deported from Serbia, possibly to the General Government in Poland or Russia. Benzler particularly requested the immediate evacuation of 1,200 Jews interned in a camp in Šabac, Serbia, 40 mi/64 km west of Belgrade on the Sava river. In reply a memorandum from the Department for German Internal Affairs signed by Franz Rademacher, Head of Division D-III, on September 13, 1941, read as follows: "I am unable to see the necessity for the deportation of the 1,200 male Jews, if not to Romania then to the General Government or to Russia, as desired by the office of the Foreign Ministry in Belgrade. Moreover, Russia, as an area of operations, is entirely unsuited for the reception of these Jews. If they are already a danger in Serbia, they will be much more so in Russia. The General Government is already over-saturated with Jews. In my opinion it ought to be possible, given the necessary harshness and determination, to keep the Jews in camps in Serbia. If the Jews continue to fan disturbances there one should proceed against them with intensified martial law. I [Rademacher] cannot imagine that the Jews will continue to conspire after a considerable number of hostages have been shot."

In view of the worsening situation in Serbia, on September 14, 1941, the German High Command of the Wehrmacht made the decision to transfer one military division from France to Serbia. Karl Ritter, Ambassador on Special Assignment in the German Foreign Ministry, sent a secret telegram to the German Legation in Bulgaria on September 15, 1941, as follows: "In connection with the rather serious and politically most undesirable disorders and armed local uprisings in Serbia it is apparent time and again that the moving forces, organizers and suppliers of arms are located outside the confines of Serbia, and from there keep the Serbian population stirred up. The Reich government has decided to strengthen the German military forces in Serbia in such a manner as to make it possible to crush and disarm the rebels and restore security within a short time. The German Foreign Minister accordingly asked the governments of Croatia, Bulgaria and Italy for their cooperation on the subject. The Embassy in Rome and the Legation in Zagreb were sent the text of this instruction on the same date."

The Yugoslav communist headquarters was relocated on September 16, 1941, from Belgrade to the Krupanj territory in western Serbia, and changed its name to supreme headquarters. However, due to German offensive, at the end of 1941 the supreme headquarters was moved into the Sandžak area. The supply of vital raw materials, especially after the destruction of the Bor mining area, northwest of Niš, caused a production loss of nearly a month's requirement of copper element for the German war industries.

The German Legation in Zagreb on September 19, 1941, was informed of Marshal Wilhelm List's visit to Zagreb for discussion with the German and Croatian authorities concerning Hitler's directive of September 16, 1941, and joint procedure for fighting the communist in Serbia. It has been decided that a further German division will be employed in Serbia in order to suppress more quickly the communist unrest.

* * * * *

~ Führer's Directive ~

Top Secret   Headquarters, September 16, 1941

1. I assign to the Wehrmacht Commander in the Southeast, Field Marshal Wilhelm List, the task of crushing the insurrectionary movement in the southeastern area. It is important first to secure in the Serbian area the transportation routes and the objects important for the German war economy, and then for the long run to restore order in the entire area by the most rigorous methods. In Croatia, up to the line of demarcation, the measures necessary against bandits are to be taken in agreement with the Croatian Government in Zagreb through the agency of the German General Edmund Glaise von Horstenau.

2. For the duration of the execution of these tasks all army forces located in the area of the insurrection or to be brought there are to be concentrated under the command of the Commanding General of the Eighteenth Army Corps, General of Infantry Franz Böhme. He will exercise executive authority in the area of insurrection itself in accordance with the directives of the Wehrmacht Commander, Southeast. All military and civilian authorities are subject to his orders to this extent. The Wehrmacht Commander, Southeast will regulate the more specific delimitation of his authority. The requirements of the Four Year Plan are to be taken into account in principle.

3. The Commander in Chief of the Army will dispatch into Serbian territory for the time being, in addition to further security forces (these also for Croatia), an infantry division, armored trained and captured tanks, and will prepare in case of need the dispatch of a further division as soon as one becomes available in the east. I request that the detailed measures be reported to the High Command of the Wehrmacht.

4. The Commander in Chief of the Luftwaffe will support as heretofore the operations in the area of insurrection with the forces available and will designate to the Wehrmacht Commander, Southeast, a leader for the tactical cooperation with General of Infantry Böhme.

5. Hungarian, Romanian, and Bulgarian army and air forces cannot be included in the operations without the permission of the High Command of the Wehrmacht; but Hungarian and Rumanian boats offered for the protection of the Danube traffic may be used in addition to the Danube flotilla. Their tasks are to be regulated in such a manner, that their contact with one another is avoided by appropriate employment of the German flotilla. The use of Croatian troops in the Serbian border areas next to Croatia has been granted by the Croatian government and can therefore take place. The Italian High Command will be advised of the intended measures and will be asked to take appropriate action in accord with the Wehrmacht Commander, Southeast, in the area occupied by the Italians.

6. The Foreign Ministry will carry out a joint political action of the Balkan countries against the communist centers [Leitstellen] in these countries. The Wehrmacht Commander, Southeast will receive further information in this matter through the representative of the Reich.

Signed: Adolf Hitler
                 Führer and Chancellor
                 Supreme Commander of the Wehrmacht

                 * * * * *

On September 20, 1941, German Gen. Franz Böhme moved his headquarters from Salonika, Greece, to Belgrade, Serbia, and one week later the 342d Infantry Division arrived from Germany. A series of offensive operations begun by Gen. Böhme succeeded in quelling the revolt in western Serbia and inflicting thousands of casualties on the guerrillas by mid-December. The guerrillas, however, were not annihilated; large numbers fled into the more mountainous regions and into Croatia, where a new center of terrorist activities was soon formed. In territory occupied by Germany, the Nazi authorities ordered that effective September 20, 1941 all Jews over the age of six must wear the Star of David. The Vichy French government cooperated fully with the Nazis in the treatment of Jews.

* * * * *

~ Conference on Resettlement ~

September 22, 1941

Conference on Resettlement, held on September 22, 1941 at the German Legation in Zagreb under the Chairmanship of the German Minister Kasche (offices represented: Foreign Ministry, Croatian government, German Legation in Zagreb, and Field Office of the Foreign Ministry in Belgrade):

The minutes of the Conference show that the numbers of Croats, Slovenes, and Serbs purportedly resettled, or scheduled for resettlement can be determined exactly only insofar as the railroad transports are concerned. The remaining figures can probably not be determined even subsequently with anything approaching accuracy. There is mutual agreement on the following figures on resettlement:

• From the Reich to Croatia (total)	26,343
Transported by railroad	9,343
Voluntary	17,000
• From Serbia to Croatia (total)	12,300
Croatians, voluntary	11,800
Slovenes, voluntary	500
• From Croatia to Serbia as of June 4, 1941 (total)	60,000
Agreed upon resettlement	30,000
Serbs to Serbia	30,000
• Serbia has received from Croatia (total)	13,111
As of August 25, 1941	12,436
August 26 until September 20, 1941	1,675
• Serbia has received Slovene resettlers from the Reich	6,720
• Croatia has received resettlers from Serbia, Macedonia, Vojvodina, Dalmatia, and the Reich	95,000
• Slovenes to be resettled from the Reich to Croatia (total):	65,000
From Lower Styria	45,000
From Carinthia	20,000

The German military command in Serbia stated that it is willing to accept 3,200 Serbs who are in the resettlement centers. The Croatian government stated that it is willing to accept 1,000 Slovene resettlers who are in the resettlement center in the Reich. Implementation will be arranged between the Croatian government and the Chief of the Civil Administration in Lower Styria.

The Croatian government and the military commander in Serbia are in agreement that all shortcomings in regard to the taking along, and arbitrary removal, of money and valuables from one territory into the other and vice versa are to be considered as settled. No further claims will be made on this score by either side.

The Croatian government states that due to the present unrest connected with the political situation makes it impossible to receive a large number of people for resettlement. On the one hand these difficulties were caused by the special situation of the littoral under Italian military administration. On the other hand Croatia had to support a very large number of refugees from insurrectionary areas. Furthermore, Croatia could not settle any resettlers in these areas of insurrection. Settling them in Srem and Slavonia, the supply areas, which have an ethnically very mixed population, was not possible for the reason that the food supplies for the whole country would be most seriously endangered thereby.

The representative of the Reich Commissar for the Consolidation of the German National Community presented the views of his office. As matters stood he was of the opinion that in these circumstances the decision could not be made in this conference. Minister Kasche stated that he would report this and submit it for decision by the Reich government and the Führer.

* * * * *

On September 26, 1941, Reinhard Heydrich, SS-Obergruppenführer, sent a telegram to Joachim von Ribbentrop stating as follows: "Concerning the resettlement work in the southeast has come to a standstill as of September 22, 1941. Croatia has deported 118,110 persons in legal and illegal transports to Serbia, whereas the Croatians have accepted 26,341 persons from the Reich, and 12,300 persons from Old Serbia. However, 12,000 German nationals (Volksdeutsche) from Kočevje are supposed to be resettled in Lower Styria. The evacuation of about 45,000 Slovenes is necessary. The Croatian government refuses to accept these people who are to be evacuated. This is jeopardizing the settlement within the country of the Volksdeutsche from Kočevje as ordered by the Führer. Please exert influence on the Croatian government so that this absolutely necessary settlement within the country of these Volksdeutsche can be concluded before the start of winter. Unfortunately, I can see no way of avoiding the issue, particularly since the troublesome inclusion of Croatia in the overall work of resettlement in the southeast, which I opposed, was brought about at the time by Minister Kasche."

* * * * *

~ Telegram to Reich Foreign Minister ~

Top Secret   Belgrade, September 28, 1941

To: Foreign Minister personally

From: German Minister with the Military Commander in Serbia

I have repeatedly requested the support of the Foreign Ministry with regard to the immediate deportation of local male Jews from Serbia, which was however denied me. Permit me to remind you that in Fuschl you expressly promised me your help in moving the Jews and also the Freemasons and pro-British Serbs, be it down the Danube or into concentration camps in Germany or in the General Government. The immediate solution of the Jewish question is the most important political task here at the moment, and is the prerequisite for a start in eliminating Freemasons and the intelligentsia which is hostile to us. The military operation in progress to put down the insurrection has now created a suitable moment for beginning the action. Furthermore, Gen. Franz Böhme as well as the military commander have again very emphatically asked me to make an effort on their behalf that the Jews be removed from the country immediately, if possible. For the time being 8,000 male Jews are involved, who cannot be accommodated in local camps because these must be used for accommodating about 20,000 Serbs from insurrectionary areas. As a result of the situation created by the insurrection it is likewise impossible to accommodate them in new camps and outside of Belgrade. We will have to cope here with the remaining approximately 20,000 Jews and their families. Deportation to an island in the Danube delta seems the simplest solution from the standpoint of transportation, since empty freight barges are immediately available. According to my information this procedure was also already used successfully in the deportation of Jews from Czechia.

I most urgently request, jointly with Edmund Veesenmayer, SS-Standartenfuhrer your support in this matter which is the first prerequisite for the lasting pacification we are striving for.

Signed: Felix Benzler

* * * * *

In September 1941, there were two underground resistances: royalist Serb-četnici and communist partisans. The former were organized on the basis of the old political and social order, which insisted in the continuation of Serbian hegemony in Yugoslavia. The communist partisans were bearers of a new social order - which was appealing in the poor provinces of Bosnia-Herzegovina, and a political order of national equality and brotherhood-which was equally attractive to two Croatian provinces, Lika and Kordun.

Tito and Mihajlović met in the village of Struganik, Serbia, on September 19, 1941, and agreed to (a) cooperate against the enemy; (b) the partition of booty; and (c) to allow the people to join either resistance force. The two terrorist leaders (Tito and Mihajlović) met again on October 25-27, 1941, in the village of Braići on Ravna Gora, where the Serb-četnici had their headquarters, to work out the specific terms of the purported agreement. The meeting was unsuccessful; the main point of disagreement remained the question of organization and administration of "liberated" territories. After a short, relatively peaceful period of coexistence, fighting gradually developed between the two underground forces, which degenerated into open civil war. The civil war began on November 2, 1941, when the Serb-četnici and the communist partisans clashed at Užice in Serbia, later renamed Titovo Užice.

After the First World War, under the Serb Karađorđević regime, the town of Jasenovac was known where innocent Croatians were slaughtered by Serbian assassins. On October 1, 1941 Jasenovac was established as a concentration camp primarily for the confinement of suspected terrorists and political prisoners. Later it was used as a transient internment of Croatian and Bosnian Jews, etc.

* * * *

Following is a secret memorandum dated October 25, 1941, from Franz Rademacher, Head of Div. D-III, Dept. for German Internal Affairs, following his visit to Belgrade to investigate the situation in Serbia, submitted to Martin Luther, Director, Dept. For German Internal Affairs:

"The purpose of the trip was to investigate on the spot whether the problem of the 8,000 Jewish agitators whose deportation was demanded by the Legation could be solved on the spot. The first discussion with Minister Benzler and State Councilor Harald Turner, German Chief of the Administrative Staff at the military headquarters in Serbia, indicated that more than 2,000 of these Jews had already been shot in reprisal for attacks on German soldiers. By order of the military commander, 100 Serbs are to be shot for every German soldier killed. In execution of this order, first of all the active communist leaders of Serbian nationals - about 50 in number - were shot, and then regularly Jews as communist agitators. In the course of the conversation it developed that not 8,000 Jews, but only about 4,000 of whom, moreover, only 3,500 can be shot. The Gestapo needed the other 500 Jews in order to maintain sanitary and security services in the ghetto to be established.

"In the first conversation it could not be clarified how the difference between 8,000 and 4,000 Jews arose. The investigations which I conducted in this matter indicated that State Councilor Turner had cited the figure of 8,000 to Minister Benzler, consisting of 1,500 from Smederevo, 600 from the Banat (a remainder from 2,000), 1,200 from Šabac and 4,700 from Belgrade.

"In this compilation a mistake was made in that the Jews from Smederevo and the Banat were counted double, and were contained once more in the Belgrade figure of 4,700; furthermore, a portion of the Belgrade Jews had in the meantime decamped for the area of insurrection.

"In the first conversation State Councilor Turner in bitter words expressed his disappointment that the first calls for help had not been immediately answered. The situation had been very precarious, and only as a result of the arrival of the German divisions had it been somewhat improved. I explained the reasons why the Jews could neither be deported to Romania nor to the General Government nor to the East. State Councilor Turner could not appreciate these reasons. He continues as before to demand the expulsion of the remaining Jews from Serbia.

"Detailed negotiations with the specialists on the Jewish questions, Sturmbannfuhrer Weimann of the State Councilor Harald Turner's office, and Standartenfuhrer Fuchs, Chief of Gestapo Office, led to the following:

"The male Jews will be shot by the end of this week; in this way, the problem brought up in the report by the Legation is settled.

"The remainder consisting of about 20,000 Jews (women, children, and old people) as well as about 1,500 gypsies, of whom the males will likewise be shot, are to be assembled in the so-called gypsy quarter, known as a ghetto, of the city of Belgrade.

"In Harald Turner's opinion the gypsy quarter of the city of Belgrade is an absolute breeding ground of epidemics, and must be burned down for hygienic reasons. Therefore the Jews and gypsies who are not shot in reprisal at first are to be assembled in the gypsy quarter and then transported at night to the Serbian island of Mitrovica. There two separate camps will be established; in one camp the Jews and gypsies are to be kept, and in the other 50,000 Serbian hostages.

133

"Then, as soon as the technical possibility exists within the framework of the total solution of the Jewish question, the Jews will be deported by water to the concentration camps (Auffanglager) in the East."

* * * * *

In a top secret telegram dated October 29, 1941, Felix Benzler, German Minister in Serbia informed the Reich Foreign Ministry as follows:

"In the past week there have been executions without trial of a large number of Serbs, not only in Kraljevo but also in Kragujevac, as reprisals for the killing of members of the Wehrmacht in the proportion of 100 Serbs for one German. In Kraljevo 1,700 male Serbs were executed, and in Kragujevac 2,300. Furthermore, in the town of Gornji Milanovac, north of Čačak there have been executions after the burning down of the buildings housing Germans. Mistakes have been made in the execution. Thus confidential agents, Croats, and the entire personnel of German armament plants have been shot, and in Milanovac also those who, relying on their innocence, had remained in contrast to the majority of the population that had fled. The executions in Kragujevac occured although there had been no attacks on members of the Wehrmacht in this city for the reason that not enough hostages could be found elsewhere. These indiscriminate executions are causing repercussions among the population which are contrary to German final political objective. The Plenipotentiary Commanding General, Franz Böhme, has thereupon issued new directives concerning the executions of hostages, which do not change anything in the ratio of one hundred Serbs for one German, to be sure, but eliminate as far as possible mistakes such as those mentioned above."

The U.S. destroyer "Reuben James" on October 30, 1941 was torpedoed by a German U-boat and sank off the coast of Iceland. This was the first U.S. warship lost in the Second World War. The U.S. Neutrality Acts (August 31, 1935, February 29, 1936, November 4, 1939) were amended on November 17, 1941 to allow merchant ships to be armed and to sail to the ports of belligerents.

Ernest von Weizsäcker, German State Secretary, on November 22, 1941, dispatched a message to Franz Rademacher, Head of Division D-III, stating as follows: "The Führer decree of April 28 last designates Minister Felix Benzler the Plenipotentiary of the Foreign Ministry as the competent authority for dealing with all questions of a foreign policy nature arising in Serbia. Specifically, it is his task to forestall any activity by Serbian political elements that might be detrimental to the interests of the Reich. Consequently, Minister Benzler, and with him the Foreign Ministry, will have to deal with the matter of the deportation of Jews from Serbia to other countries. However, it lies

134

outside the responsibility of Benzler and the Foreign Ministry to do anything actively about the way the Jewish problem inside Serbia is being handled by the military and administrative authorities concerned. They receive their instructions in this matter, as we know, through channels other than the foreign ministry. I have talked to Minister Benzler about this today. It will be advisable also to give him the appropriate instructions in writing."

In Berlin, on November 25, 1941, a conversation between Joachim von Ribbentrop, Reich Foreign Minister, and Galeazzo Ciano, Italian Foreign Minister; a question from Ciano as to the German attitude toward Croatia, Ribbentrop replied that, conditions were becoming more and more stable in Croatia, as the German Minister Kasche in Zagreb reported. This caused Ciano to remark that the Duce was not satisfied with developments in Croatia where a certain anti-Italian trend had developed. When Ciano once more inquired as to Germany's views concerning Croatia, Ribbentrop replied, with reference to the declaration already made in Vienna, that Germany regarded Croatia as belonging to Italy's sphere of interest. At Ciano's request, Ribbentrop promised that he would speak with the Croatians accordingly, and that Ribbentrop had given to Minister Kasche very clear instructions on this matter as late as August 21. Ribbentrop knew that Croatian elements who had formerly lived in Germany (among others, Minister Branko Benzon, Croatian Minister in Germany, May-November 1941, now about to leave Berlin), were not adverse to intrigues in which Germany and Italy were played off against each other.

* * * * *

~ Situation in Serbia ~

Confidential   Belgrade, December 3, 1941

To: German Foreign Minister

From: Counselor, German Legation in Yugoslavia

I. Military

The successful conclusion of the operations against the communist bands operating in the areas of Čačak and Užice, which had their main bases in these cities, represents an important stage in the suppression of the insurrection in Serbia. After the Plenipotentiary Commanding General, as his first action after assuming command, had deprived the rebels of an important supply base by mopping up the area around Šabac in the Sava-Drina bend and had further driven them out of the Čer mountains, the capture of Užice is a new heavy blow that has fallen on the actual base of the communist resistance. The victory, which cost the enemy more than 1,500 dead, was bought with very few casualties of our own. The operations are being continued successfully toward the south. Today our troops have already reached Raška and are advancing on Novi Pazar, so that this area of unrest, too, is approaching pacification. The impression made by these successes is strong all over the country. It would be greater still if a

135

considerable portion of the communist bands had not slipped out of the threatened encirclement and escaped to Croatia. The open border toward Croatia is one of the greatest difficulties with which the fight against the rebellion in the Serbian area has to cope. Full pacification is possible here only if quiet is restored everywhere in Croatia, too, and the border between the two countries is closed off.

While the Plenipotentiary Commanding General was carrying out the operations in the west, Prime Minister Milan Nedić, in full accord with him, contributed very essentially with the Serbian gendarmerie and the volunteers in numerous small engagements and mopping-up actions to putting down the uprising in central Serbia and in the northeastern part of the country. A rough mopping-up operation was carried out in these areas, too. The Serbian auxiliary forces have shown themselves to be exceedingly useful and skillful in this respect and have proved their reliability. What they achieved is to be appreciated all the more since in numbers and in their armament they cannot, of course, be compared with German troops, and they were often inferior in this respect even to the rebels. The bloody losses which they have so far inflicted upon the rebels are probably about as large as those the German troops have inflicted upon them. On the other hand the losses of the Serbian gendarmerie and volunteers are considerably larger than the German losses.

Although according to the foregoing the military situation in Serbia can be termed satisfactory, the country is still far from real pacification. Up till now only the large communist bands have been defeated and the main communist bases taken. However, one cannot speak of an annihilation of the enemy. In many places there are still small bands roving about, attacking villages and isolated police units and interfering with the traffic on the roads and railroads. Furthermore there exists in the person of Colonel Draža Mihajlović a rallying point for all insurgents with nationalist leanings. This person, who is said to have his headquarters in the mountains between Čačak and Valjevo in the village of Ravna Gora, has not many followers any longer, but should nevertheless not be underestimated, since many nationalistically minded Serbs sympathize with him. Whereas the communist bands get their instructions from Moscow, with which they are in connection not only by radio but also by courier via Bulgaria - probably through the Soviet legation in Sofia - Colonel Mihajlović is the exponent of King Petar and the Šimović Government in London and is being supported particularly by the radio there and in the one of Boston. True, at the moment he does not present any acute danger, particularly as he has become an enemy of the communists, with whom he at first cooperated, and is indeed fighting them. In the long run, however, he might become dangerous.

II. Administrative

It is evident from what has been said that thorough measures are still needed in order really to pacify Serbia. These measures, to be sure, will have to be more in the sphere of the police than in the military field. In particular it is necessary to establish again a disciplined administration all over the country and to comb through systematically, thoroughly, and continuously the areas which had been roughly cleaned up in order to remove all undesirable elements and force the surrender of arms. What is necessary is demonstrated by the example of the city of Belgrade, where an energetic police chief has seen to it that so far tranquillity has never been the focus of the unrest in the country, and although the population is freezing and starving. Here, however, it has been possible to maintain tranquillity and order through disarmamemt of the inhabitants, constantly repeated searches for communists, severe actions against Jews, Freemasons and anti-German elements from the old political parties of Yugoslavia and through the arrest of numerous hostages. Similar measures are necessary for the whole country so as to put through a real pacification and to prevent the insurrection from breaking out anew in the spring. Certainly much has already been done in this respect, as is indicated alone by the number of executions which have probably exceeded 20,000 at the present time. But there is still much to be done.

The question is who is to do it, Germans or Serbs. It would be in the interest of the Reich to leave the carrying out of the necessary operations largely to the Serbs, in order to save

136

her own forces. A prerequisite for this is that one trust them sufficiently. In this respect, it can be said today after General Nedić has been Prime Minister for three months that so far he has justified the trust placed in him. Called upon at the most difficult time, he has proved to be resolute and of firm character in carrying out the thankless task once he undertook it. Unperturbed by all the hostility, unshaken by the abuse that comes from London, this old soldier goes his difficult way. Today he is so much identified with Germany in the eyes of the Serbian people that it is hardly possible for him any more to abandon this line.

He has shed Serbian blood in fratricidal struggle, and with this his position is fixed once and for all. In his government there are men like Minister of Interior Aćimović, an experienced police expert who for many years has taken the German line; also Minister of Economics Olčan, a follower of Ljotić, who as Minister has himself fought successfully at the head of volunteer units against the communist bands; and Minister of Education Jonić, who through the university law has made an important contribution to the clean-up of academic life in Serbia which had been infected for a long time. Furthermore the Nedić government can rely upon the support of the Četnik leader Pećanac, who has led a large number of these volunteers to the cause of tranquillity and order. Also to be mentioned, and not in the last place either, is Dimitrije Ljotić, leader of the "Zbor" movement in Serbia, who has not joined the government himself, to be sure, because he is evidently keeping himself in reserve for a later time, but who has made available a number of his followers for important ministerial posts and has placed his authority in the scales in favor of Gen. Nedić. Ljotić, the old enemy of the communists, Freemasons and Jews in Serbia, represents a moral force which must not be underestimated. He is particularly valuable to the Nedić government, to which he has also made available numerous volunteers from his movement.

III. Prospects

If one surveys all of these forces one can say without exaggeration that they doubtless represent the best that this country possesses in the way of men in public life. They are the nucleus for the establishment of a new Serbian nation that has learned from the mistakes of the past and seeks its course in the direction which the German Reich has indicated. To be sure, the good elements are still weak in this country, and it would be desirable to reinforce them from the ranks of those who are at present sitting idle in German prisoner of war camps. There are still numerous men there who are indispensable for the work of reconstruction here. The problem is simply to choose the right ones.

Although it is impossible today to predict how things will develop here in Serbia, one can nevertheless determine that a beginning has been made in the right direction. The credit for this belongs largely to Prime Minister Nedić, and one can therefore justify giving him the trust which he needs in order to continue his work successfully. It is self-evident that such trust must not be blind and that under the existing war conditions a German force capable of putting down at once any new major attempt at insurrection must remain in such a restless country as is Serbia.

Signed: Gerhard Feine

* * * * *

At 7:55 on Sunday morning December 7, 1941, Japanese Military Forces attacked the U.S. Pacific Fleet at Pearl Harbor, Hawaii. The Japanese fleet returned to their naval base, and the United States was for the time being without naval power in the Pacific. Also, in the Pacific Ocean an attack on Wake Is. (Northern Marshall Is.) and Guam Is. (Southern Mariana Is.) began December 7, 1941 on the west side of the international date line. After the attack on Pearl Harbor, the Republic of Panama declared war against Japan. On December 8, 1941 United States, England and Canada declared war on Japan. In accordance with the Tripartite Pact signed on October 25, 1936, Germany and Italy declared war on USA, and on December 11, the USA reciprocated by declaring war on Germany and Italy. Within 48 hours the following countries declared war on Japan: Colombia, Costa Rica, Cuba, Domenican Republic, Guatemala, Haiti, Honduras, Nicaragua, and El Salvador. Later, these same nations declared war against Germany and Italy.

U.S. President Franklin D. Roosevelt on December 8, 1941 appeared before Congress and asked for an immediate declaration of war against Japan. The declaration of war was promptly approved, unanimously in the Senate and with one dissenting vote in the House of Representatives.

Concerning the deportation of Jews from Serbia, the Department for Internal Affairs sent a telegram on December 8, 1941 to Martin Luther, Under Secretary, German Foreign Ministry, advising as follows:

"Herewith is a copy of the record of telephone conversation between Felix Benzler and Franz Rademacher":

Minister Felix Benzler, German Minister with the military commander in Serbia, communicated the following:

"In the plan for the future treatment of the matter of the Jews in Serbia, a change had occurred since Rademacher's official trip to Belgrade, October 25, 1941, in that the Jews now would not be sent to a Serbian island, but rather to the Zemun camp. Minister Benzler requested on that account the Jews should be taken away to the east at the earliest. Rademacher replied that this was completely out of the question before next spring because the deportation of the Jews from Germany had priority. Even next spring such a transfer would still be doubtful."

* * * * *

~ Message by Franklin D. Roosevelt ~

Washington, D.C., December 9, 1941

Radio Address to the Nation by U.S. President Franklin D. Roosevelt, following a Declaration of a State of War with the Japanese Empire:

"The sudden criminal attacks perpetrated by the Japanese in the Pacific provide the climax of a decade of international immortality. Powerful resourceful gangsters have banded together to make war upon the whole human race. Their challenge has now been flung at the

United States of America. The Japanese have treacherously violated the long-standing peace between us. The course that Japan has followed for the past 10 years in Asia has paralleled the course of Hitler and Mussolini in Europe and Africa:

In 1931,   Japan invaded Manchukuo - without warning.
In 1935,   Italy invaded Ethiopia - without warning.
In 1938,   Hitler occupied Austria - without warning.
In 1939,   Hitler invaded Czechoslovakia - without warning.
           Later in 1939, Hitler invaded Poland - without warning.
In 1940,   Hitler invaded Norway, Denmark, Holland, Belgium, and Luxemburg - without warning.
In 1940,   Italy attacked France and later Greece - without warning.
In 1941,   the Axis Powers attacked Yugoslavia and Greece and they dominated the Balkans - without warning.
In 1941,   Hitler invaded Russia - without warning.
Dec. 1941 Japan attacked Malaya, Thailand, and the USA without warning."
           [Note: Thailand declared war on the USA and Britain on January 25, 1942.]

* * * * *

President Roosevelt in his radio message revealed only the half-truths. The Axis Powers committed barbaric deeds against the world community to benefit territorial gains and achieve political, military, and economic interests. It is unfair to omit identifying other culpable parties who also contributed or committed territorial conquests. Preceding the Second World War, under the pretext of peace, friendly and foe nations invaded whatever territories they deemed convenient in flagrant violation of international laws:

Sept. 29, 1938,   Hungary annexed southern Slovakia.
Oct.   2, 1938,   Teschen on Olsa river (Eastern Austrian Silesia) was divided as follows: Cieszyn under Poland, and Česky Těšín under Czechoslovakia.
Mar. 16, 1939,   Bohemia and Moravia made a German Protectorate.
Mar. 23, 1939,   Germany occupied Memel, Lithuania.
Sept. 17, 1939,   USSR invaded eastern Poland.
Oct. 10, 1939,   USSR occupied Vilnius, Lithuania.
Nov. 30, 1939,   USSR invaded Finland.
Dec. 14, 1939,   USSR was expelled from the League of Nations (today's United Nations) for invading Finland and committing crimes against humanity.
Jun. 27, 1940,   USSR seized Bessarabia and northern Bukovina from Romania.
Aug.   3, 1940,   USSR annexed Estonia, Latvia, and Lithuania.
Aug. 21, 1940,   Romanian territory of Dobruja was seized by Bulgaria and Transylvania by Hungary.

The Japanese after attacking the island of Guam, the largest and southernmost of the Mariana Islands in the western Pacific Ocean, occupied the island on December 10, 1941. On the same date Japanese forces landed on the Island of Luzon, the main island of the Philippines. The Wake Island an atoll in the northern Pacific Ocean, located midway between Hawaii and Guam Islands, was captured by Japanese on December 23, 1941. The islands of Guam and Wake were both retaken by U.S. forces on August 20, 1944. U.S. Congress passed the War Power Act on December 18, 1941 which authorized the U.S. President to impose censorship; award and terminate defense contracts; realign functions of federal agencies except the General Accounting Office (GAO); and freeze foreign credits.

The two small islands of Saint Pierre and Miquelon belonging to the Republic of France, located in the Atlantic Ocean just south off the coast of Newfoundland, Canada, were seized by "Free French" forces on December 24, 1941, and in 1946 these islands (93 mi^2/241 km^2) were classified by French Constitution as a territory of the Fourth Republic.

Although Croatia officially was declared an independent nation, its territory was partitioned into two distinct areas, one under the military auspice of Germany and the other under Italy. The Independent Republic of Croatia, upon request by the Axis Powers (specifically, Germany and Italy), declared war on December 15, 1941 on the Allied Powers

The first regular unit, the proletarian brigade of Yugoslavia, was formed at the end of 1941. Although some communist partisans fought for excitement, adventure, and revenge; others were compelled at gun point to join the resistance movements; some volunteered to prevent assassination or deportation to labor camps; the fanatic few were motivated to support the proletarian revolution propagandized by Karl Marx (1818-1883), hoping to collect the fruits promised by Vladimir Iljich Uljanov "Lenin" (1870-1924); thence implement Tito's communism.

Twenty-six nations gathered in Washington, D.C. (USA) on January 1, 1942, signed the Declaration of the United Nations, pledging to fight against the Axis Powers and never to sign a separate peace treaty.

* * * * *

~ United Nations Declaration ~

January 1, 1942

The Declaration by the United Nations joins together the purpose and will of 26 nations, representing the overwhelming majority of the inhabitants of all six continents. The text of the United Nations Declaration:

The Governments signatory hereto,

Having subscribed to a common program of purposes and principles embodied in the Joint Declaration of the President of the United States of America and the Prime Minister of the United Kingdom of Great Britain and Northern Ireland dated August 14, 1941, known as the Atlantic Charter.

Being convinced that complete victory over their enemies is essential to defend life, liberty, independence and religious freedom, and to preserve human rights and justice in their own lands as well as in other lands, and that they are now engaged in a common struggle against savage and brutal forces seeking to subjugate the world, declare:

1. Each government pledges itself to employ its full resources, military or economic, against those members of the Tripartite Pact and its adherents with which such government is at war.

2. Each government pledges itself to cooperate with the governments signatory hereto and not to make a separate armistice or peace with the enemies.

The foregoing declaration may be adhered to by other nations which are, or which may be, rendering material assistance and contributions in the struggle for victory over dictatorship.

* * * * *

In the German zone of interest in Croatia, the Germans planned a large-scale operation designed to annihilate the guerrillas in place or drive them into strong Italian blocking forces to be brought up to the Italian side of the demarcation line. Well planned, with typical anti-guerrilla measures, the operation conducted from 15 to 16 January 1942, had the advantage of cold weather, inconvenient for the Germans but disastrous for the guerrillas, who lacked proper clothing and equipment for operations in the snow. The guerrillas were estimated at 4,000 men and women, concentrated about Sarajevo and Višegrad and the area to the north. Meeting strong resistance, the Germans suffered a total 25 dead, 131 wounded, and almost 300 cases of frostbite; against 521 guerrilla dead and 1,331 captured. The Germans seized a booty which included 855 rifles, 22 machine guns, 4 field pieces, 600 head of livestock, and 33 draft animals. Although a tactical success, the operation failed to achieve its purpose when the Italian forces against which the guerrillas were to be driven did not arrive in time to prevent the escape of large numbers of the guerrillas into the Italian zone of interest in Croatia.

Representatives empowered by Hitler to work out plans to implement a "final solution" (Endlösung) of what to do with the very large number of persons, mostly Jews being held in concentration camps, met on January 20. 1942, at lake resort of Wannsee (10 mi./16 km from the city of Zehlendorf, southwest of Berlin Germany). Representatives recommended using "Zyklon B" gas for the systematic extermination of prisoners, thereby sealing the fate of European Jews.

A serious military situation in Russia made it necessary for the Germans to transfer from Serbia two Infantry Divisions by the end of January 1942. This reduction of forces prompted the German Armed Forces High Command to request the Bulgarians to move troops into southeastern Serbia. The Bulgarians assented and immediately shifted their First Corps from Thrace. Since it was occupying that part of Serbia allocated as an occupation zone of the Germans, the Bulgarian First Corps later came under the operational control of the German Military Commander in Serbia.

In February heavy fighting at Valjevo (45 mi/72 km southwest of Belgrade), caused the Germans almost 500 casualties, as compared to 3,500 guerrillas killed in action or shot in reprisal. Following field combat mistakes attributed to lack of integrated operations and cooperative support, the decision was made to establish a joint German-Italian-Croatian operation under a combined command to fight the resistance forces in eastern Bosnia. Gen. Paul Bader, the Commander of all German Forces and Administrative Authority in Serbia, was named Task Force Commander Under Operational Control of the Italian Second Army for the period of the operation.

Regarding the British government's attitude toward Gen. Mihajlović's position, Winston S. Churchill, British Premier expressed his government's concern to King Petar II of Yugoslavia regarding the lack of unity in fighting the Axis occupation forces. The following reports received from Yugoslavia concerning the activities of Gen. Mihajlović's "Lieutenants" were largely responsible for the British government's concern in the matter: (a) that Gen. Blasi Đukanović (the "Quisling" of Montenegro) was the main liaison between Mihajlović and the Italian military occupation forces, resulting in Mihajlović's forces raiding through the Croatian Littoral, and Herzegovina; (b) that Mihajlović's "Lieutenants" were cooperating with the Italian military authorities in forming organizations to fight the Croats who were engaged in fighting the Italians, Germans, and the partisan communists; Jevđević (former leader of the pro-fascist organization in Bosnia and Serbia) and Colonel Mihić (General Staff Officer) were operating at Abbazia (Opatija). Bircanin (former President of National Defense, "Narodna odbrana") was operating at Split; Grđić (Secretary General of "Narodna odbrana") was operating from Division Headquarters at Mostar. Foreign Minister Nincić, when confronted with the foregoing information, had defended Mihajlović on the grounds that Nincić was not aware of these activities on the part of Mihajlović's "Lieutenants."

In February 1942, the government of Canada ordered the arrest of all ethnic Japanese (an estimated 21,000 of whom 90% were Canadian citizens) living in Canada to be deported to isolated areas in the interior of Canada. None of the deportees had been charged with any criminal or subversive acts. In the United States, grave injustice was done to both U.S. citizens and permanent resident aliens of Japanese ancestry during WW II. A total of 120,313 individuals were confined, held in custody, relocated, or otherwise deprived of liberty as a result of Executive Order No. 9066, signed by President Franklin D. Roosevelt on February 19, 1942. These actions were carried out without adequate security reasons and without any acts of espionage or sabotage, and were motivated largely by racial prejudice, wartime hysteria, and a failure of political leadership. With the Civil Liberties Act of 1988 (Public Law 100-383, dated August 10, 1988), Congress implemented recommendations of the Commission on Wartime Relocation and Internment of Civilians. The purpose of this Act was to - acknowledge the fundamental injustice and apologize on behalf of the people of the United States; make restitution to those individuals of Japanese ancestry; make restitution to Aleut residents of Pribilof Islands and the Aleutian Islands west of Unimak Island; discourage the occurrence of similar injustices and violations of civil liberties in the future; make more credible and sincere any declaration of concern by the U.S. over violations of human rights committed by other nations; and authorize each eligible individual (or surviving spouse, children, parents, etc.) the sum of $20,000 in compensatory payment.

On February 23, 1942, the first meeting of the Croatian State Parliament was convened at Zagreb, and concluded: "The Croatian State Parliament declares that all the acts made from December 1, 1918, and until the establishment of the Independent State of Croatia (Nezavisna Država Hrvatska) on April 10, 1941, are null and void."

Sixteen U.S. Army B-25 bombers on April 18, 1942, took off from the U.S. aircraft carrier Hornet (operating 650 mi./1,046 km east of Japan), bombarded the cities of Tokyo, Nagoya, and Kobe. Due to insufficient supply of fuel for returning to the Hornet, the B-25 bombers purposely landed in China. Of the 82 aviators on the mission, only 70 returned. Three airmen were captured and executed by the Japanese.

The Bulgarian command in Serbia had a pacification problem similar to that of the Germans. Consequently, the Bulgarians undertook a number of anti-guerrilla operations on their own initiative, informing the Germans through liaison officers of the results of their efforts. In general, these were so savage as to quell the growth of any resistance movement of significance until late the following year. Extending from 20 April to 3 May 1942, the operation was considered a success from the German standpoint, with 168 enemy dead, 1,309 prisoners taken, and stocks of weapons, ammunition, and equipment captured. However, large numbers of guerrillas managed to escape through the Italian units assigned to block their flight and to make their way into the Italian zone of interest.

After the sinking of two Mexican tankers by German U-boats, on May 22, 1942, Mexico entered the war on the side of the Allies.

In London the Czech government-in-exile ordered the assassination of Reihard Heydrich (1904-1942), SS-Gruppenführer Deputy Reich Protector in Bohemia and Moravia. Under a covert mission on May 31, 1942, agents of the Czech resistance movement ambushed and critically wounded Heydrich, during his routine travel to his office at Hradčany Castle in Lidice (approximately 10 mi./16 km northwest of Prague, Czech Republic). On June 4, 1942 Heydrich died from wounds received four days earlier. In retaliation during June 9 and 10, 1942 the Nazi Gestapo apprehended and executed all the 188 men inhabitants of Lidice, sent all the women to concentration camps, and all the children to German orphanages. In the process, the Gestapo completely destroyed the village.

The major naval battle of Midway (1,100 mi./1,770 km northwest of Hawaii) was fought June 3-4, 1942 by the USA and Japanese fleets. Concurrently, the Aleutian campaign commenced when Japanese carrier-based aircraft bombarded and strafed Fort Mears and Dutch Harbor on the Aleutian Islands southwest of Alaska, damaging fuel installations and U.S. naval base, causing less than 100 casualties. On June 7, 1942, Japanese force landed 2,500 troops and occupied the islands of Attu and Kiska in western Aleutian Island (formerly: Catherine Archipelago). These were the only U.S. territories occupied by the Japanese during the Second World War. On May 11, 1943, U.S. forces landed at widely separated points on Attu. After heavy fighting and the bloodiest battles, the organized Japanese resistance collapsed and Attu was retaken on May 31 by U.S. forces. On July 28, 1943, Japanese garrison of Kiska had withdrawn by sea without being detected by U.S. forces. On August 15, U.S. and Canadian forces arrived off Kiska and began landing without encountering enemy opposition. On August 17, the main enemy camp on Kiska was found to be deserted. Uneventful search for enemy on Kiska was completed August 22, 1943.

A major countermeasure by the Italian occupation forces against the resistance was undertaken in July 1942 when Lt. Gen. (Generale di Corpo d'Armata) Mario Robotti launched a drive against the communist partisans in Slovenia. General Robotti's forces managed to surround the partisans, causing several thousand casualties on the partisans, and the survivors were routed. The partisans in Slovenia suffered a major military setback.

Two years after the initial suggestion by Albert Einstein and others, on August 13, 1942 the Manhattan Engineering District (MED) code name "Manhattan Project," was placed under the U.S. Army for the "development of substitute materials" (DSM). General Leslie R. Groves was the Commanding Officer in charge of administering and coordinating the entire nuclear energy project at Hanford, WA and at Oak Ridge, TN. The atomic bomb is an awesome destructive power by harnessing atomic fission and the splitting of atoms as uranium 235, heavy element which is radioactive. The price on the project for developing the atomic bomb was $2 billion. The first controlled and sustained nuclear chain reaction was produced on December 2, 1942, amid the wartime secrecy, in a reactor built inside an old court beneath Stagg Field at the University of Chicago, Illinois.

On August 22, 1942, Brazil joined the Allied cause, thus making it possible for the U.S. Navy to establish a naval station at the naval and military base of Recife (formerly Pernan/Buco), Brazil, easternmost point of South America. Brazil was the only South American nation with a small infantry unit which fought in Europe.

The communist guerrillas, hiding behind the patriotic symbol of National Liberation Front, surreptitiously gained absolute mastery over the liberation movement in 1942. This constitutes a classic example of how communists can encourage the formation of broadly based popular movements and then capture these movements by stealth and by fraud. In 1942 when the communist character of the National Liberation Front became clearer, and when this communist minority began to harrass the non-communist and peaceful peasants with requisitions, drafting, taxation, and extermination, the latter took hidden arms to defend themselves. Peasants were put between the hammer and anvil: if they cooperated with the communists they had to suffer horrible reprisals by the Axis occupiers; if they did not comply, they were marked as traitors and had to suffer reprisals by the partisans. Consequently, the first village guards were formed. These guards were at first a strictly defensive instrument and remained without any central command. However, the Italians soon put them under a unified command and, in 1943, the Germans transformed them into a home guard (domobranska vojska), they were given ammunition by the Germans to protect themselves, property, and their homes against marauders. Partisans accused them of collaborating with the enemies.

The German forces in Croatia and Serbia carried on a series of small-scale operations throughout the remainder of the year 1942, without achieving any marked success in eliminating the guerrilla movement. A new headquarters was created in October 1942, Commander of German Forces in Croatia under Gen. Rudolf Leuters; however, this headquarters did not become operational until shortly after the end of the year.

Operation code "Torch" under Gen. Dwight David Eisenhower (1890-1969), Thirty-fourth President of the United States (1953-1961), commenced on

November 8. 1942 with the landing of Allied Expeditionary Forces at Casablanca in French Morocco, Oran and Algiers in Algeria.

The Supreme Headquarters of Partisan Detachments on November 20, 1942 assumed the name of the Supreme Headquarters of the National Liberation Army (NLA). All units had their own political commissars, as well as military commanders. The most powerful factors in the NLA were the political commissars, nominated by the Central Committee of the Communist Party or by its Politburo selected from among the most reliable and trustworthy communists. The same criteria was true for the nominated provincial National Liberation Committee which had already been formed. In November 1942, the partisans launched their offensive which resulted in the temporary occupation of the town of Bihać in northwestern Bosnia, including the territory surrounding the town. The town of Bihać was the venue for the first session of the Anti-Fascist Council for the National Liberation of Yugoslavia - ACNLY (Antifašističko Vijeće Narodnog Oslobođenje Jugoslavije - AVNOJ), held on November 26-27, 1942. It's task was to convert and indoctrinate the guerrilla forces into the NLA, thus organized a political mobilization against the Axis occupation. Thereafter, the NLA began to improve their strategic initiative and slowly turn the military and political situations to its advantage. This occurred at a time when the Axis forces were suffering major defeats at El Alamein (Egypt), Stalingrad (Russia) and Midway (Pacific Ocean).

A discordant note was introduced into the resistance relationship by the increasing activities of communist partisans which came into prominence in the last six months. These small groups of communists were mostly located along the Dalmatian coast and in Croatia; they were under local leadership who at first confined themselves to attacks on the Serb-četnici of Mihajlović. Naturally, the Royal Yugoslav government-in-exile was hostile to the communist partisans because of their relentless attack on the Serb-četnici of Mihajlović. Similarly, the British had, of necessity, accorded full backing to Mihajlović because they were members of the recognized Royal Yugoslav government-in-exile at London. On the other hand, the Soviet government saw fit to give encouragement to the communist partisans, as evidenced by various radio messages from Moscow. It's important to understand that the Soviet's support of the communist partisans was not only a source of deep embarrassment to the British and United States governments, but also it was not a good omen for the future democratic institutions in the Balkans. The Soviet government aimed to capitalize on the Yugoslav situation and to foment communist disturbances, it indicates further activities along these lines in the future as well as imposing additional chaos in Europe at the conclusion of the war. The British government had directly approached the Soviet Embassy in London regarding Soviet support of the Yugoslav communist partisans and the attacks on Serb-četnici of Mihajlović. The Soviets (in conformity with their consistant pathological behavior and deep passion for big lies) claimed that they had no influence or communication with Tito's communist partisans.

A mass grave containing 9,000 corpses was discovered in 1943 near the city of Vinnitsa, Ukraine. All had died during Stalin's Great Purge, and had been killed by shots in the back of the neck.

Early in January 1943, Constantin Fotić Ambassador of Yugoslavia in Washington, D.C., called to see Sumner Welles, U.S. Under Secretary of State. During the meeting, the Ambassador referred to his conversation with Cordell Hull, U.S. Secretary of State, and inquired whether any decision had been reached by the U.S. government with regard to the issuance of some official statement regarding Gen. Mihajlović. Ambassador Fotić said that he had received two messages from his royal government-in-exile, one of them directly from King Petar II, requesting the Ambassador to see the U.S. President Roosevelt personally in order that the President might be informed of the very great importance which King Petar and the members of his cabinet attached to the official statement desired from the U.S. Government. In view of the fact that the White House had referred the Ambassador to the Dept. of State, the Ambassador did not wish again to request an interview with the President on this matter. Sumner Welles told the Ambassador that the best way of indicating that Mihajlović was rendering a service of military value to the United Nations was for Gen. Dwight D. Eisenhower, Commander in Chief, Allied Expeditionary Force, North Africa, to send some message to Mihajlović similar to that sent to Mihajlović recently by Gen. Harold Alexander, Commander in Chief of the British Forces in the Middle East. A suggestion of this kind had been made to Gen. George C. Marshall, Chief of Staff of the U.S. Army, but no action was contemplated.

On January 12, 1943, Anthony J. Drexel Biddle, Jr., U.S. Ambassador to the Yugoslav government-in-exile at London, had a meeting with Slobodan Jovanović, Yugoslav Premier. During their conversation Yugoslav diplomatic representatives were warned regarding separatist tendencies and instructed them to play an active part in and interests of Yugoslavia as a whole. Regarding the question of a political directive to Gen. Mihajlović, envisaging the coordination of action between the forces of resistance in Yugoslavia, the Jovanović replied that the Yugoslav government had devoted much thought to the subject; that they had taken into consideration previous informal suggestion of a possible basis for an agreement between Mihajlović and Tito (a) to cease fighting one another; (b) to coordinate their respective plans of action against the Axis; (c) to conduct their respective campaigns in their respective theaters of operation; and (d) to declare an armistice with each other in any given areas where their respective forces were at grips with one another.

U.S. President Franklin Roosevelt, British Premier Winston Churchill, and Charles DeGaulle of France held a conference January 14-24, 1942 at Anfa, near Casablanca, Morocco. The conferees made plans for an invasion of the Island of Sicily, Italy, and asserted the "unconditional surrender" of Axis nations is irrevocable.

Following the siege of Volgograd (formerly, Stalingrad), most of the German army on January 31, 1943 surrendered to the Soviet military forces. In February 1943, intelligence reports identified Soviet Union aspirations in Europe, which indicated that Stalin's post war plan vis-a-vis the Danubian Basin envisaged a Soviet Union of Southern Slav States. In order of preference, Stalin aimed at bringing Bulgaria, Macedonia, Serbia, and Montenegro under Soviet control, because of their eastern culture, the eastern orthodox church, Russian assimilative traditions. The other two regions with their western culture and traditions, catholic religion, and strong desire for personal freedom and democratic ideas, Croatia and Slovenia will be involved in case Stalin succeeded in Sovietizing the Danubian Basin. The Sovietization of the Danubian Basin was being pressed for the Comintern as far as Yugoslavia was concerned. The communist partisans declared that they as communists must continue fighting to protect the USSR interests against Western Europe and ensure an irrevocable future with their proletarian brothers of the USSR.

* * * * *

~ Serb-Četnici of Mihajlović ~

Telegram   London, March 30, 1943

To: U.S. Secretary of State

From: U.S. Ambassador to Yugoslav Government in Exile

British Foreign Office informs me it is today handing note to Yugoslav government to the following effect: (a) that the British government was seriously disturbed over developments in Yugoslav affairs and increasingly concerned regarding the future, unless measures were adopted to bring about a greater degree of unity among the resistance elements within Yugoslavia, the Croats, Slovenes and Serbs, and among Yugoslav circles abroad in general, the government in particular; (b) that as regards the situation inside Yugoslavia, the British government felt obliged to inform the Yugoslav government of certain views recently expressed in a speech by Gen. Mihajlović, and suggest that the Yugoslav government take the necessary steps at once, to inform the General of his government's views, and to instruct him to adopt a line more in accord with the attitude both of his own and the British government; and unless Mihajlović were prepared to revise his policy vis-a-vis the Italians and his compatriots [Tito's communists] now resisting the enemy, the British government might find it necessary to revise its present policy of favoring Mihajlović to the exclusion of other resistance elements in Yugoslavia.

In connection with the foregoing, the note draws attention to the British government's recent report from Colonel Bailey, British Liaison Officer to General Mihajlović, to effect (a) that a virtual state of civil war continued between the forces of Mihajlović and other resistance elements, that in this conflict Mihajlović had associated himself, directly or indirectly, with the Italian occupying forces, that this association had been confirmed by the General himself in an address he had delivered at a local gathering on February 28, 1943 (which, on the whole, amounted to a tirade against the western democracies and the Partisans).

The note goes on to summarize the General's speech, of which the following are the main points: (a) that the Serbs were now completely friendless; that the British to suit their own strategic purposes, were pressing them to engage in operations without any intention of helping them, either now or in the future; that the British were trying to purchase Serb blood at the cost of a trivial supply of munitions, that he needed no further contact with the western democracies, whose sole aim was to win the war at the expense of others; (b) that King Petar and his government were not guests, but virtually prisoners of the British, who were shamelessly violating Yugoslav sovereignty by conducting negotiations on internal Yugoslav problems directly with Moscow; (c) that the hypocritical and anti-Yugoslav activities of the partisans was a satisfaction for the Allies' lust for fraud; however, nothing the Allies could do or threaten, could divert the Serbs from their vowed and sacred duty of annihilating the partisans; (d) that as long as the Italians comprised his only adequate source of help generally, nothing the Allies could do would force him to alter his attitude towards them; (e) that his enemies were the Ustashi, the partisans, the Croats and the Moslems; that when he had dealt with these, he would turn to the Germans and the Italians.

I understand that, while the British government has no intention to deviate from its past 2 years' policy of supporting Mihajlović in his conflict against the Axis, and of rendering him every possible material help, it feels that the General should be brought to a sense of reality and "pulled up" as a result of his recent outburst. Besides, it feels it could never justify to British public opinion or to Britain's other Allies its continued backing of a movement, whose leader declared publicly that their enemies were his Allies and that his enemies were not the German and Italian invaders, but his fellow Yugoslavs. Should information concerning this declaration reach Soviet ears, Moscow and the Communist press abroad may, to my mind, be expected to exploit it vis-a-vis the Yugoslav government in light of Mihajlović's position as war minister, and even as pressure on London to withdraw whatever support Moscow may suspect London is rendering the General.

I furthermore understand that the note is motivated by the hope that it may serve to bring the Yugoslav government to face squarely the necessity for a greater degree of unity of thought and action. The conflict in the cabinet has now resolved itself into an intra-Serb affair between two conceptions of the Serb extremists; the pro-Yugoslav and the pan-Serb.

Signed: Anthony J. Drexel Biddle, Jr.

* * * * *

In order to reverse the precarious military and political situation to their own advantage, early 1943 the communist partisans began to strive and gain the long sought strategic initiative. The Axis not about to be outmaneuvered, decided to counterattack, thus the Battle of Neretva and Sutjeska in the central part of Yugoslavia, lasted almost continuously from January 1943 to the middle of June 1943. The partisans suffered heavy casualties and hardships. During the Battle of Sutjeska June 9, 1943, at the slopes of Mount Ozren, Bosnia-Herzegovina, Marshal Tito was wounded in the left arm by an exploding bomb.

The German military on April 13, 1943 revealed that they had found a mass grave in the Katyn forest (10 mi./16 km west of Smolensk, Russia), containing several thousands of Polish army officers. An International Commission confirmed that they had found 4,443 bodies buried in large common graves. The Russian communist government not only denied having committed the crimes, but blamed the Nazis for the atrocities. In 1952, an inquiry by the Polish communist government concluded that the Nazis were to blame. However, in February 1989, the Polish Red Cross commission had exhumed over 15,000 bodies from the mass graves and concluded, after a thorough investigation, that the victims had been killed between the end of March and the beginning of May 1940 when the Soviet military were in control of the territory. Another 10,500 Polish army officers disappeared at the same time of the Katyn massacre, and have never been found. Finally, on April 15, 1990 the Russians admitted that on Stalin's orders the Soviet secret police committed the atrocities at Katyn, but is not ready to apologize or make compensation, and cannot determine the fate of the missing 10,500 officers. On Sunday, May 7, 1995, Polish President Lech Walesa lay a cornerstone for the cemetery of 4,443 officers shot en masse and to commemorate the 1940 Soviet mass murder of 15,000 Polish officers captured during the Soviet Red Army's 1939 invasion of Poland.

The International Trident Conference held in Washington, D.C. (USA) ended on May 25, 1943. The conferees selected May 1, 1944 as target date for implementation of operation code "Overlord," Cross-Channel invasion of northwestern Europe. Large-scale air offensive from England will precede operation Overlord. After the capture of the Island of Sicily, Italy, operation "Husky," would knock Italy out of the war. Moreover, the center of important oil fields, oil refineries, and petrochemical plants in Ploesti, Romania, were to be bombed from Mediterranean military bases.

According to 1939 statistical data of Jewish population, there were 5,500,000 in the USSR; 4,500,000 in USA; 1,250,000 in Poland; 750,000 in Hungary; 450,000 in France; 400,000 in England; 185,000 in Germany; etc. During April 9 - March 16, 1943 about 250,000 Jews (including long established population and refugees) inhabited the so-called Warsaw ghetto in Poland, took up arms against the Nazi conquerors. The Germans reinforced their garrison with troops and tanks to squash the uprising. On May 16, 1943, the Jewish resistance ended after the Nazi burned and destroyed the ghetto, executed an estimated 7,000 Jews, and dispatched 56,065 Jews to concentration and labor camps. An unknown number of Jews perished.

During the spring of 1943, the Allied Command established contact with Tito's partisan supreme headquarters, sending a British mission to the communist partisans. This was followed by the arrival of joint military missions representing the United States and Britain in the Autumn of 1943, followed in February 1944 by a Soviet Mission. The missions concluded that, military successes against Axis forces were achieved primarily by Tito's communist partisans, not by Mihajlović Serb-četnici as previously attributed.

Following the preinvasion and heavy air and naval bombardments against the Island of Sicily (Sicilia), resulted in Allied air superiority over Axis forces. Operation "Husky" was implemented during the night of July 9-10, 1943. The 15th Army Group: main invasion forces of U.S. Seventh and British Eighth Armies with close support by Allied aircraft and navies, landed July 10 on the southeast coast of Sicily, establishing bridgeheads from west of Licata to south of Syracuse (Siracusa). U.S. parachute task force under Col. James Maurice Gavin (1907-1990), were dropped from two hundred twenty-six C-47's to take high ground near Ponte Olivo airfield. Eventually Allied victory had become more obvious to the Southeastern European population. The successful Allied lodgment in Sicily on July 10, 1943, and the worsening internal situation in the Balkans again raised the specter of western Allied forces landing along the eastern Adriatic coast. Accordingly, the German OKW, on July 26, 1943, issued a directive introducing major organization changes and centralizing authority for the defense of the entire Balkan Peninsula. Marshal Maximilian von Weichs, formerly commander of Army Group B in southern Russia, became Commander-in-Chief, Southeast, replacing Gen. Loehr, whose Army Group E was now restricted to Greece and the islands of Greece. Marshal von Weichs, with headquarters at Belgrade, Serbia, also commanded the Army Group F, controlling occupational troops in Yugoslavia and Albania.

On July 25, 1943, Benito Mussolini (1883-1945) "Il Duce," Premier of Italy (1922-1943), was overthrown, and Vittorio Emmanuele III, King of Italy, named Gen. Pietro Badoglio (1871-1956) Premier of Italy. Ironically and unparalleled, Gen. Badoglio as a former Italian Chief of the General Staff, was blamed for the Italian ill-fated invasion of Greece in December 1940, prompting Mussolini to dismiss him.

Under operation code "Tidalwave," on August 1, 1943 the oil field and refineries in Ploesti, Romania, were targets of mass assault by Allied Air Force heavy bombers. A total of 177 B-24 Liberator Bombers under control of the 9th USAF based in Bengasi, Libya, carried out a low-level bombardment causing severe damage to the oil refineries. The costs of the operation were high, resulting in the loss of 54 aircraft. In addition seven disabled aircraft made their emergency landing in Turkey.

After Mussolini was forcibly dismissed from office he was arrested and incarcerated. Ever since the overthrow of Mussolini, the relations between the Axis (German-Italian) partners continued unsatisfactory as ever. The Germans remained suspicious of Italy's intentions. The Italian declaration of Rome as an open city on August 14, 1943, seemed to be related in some fashion to peace moves, and of course bode no good for the Germans. On August 17, 1943, Hitler revealed, "I have clear proof that Badoglio [Premier of Italy] is already negotiating an armistice with the Allies." Foreknowledge of Allied landing, the strategical evacuation of Sicily was completed when 40,000 German troops plus their weapons and vehicles of the XIV Panzer Corps retreated toward southern Italian terrafirma of Calabria. Accordingly, the German Army Group B commanders were warned to be alert and ready to act against the Italians should the political situation change.

After weeks of planning, on August 17, 1943, Waffen-SS Colonel Otto Skorzeny (1908-1975) learned that Mussolini was being held prisoner on the Sardinian island of Maddalena, near Elba. Skorzeny was preparing to raid Maddalena and rescue Mussolini. Ten days later, on August 27, 1943, the German OKW learned that Mussolini had been transferred to Monte Gran Sasso d' Italia near the city of L' Aquila, in central Italy. On September 12, 1943, Hitler ordered the execution of a successful commando unit of glider planes led by Waffen SS Colonel Otto Skorzeny to rescue Mussolini and deliver him safely to Vienna, Austria. The mission was accomplished. Subsequently, Hitler installed Mussolini as the titular head of the Italian Socialist Republic with headquarters in the town of Salo, located at the resort of Lako di Garda (Lake of Garda) in northcentral Italy.

The German OKW issued a directive on August 17, 1943, made Marshal Erwin Rommel (a.k.a. "Desert Fox"), and Army Group B, in conjunction with the Commander-in-Chief, Southeast, responsible for destroying the guerrilla forces in Istria. Rommel moved his headquarters from Munich (München) in Germany to Garda in Italy, not far from the Bremer-Verona railway. Army Group B controlled operational and occupation forces in northern Italy until November 1943, when it was replaced by Army Group C. Further, to strengthen the German Forces in the Balkans, the Commander-in-Chief, Southwest (under the command of Marshal Albert Kesselring), was to turn over to Marshal von Weichs all captured tanks and other armored vehicles unsuitable for use against Allies in the Italian theater. This plan was designed to eliminate the resistance movement in Slovenia (NW Yugoslavia) and in Istria along the Yugoslav-Italian border area. The contemplated transfer of several divisions from Army Group B to the Commander-in-Chief, Southeast, was thwarted by developments in Italy and the immediate departure of Marshal Rommel and his staff to France.

On August 24, 1943, after the guerrilla bands attacked a 24th Panzer Division supply train near Ljubljana in northwestern Yugoslavia, the German OKW instructed Emil von Rintelen to protest to the Italian Armed Forces High Command (Comando Supremo) and to indicate to the Italians that the Germans would have to reinforce the troops protecting the Travis-Feistritz-Ljubljana passes. Though an Allied invasion was an everpresent danger, the Germans regarded the prospect of Italian treachery as the graver threat. Marshal Kesselring, while not unmindful of the possibility that he could be wrong, continued to accept in good faith repeated Italian assurances.

The German OKW, on August 30, 1943, made what turned out to be its final revision of operation "Achse," (Axle) the plan to seize control of Italy. Also, the Army Group B was to reinforce the German troops at all the passes leading into Italy, occupy the cities of Trieste, Fiume (Rijeka), and Pola (Pula), and pacify northern Italy.

After the conquest of Sicily, Allied troops landed on the west coast of the Province of Calabria, advancing toward the Italian mainland. On September 3, 1943, a secret short-term armistice was signed between the United States and the British government on the one hand, and the Italian Government on the other hand; hostilities were suspended between Italy and the United Nations on certain terms of a military nature. The Instrument of Armistice was signed at Cassibile, near Siracusa, Sicily, by Gen. Walter Bedell Smith (1895-1961) on behalf of Gen. Dwight David Eisenhower (1890-1969) and by Gen. Guiseppe Castellano on behalf of Marshal Badoglio. Negotiations between the Allies and the Badoglio government were conducted in great secrecy, thus on September 8, 1943, when it was announced that Italy capitulated, the shocking news caught both Italian and German military and political leaders by surprise. The immediate German reaction was to put into effect operation "Konstantin" seizing control of the Italian-occupied areas, reinforce German troops in the Balkans theater; and implement operation "Achse" (Axle) to take over control of Italy, thereby, disarming Italian units that refused to continue the war on the German side.

Though Italians were in the process of withdrawing from Albania, Greece, and Yugoslavia at the time the fascist government capitulated, the Italian forces still held most of Albania; portions of Slovenia, Dalmatia, and Montenegro; the Ionian Coast and Islands of Greece; and a number of the Aegean Islands. In addition, they had troops in the Italian zone of interest in Croatia, in the interior of Greece, and under German command on the island of Crete (Kriti, a.k.a. Candia). September 1943 was an important favorable event for the Yugoslav communist resistance movement. Tito's partisans gained substantial military strength which was facilitated mostly by the acquisition of a large quantity of war equipment obtained from Italian troops in complete chaos. The opportunity to procure much-needed weapons, equipment and supplies was not lost by the guerrillas, who immediately, at the time of the Italian armistice, called upon the Italian garrisons to surrender. Fearful of guerrilla vengeance, however, many Italian units waited in place to be disarmed by the Germans, and the situation developed into a race between Germans and guerrillas to reach the acquiescent Italians. Incensed by what they considered treachery on the part of their former allies, the Germans made it a point to single out Italian units and installations in their continuing anti-guerrilla operations. Italian troops disarmed by the guerrillas were bombed and strafed in their unit areas by German Luftwaffe, and German ground troops hunted down Italian units and groups.

The Dalmatian city and port of Split, with enormous stocks of food, clothing, fuel, and ammunition for the Italian occupation forces fell to the partisans, dock workers, and left-wing elements of the population. Though the partisans were forced to evacuate Split, they managed to remove considerable quantities of stores before the arrival of German forces. The confused situation and sporadic fighting of the next few weeks ended with the Germans in control of the ports, main centers of population, and coastal areas. The partisans, laden with the loot, were busily re-equipping and regrouping their forces in the mountains and carrying on a harrassing campaign against the occupation troops. Nor were the Serb-četnici idle during this period of changing authority. Strong detachments moved into southern Dalmatia, seizing stretches of the coastal areas and obtaining stocks of arms from Italian units sympathetic to theSerb-četnici in the past.

The Croatian state, truncated by the Italian annexation of Dalmatia, moved its military forces into the coastal areas. The Poglavnik Ante Pavelić had to impress his population, and a show of force against the Italians in their weakened state appeared to be an ideal opportunity. In Slovenia and Dalmatia, to relieve their own troops of many routine security duties, the Germans banded together the former Italian-sponsored "White Guard" of Rupnik and the "Blue Guard" of Novak, the latter a četnik commander, into the "Domobran," a home guard-type organization. Exhausted by long marches and intermittent fighting to gain the areas vacated by the Italians, the German troops were in no condition to pursue the guerrillas into the mountains. Instead, German commanders hurried to set up a defense against Allied landings, allocated units specific areas of responsibility, and organized mobile forces to seek out and destroy the guerrilla bands.

Experience gained in operations in the Balkans and in Russia enabled the Germans to devise more effective anti-guerrilla measures than had their Italian predecessors. They resolved to contain the guerrillas and keep up the flow of bauxite and other strategic raw materials produced in the Balkans to the German war machine. A highly effective offensive weapon was found in the newly organized German Ranger Commando, designed to seek out and destroy resistance bands. Personnel of the rangers were young, physically strong and trained to live in the open field for extended periods of time, they depended little on supply columns and could pursue the guerrillas. When the situation required, the rangers would put on civilian clothing, disguising themselves as appropriate, to work their way closer to the wary enemy. In event the rangers came upon major enemy forces, the rangers would keep the enemy under surveillance, gather intelligence information while awaiting German reinforcement units.

On September 15, 1943, King Petar II Karađorđević accompanied by members of his Yugoslav Royal Government left London, England, to establish a new headquarters in Cairo, Egypt. On November 12, 1943, the U.S. Senate confirmed the nomination of Lincoln MacVeagh as U.S. Ambassador to the Yugoslav government-in-exile in Egypt.

With the capture of the Italian cities of Foggia and Brindisi and their great air bases and seaports, situated along the southern coast of the Adriatic, the Allies made it imperative for the Germans on September 20, 1943 to secure control of the Dalmatian coast and its seaports without delay. On September 29, 1943 aboard the British battleship "H.M.S. Nelson" anchored in Valetta harbor, Malta, the second long-term Italian surrender document with the Allies was signed by Gen. Dwight David Eisenhower, and Marshal Pietro Badoglio, Head of the Italian Government. The additional conditions provided in the Armistice made the Italian Government bound to comply with political, economic and financial matters. As a result, Italy became a cobelligerent of doubtful value if judged in terms of material military resources - the Italian Army was virtually ineffective; the Air Force was obsolete; only the Navy and merchant marines made substantial contributions to Allied power. Meanwhile, the newly established Italian government located at Brindisi (a city on Italy's southeastern coast in the Adriatic Sea), on October 13, 1943 declared war against Germany.

In preparation of military commitment in southeastern Europe, the Allied Air Force carried out continuous air bombardments against shipping and seaports along the eastern coast of the Adriatic Sea. Purportedly, aerial bombardments were directed toward military targets but, in the northern major city and seaport of Zadar, Dalmatia, Allied aerial attacks wreaked havoc on the city and inflicted thousands of civilian casualties but very few military casualties. Therefore, during the course of the war, aerial attacks on civilians became known as the "mystery" of war. Case in point, there were two active and fully staffed anti-aircraft artillery installations located at the city's periphery, one south and the other northeast of the city. Although 75%

of the city was destroyed and its suburbs sustained heavy damages by constant Allied aero-bombardment, these two anti-aircraft installations were never (not even once), deliberately or fortuitously targeted for destruction by the Allies or anybody else.

The Bulgarians also became a problem to the Germans during November 1943, with whole units disaffected. On one occasion, the 24th Bulgarian Division had to be withdrawn from an operation against the communist partisans when it refused to obey the order of the German task force Commander. Desertions to the guerrillas became more frequent, and several communist bands of Bulgarian deserters were organized to operate against German forces and their own Bulgarian government in southern and western Bulgaria from bases on Yugoslav soil.

On November 29, 1943, the second session of AVNOJ attended by 208 delegates from various parts of Yugoslavia was held at Jajce in Bosnia-Herzegovina. It was decided that (a) AVNOJ constitute the supreme legislative and executive body; (b) National Committee for the Liberation of Yugoslavia was established as a provincial government headed by Josip Broz Tito (promoted to the rank of Marshal of Yugoslavia); and (c) organized the communist state of Yugoslavia based on democratic federal principals as a community of equal nations.

The Big Three, Roosevelt, Churchill, and Stalin, accompanied by their top political and military advisers attended the Tehran Conference (code name "Eureka") which was held from November 28-30, 1943. Among others, they reached the decision: to recognize the National Liberation Army (NLA) of Yugoslavia and extend substantial military and economic assistance to Marshal Tito and his communist partisans.

After occupation of Bari, Italy, by Montgomery's British Eighth Army on September 14, 1943 the Allies became careless in the effort to protect their shipping along the Adriatic Sea. During the night of December 2 and 3, 1943, about 30 German aircraft launched a raid against the crowded harbor of Bari inflicting heavy damage. The Luftwaffe blew up two ammunition ships and caused the loss of 17 other ships loaded with valuable cargo.

On December 24, 1943, Gen. Dwight D. Eisenhower was appointed Supreme Commander of Allied Forces in Europe in charge of operation "Overlord," meaning the invasion of Normandy, France.

Military assistance from the United States and England began arriving to Yugoslavia in accordance with the decision reached at Teheran Conference by Roosevelt, Churchill, and Stalin which concluded that Tito's communist partisans must be given food, medicine, and military supplies in recognition as a full member of the Allied army and anti-Axis coalition. Direct military cooperation was established between the partisans and the Allies.

United States and British amphibious operation code name "Shingle" on January 22, 1944, landed at Anzio, Italy (33 mi./53 km southwest of Rome) with the purpose to disrupt German forces at Cassino. Meanwhile, on February 1, 1944, the U.S. Fifth Army, the British Eighth Army and units of Free French, New Zealand, and Polish, with the support of artillery and air attacks were unsuccessful in breaking the German defense of "Gustave Line". A key point on the Gustav Line was the Benedictine Abbey of Nursia on the hill of Monte Cassino. Believing that the Benedictine Abbey was being used by the Germans as an observation post, the Allies commenced on May 11, 1944, a second battle by bombing and destroying the monastery on May 17, 1944. It was later found that the Germans did not use the famous Abbey until after the Allied bombardment, when its ruins provided an almost insurmountable obstacle to Allied tanks.

In the Eastern front, on January 27, 1944, the Soviet Red Army broke the siege of the city of Petersburg (formerly, Leningrad), and their armies advanced toward Estonia, Latvia, and Lithuania.

An Allied Commando party successfully raided the Island of Hvar in the Adriatic Sea during the night of January 27-28, 1944. Allied naval base for coastal craft was established January 29, 1944, on the Island of Vis in the Adriatic Sea for supplying Tito's communist forces in Yugoslavia.

German troops on March 19, 1944, invaded Hungary, in part because Hungary was contemplating to withdraw from fighting the war, and in part because the Soviet forces were drawing ever near the Hungarian border. U.S. aircraft flying from air bases in southern Italy, on April 15, 1944 raided the Ploesti oil fields in Romania, suffered heavy losses.

The Allied forces, by their heavy attacks against German troops in Italy, helped the cause of Tito's communist partisans. Late March and early April 1944, four Allied squadrons of C-47's (60th Troop Carrier Group) arrived at Brindisi, Italy, from North Africa. Immediately, the Troop Carrier Group went into action, flew hundreds of sorties dropping propaganda leaflets over Yugoslavia, and carried out hundreds of military missions by delivering thousands of tons of supplies to Yugoslav partisans. The supplies consisted mainly of dynamite, weapons, ammunition, medical supplies, food, clothing, and other materiel needed by the partisans to carry out the guerrilla warfare. It was at this time that a number of the Allied liaison officers were withdrawn from the Serb-četnici of Mihajlović, and with the departure of military advisors the supply of weapons and equipment from Allied forces were reduced, with much of the Allied military assistance diverted to the communist partisans. Under constant attack by Tito's forces, the military and political position of the Serb-četnici began to deteriorate. Though the Serb-četnici still held a large part of Serbia and some of the Montenegro territory, their strength waned with battle losses and mass desertions.

Although British Special Operations Executive (SOE) agents dominated operations in the eastern Mediterranean, the Office of Strategic Services (OSS) still played an important role there. Seeking to pin down German forces far from the Cross-Channel invasion, operation "Overlord," U.S. operatives agreed to provide arms to communist and socialist guerrillas in Greece as early as October 1943. While the guerrillas activities increased, operational groups began to infiltrate into Greece early in 1944 to conduct a series of raids against German transportation and communications in Macedonia, Thessaly, and the Peloponnese.

Beginning of 1944, the Balkan occupation became a heavy burden to the Germans. The Wehrmacht was loosing on Russian battlefields; the United States, British, Canadian, and other Allied forces were firmly established in Italy since their landing, operation "Husky" in Sicily on July 10, 1943, and the Allied Forces invasion of France was a few months away from "D-Day" June 6, 1944 in Normandy Peninsula.

Tito's communist partisans had grown to a force able to hold an area of the country by themselves, including important transportation, communications, and depot facilities, just enough to set up a provisional government for propaganda purposes. On May 13, 1944, Tito created the Department for the Protection of the People (Odelenje za žastitu narodna, OZN-a) to assimilate the odious and despicable national police in the Soviet Union. From its inception, the OZN-a committed innumerable crimes against humanity, and launched an aggressive campaign of persecution against anyone who was not in favor, or unsympathetic to the communist cause. The centralized organization of OZN-a became the sharp sword of Tito's communist revolution. Lenin defined the dictatorship of the proletariat as "power based on violence." So, Tito like Stalin, used the secret police to be the final interpreter of the government tyranny.

In Italy, Allied Forces launched assaults after assaults but failed to pierce the German "Gustav Line." Finally, the German stubborn resistance collapsed during the battles fought from May 11 to 18, 1944. On May 23 the Allies broke out of the Anzio beachhead and advanced toward Rome.

Small-scale operations by the various German divisions and smaller units against the partisans met with some success, but the center of the partisan movement, in the Knin-Jajce-Bihac-Banja Luka area, remained a refuge to which Tito's partisans planned to withdraw whenever German pressure became too great in any other area. Therefore, to regain at least some of the initiative now all but lost, and to strike the partisans a blow from which they would not soon recover, Marshal von Weichs ordered the Second Panzer Army to destroy the Tito forces in their main stronghold at Drvar in Bosnia. On the morning of May 25, 1944, the German forces under the Command of Gen. Lothar Rendulic (1887-1971), who served on the Eastern Front since 1941, was transferred in August 1943 to the Southeastern European theater, launched a combined airborne and ground operation, code name "Rösselsprung" (Knight's Move), against Tito's communist partisans. Parachutists and glider troops were dropped on Tito's headquarters at Drvar (Bosnia-Herzegovina), while tanks and infantry units from the towns of Bihać, Banja Luka, and Livno converged to capture or kill Tito at his mountainous headquarters hideout. Although the Germans captured Tito's supreme headquarters with its extensive communication system, Tito together with his staff and the Allied mission managed to escape to the nearby Prekaja mountains. However, Ivan Lola Ribar, one of Tito's close revolutionary associates, was killed. The Allied 334th Wing flew emergency supplies to the encircled partisan leaders.

On June 3, 1944, a Soviet aircraft-transport arrived from Bari, Italy, and landed at the emergency air strip constructed in the Kupreško Polje (Valley), Bosnia-Herzgovina, took Tito and members of his staff and delivered them safely to Bari. During the same night, three C-47 aircraft of the United States 60th Troop Carrier Group safely evacuated the military and political members of the communist partisans and members of the Allied mission. Subsequently, additional flights by C-47 aircraft continued to evacuate remaining wounded personnel until the night of June 5, 1944, when the Germans captured the transient partisan headquarters. Though not a fatal blow, the operation "Knight's Move" did achieve its purpose in that the communist partisan chain of command was temporarily broken until Tito could re-establish himself on the island of Vis off the Dalmatian coast under British protection. The heavy personnel and materiel losses forced the communist partisans to withdraw from active operations in the area to reorganize and regroup their guerrilla forces.

Subsequent to extensive diplomatic maneuvering, U.S. Ambassador in USSR, Averill William Harriman (1891-1986) on February 2, 1944, in conversation with Joseph Stalin (1879-1953), Premier of the USSR (1922-1953), succeeded in getting the Soviets to accept the implemention of shuttle-bombing, operation "Frantic." Reluctantly, Stalin agreed to allow three airfields inside Ukraine: Poltava, Mirgorod, and Piryatin to be used for shuttle bombing purpose. Construction and improvements went ahead rapidly. By the end of May 1944, the bases were in adequate condition to accommodate heavy bombers. The U.S. Fifteenth Air Force got the assignment: fly from Italy to Russia and return to Italy. B-17's from the 4th Wing of the Fifteenth Air Force and a reinforced P-51 group from the 306th Wing were organized into a task force to fly to USSR. On the way they would attack a railway center in Debrecen, Hungary. All the 130 bombers would land at Poltava or Mirgorod and the 70 fighters would base at Piryatin. At 0655 on June 2, 1944, the first "Frantic" task force took off from the military air base in southern Italy. The aircraft reached Debrecen, Hungary, soon after 0900, and dropped a thousand 500 lb./227 kg bombs from altitudes ranging from 21,000-25,000 ft. / 6,400-7,620 meters. No German Luftwaffe fighters appeared in the air, but one B-17 fortress unaccountably exploded. It was the only loss. By early afternoon the main group of B-17's landed at Poltava, Ukraine. A force of one hundred four B-17's and forty two P-51's of U.S. Fifteenth Air Force on June 6, 1944, attacked an airfield at Galatz, Romania, staging from bases in USSR. Two Mustang P-51's were shot down. However, the U.S. pilots destroyed eight German aircraft. The task force returned to Italy on June 11. On the way the task force bombed the airfield of Foscani in northeastern Romania. One B-17 bomber was lost.

On June 6, 1944 commenced the D-Day for operation "Overlord" meaning the Allied Cross-Channel invasion of Normandy, France. An armada of 4,600 warships, transports, supply ships, and landing craft put 175,000 Allied troops ashore. The troops landed on five beaches of Normandy: on the west Utah and Omaha beaches were U.S. troops objectives; to the east, the British landed on Gold and Sword; while the Canadians hit Juno, between Gold and Sword. Shortly before the landing two U.S. and one British airborne divisions were dropped behind the beachheads to destroy German communications.

Germany on June 13, 1944, introduced the V-1 (Vergeltenungswaffe Ein), a pilotless flying bomb powered by a jet engine. On September 13, 1944, Germany introduced the V-2 propelled by a liquid fuel rocket. The V-2 (Vergeltenungswaffe Zwein) 12-ton rocket-propelled carrying one ton of explosives warhead, flew higher, farther, and faster (circa 3,500 mph) than the V-1. The V-2 projectile burned a mixture of alcohol and oxygen.

In Asia, China based United States B-29 bombers on June 15, 1944, accomplished their first attack on Japan, dropping 231 tons of bombs on Imperial Iron and Steel Works' Jawata plant on the island of Kyushu.

U.S. bombers based in England raided Berlin on June 17, 1944, and continued their flight to Russia, where they refueled and rearmed, and made another raid over Berlin on their way back to England. On June 21, 1944,

U.S. Eighth Air Force began shuttle raids between England and Soviet bases. Squadrons of one hundred fourteen B-17's and seventy P-51's, after bombing oil targets at Ruhland, south of Berlin, landed at USSR bases. The Germans discovered the secret Allied airbase at Poltava, Ukraine, and during the night of 21 and 22 June 1944, made a highly destructive attack on it by utilizing the light of flares, causing heavy damage to U.S. aircraft and stores of ammunition and gasoline. Planes of the Eighth Air Force left USSR air bases on June 26, 1944, and on their way to Italy, bombed oil plants at Drohobycz, Poland. Upon reaching Italy, the planes remained long enough to fly one more mission with the Fifteenth Air Force before returning to their airbase in England.

Delegates from 44 nations met on July 1-15, 1944, at Bretton Woods, New Hampshire (USA), to plan postwar financial matters. They agreed to establish an International Monetary Fund (IMF) and also an International Bank for Reconstruction and Development (a.k.a. the World Bank).

After a lapse of about a month, on July 22, 1944, the shuttle bombing was renewed, whereby seventy-six P-38's and fifty-eight P-51's of U.S. Fifteenth Air Force attacked airfields in Romania, claiming destruction of 56 enemy planes, and landed at Soviet bases. At the same time, heavy bombers of the same airforce squadron attacked oil industry targets of Ploesti, Romania. On July 25, 1944, U.S. Fifteenth Air Force fighter bombers from Soviet bases attacked the airdrome of Mielec, Poland, near Lwow (Lemberg), with good military effect. While returning to Italy from USSR on July 26, 1944, the U.S. Fifteenth Air Force fighter bombers, made a successful sweep over Ploesti and Bucharest areas of Romania.

In response to the first Soviet Union direct request for air support, on August 4, 1944, a group of U.S. Fifteenth Air Force fighter bombers attacked many airfields in Romania and then landed at Soviet air bases. On August 6, 1944, the U.S. Eighth Air Force planes bombed the seaport of Gdynia (Gdingen) on the Gulf of Danzig, and on August 7th some of the planes bombed oil refineries at Trzebinia (Poland) and then landed at Soviet air bases. Upon returning from the Eastern Command bases in USSR to England via Italy on August 8, the planes attacked airfields in Romania.

Tito, after his arrival to Italy on August 12, 1944, visited British Premier Churchill at Naples, and also conferred at Caserta with Gen. Henry Maitland Wilson, Supreme Commander of the Allied Forces in the Mediterranean (SACMED) theater. The Headquarters of the Allied High Command was located in Caserta's royal palace, situated at the foot of Mount Tifatini, built in 1752 for the Bourbon ruler, King Charles III of Naples and Sicily. During the meeting with Churchill and other British military leaders, Tito repeated his statements of falsehood that he as a fervant Marxist-Leninist had no intention to establish a communist regime in Yugoslavia. Everybody should know that Tito was a classic, pathetical liar in communist clothing.

Strong concentrations of communist partisans in Montenegro compelled the Germans to plan another large-scale operation, under the code name "Ruebezahl." However, before "Ruebezahl" could be launched, the movement of partisans toward the Macedonia region compelled immediate and effective action. On August 12, 1944, Operation "Ruebezahl" finally got underway, holding the major part of the advancing partisans and then driving them back across the Lim River in southcentral Yugoslavia.

On August 23, 1944, King Michael of Romania surrendered unconditionally to the Soviet forces. Ploesti, center of Romanian oil industrial complex, on August 30, 1944 was captured by troops of the Second Ukrainian Front.

The city of Paris, France, was abandoned by the German troops, and on August 25, 1944 the Allies led by Free French units entered the capital city. Five days later Gen. Charles de Gaulle arrived triumphantly in Paris and established his provisional French government.

After visiting the Allied in Italy, Marshal Tito went to the Island of Vis where he conducted diplomatic activities for the recognition of post-war Yugoslavia. Tito and Ivan Šubašić (for the Karađorđević government-in-exile) signed the Vis Agreement on August 26, 1944. Consequently, King Petar abolished the Serbian military establishment of Gen. Mihajlović, recognized the National Liberation Army (NLA) of Yugoslavia, and publicly called on his loyal Serbian people to support Tito and his communist organization. In September 1944, Tito flew to Moscow, Russia, for talks with his mentor and tyrant Stalin to plan a strategy for postwar communist takeover.

Allied successes in eastern European fronts, particularly those of the Red Army, forced the German Army Group F to begin withdrawal from Greece proper and the islands of Ionian and Aegean Seas on September 1, 1944. The main withdrawal route, railroad through Skopje and Belgrade was so effectively hit by the U.S. Fifteenth Air Force during the first half of September that the German Luftwaffe was constrained to withdrawal from all three airfields in Athens, which were rendered unserviceable by the Fifteenth Air Force attacks during the latter half of the month.

On September 5, 1944, USSR declared war on Bulgaria. Soviet forces reached the Romania-Yugoslav frontier at Turnu-Severin, Romania on the Danube River at the Iron Gate on September 6, 1944, and other Red Army troops occupied Ostroleka, Poland.

Bulgaria declared war on Germany on September 7, 1944, and requested a cessation of hostilities with the Allies. The USSR accepted the armistice effective September 9, 1944.

The U.S. Eighth Air Force completed the last of its shuttle-bombing missions on September 11, 1944, by using seventy-five B-17's and sixty-four P-51's to attack the armament plant at Karl-Marx-Stadt (Chemnitz), Germany, and proceeding to designated "Frantic" air bases in the USSR.

On September 12, 1944, Romania signed an armistice with the Allies, and agreed to cooperate in the war effort against Germany and Hungary, and to pay undetermined reparations. Boundary between USSR and Romania established by the Soviet-Romanian agreement of June 28, 1940, the USSR promised to return the territory of Transylvania to Romania.

British special detachment on September 14, 1944, temporarily landed on Pelješac Peninsula in the Dalmatian littoral and shelled the town of Trpanj, a withdrawal point for German occupation forces.

On September 16, 1944, Soviet forces of the Third Ukranian Front, advanced westward to block enemy withdrawal from Yugoslavia, and occupied Sofia, capital of Bulgaria. Troops of the Third Ukranian Front, having secured the Iron Gate-Turnu-Severin-Orsova area in Romania, where the Danube passes through the Transylvanian Alps, crossed the Danube on September 30, 1944, and pushed toward Belgrade; succeeded in cutting the Niš-Belgrade railway at Velika Plana on October 10, 1944.

Serb-četnici lost their battle for Serbia in September 1944, when the Soviet Red Army entered northern Serbia and the Bulgarian Army entered southern Serbia. The Serb-četnici hurriedly split into two groups. One group retreated to the north, unaware of wrongdoing, tried to reach the Soviet communist forces and surrender to them rather than to Tito's communist partisans. The fate of prisoners of war in the Yugoslav Marxist revolutionary war was putting into effect the communist's law of execution. In the life-and-death struggle, there were few prisoners taken. Most of them when captured were annihilated by Tito's communists. Only a part of the Serb-četnici that fled north reached the Red Army. At any rate, the fate of those captured by the Soviets or by Tito's partisans did not vary - they all unceremoniously disappeared. The second group of Serb-četnici, under the command of Gen. Mihajlović eluded being captured and remained fugitives in central Bosnia in the same mountains where Tito's partisans had engaged in guerrilla tactics during the earlier years.

Thinking about the post-war balance of power and sphere of influence in southern Europe, the British focused their attention on northeastern Adriatic and the ports of Trieste, Pola (Pula), and Fiume (Rijeka) within the region coveted by Tito and his communist partisans. The British were purportedly determined to keep these strategic ports out of communist control so as to prevent the possibility that they become naval bases from which a Soviet fleet might dominate the Adriatic sea.

By the end of October 1944, it seemed unlikely that the Allied armies in Italy would wrest control of the Po Valley before winter from the German forces under Kesselring, Commander in Chief, Southwest (Oberbefehlshaber, Suedwest), who was responsible to the Armed Forces High Command through the Armed Forces Operations Staff (Wehrmachtführungsstab-WFSt) for operations and nominally had full tactful authority over all units of the Army, Navy, Air Force (Luftwaffe), and Waffen-SS (Schutzstaffeln military units of the Wehrmacht) in Italy. Marshal Harold R.L.G. Alexander revived his earlier British concept of a trans-Adriatic amphibious operation. This large-scale turning maneuver was to outflank the German forces in northern Italy, concurrently, open up roads into the mid-Danube basin and possibly reach the Austrian's capital city of Vienna before the Soviet Red Army.

For logistical support, the landing craft that had been employed earlier to convey troops and equipment from ship to shore in southern France (under designation code "Dragoon") would be made available for an amphibious operation against the Istrian peninsula and the Dalmatian littoral; but since that same shipping would soon be needed for the Pacific theater, the USA high commands placed a time limit on its availability. For that reason the Supreme Allied Commander in the Mediterranean (SACMED), namely the British Gen. Henry Maitland Wilson, had to make his decision by October 10 whether to undertake an amphibious assault in eastern Adriatic. British Premier Churchill summoned Marshal Alexander and Gen. Wilson to meet with him on October 8 at Naples, Italy. At Naples the British made a preliminary survey of ways to undertake a trans-Adriatic attack. The survey disclosed two possible courses of action: a seaborne attack on the Istrian peninsula, including the capture of Trieste; or a landing south of Fiume (Rijeka) followed by a thrust northward toward the city. Marshal Alexander believed he would be able to occupy the Dalmatian ports of Zadar, Šibenik, and Split. As part of the Allied offensive, the British Eighth Army could pass through these ports in Dalmatia and advance rapidly on to Fiume (Rijeka) in Istria and Ljubljana in Slovenia and thence into Austria.

Gen. Wilson was assigned to undertake a study concerning the feasibility of an amphibious operation in the light of the rather short time limit placed on the use of the sealift in the Mediterranean theater. Two days later, on October 10, Wilson submitted a report that offered little comfort to the advocates (Churchill and Alexander) of amphibious operations on the Adriatic flank. Since the British intervention in the Greek civil war in October, the German Armed Forces Operations Staff (WFSt) believed that Allied forces in the Mediterranean theater lacked the strength to support landings either in Istria, south of Fiume (Rijeka), or along the Dalmatian littoral while at the same time supporting the Greeks and maintaining an active front in Italy. Allied schemes for trans-Adriatic operations were known to the Germans, but had not been taken seriously. Many areas along the Dalmatian beaches became dangerous zones because the Germans had laid explosive mines as defensive precognition measures to impede possible Allied invasion.

In Yugoslavia, the German Army Group E, commanded by Marshal von Weichs consisted of about 200,000 troops divided among 15 multinational divisions. Opposing the Germans and their allies were approximately 200,000 communist partisans under Marshal Tito.

Troops of the Second Ukranian Front on October 11, 1944, forged along Tisza (Tisa) River at Szeged, Hungary's second largest city, seriously threatening the capital city of Budapest, Hungary; orders were to advance toward Debrecen, east of Budapest; other units, assisted by Romanian forces, are ordered to take Cluj, capital of Transylvania, Romania. On October 12, 1944, the above troops occupied Oradea, Transylvania, and continued to battle for Debrecen, Hungary, breaking the Belgrade-Budapest railway at Subotica. British commando forces, on October 12, 1944, landed on the Island of Corfu (Kerkyra), Greece, and in the Sarandë, Albania.

With the fall of Sombor, southwest of Subotica in Vojvodina, on October 14, 1944, Soviet forces controlled most of the east bank of the Danube as far north as the Hungarian town of Baja. The combined Soviet and Yugoslav communist forces, on October 14, 1944, were converging on the capital city of Belgrade, Serbia, which was encircled. On October 16, 1944, the combined forces were fighting side by side in the streets of Belgrade. In the meantime, the city of Niš, on Sofia-Belgrade railway line, was taken from the German occupation troops. On October 20, Belgrade was occupied by combined forces of the Third Ukrainian Front and Tito's Yugoslav Army. The Yugoslavs announced the capture of the Dalmatian city and seaport of Dubrovnik. Henceforth, the Yugoslav communist movement, their ranks swelled to over 220,000 men and women, were ready to fight as organized units alongside Stalin's Red Army, and Tito and his communist partisans would no longer be as dependent as before upon Allied assistance.

Acting on Premier Churchill's instructions, Gen. Wilson proposed to the Combined Chiefs of Staff (CCS) on October 24, 1944 that the Allied armies establish their defense along or near the La Spezia-Bologna-Ravenna line;

Marshal Alexander then could withdraw from the front up to six divisions, sufficiently trained and equipped, with which to mount an amphibious operation along the coast of Dalmatia. Once the Allied landing force had established a beachhead at Zadar, three or four divisions could pass through to begin an overland advance on Fiume (Rijeka), Pola, and Trieste, then continuing northward to cut the line of communications of German forces in Italy with Austria and Gen. Weichs' Army Group E in the Balkan. For Marshall Alexander and his staff, that plan found no more favor with the CCS than had the previous plan. Premier Churchill was disappointed by Gen. Wilson's apparent inability to undertake amphibious operations across the Adriatic.

Bulgaria signed the armistice with the Allies on October 28, 1944. By the armistice terms, Bulgaria agreed to relinquish portions of Greece and Yugoslavia territories acquired in 1941, make certain reparations to be determined, and place Bulgarian armed forces at the disposal of the Soviet authorities. The reorganized Bulgarian army helped the Soviet and Yugoslav communists to conquer the eastern parts of Serbia and Macedonia. On the same day, Yugoslavia announced the capture of the city and seaport of Split, Dalmatia, by Tito's partisan forces.

After the withdrawal of the German troops on November 1, 1944, from Florina (Phlorina) and Salonika (Thessaloniki), Greece, only German rear guard remained south of the Yugoslavia border. On November 1, 1944, Tito and Šubašić concluded an agreement for establishing a joint democratic government under a regency that would be appointed to act until a plebiscite could be held. The part of the Agreement which concerned specifically the Elections for the Constituent Assembly, reads in part as follows: "Elections for the Constituent Assembly will be decided upon within three months of the liberation of Yugoslavia. The elections will be held in accordance with the Law on Elections for the Constituent Assembly which will be enacted in good time. This law will guarantee complete freedom of election, freedom of assembly and speech, liberty of the press, franchise for all and a secret ballot, as well as the right of independent or united political parties, cooperations, groups or individuals - who have not collaborated with the enemy - to present lists of candidates for the elections. All those whose collaboration with the enemy will have been proved, will be deprived of both the right to elect and to be elected. The new government will publish a declaration proclaiming the fundamental principles of democratic liberties and guaranteeing the application. Personal freedom, freedom from fear, freedom of worship, liberty of conscience, freedom of speech, freedom of the press, freedom of assembly and association will be specially emphasized and guaranteed; and in the same way the right of property and private initiative." Again, Tito lied professionally.

During the early morning of November 2, 1944, the communist partisans entered the Dalmatian city and seaport of Zadar without firing a single shot; because during the nights of November 1 and 2, 1944, the small German garrison quietly and unceremoniously abandoned the town without being forced out by Tito's communist partisans. There were no welcome civilian committees or ceremonial greeting parties. A tall-slim soldier was the only known German noncommissioned officer and catholic priest, left behind who sought refuge to prevent being captured and executed by the communists.

The city of Šibenik, on the Dalmatian coast, fell to the communist partisans on November 4, 1944. Kumanovo, a town in Macedonia on the Skopje-Niš railway line, on November 12, 1944, was occupied by communist partisans. On November 14, 1944, communist partisans announced the fall of the city of Skopje, a staging point for the German troops withdrawal from Greece.

On November 26, 1944, Tito authorized Allied naval and air force personnel to temporarily use certain ports and airfields inside Yugoslavia. The valley south of the village of Skabrnje and north of Nadinsko Mud (Blato) was used during 1944-45 as a staging area "emergency airport" for USA and British military aircraft in bombing missions over eastern European targets.

Forces of the Third Ukrainian Front, November 29, 1944, joined in offensive to the left flank of Second Ukrainian Front and, in conjunction with Yugoslav partisans, crossed the Danube river near the Yugoslav-Hungarian frontier south of Budapest and advanced toward Lake Balaton, Hungary, north of the Drava River. The cities of Mohacs and Pecs in south Hungary were no longer under German occupation. On December 5, 1944, the Third Ukrainian Front progressed rapidly in the center of Hungary, where forward elements reached Lake Balaton; left flank elements driving along the north bank of the Drava River overran Szigetvar, west of Pecs. In northeastern Croatia, on December 10, 1944, the Soviet and Yugoslav communist partisans advanced toward Vinkovci, and penetrated into Vukovar, on the Danube River.

Every nation at war shares some blame for crimes committed against humanity. The Croatian people were victims of circumstances and cannot be blamed for all the horrible tragedies of war. Those who find comfort in describing the Croatians as fascists or nazis because some of them fought on the side of the Axis, then the people of Belgium, Bulgaria, Denmark, Finland, France, Greece, Hungary, Norway, Romania, Serbia, Slovakia, etc., should be classified as fascists or nazis. To apply the above maligned logic, the people of those nations that were allied with Stalin's communist tyranny (responsible for exterminating at least 10 million people) should be characterized as communists. The moral of the story is - think, get the facts, analyze, don't muddy the waters, and leave the Croatians alone.

CHAPTER 5

COMMUNIST YUGOSLAVIA, 1945 - 1990

The Socialist Republic of Croatia (1945-1990) was a patchwork of one of the six constituent republics which comprised the former Socialist Federal Republic of Yugoslavia - SFRY (Socijalisticka Federativna Republika Jugoslavija - SFRJ), better known as "Communist Yugoslavia."

To thwart annihilation, the Germans decided to continue fighting with all their power against communist forces and strategically withdrew their military troops. Heavy fighting continued on January 14, 1945, along the banks of the Danube River in the city of Budapest, Hungary, with German garrisons slowly giving up territory. Meanwhile, the Germans were steadily but slowly withdrawing troops from Yugoslavia.

On January 20, 1945, the Provisional National Government of Hungary signed an armistice agreement in Moscow with England, USA, and USSR. Early in March 1945, the government of Democratic Federal Yugoslavia was formed in Belgrade, with Marshal Tito as Premier of Yugoslavia.

During the "Yalta Conference" held at Yalta in the peninsula of Crimea (Ukraine) from February 4 to 11, 1945, U.S. President Roosevelt, British Premier Churchill, and Soviet Chairman Stalin issued a communiqué with specific provisions concerning Yugoslavia that, (a) the agreement made between Marshal Tito and Ivan Šubašić be put into effect immediately; (b) the new government be formed on the basis of that Agreement; (c) the Anti-Fascist Assembly of National Liberation be extended to include members of the last Yugoslav Parliament, those forming the body to be known as a Temporary Parliament; and (d) legislative acts passed by the Anti-Fascist Assembly of National Liberation will be subject to subsequent ratification by a Constituent Assembly. In addition to these specific stipulations concerning post-war Yugoslavia, there was a paragraph in the communiqué of the Yalta Conference entitled, "Declaration on Liberated Europe" where the principle of the Atlantic Charter of August 12, 1941, the right of all peoples to choose the form of government under which they will live, were reaffirmed. At the Yalta Conference, Stalin achieved great success. Unfortunately, President Roosevelt and Premier Churchill were outsmarted, outmaneuvered, and manipulated by their friendly communist counterpart. During the discussions, Stalin got most of his wishes realized whereby the postwar Europe would be divided into two geopolitical influences - Eastern and Western Europe. To prevent Germany's possible resurgence, the three Allied leaders agreed to punish, divide, occupy, and place the territory of Germany under Allied administrations. France did not take part at the Yalta Conference or later at Potsdam in July 1945, but the United States and Britain suggested that France be made full partner of Allied occupation forces. Stalin agreed to give France a piece of German territory, provided their portion was taken from that part designated to western zones. Also, the city of Berlin (formerly the capital of Germany) was divided among the four occupation forces.

Concerning the Far East, Japanese territory was placed under United States administration. The islands off the western coast of Russia, the Kurile and southern part of Sakhalin, was placed under the Soviet Union. The Korea Peninsula was divided in two areas, along the 38th parallel, northern territory under the Soviet Union and southern under the United States. Because President Roosevelt feared a possible French and British ambitious goal and colonial influence in the Pacific territories.

With the conclusion of the Second World War, most of the colonial possessions, including those of the two victorious military powers such as France and Britain, proceeded toward their dismantlements. Conversely, the Soviet Union in typical communist action of the proletariat, ruthlessly and systematically annexed the eastern half of Poland and northeastern Prussia. Subsequently, the Soviet Union occupied Eastern Europe which included Eastern Germany where Stalin set up his communist tyranny by proxy.

Not surprising, the fundamental principles of democratic liberties mentioned in the Agreement of November 1, 1944 between Tito and Šubašić were completely ignored by communist Tito. In conformity with communist principles, there was no such right as personal freedom, freedom from fear and liberty of conscience under a regime where a state political police known as the Department for the Protection of the People (Odeljenje zaštite naroda, OZN-a) aimed incessantly to destroy the so-called reactionaries and anti-communist elements. There was no freedom of the press, as the press was entirely under government control, and even the few owned by foreign citizens received equal treatment by being put under the control of Yugoslav government authorities. The entire Yugoslav communist administration had been taken over by the National Liberation Committees. These committees were organized for the cities as well as for the smallest communities and villages which in turn elected among themselves representatives for the county Liberation Committee and from there on for the district and the provincial Liberation Committee, exactly according to the pattern of elections practiced in the USSR.

Early in 1945, the Montenegrin četnici, under the command of Pavle Đurišić, decided to escape and marched northward, but after they had lost contact with the main forces of Mihajlović they entered the area controlled by Croatian ustaše, consequently the četnici were destroyed by the ustaše near Lijevče Polje, between the Vrbas and Sava Rivers, in northern Bosnia.

The island of Iwo Jima, located in the Western Pacific, 775 mi./1,247 km south of Tokyo, Japan, heavily fortified and strongly defended by a garrison of 22,000 Japanese soldiers, was the scene of one of the bitter campaigns during the Second World War. Subjected to constant heavy bombing by U.S. naval and airforce beginning December 1944, thru January and February 1945, the U.S. 5th Amphibious Corps landed on February 19, 1945. The U.S. 4th and 5th Marine Divisions (the 3rd Marine Division in reserve) landed on the southern coast of the island, and were compelled to fight with great intensity a battle which was highlighted by members of the 5th Marine Division raising the U.S. flag on the top of Mount Suribachi at 0930 on March 14, 1945. Motoyama airfields was taken February 26, and the island was declared secure at 1800 hours on March 16, although pockets of Japanese resistance (confined to a small area on the northern coast of the island) continued until March 26, 1945. The Japanese commander, Gen. Tadamichi Kuribayachi, while hiding inside a cave, committed ritual hiri kiri suicide. The Iwo Jima victory provided the U.S. an air base for operations against the Japanese forces in the Pacific.

Three Regents, all being Tito's candidates, were appointed on March 2, 1945 to the Regency Council which was composed of Srđan Budisavljević, a Serb, former member of the Independent Democratic Party; Ante Mandić, a Croat, former member of the Croatian Peasant Party; and Dušan Sernec, a Slovene and former member of the Slovenian Popular Party.

In a move designed to appease the Western public opinions, on March 7, 1945, the wartime partisan leader Josip Broz, alias Tito, formed a provisional government which consisted of representatives from Antifascist Council for the National Liberation of Yugoslavia-ACNLY (Antifašističko vijeće narodnog oslobodjenja Jugoslavije-AVNOJ) and three members of the royalist government-in-exile, thus giving the appearance that Yugoslavia was some type of socialist democracy. The Regency Council appointed a new government, headed by Marshal Tito, as proposed by the Presidium of the AVNOJ. This was the first and the last act of the Regency Council. The new government was composed of twenty-eight ministers, the great majority of them being Tito's partisans. Only five ministers did not belong to the National Liberation Movement. Tito's Communists had absolute control of the government; the seizure of power by the Communist Party of Yugoslavia was acheived. The Premier and Minister of National Defense, Tito broadcast from Belgrade a declaration of the policy which the government of Federal Democratic Yugoslavia would follow: "the new government will try to rally all those not compromised by collaboration with the invader and their servants."

The situation in Yugoslavia since the formation of the new tyrannical government had rapidly deteriorated, measured by any standards commonly used in the civilized Western Hemisphere. It was common knowledge that in communist Yugoslavia not one of the freedom guarantees was carried out. Accordingly, Tito's communist government of Yugoslavia became the copycat of the previous Yugoslav government under the Serbian Karadordević monarchy, both were a farce and a mockery. Communist committees exercised full power in matters concerning the administration. They also had full powers in handling juridical cases and sat as a tribunal and pronounced decrees and regulations entrusted usually to a legislative body. The National Liberation Committees acting as courts of justice did not apply the civil code or the criminal code. Those laws had been out of force by the Central Committee of National Liberation. They passed their judgement "according to their communist conscience." The prevailing conditions could hardly be called conditions of internal peace, as the action of these committees were mainly aimed at breaking down any resistance to the newly introduced communist organization. Everyone who was not in "line" with communist policy was considered a reactionary; their resistance had to be broken or suffer the consequences.

It was evident that the communist administrative organization could hardly carry out any emergency measures for relief because all economic assistance had to be arranged by the new administration who purposely discriminated in favor of communist party members. The communist apparatus had even established three kinds of ration cards: one for partisans, another for pre-communists, and the third for the ordinary people. The amount of rationing was determined by the status, the partisans received three times as much as other citizens. Urgent projects for solving relief problems could not be fulfilled for lack of organization.

Some elements of the Third Ukrainian Front (parts of the Soviet Red Army), on March 30, 1945, advanced into Austria from the vicinity of the town of Koeszeg, Hungary, while other units gained territory west of Lake Balaton; still others assisted by Bulgarian troops, thrust southward from Lake Balaton to the Drava River along the border of Hungary and Yugoslavia. On April 3, 1945, troops of the Second Ukrainian Front continued west toward Vienna, Austria; those north of the Danube in Czechoslovakia occupied the eastern suburb of Bratislava, and those to the left overran Kremnica with the support of Romanian troops; elements south of the Danube crossed the Austro-Hungarian border south of Bratislava. Troops of the Third Ukrainian Front in Austria, on April 3, 1945, overran the important industrial center of Wiener Neustadt and controlled the roads and railway lines connecting Wiener

171

Neustadt with Vienna. Left flank elements of the Third Ukrainian Front and Bulgarian troops continued clearing the area southwest of Lake Balaton in Hungary; and the forward units crossed the Hungarian-Yugoslav border.

In the British Eighth Army's 13 Corps area, the New Zealand's 2d Division occupied Padova (Padua) April 29, advanced northward, reaching the Piave River, the 56th Division of the 5th Corps occupied Venezia (Venice). On April 31, 1945, the 2d Corps was reinforced by the 85th Division. The 91st Division advanced toward Treviso, north of Venice. This ended the eastward drive of the 2nd Corps. New Zealand 2d Division crossed the Piave River and continued to the town of Portogruaro, on route to Trieste, Italy. Pursuing forces of the 6th Armed Division established contact with U.S. forces at Treviso and thrust toward Belluno and Udine in Italy.

To prevent being captured by Allied armies, Mussolini tried to escape to Switzerland. On April 28, 1945, Mussolini and his mistress Clara Petacci (1912-1945), were captured by partisans at Dongo, executed, and then hanged up-side-down. Adolf Hitler (1889-1945) and his wife Eva Braun Hitler (1910-1945) committed suicide on April 30, 1945. However, before his death, Hitler designated Admiral Karl Dönitz (1891-1980) as his successor.

In the closing days of the war, the U.S. 7th Army crossed the Danube river on April 22; captured the city of Munich, Germany, on April 30; Innsbruck, Austria, on May 3; and Salzburg, Austria, on May 4, 1945. The U.S. 3rd Army operating in southern Germany, at the left flank of the U.S. 7th Army, advanced southeastern and captured Karlsbad, Germany, and the armament center of Pilsen, Czechoslovakia.

In the Italian theater, the New Zealand 2nd Division and the U.S. 5th Army converged toward Trieste; after occupying Monfalcone, made contact with Yugoslav communist units and proceeded until they reached Trieste and Gorizia on May 2, 1945. After brief negotiations, German forces in northern Italy agreed to the Allied terms of unconditional surrender on May 2, 1945.

* * * * *

~ Memorandum from Grew to Truman ~

Washington, May 1, 1945

To: The U.S. President, Harry S.Truman

From: U.S. Acting Secretary of State

In March the Italian Ambassador asked President Roosevelt and the Secretary of State what would be the attitude of this government toward an Italian declaration of war upon Japan. In arriving at a decision on this question the Department sought the views of the War and Navy

Departments through the State-War-Navy Coordinating Committee. The views of the State, War and Navy Depts., as well as those of the Joint Chiefs of Staff, may be summarized as follows:

From the political point of view, the participation of Italy in the war against Japan along with the United States would further identify Italy with the United Nations and the victorious powers. The prestige of the present Italian Government would thus be strengthened and increased support for it acquired in Italy at a time when the North of Italy is being liberated and when the Government in Rome will require the greatest possible stability. Italy is trying to "work her passage" back to a respectable place in the family of nations. It has been given an opportunity to do this through its contribution to the war against Germany. Participation in the war in the Far East after the defeat of Germany will give the Italian Government and people an increased and prolonged opportunity to contribute to the common war aims of the United Nations and to increase Italy's chances for an early and more secure place among them.

For political reasons it is recommended that the Italian Government should be informed that the United States Government would welcome an Italian declaration of war against Japan but that such action involves no commitments with respect to Allied resources or shipping. It is further recommended that the United States Government obtain the concurrence of the British and Soviet Governments to this policy before replying to the inquiry of the Italian Government.

If you concur with these recommendations, I will instruct our Ambassadors in London and Moscow to inform their Governments accredited of our position and to ask for assurances from the British and Soviet Governments that such a reply to the Italian Government would not be contrary to their views on this subject.

Signed: Joseph C. Grew

* * * * *

On May 6, 1945, members of the Croatian government entourage departed from Zagreb, followed by tens of thousands of Croatian soldiers accompanied by members of their families to seek protection of western military occupation armies in Austria. Anti-communist forces, comprising Croatian Ustaše, Slovenian Home Guards (Domobranci) of Gen. Leon Rupnik, and Serbian nationalists of Dimitri Ljotić (Zbor Movement), Gen. Milan Nedić's četnici, retreated toward Austria which was occupied by British forces. Upon their arrival in the province of Carinthia, Austria, they were met by British occupation army. No longer having means of defense, the Croatian soldiers immediately lay down their arms and surrendered to the British military authority, thus considering themselves prisoners of war (POWs). Meanwhile, thousands of civilian refugees arrived daily, humbly requesting humanitarian consideration and political protection. The British military authorities kept the POWs and refugees under confinement near the village of Bleiburg in southern Austria under the pretense of conducting the necessary screening and processing before transferring them to Palmanova, Italy. In reality, this tactical procrastination was an unequivocal British betrayal

173

in order to postpone any decision until Tito's communist units arrived inside Austria. In the meantime, a significant number of POWs and refugees succeeded in avoiding death by fleeing, to Germany, Italy, and other western countries.

Envoys of the German Government arrived pre-announced at the Headquarters of Gen. Eisenhower, Commander of Allied Forces in Western Europe located at Reims (on the Vesle river 80 mi./130 km NE of Paris, France), to discuss terms of surrender. After communicating and receiving authorization from Karl Dönitz, Germany agreed to capitulate to the Allied demand of unconditional surrender. The Instrument of Surrender was concluded at 0240 French time on May 7, 1945, (with hostilities to cease at midnight on May 8), and signed by Gen. Wilhelm Jodl, Chief of Staff of the German Army, representing the Reich; Gen. Walter Bedell Smith, Eisenhower's Chief of Staff, representing the Supreme Allied Command; Gen. Francois Sevez, representing France; and Gen. Ivan Susloparov, representing the Soviet Union. At insistance of Stalin, copy-cat of Mussolini's dual ceremonial of Greece's unconditional surrender in 1941 to the Axis Force, on May 8, 1945 at 1100 hours the second signing of German capitulation was formally reinacted in Berlin, Germany, officially ending the war in Europe, V-E Day (Victory - in - Europe). The Instrument of Surrender was signed in Berlin by: Gen. Wilhelm Keitel, Chief of the High Command, and Adm. Hans G. Friederburg, Chief of the Navy and Paul Stumpf, Chief of the Air Force, representing the Reich; Marshal Arthur Tedder, Deputy Supreme Commander of Allied Forces in Western Europe, representing the USA; and Marshal Gregori K. Zhukov, Commander of the First White Russian Army, representing the USSR. Signatures were witnessed by Gen. Carl Spaatz, Commander of U.S. Strategic Air Force; and Gen. Jean de Lattre de Tassigny, French First Army Commander. Hostilities in all battlefields ceased except along northern Yugoslavia, central Austria, and Czechoslovakia where German units were unwilling to desist fighting. Although Germany officially surrendered to the Allies on May 8, 1945, fighting in Yugoslavia continued until the 15th of May, because the German Balkan Group kept their fighting spirit and refused to lay down their arms.

Alexander C. Kirk, Political Advisor to the SACMED Theater in Caserta , Italy, transmitted a telegram dated May 9, 1945 to the U.S. Secretary of State stating: "At this morning's conference in the Supreme Allied Commander (SAC), Mediterranean Theater office to discuss Gen. Frederick E. Morgan's report, SAC was vehement in his determination not to make any further concessions to Tito, and at the end of the meeting Morgan had lost all patience with the Yugoslav dictator and was ready to drive him and his forces out of Venezia Giulia if he could get Washington and London to Agree."

On May 16, 1945 the occasion of suffering began when the bloodthirsty Yugoslav communists reached the fields of Bleiburg, Austria, and in cahoots with their British comrades-in-arms carried out the final solution of the Croatian people. Unceremoniously, contrary to civility and international laws, the barbarous and unscrupulous British military authorities extradited en masse hundreds of thousands of anti-communist soldiers and civilians without any distinction as to who had or had not collaborated with the Axis forces, and who had legitimate claims as civilian refugees (non-combatants such as children, expectant mothers, wounded and sick, and elderly citizens), they were transferred to the communist henchmen of Tito's Yugoslavia who were eagerly awaiting implementation of the most massive slaughter perpetrated against Croatians. The survivors were transported from Austria to Yugoslavia in secured military vehicles and railway box-cars. The extradited people were anti-communist, soldiers, and civilians who were liquidated without any trial. Henceforth, inside the Yugoslav communist territory, the prisoners were divided into separate columns and compelled to move by endless "death marches." Commencing at Maribor and after unscheduled interruptions, additional executions were carried out, the prisoners continued their death march until the "final solution" was consummated, which undoubtedly met with prior approval of the British government. Croatia shall remember the Bleiburg-Maribor massacres.

The May 1945 commemoration of V-E Day (Victory-in-Europe), unlike most other nations to whom freedom and democracy were restored, signified for Croatia the arrival of the Marxist-Leninist totalitarian regime, a new beginning of persecution, imprisonment, and the execution of innocent people merely because they were not communists.

The first man-made atomic bomb was detonated successfully at 0530 on July 16, 1945 from the top of a 100 ft/30.5 m steel tower at the Trinity site northwest of Alamogordo, located in south central New Mexico, northeast of White Sands National Monument and Holloman Air Force Base. A team of cryptanalysts of the U.S. Army Signal Intelligence Service, a forerunner of the National Security Agency (NSA), in 1944 under code name "Venona" intercepted and decoded communiques that provided evidences that a Soviet espionage ring, between Moscow and its KGB operatives in Washington, D.C. and New York, had stolen "top secret" blueprints from the United States to build the atomic bomb. Code name "Enormous" was assigned by the Soviet Union for the Manhattan Project established on August 13, 1942.

The Potsdam Conference held from July 16 to August 2, 1945, attended by representatives of the USA, Britain, and the Soviet Union was called to draw up terms for the Japanese surrender and to discuss military and political issues connected with the termination of hostilities. On July 26, the Allies issued an ultimatum, calling for Japan to surrender unconditionally or face "utter destruction." On July 30, Japan rejected the Potsdam ultimatum. Gen. George C. Marshall, in behalf of the Joint Chiefs of Staff, directed Generals Douglas MacArthur and Albert C. Wedemeyer and Adm. Chester W. Nimitz to coordinate plans for Japan's surrender.

On June 18, 1945, Tito, accompanied by the Soviet Ambassador to Yugoslavia, visited several towns in Serbia. In the town of Mladenovac, Tito stated, "Our country is faced with great difficulties. First the greater part of our most able brothers and sisters are still serving in the armed forces. We cannot send them home yet because they must keep guard." Further, he continued, "The USSR, headed by the great leader Stalin gave us moral and material support and is still giving it today in full measure so that we can be assured that we shall carry out our duty in completely settling and reconstructing our country." No mention had been made throughout the speech of any help distributed during or after the war from Western Allies. Tito continued further to admit the unfavorable results of his proletarian communist administration by telling, "Our Federal Democratic Yugoslavia has not yet been able to give anything to the people, not because it did not wish to do so, but because it has not yet had time, and because it has not yet been able to do so." By factual accounts, simply stated: the communist system is the cause of social economic disaster.

The United Nations (UN) Charter was signed in San Francisco, CA on June 26, 1945, and came into effect on October 24, 1945. The purpose of the United Nations is (a) maintain international peace and security, take effective collective measures for the prevention and removal of threats to the peace, and suppress acts of aggression; (b) develop friendly relations among nations based on the principle of equal rights and self-determination; and (c) achieve cooperation in solving international problems of an economic, social, cultural, or humanitarian character, and in promoting and encouraging human rights and freedoms for all regardless of race, sex, age, language, or religion. On July 28, 1945, the U.S. Senate ratified the United Nations Charter by an overwhelming vote of 89 to 2.

Winston S. Churchill (1874-1965), Premier of Britain (1940-1945) guided Britain to victory during the Second World War. But, British election in July 1945 resulted in Churchill's defeat, and Clement Richard Attlee (1883-1967), leader of the Labor Party became British Premier (1945-1951), replacing Churchill at the Potsdam Conference. Hitler and Mussolini were unable to defeat Churchill, but the British people did not think that Churchill was a hero because they defeated him at the ballot boxes. It must have been a humiliating defeat imposed by the people of Britain against Churchill, but in 1951, he was re-elected as Premier, and served until 1955.

A lone B-29 Superfortress aircraft of the 509th Composite Group U.S. Air Force, named the "Enola Gay" (named for the pilot's mother), piloted by Col. Paul W. Tibbets, Jr. took off from the Tinian airbase on Tinian Island (Marianna Islands), and on Monday at 9:15 a.m. August 6, 1945 the first atomic bomb (the power of approximately 20,000 tons of Trinitrotoluene-TNT) was dropped on the city of Hiroshima, Japan. Aerial photography showed that the bomb destroyed an area of more than 4 mi^2/10 km^2 of Hiroshima. Subsequently, reports confirmed that approximately 75,000 persons were killed or died later from the effect of radiation.

Taking advantage of dictating the conditions of the peace treaty, on August 8, 1945, (agreed at Yalta on February 11, 1945 by the Three Big Powers), the Soviet Union declared war on Japan, effective on August 9 Soviet troops invaded the Kurile island, Manchuria, and moved into northern Korea.

President Truman warned the Japanese that the use of the first atomic bomb on Hiroshima was "a warning" and that the United States would drop more bombs unless Japan surrendered unconditionally. As promised, a second bomb was dropped this time on Nagasaki, Japan, on August 9, 1945, killing 40,000 persons and destroying 30 percent of the city's industrial area, including the Mitsubishi steel and iron works. The dropping of two atomic bombs caused Japan to request on August 14, 1945, their unconditional surrender. On the same day, President Truman appointed General of the Army Douglas MacArthur (1880-1964) as the Supreme Commander for the Allied Forces in Asia. The Protocol of Surrender was officially signed on September 2, 1945, aboard the battleship "U.S.S. Missouri" anchored in Tokyo Bay. Foreign Minister Shigemitsu Mamoru and Gen. Umezu Yoshijiro signed for the Japanese Imperial government. Gen. Douglas MacArthur signed for the Allied Powers, officially ending the war in Asia, V-J Day (Victory-over-Japan).

The end of the Second World War created a post war chaos in Yugoslavia, and with the absence of an organized democratic political opposition, enabled Tito's communists to consolidate their position and establish an undisputed control over Yugoslavia. The third session of the AVNOJ was held at Belgrade on August 7, 1945, its membership was increased to comprise thirty-six members of prewar Assembly and seventy members of prewar political parties. The AVNOJ, as the People's Provisional Assembly (Privremena narodna skupstina), enacted legislation for the convocation of a Constituent Assembly, electoral eligibility, and agricultural land reforms. Under electoral law all citizens over eighteen years of age and all members of the armed forces were eligible to vote. Considerable number of persons regarded as former collaborators with the enemy, or were unfriendly to communist ideas, or were of questionable political preference, were not eligible to vote. Land reform was implemented by liquidating large estates, land holdings in excess of twenty-five acres by religious and other institutions, and properties held by collaborators.

To conceal the communist intentions, Tito assigned Edvard Kardelj, the leading theoretician of Yugoslav communism, to conduct the campaign for the November 1945 elections and to keep deceiving the Western Allies. The communists promoted themselves as the National Liberation Front and not as the Communist Party. The word "communism" was never used during the national election. Under strong communist control the People's Front (Narodni Front) organized a nationwide political gimmick to enhance the appeal for a sure victory, and to eliminate foreseeable anti-communist opposition. As expected, the anti-communist resistance was not a factor in the outcome since they did not participate in the election. Voters were offered a long list consisting only of faithful candidates of the People's Front, who were approved in advance by the Communist Party. The outcome of the election was an overwhelming victory for Tito and his conspirators.

The proposal made by the U.S. government on November 10, 1945 to recognize the Albanian regime headed by Gen. Enver Hoxha specified as a condition that the Albanian authorities affirm the continuing validity of all treaties and agreements in force between the United States and Albania as of April 7, 1939, the date of the Italian invasion of Albania. The requirement of such an assurance from the Albanian regime as a prerequisite to United States recognition was in accord with the established practice of the U.S. government to extend recognition only to those governments which had expressed a willingness to fulfill their international obligations. The Albanian regime on August 13, 1946 indicated its acceptance of the multilateral treaties and agreements to which both the United States and Albania were parties, but it failed to affirm its recognition of the validity of bilateral instruments between the United States and Albania. In view of the continued unwillingness of the Albanian regime to assume these bilateral commitments and obligations, which were in no instance of an onerous character and concern such customary subjects as arbitration and conciliation, naturalization, extradition, and most-favored-nation treatment, the U.S. government concluded that the American Mission can no longer serve any useful purpose by remaining in Albania. This decision was made to notify Gen. Hoxha in a letter of November 5, 1946 by the Acting American Representative in Tirana, George D. Henderson. Therefore, the American Mission to Albania was withdrawn.

The International Military Tribunal-IMT (a.k.a. Nuremberg War Trial) was established pursuant to the London Charter signed on August 8, 1945 by representatives of USA, Britain, France, and USSR, and adhered by nineteen other nations: Australia, Belgium, Czechoslovakia, Denmark, Ethiopia, Greece, Haiti, Honduras, India, Luxembourg, Netherlands, New Zealand, Norway, Panama, Paraguay, Poland, Uruguay, Venezuela, and Yugoslavia. On October 18, 1945, the four prosecutors filed an indictment against 24 German citizens and six German organizations. The IMT held in Nuremberg (Nürnberg), Germany, lasted ten months, convened on November 20, 1945 and ended on October 1, 1946. The war crimes prosecution relating to the Second World War in the European theater, counterpart of the second IMT held in Tokyo, Japan, indicted 24 leading political and military officials of pre-war and wartime German government. The most famous Nazi leaders, Adolf Hitler (1885-1945), Josef Paul Goebbels (1897-1945), and Heinrich Himmler (1900-1945) were not indicted, tried, nor sentenced as they had all committed suicide in the closing days of the war. Sitting in judgment on the IMT bench were four judges, each representing one of the four aggrieved nations: USA, Britain, France, and USSR. The presiding judge was Geoffrey Lawrence, the British member of the IMT. The IMT was conducted in four languages: English, German, French, and Russian. The charges against the defendants fell into four counts: (1) Conspiracy; (2) Crimes Against Peace; (3) War Crimes; and (4) Crimes Against Humanity. Of the 24 persons indicted, 22 were tried, including Bormann in absentia, formally pronounced dead by a German court in April 1973; Göring committed suicide on October 15, 1946, by biting on a vial of poison before the verdict; Krupp was declared unfit to stand trial due to his physical and mental conditions; and Ley committed suicide in prison on October 25, 1945. All defendants, except Bormann and Ley who were not present, pleaded "not guilty." In accordance with Article 27 of the London Charter, the President of the IMT, at its concluding session of October 1, 1946, pronounced the verdict: twelve were condemned to death by hanging (executed on October 15, 1946); three were sentenced to life imprisonment; four sentenced to lesser prison terms; and three were acquitted. For the final adjudications, see below:

The Defendants	YOB - YOD	Sentences
Bormann, Martin	(1900-1973)	Death by hanging
Dönitz, Karl	(1891-1980)	10 yrs. imprisonment
Frank, Hans	(1900-1946)	Death by hanging
Frick, Wilhelm	(1877-1946)	Death by hanging
Fritzsche, Hans	(1900-1953)	Acquitted
Funk, Walter	(1890-1960)	Life imprisonment
Göring, Herman Wilhelm	(1893-1946)	Death by hanging
Hess, Rudolf Walter Richard	(1894-1992)	Life imprisonment
Jodl, Alfred	(1890-1947)	Death by hanging
Kaltenbrunner, Ernst	(1903-1946)	Death by hanging

Keitel, Wilhelm	(1882-1946)	Death by hanging
Krupp, Alfreid von Bohden	(1907-1967)	Unfit to stand trial
Ley, Robert	(1890-1945)	Strangled himself
Neurath, Konstantin von	(1873-1956)	15 yrs. Imprisonment
Papen, Franz von	(1879-1969)	Acquitted
Raeder, Erich	(1876-1960)	Life Imprisonment
Ribbentrop, Joachim von	(1893-1946)	Death by hanging
Rosenberg, Alfred	(1893-1946)	Death by hanging
Sauckel, Fritz	(1894-1946)	Death by hanging
Schacht, Hjalmar	(1877-1970)	Acquitted
Schirach, Baldur von	(1907-1974)	20 yrs. imprisonment
Seyss-Inquart, Arthur	(1892-1946)	Death by hanging
Speer, Albert	(1905-1981)	20 yrs. Imprisonment
Streicher, Julius	(1885-1946)	Death by hanging

Based on the indictment, the following four elements of the Third Reich were declared criminal organizations: the Nazi Party Leadership Corps; Schutzstaffeln (SS), or elite guard; Sicherheitsdienst (SD), or security service; and the Geheime Staatspolizei (Gestapo), or secret state police. However, the IMT refrained from declaring guilty the following elements considered to be legitimate and not criminal organizations: Reich Cabinet (Die Reichsregierung); Sturm-Abteilungen (SA), or Storm-trooper (Brown Shirt); and the German High Command of the German Armed Forces (Oberkommando der Wehrmacht). Between December 1946 and March 1949, approximately 190 other German political, military, and civilian individuals - government ministers; jurists; ambassadors; physicians; army and airforce generals, and navy admirals; industrialists; etc. - were indicted and tried at Nuremberg by 12 diffirent tribunals, presided by United States judges. The final report revealed that four defendants were declared too ill to stand trial, and four others committed suicide. Of the 182 remaining, 25 were condemned to death, 21 were sentenced to life imprisonment, 99 sentenced to lesser prison terms, and 37 found not guilty. In many countries national tribunals tried war criminals, military or civilian, for war crimes during the Second World War.

Elections for the FPRY Constituent Assembly were held on November 11, 1945, candidates of the National Front (Communist Group) received an overwhelming majority of the votes. At its first session held on November 29, 1945, the Constituent Assembly abolished the Serbian Karađorđević monarchy and approved a new communist state "Federativna Narodna Republika Jugoslavija-FNRJ" (Federal People's Republic of Yugoslavia-FPRY).

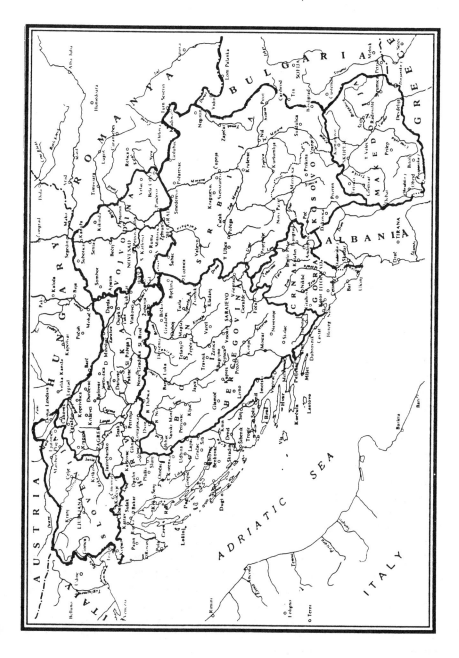

Based on the Yugoslav Constitution of 1946 the supreme state authority was the People's Assembly of the FPRY which comprised of representatives from six constituent republics: Bosnia-Herzegovina, Croatia, Macedonia, Montenegro, Serbia, and Slovenia, and two autonomous provinces, both included in the republic of Serbia. On January 31, 1946, the Assembly unanimously approved the first postwar Yugoslav Constitution patterned to the principles as those formulated in the Constitution of the Soviet Union dated December 5, 1936. Despite repeated assurances that Yugoslavia was not a communist state, Tito kept restructuring his regime along the same lines as those of his patron Stalin.

Tito's Yugoslav government was a national political organization under Tito's Yugoslav communist party. The theory of people's government was just a smoke screen used by Marxist proletarians to maintain a dictatorship of the communist party. On March 24, 1946, Aleksandar Ranković, Yugoslav Minister of Interior (Head of the Communist Secret police), announced to the Yugoslav People's Assembly in session that General Dragoljub Mihajlović, leader of Serb-četnici, was captured on March 10, 1946. Mihajlović was put on trial for collaborating with Axis forces, condemned to death as a traitor and executed by firing squad on July 17, 1946. Soon after the trial of Mihajlović ended, his defense attorney Dragić Jokšimović was imprisoned as a "people's enemy" and sentenced to three years in jail. Jokšimović died of unknown causes while serving his sentence.

The International Military Tribunal (IMT) for the Far East was established on January 19, 1946, by General of the Army Douglas MacArthur, Supreme Commander of the Allied Power (SCAP) in Japan. The IMT held in Tokyo, lasted two and one-half years, convened on May 3, 1946, and delivered its judgement on November 21, 1948. The war crimes prosecution relating to the Second World War in East Asia, Indian Ocean, and the Pacific theaters, counterpart of the first IMT held in Nuremberg (Nürnberg), Germany, indicted 28 leading political and military officials of pre-war and wartime Japanese government. Sitting in judgment on the IMT bench were eleven judges, each representing one of the eleven aggrieved nations: Australia, Britain, Canada, China, France, India, Netherlands, New Zealand, Philippines, USA, and USSR. The presiding judge was William Webb, the Australian member of the IMT. The charges against the defendants fell into four counts: (1) conspiracy; (2) crimes against peace; (3) war crimes; and (4) crimes against humanity. Of the 28 persons indicted, 25 were tried and found guilty, two defendants died during the trial, and one was declared unfit to stand trial due to his health conditions. The verdict of those defendants found guilty was: seven were condemned to death by hanging; 16 were sentenced to life imprisonment; one sentenced to 20 years in prison, and another to seven years in prison. For the final adjudications, see below:

The Defendants	YOB - YOD	Sentence
Araki, Sadao	(1877-1966)	Life imprisonment
Doihara, Kenji	(1883-1948)	Death by hanging
Hashimoto, Kingorō	(1890-1957)	Life imprisonment
Hata, Shunroku	(1879-1962)	Life imprisonment
Hiranuma, Kiichirō	(1867-1952)	Life imprisonment
Hirota, Kōki	(1878-1948)	Death by hanging
Hoshino, Naoki	(1892-1978)	Life imprisonment
Itagaki, Seishirō	(1885-1948)	Death by hanging
Kaya, Okinori	(1889-1977)	Life imprisonment
Kido, Kōichi	(1889-1977)	Life imprisonment
Kimura, Heitarō	(1888-1948)	Death by hanging
Koiso, Kuniaki	(1880-1950)	Life imprisonment
Matsui, Iwane	(1878-1948)	Death by hanging
Matsuoka, Yōsuke	(1880-1946)	Died during trial
Minami, Jirō	(1874-1955)	Life imprisonment
Mutō, Akira	(1892-1948)	Death by hanging
Nagano, Osami	(1880-1947)	Died during trial
Oka, Takasumi	(1890-1973)	Life imprisonment
Ōkawa, Shūmei	(1886-1957)	Unfit to stand trial
Ōshima, Hiroshi	(1886-1975)	Life imprisonment
Satō, Kenryō	(1895-1975)	Life imprisonment
Shigemitsu, Mamoru	(1887-1957)	7 yrs. Imprisonment
Shimada, Shigetarō	(1883-1976)	Life imprisonment
Shiratori, Toshio	(1887-1949)	Life imprisonment
Suzuki, Teiichi	(1888-1989)	Life imprisonment
Tōgō, Shigenori	(1882-1950)	20 yrs. Imprisonment
Tōjō, Hideki	(1884-1948)	Death by hanging
Umezu, Yoshijirō	(1882-1949)	Life imprisonment

In addition to the major Japanese trial, the Allies conducted several thousand minor trials. Of approximately 6,000 Japanese accused of alleged atrocities, committed either in battle, during military occupation, or against prisoners of war (POW), a total of 927 were sentenced to death and executed. Furthermore, thousands of Japanese citizens, believed to be culpable, were arraigned on charges of having allegedly contributed to war crimes, and were barred from holding government positions.

On April 19, 1946, the government of the United States of America formally recognized the communist government of the Federal People's Republic of Yugoslavia (FPRY).

During the Second World War the Yugoslav communists deemed it expedient not to disseminate anti-religious propaganda and denounce or condemn religious activities. Immediately after the war, Tito's communist regime implemented a firm course of actions aimed to eliminate the influence that church organizations had heretofore exerted. Hereafter, Tito launched his anti-religious campaign against adherence to religion in both belief and practice. Consequently, hundreds of priests, bishops, and civilians were arrested and tried on charges of war crimes, crimes against the people and state, incitement of religious hatred, and anti-government activities. Perhaps the most notorious trial of religious personages was that of Roman Catholic Archbishop Aloysius (Alojzije) Victor Stepinac, Primate of Croatia.

Aloysius Stepinac was born on May 8. 1898 in Krašić, a village near Zagreb, Croatia, which was under the imperial monarchy of Austro-Hungary. After completing elementary school in his native village of Krašić, he enrolled at the Gymnasium in Zagreb. In 1916 having reached the age of eighteen, he was inducted in the Austrian Army (member of the Central Power during the First World War), and transferred to a combat unit to fight against Italian forces in northern Italy where he was captured and sent to a prisoner of war (POW) camp. During his short stay in prisoner camp, he enlisted in a South-Slav military unit and transferred to Salonika, Greece, ready to fight in the eastern front against Austria. However, before his unit arrived to the front line, the First World War ended. Stepinac returned to Zagreb where he continued his education; graduated from the Gymnasium and enrolled at the University of Zagreb. In 1924 at the age of 26, young Stepinac decided to study for the priesthood, entered the Gregorian University in Rome, Italy, where in 1927 he earned a doctorate in philosophy, became an ordained priest on October 26, 1930, and in 1931 earned a doctorate in theology. In 1931 Stepinac returned to Croatia, at that time under the dictatorship of the Karađorđević dynasty of Yugoslavia, was assigned as parish priest and later reassigned as secretary to Antun Bauer, Archbishop of Zagreb. On June 24, 1934, the thirty-six year old Stepinac was consecrated Archbishop-coadjutor of Zagreb with the right of succession. When Archbishop Antun Bauer died on December 7, 1937, Stepinac became the Archbishop of Zagreb, the Metropolitan of Croatia, and the President of the Conference of the Croatian Episcopate. During the German and Italian occupation of Croatia, Stepinac was Vicar General of the Croatian Army which was the military organization of the Independent State of Croatia under the titular authority of Ante Pavelić. Although, Stepinac welcomed and supported the Independent State of Croatia, established on April 10, 1941, he openly criticized its brutal excesses. Similarly, after Tito's communist partisans assumed control of Yugoslavia in 1945, Stepinac openly denounced communism for its brutal excesses. Thus began the dialogue of accusations, charges and counter-charges that continued for the next year. Croatian and Yugoslav Bishop's pastoral letters condemned the acts of savagery committed by Tito's henchmen and demonstrated that the Bishops and Stepinac in particular, were not about to give up their rights of freedom of speech and fold under the encroachments of the communist tyranny. As a result of this outspoken criticism against Tito's communist government, Stepinac was accused of collaboration with the Nazis and Fascists occupation forces (from 1941 to 1945), supporting the Independent State of Croatia, and attempted conversion of Eastern Orthodox believers.

On September 18, 1946, Stepinac was arrested by the communist police. As a result of political expediency, after twelve days of rigged trial held at the People's Court in Zagreb, on October 11, 1946, Stepinac was sentenced to sixteen years imprisonment in Lepoglava. Relations between the Vatican and Tito's communist Yugoslavia remained tense until Stepinac's release from Lepoglava prison in December 1951, but he remained under house arrest and confined to his native village of Krašić, On November 29, 1952, the Vatican announced that Archbishop Stepinac was named to the rank of Cardinal. On December 17, 1952, Eugenio M. G. G. Pacelli (1876-1958), Pope Pius XII (1939-1958) elevated Stepinac to the College of Cardinals, thus provoking the Yugoslav government to break off diplomatic relations with the Vatican. Cardinal Stepinac died in Krašić on February 10, 1960, and was buried on February 13, 1960 behind the main altar inside the Cathedral of St. Stephen (Sveti Stjepan) in Zagreb.

The development of the statehood of the constituent Yugoslav republics was expressed in the adoption of their constitutions; the Republic of Croatia was the last republic to adopt the communist constitution on January 18, 1947. After years of deliberations, the peace treaty was signed in Paris, France, on February 10, 1947. Italy dispossessed the territories in the eastern Adriatic and the Istrian penninsula to Yugoslavia. However, provisions of the peace treaty concerning the Free Territory of Trieste were not realized (the city of Trieste and a narrow coastal area known as Zone A came under the British and USA military authority; while the area south of Trieste known as Zone B came under the military administration of communist Yugoslavia. March 7, 1947, the communist Yugoslav police arrested Monsignor Pietro Doimo Munzani, Archbishop of Zadar, on charges of supporting the fascists.

To consolidate Soviet control over European communists, Stalin ordered the creation of a Soviet-dominated alliance. Thus, in September 1947 the communist parties of Bulgaria, Czechoslovakia, France, Hungary, Italy, Poland, Romania, Soviet Union, and Yugoslavia founded the Cominform (Communist Information Bureau, as successor to the prewar Communist International-Comintern). The city of Belgrade was established as the Cominform headquarters to strengthen the image and give the perception that Yugoslavia was the staunch Soviet ally. Stalin's unsuccessful attempts to influence and subordinate the Communist Party of Yugoslavia (CPY) to his own direct interests were exemplified on March 19, 1948 by the withdrawal of Soviet military and civilian advisors from Yugoslavia. At the meeting of the Communist Information Bureau (Cominform), on June 28, 1948, a Resolution of the Situation in the CPY was unanimously adopted, whereby the CPY was expelled from the Cominform. In July 1948, the Fifth Congress of the CPY convened in Belgrade, offered unanimous support to the CPY central committee and to their leader, Marshal Tito. After declaring political independence from the Soviet Union in 1948, Tito modified Yugoslavia's communist economic system by allowing worker organizations limited control in a self-management system. Although dominated by the CPY, the self-management system brought some economic growth during the years of 1950 and 1970. The most important economic policies which contributed to the growth was allowing citizens to emigrate to Western Europe as guest workers which brought substantial hard currency into Yugoslavia and relieved labor surpluses at home.

After the CPY was expelled from the Cominform, Tito implemented changes in order to consolidate his control, thus the Yugoslav security forces were reorganized. Under the new Law on State Security enacted January 5, 1949, the name of the Department for the Protection of the People (Odelenje za žastitu naroda, OZN-a), was changed to the Administration of State Security (Uprava državne bezbednosti, UDB-a). By this law the secret police were charged not only with fighting anti-communist elements, but also with infiltrating and uncovering counter-revolutionary activities within the Yugoslav communists. Subsequently, members of CPY were investigated, screened, and imprisoned, but nobody knows how many were liquidated.

The North Atlantic Treaty Organization (NATO) was created on April 4, 1949, became effective August 24, 1949. The original members were: Belgium, Canada, Denmark, England, France, Iceland, Italy, Luxembourg, Netherlands, Norway, Portugal, and the U.S.A. Subsequently, Greece, Turkey, West Germany, and Spain have joined. The members agreed to regard an attack on one as an attack on all. The NATO Headquarters was in Paris, France, from 1950-1957. However, after announcement in 1966 of French withdrawal from most military affairs of NATO, the Headquarters moved to Brussels, Belgium. On September 8, 1951, a Peace Conference held in San Francisco, CA concluded with the Peace Treaty signed by 48 nations, except the USSR and India refused to sign the instrument, while separate arrangements were made to complete a peace treaty between China and Japan. Following the ratification of the Peace Treaty, the Allied military occupation of Japan officially ended on April 28, 1951, and Japan regained its sovereignty.

Federalism was largely theoretical, as the powers of the six republics were totally subordinated to the central government in all matters of importance. In those limited areas left to the republics, close supervision was exercised by the central government. In January 1953, the constitution was amended to partially replace the constitution of 1946, following the promulgation of a special Constitution Law.

* * * * *

The following Statement of Policy by the National Security Council (NSC) was one of several parts of NSC 5406/1. The other parts, were a 2-page Financial Appendix; a 32-page Staff Study; a cover sheet; and a memorandum of February 6, 1954 from Everett S. Gleason, Deputy Executive Secretary of the NSC, in which he noted that the President that day had approved the Statement of Policy, and directed its implementation by all appropriate executive departments and agencies, and had designated the Operations Coordinating Board (OCB) as the coordinating agency. He also noted that NSC 5406/1 accordingly superseded the existing NSC policy papers on Yugoslavia, NSC 18/2, "Economic Relations Between the United States and Yugoslavia," February 17, 1949, and NSC 18/6, "The Position of the U.S. With Respect to Yugoslavia," March 7, 1951.

~ U.S. Policy Toward Yugoslavia ~

Top Secret (NSC 5406/1)   Washington, February 6, 1954

U.S. policy toward Yugoslavia may be seriously affected by the future course of the Trieste controversy. However, the following statement of policy was prepared on the assumption that its implementation would not be precluded by developments connected with Trieste.

General Considerations

1.The continued denial of Yugoslavia to the Soviet bloc is of great strategic importance to the security of the Free World. Because of its geographic position and potentially strong army, an independent Yugoslavia denies important assets to the Soviet bloc and reduces the Soviet threat to the internal and external security of Greece and Italy, etc.

2. Politically and psychologically, the "Tito heresy" has provided the West with an important asset. It represented the first defection of a Communist Government from the Soviet orbit, challenging Kremlin control of world communism as an instrument of Soviet imperialism. The continued independence of Yugoslavia offers a standing example of successful defiance of the Kremlin and is proof that there exists, for nationalist communist leaders, a possible alternative to submission to Soviet Control.

3. The United States, and to a lesser degree Britain and France, have extended military and economic aid to Yugoslavia in order to insure the retention of the foregoing benefits through strengthening the will and ability of the Yugoslav nation to defend its independence. With short term objectives in mind, U.S. aid programs have been continuously reviewed on a year-to-year basis, thereby enabling the United States to influence the policies of the Tito regime in some degree. Retention of Yugoslav cooperation with the West, and maintenance and improvement of

187

the Yugoslav armed forces, can be expected to require outside assistance. Continued drought may further aggravate the economic situation.

4. Yugoslavia remains a communist dictatorship with the strength and stability of the regime due in large measure to Tito's dominant position. In the event of Tito's death, a successor regime would probably attempt to continue the main outlines of his internal and external policies. However, it is possible that a struggle for power would develop, with results which cannot now be estimated.

5. The nature of the regime makes full exploitation of Yugoslav potentialities in the Western system of defense difficult to achieve. Nevertheless, under present conditions it is in the security interest of the United States to support Yugoslavia, despite its communist regime and U.S. opposition in principle to such a regime. The balance of probability is that Yugoslavia, even if not initially attacked, would cooperate with the West in the event of general war.

6. The majorityof the people of Yugoslavia are opposed to the principle and domestic policy of their communist dictatorship, under which they perceive little hope of obtaining political and economic freedom. Nevertheless, on issues which arouse nationalist feelings the regime can count on widespread support. In the event of a Soviet or satellite invasion, there is little doubt that the Yugoslav people initially would rally to the support of Tito, and that the Yugoslav forces would offer vigorous resistance. However, under the impact of military defeats or the pressure of a long war, the possibility exists of the breakdown of organized military resistance under the Tito regime. This possibility must be regarded as an acceptable risk.

7. The death of Stalin and the apparent shift in tactics by his successors raise the possibility of a Yugoslav rapprochement with Moscow. While it would be unwise to exclude such an eventuality, it is considered unlikely as long as the Tito regime remains in power. The Kremlin may be expected to continue its efforts to undermine Tito's domestic position and to weaken his ties with the West.

8. Although the Tito regime appears to be increasingly inclined toward greater participation in over-all European defense arrangements, the extent of Yugoslav participation is limited by such factors as Tito's fear of alienating doctrinaire Yugoslav communists and by his unwillingness to have Yugoslav forces serve under non-Yugoslav command. On the Western side, some non-communist nations are reluctant to deal with Tito as an equal and an ally. Current strained relations between Italy and Yugoslavia, aggravated as they are by the Trieste issue and by Yugoslav fear and distrust of Italy's ambitions in the Balkans, constitute a major stumbling block to realization of the full benefits of Yugoslavia's association with Western defense.

9. An attack on Yugoslavia by organized Soviet or satellite forces would probably result in general war.

Prepared by: National Security Agency

* * * * *

After intensive diplomatic brinkmanship a "Memorandum of Understanding" was signed on October 5, 1954, ending the military administration in Zone A and B. Thus, a legal and de facto situation was established: Zone A was annexed to Italy and Zone B to Yugoslavia.

~ U.S. Policy Toward Yugoslavia ~

Washington, April 13, 1955

Period Covered: May 7, 1954 through April 13, 1955

This report is prepared pursuant to U.S. policy approved (NSC 5406 February 6, 1954) by President Dwight D. Eisenhower.

Summary of Major Actions and Decisions:

1. Since, in major respects, the implementation of U.S. policy towards Yugoslavia was either held in abeyance or seriously curtailed by the existing impass over Trieste, the focus of our efforts within the period under review was upon a solution of this problem. Diplomatic negotiations of eight months duration, in which the U.S. and Britain laboriously promoted an Italian-Yugoslav accord on Trieste, culminated October 5, 1954 in a four-power understanding which resolved the issue in a manner not only acceptable to Italy and Yugoslavia but also favorable to U.S. interests. It is hoped that the disposal of the Trieste problem, in terms accepted by both Yugoslavia and Italy, established the basis for Italian-Yugoslav rapprochement and cleared the way for planning and action with respect to other phases of U.S. policy towards Yugoslavia.

2. On August 9, 1954, Yugoslavia, Greece and Turkey concluded a treaty for a military elaboration of the Balkan (Ankara) Pact. From the outset, the U.S. assumed a sympathetic attitude toward the development of the Balkan Entente into a formal military alliance. Our influence was exerted in concert with Britain and France to the end that the conclusion of the Alliance should not impede the achievement of other important objectives of U.S. policy. Although the establishment of the Balkan Alliance provices no organic connection with NATO, it aligns Yugoslavia indirectly with the general scheme of Western defense.

3. In continuation of U.S. military aid to Yugoslavia, the cumulative amount programmed from the beginning in FY 1951 through February 28, 1955 reached $787.7 million. During the period of April 30-January 31, 1955 materials delivered increased from 47 to 65 percent of the total value of end-items programmed since FY 1951; dollar value of end-items delivered by January 31, 1955 was $513.1 million. Deliveries within the period amounted to $144.3 million.

4. At the end of the period under review, the cumulative total of U.S. economic assistance which had been programmed and allotted for Yugoslavia since the beginning of the U.S. aid programs in 1950 amounted to $475.485 million. At the end of February 1955, $435.6 million had been shipped. (These figures include surplus agricultural commodities provided under the Agricultural Trade Development and Assistance Act of 1954, approved July 10, 1954, as outlined in paragraph 5). The cumulative total of contributions by Britain and France to the tripartite economic aid program for Yugoslavia reached the equivalent of $77 million ($48.2 million from Britain and $28.8 million from France). During this period a final allotment of $10 million was made under the Mutual Security Program (MSP) for Fiscal Year 1954, which totalled $65 million. The MSP planning figure for Yugoslavia in FY 1955 is $45 million plus $500,000 for technical exchange activities. Allotments for MSP FY 1955 funds for economic aid as of April 15, 1955, totalled $36 million. The $40.5 million for economic aid requested for FY 1956 will allow a somewhat greater proportion of aid for direct strengthening of the economic and defense structure of Yugoslavia than in past years when aid has been almost exclusively concentrated on food and raw materials for subsistence purposes.

5. In November 1954, discussions were held in Washington on economic matters

between high-level representatives of the U.S. and Yugoslav Governments. The head of the Yugoslav delegation made an extended presentation of Yugoslavia's economic difficulties. The question of Yugoslavia's medium and short-term indebtedness, which was discussed at the Washington talks, is under further study. Following the talks, an agreement was signed under which 425,000 tons of wheat and $10 million worth of cotton from surplus stocks were provided to Yugoslavia under Title I of PL 480. Funds were authorized in the amount of $44.185 million to cover this wheat and cotton, and the ocean tranportation thereof. The furnishing of these commodities was in addition to 275,000 tons of wheat (at a cost of $32 million) provided under Title II of PL 480, and 150,000 tons (at a cost of $9 million) provided in the MSP, bringing the total of FY 1955 wheat to 850,000 tons as of the end of Current Year 1954. In February 1955 the Yugoslav Government requested an additional 286,000 tons to meet its needs until the new crop was harvested. As of April 13, 1955, this question had not been finally decided, but it appeared likely that this request would be given favorable consideration.

6. The United States Information Service program emphasized (a) growing military and economic strength of the West wi th U.S. support, (b) the values of cooperation among the free world powers, (c) U.S. measures of economic, technical and flood relief assistance to Yugoslavia, and (d) the dangers of too close a rapprochement with the Soviet bloc. As part of an extensive program of cultural relations, the stage play "Porgy and Bess" was performed with significant success in Yugoslavia. The U.S. is sounding out the Yugoslav Government with a view to sending an "Atoms for Peace" exhibit to Yugoslavia beginning with the Zagreb Trade Fair in September, 1955.

Prepared by: Operations Coordination Board

* * * * *

Germany in 1945 was partitioned into four zones of occupation, one zone "East Germany" under the USSR formed the German Democratic Republic-GDR (or Deutsche Demokratische Republik); and three zones "West Germany" under the USA, British, and French formed the Federal Republic of Germany-FRG (Bundesrepublik Deutschland). On May 5, 1955 the FRG attained its sovereignty and became a member of NATO.

The Warsaw Pact was created on May 14, 1955 in opposition to NATO. The members were: Albania (which withdrew in 1961), Bulgaria, Czechoslovakia, East Germany, Hungary, Poland, Romania, and the USSR. After the communist disintegration of the USSR and its East European satellites the Warsaw Pact was dissolved on March 31, 1991.

* * * * *

~ Yugoslavia's International Position ~

Washington, September 7, 1955

The Problem - To assess Yugoslavia's international position and to estimate the probable effects of U.S. courses of action with respect to Yugoslavia. In conclusion:

1. We believe that the dominant concerns of the Yugoslav regime, at least so long as Tito remains alive, will be to insure its own survival free of foreign domination and to advance its own influence and prestige on the world scene. Despite Tito's Marxist world outlook, we believe that he will continue to regard his interests to be best served from a flexible position in which Yugoslavia can achieve benefits from both power blocs with a minimum of commitments to either.

2. We have carefully considered the possibility that Tito may have decided that his interests can best be served from a position within rather than outside the communist orbit, and that he has made an agreement with Moscow to rejoin the Bloc. His present mawneuvers might thus be designed to prepare the way for open acknowledgment of such an agreement. We consider it unlikely, however, that Tito has come to this decision or has made an agreement with Moscow. Even if he were fully convinced that the USSR was prepared to take Yugoslavia back, not as a Satellite but as a partner, a position in the Bloc would still offer Tito and his key associates great personal danger and would be unlikely to offer any great advantages to compensate for the loss of world-wide influence and prestige.

3. Tito will continue to take advantage of opportunities to profit by the USSR's present show of friendship, to test Soviet good faith, and to encourage the readjustment of Soviet relationships with the Satellites and with the non-communist world which he hopes is in the making. This process is likely to increase not only by further economic and cultural cooperation but also by cautious moves toward re-establishment of party-to-party relations.

4. However, we believe that as long as Tito is in power this process of political rapprochement will not result in Yugoslavia's realignment with the Bloc unless the USSR proves willing to make such modifications in the nature of its relationships with the Satellites as to convince Tito that he would have real opportunities for independent leadership and influence in the communist world. We feel safe in estimating that there is a pro-Soviet element in the Yugoslav Communist Party that is now pressing for closer ties with Moscow, but we are uncertain as to its leadership and extent. However, Tito is clearly in firm control.

5. Given a continuation of the USSR's present conciliatory behavior, Yugoslavia will probably continue to preach "peaceful coexistence" and may toy with the idea of some form of buffer alignment in Europe. It will support various Soviet and Chinese Communist diplomatic moves, and will display increasing indifference toward its military ties with the West. However, it will still wish aid and trade ties with the West, will display continuing interest in economic regional cooperation with Western states, and will look to the West as a potential source of support against possible Soviet designs.

6. Yugoslavia's adherence to its Balkan Alliance commitments in time of war is doubtful, and its wartime usefulness to the West is uncertain. Therefore, we believe that the Yugoslav regime would endeavor to remain neutral in a general war, at least until the situation clarified. We also believe, however, that Tito would fight if directly attacked, and might also enter the war, not because of his Balkan Alliance commitments, but as a consequence of his judgment as to the course of hostilities and as to the advantages which he might gain from participation. Ultimately, Tito might consider it advantageous, and perhaps even essential for the survival of his regime, to join the winning side before the end of hostilities.

7. Present U.S. ability to affect the process of readjustment in Yugoslavia's international position is limited: (a) Although the Yugoslavs desire additional U.S. military and more particularly economic aid, they would almost certainly refuse to make more than minor concessions to obtain it. They are probably prepared to accept a substantial reduction in military aid. (b) Should a substantial reductioon in economic aid actually take place, Yugoslavia's ability to pursue major economic goals would be severely limited, and its tendency to look to the Bloc for increased trade and credits, which will in any case be evident, would be intensified. However, such a cut would not critically endanger Yugoslavia's economic viability if the regime accepted the need for austerity

measures, and we do not believe that Tito would allow himself to become economically subservient to the Bloc. (c) A substantial reduction in U.S. economic aid would cause considerable Yugoslav resentment and would somewhat impair Tito's bargaining position as against Moscow, though it would not in itself impel the Yugoslavs to move politically closer to the Bloc.

Prepared by: National Intelligence Estimates

* * * * *

On October 23, 1956, anti-communist demonstrations in Budapest, Hungary, developed into open revolt. Premier Imre Nagy formed a new government, declared Hungary's neutrality, withdrew from the Warsaw Pact,and appealed to the United Nations for help. On November 4, 1956, Soviet forces (200,000 troops with 2,500 tanks and armored vehicles) launched a massive and barbaric attack against the twin city of Buda-Pest. After bloody street fighting, 185,000 Hungarians fled their country, and Cardinal Józef Mindszenty (1892-1975) released from prison took refuge in the U.S. Embassy. Nagy was executed by the Soviets. In the spring of 1963, the regime granted amnesty to the captive anti-communist elements. In 1968, Hungarian troops participated in the Warsaw Pact invasion of Czechoslovakia. Finally, the last Soviet soldiers departed from Hungary in June 1991, thereby ending almost 47 years of communist tyranny.

John Foster Dulles (1888-1959), U.S. Secretary of State, spent Sunday, November 6, 1955 at Brioni Island, as Tito's guest. They talked about various international subjects. At the press conference held on Brioni following the meeting, Dulles stated in part "that the final subject of their talk was the problem of the States of Eastern Europe. They [Dulles and Tito] reached common accord on recognizing the importance of independence for these States, noninterference from the outside in their internal affairs, and their right to develop their own social and economic order in ways of their own choice." On November 8, 1955 Dulles and Tito met in Geneva, Switzerland. Tito spoke about his relations with the Soviet Union, saying that having once been in their clutches he would never risk getting there again. Dulles said the principal difficulty in United States arose from Catholics who felt that he [Tito] was persecuting their religion. Then, Dulles asked whether it was not true there was very large freedom of religion. Tito replied "there was and that Catholics, Muslims, and Serb Eastern Orthodox all had complete freedom." Tito proceeded by saying "that the trouble arose about Aloysius Stepinac, Archbishop of Zagreb, who was proved to be a collaborator with Germans, who had been condemned to ten years in prison and whom he [Tito] had released after four years, now Stepinac is free and serving in a church, and free to go to Rome." In connection with this matter, Tito showed the first sign of emotionalism he had exhibited during the entire visit. He spoke with considerble heat. For the record, Archbishop Stepinac was sentenced on October 11, 1946 by the communist tribunal to sixteen years imprisonment, released in December 1951, but remained under house arrest and confined to his native village of Krašić. On December 17, 1952 Stepinac was elevated to the College of Cardinal, he died on February 10, 1960.

* * * * *

~ U.S. Policy Toward Yugoslavia ~

Washington, November 23, 1955

Period Covered: April 13, 1955 through November 23, 1955

Pursuant to the Operating Coordinating Board (OCB) in the latest prior progress report, April 13, 1955, the basic policy has been under review during the past four months. A national Intelligence Estimate (NIE) for the National Security Council (NSC) and the Joint Chiefs of Staff (JCS) reevaluation of the military significance has been prepared.

1. Policy Review. Pursuant to the recommendations of OCB in the latest prior progress report, April 13, 1955, the basic policy has been under review during the past four months. A National Intelligence Estimate was prepared for the NSC and a JCS reevaluation of the military significance has been prepared.

2. Military Assistance. The total accumulative amount of U.S. military assistance to Yugoslavia programmed for end items through September 30, 1955 reached $812.7 million. The dollar value of end items delivered by August 31, 1955 was $587.2 million. Shipments during calendar year 1955 (through August 31) totaled $76.7 million.

3. The Department of Defense after coordination with the Department of State issued instructions on June 13, 1955 to accord lowest priority to Yugoslavia for the receipt of Mutual Defense Assistance Program (MDAP) equipment except for (1) material essential for the maintenance of MDAP equipment previously furnished or required for training, and (2) the MDAP equipment in the supply pipelines.

4. Economic Assistance. At the end of the period under review the cumulative total of U.S. economic assistance amounted to $525.1 million, of which $484.0 million had been shipped by June 30, 1955. The bulk of this assistance was in the form of surplus agricultural commodities, i.e., wheat and cotton.

5. Discussions with the Yugoslav Government regarding continued economic assistance under FY 1956 MSP and PL 480 were not undertaken until basic U.S. policy review indicated the desirability of continued economic aid.

6. Mission of Deputy Under Secretary Murphy. The Deputy Under Secretary of State conducted negotiations with the Yugoslav Government in Belgrade during the week ending October 1 and reached an understanding on the following major matters: (a) No change in policy of either nation toward the other. (b) Facilitate operation of American Military Assistance Staff. (c) Strengthen mutual economic cooperation - U.S. to furnish immediately 300,000 tons of wheat and to negotiate on further economic aid this year. (These discussions have begun). (d) U.S. willingness to discuss program for peaceful uses of atomic energy. (e) Department of State to support Yugoslav application for Export-Import Bank Loan.

7. Information Programs. USIA continued its efforts to disseminate the U.S. foreign policy viewpoint in Yugoslavia through its press bulletins, Voice of America (VOA) broadcasting, exhibits, backgrounders, book presentations, and related activities. In September and October 1955, the U.S. atoms-for-peace exhibit was shown to large audiences, including key government officials.

Prepared by: Operations Coordinating Board

* * * * *

* * * * *

~ U.S. Policy Toward Yugoslavia" ~

Washington, April 24, 1957

Period Covered: September 6, 1956 through April 24, 1957

1. Operations Coordinating Board (OCB) Recommendation Regarding Policy Review. The OCB notes the National Security Council (NSC) directive for a review of NSC 5601, but considers that in the light of operating experience to date, and of anticipated future developments, there is no urgency for a review from the OCB standpoint.

2. Summary Evaluations. On October 15, 1956 the President issued the finding with regard to continued aid to Yugoslavia required by Section 143 of the Mutual Security Act of 1954 as amended. This action was based on a determination that Yugoslavia remained independent of Soviet control and that U.S. objectives would, on balance, continue to be served by U.S. support of Yugoslavia. The finding permitted economic aid to Yugoslavia to go forward, but deferred a decision with regard to military aid with the exception of spare parts and maintenance items.

(a) U.S. officials now feel more confident of the Yugoslav will and ability to maintain independence than they did in the period when the Yugoslavs were eagerly reciprocating the Soviet-initiated rapprochement. In the last six months the Soviet threat to Yugoslav independence has changed its character. It now is exerted through economic pressures and "idealogical" polemics instead of taking the form of economic inducements and other blandishments, as it had after late 1954. The Soviets have blamed the events in Poland and Hungary in part on Yugoslav influence. The result has been a mounting Soviet bloc pressure on the Yugoslavs for ideological (and, hence, political) subservience to Moscow. This pressure was first manifested on an ideological level and exercised through speeches and editorials, but it now gives clear signs of being extended to the state level, where it is evidenced by the refusal of the USSR and East Germany to implement fully previously-granted credits and development loans. The Yugoslavs have indicated clearly that they do not intend to submit to this pressure.

(b) Recent events in Eastern Europe and the strong anti-Yugoslav Soviet reaction thereto have provided evidence of the extent of Yugoslav influence. Polish nationally-minded communists have been influenced by the Yugoslav example and advice in their so-far successful bid for greater independence and, moreover, from all reports, have been greatly heartened by the fact of U.S. support for Yugoslavia and the nature of U.S.-Yugoslav relations. The Yugoslav example had an important role in encouraging those in intellectual elements which first instigated the Hungarian revolt with their demands for greater national and intellectual freedom.

(c) Considered in relation to the NSC objectives and that Yugoslav potentialities be developed on behalf of U.S. and other free world aims, Yugoslav foreign policies seem to call neither for great concern nor for enthusiastic approval. Yugoslavia has not recognized

194

the (East) "German Democratic Republic," but remains willing to accept economic relations with it not leading to recognition. In general, the neutralist bent of Yugoslav foreign policy continues as before and seems to be dictated by the Yugoslavs' view of their country's needs as a small country balanced between East and West. Yugoslavia has supported United Nations actions in the Middle East, but its attitude in regard to UN action on Hungary has been somewhat ambiguous. While disapproving of Soviet intervention there in principle, Yugoslav officials have explained their abstention on most General Assembly votes condemning the Soviet Union by claiming that UN action could only exacerbate the situation, would not influence the USSR, and could not help Hungary in any case. Besides this rationalization of their position, the Yugoslavs indicated to the United States last November their apprehension about possible Soviet military actions against them or other nearby countries.

(d) No concrete measures toward liberalization of the regime took place during the reporting period. On the contrary, the arrest and conviction of Djilas for his criticism of the basic tenets of communism, whether of the Yugoslav or Soviet variety, points up the lack of political freedom which prevails. There are signs, however, that Djilas' message and the impact of events in Hungary and Poland were not lost on Yugoslav leaders. Although Yugoslav communists have been realistic enough, apparently, to recognize the desires of the people for improvement in living standards and for some measure of freedom, such recognition has not yet resulted in any material improvement in the conditions of life in Yugoslavia.

3. Status of and Progress on U.S. Commitments for Funds, Goods or Services and Other Programs.

(a) Military assistance to Yugoslavia is still limited to spare parts and maintenance items in accordance with the policy set by the Presidential determination on aid of October 15, 1956. Pending a decision by the executive branch, deliveries of ammunition, major items, and aircraft remain suspended.

(b) Defense support for Yugoslavia for FY 1957 amounts to $15 million, of which $1.5 million has been approved for technical assistance and $13.5 million approved for wheat and cotton, bringing total non-military MSP assistance to approximately $445 million since 1950.

(c) A PL 480 agreement for FY 1957 in the amount of $98.3 million was signed on November 3, 1956, and is being carried out on schedule. This will bring total PL 480, Title I, assistance to Yugoslavia to a cumulative total since 1954 of approximately $221.5 million. In response to a Yugoslav request, the Department of Agriculture agreed in January to shift $5 million from wheat to ocean freight, and the Yugoslavs were promised that the U.S. would consider the problem of additional wheat when supplementary PL 480 funds are voted by Congress.

(d) Commitments for military, economic and technical aid have totalled about $1.5 billion from 1949 to the present.

4. New U.S. Commitments for Funds, Goods or Services Entered Into During the Reporting Period. No new commitments.

5. Hungarian Refugees. As of March 1, 1957, there were over 17,000 Hungarian refugees in Yugoslavia. UN observers have reported that conditions of housing and feeding provided by the Yugoslavs are roughly comparable to Austrian standards. New refugee flow has been reduced to a trickle and it is unlikely that the number in Yugoslavia will exceed 20,000. To date, about 400 have settled permanently in Yugoslavia, over 250 have gone from Yugoslavia to Western countries other than the United States, and almost 1,800 have voluntarily returned to Hungary. The Yugoslavs complain that the refugees represent a heavy economic burden to them, and continue to press the West for financial and material assistance in caring for the refugees, as

well as for action to remove some of the refugees to the countries of second asylum. No refugees will be taken directly into the U.S. from Yugoslavia on parole, at least until the proposed amendments to the Immigration and Nationality Act have been acted upon. However, the Department of State is seeking to work out a plan (for which $2 million has been allocated) for helping the Intergovernmental Committee for European Migration to move 10,000 Hungarians from Yugoslavia to countries of permanent resettlement or secondary asylum. Some U.S. assistance for interim care and maintenance of the refugees is also being considered.

6. Military Aid. The resumption in March 1956 of previously programmed deliveries, following a 10-months' suspension, continued for less than four months before another partial suspension was instituted on the basis of Congressional hesitancy about aid for Yugoslavia. In October 1956 this partial suspension was extended to all items except spare parts and maintenance equipment. The Departments of State and Defense have reviewed this situation a number of times in recent months, and an early decision on a resumption of relatively normal shipments appears probable. Such a decision is required to avoid expensive prolonged storage of jet aircraft incorporated in prior programs. On the political level the Yugoslavs have requested a decision and on the working level Yugoslav military officers have made it apparent to American Military Assistance Staff officers in Belgrade that the present stoppage is materially affecting the tactical efficiency of the Yugoslav Air Force. A similar problem exists concerning three OSP minesweepers which have been completed for the Yugoslavs in French yards and which are now using up urgently needed harbor space.

Submitted by: Operations Coordinating Board

* * * * *

On August 13, 1961, the puppet communist government of East Germany sealed off most of the crossing points between East and West of the divided city of Berlin with a barbed wire fence. The barrier was later reinforced with concrete (called the "Berlin Wall") by the Soviets to prevent inhabitants of East Germany from escaping to West Germany seeking freedom and economic opportunities. On November 9, 1989, the East German government could no longer stop the exodus of its citizens to the West, opened its borders and the "Wall" was gradually dismantled.

One of the most tragic events of the twentieth century occurred when the 35th President of the United States (1961-1963), John Fitzgerald Kennedy (b. May 29, 1917), while riding a motorcade in Dallas, Texas, was assassinated on November 22, 1963 by Lee Harvey Oswald (1939-1963) who was fatally shot on November 24 by Jack Ruby (1911-1967). According to Article XXV, Section 1 of the U.S. Constitution, "In case of the removal of the President from office or of his death or resignation, the Vice President shall become President. On November 22, Vice-President Lyndon Baines Johnson (1908-1973) became the 36th President of the USA (1963-1969).

In conformance with the constitution of 1963, the official name of Yugoslavia was changed to the Socialist Federal Republic of Yugoslavia (SFRY). A major communist purge in 1966 effected the Yugoslav internal security force.

Aleksandar Ranković, head of the Administration of State Security (Uprava države bezbednosti-UDB) was promptly dismissed. The official communist announcement stated that the UDB was responsible for ethnic brutality and repression against the Albanian population of Kosova. The UDB was purged and its name changed to the State Security Service (Služba državne bezbednosti, SDB). Coincidentally, the Military Counter-Intelligence Service (Kontra baveštajna služba, KOS) was instrumental in exposing the UDB's unauthorized covert activities. The SDB actively pursued its mission of identifying and neutralizing émigré organizations in foreign countries to inhibit their efforts to establish contacts and support inside Yugoslavia. In 1966 the repressive Yugoslav secret police organization of Aleksander Ranković had been dismantled, yielding political liberalization that led to resurgence of nationalism which took place in Kosova in 1968.

After the death of Stalin and the relaxing of Soviet controls, Czechoslovakia witnessed a nationalist awakening. In January 1968 an anti-communist movement spread through Czechoslovakia. A chain reaction resulted whereby, political leaders were deposed, succeeded and resigned in succession. In July, the Soviet Union and the Warsaw Pact nations demanded an end to liberalization. On August 20, 1968 an estimated 250,000 troops of Bulgaria, East Germany, Hungary, Poland, and Russia invaded Czechoslovakia. In 1973, amnesty was granted to 45,000 who fled their country after the 1968 vicious defeat of the liberalization movement. In 1977, more than 700 Czechoslovak (Czech and Slovak) intellectuals and former communist party leaders signed a human rights manifesto, "Chapter 77." Finally, the last Soviet soldiers departed in June 1991.

Croatian resurgence of nationalism, and demands for political and economic autonomy brought prompt and forceful suppression by Tito in 1971 and 1972. In the aftermath, many Croatian officers who actively or tacitly supported Croat nationalists were purged from the YPA, CPY, and many were sentenced to years of prison.

During the 1970s, Tito began restructuring his communist regime to prepare it for a power-sharing government. The Constitution of February 21, 1974 delegated new power to the six republics and two autonomous provinces, which obtained veto power over federal legislation. There were differences between the previous Constitutions and the 1974 Constitution, the most obvious being the composition of the executive branch of the federal government. To ensure that after Tito's death no person or group of persons could impose their will, Tito rejected a strong president and vested the executive power in an eight-member council, represented by a member of each of the eight national divisions in an attempt to forestall any rebellion against overwhelming Serbian domination.

197

Tito designed a system in which the federal government and governments of the six republics and two autonomous provinces shared power and authority. Political candidates were included on the election list, but only after they were accepted by the communist authority, that is by the Socialist Alliance of the Working People of Yugoslavia (SAWPY). The League of Communists of Yugoslavia (LCY) encouraged the Serbian Eastern Orthodox Christian Church to forgo christianity, concentrate on their adherance to anti-western ideas, and promote the cause of the communist Marxist teachings.

The Federal Executive Council (FEC) acted as cabinet; its president was Prémier of Yugoslavia and de facto head of government. The legislative branch was bicameral Federal Assembly (Skupština), representing republics and social organizations. The legal political power was the League of Communists of Yugoslavia (LCY), until 1952 was called the Communist Party of Yugoslavia. Until his death on May 4, 1980, Tito served as President of the Socialist Federal Republic of Yugoslavia (SFRY) and President of the Presidency (Chief of State). Tito, like a true disciple of Stalin, did not designate his trustworthy successor, but established a collective presidency. The SFRY Constitution of 1974 provided that after the termination of the Office of the President of SFRY, the Vice-President of the Presidency became President of the Presidency. The posts of the President of the Presidency and the Vice-President of the Presidency were rotated annually on May 15th in the prescribed order by the eight members of the Presidency representing six republics and two autonomous provinces. The President of the SFRY was also the Commander-in-Chief of the Armed Forces and Chairperson of the Council of National Defense. The Federal Executive Council - FEC (the Cabinet), was the executive body of the SFRY. The President of the FEC (Premier and head of the government) was elected for a four-year term by the Chambers of the Federal Assembly (Savezna Škupština) at the proposal of the Presidency of the SFRY.

In 1978, communists in Afghanistan took power in a bloody coup d' état and concluded an economic and military treaty with the Soviet Union. In December 1979, the adventurous, troublemaker Soviets commenced a massive military airlift into Kabul, capital of Afghanistan. On December 27, the Soviets executed a second coup d' état by overthrowing the three-month old regime of Halizullah Amin and replacing him with Babrak Karmal, a pro-Soviet puppet. Soviet troops, estimated at between 80,000-100,000, fanned out over Afghanistan. The Soviet invasion was met with fierce resistance from the Afghan population. The communists had to fight Afghan "Mujaheddin" (Holy Warriors). The fighting continued as the Soviets found themselves trapped in a protracted guerrilla war. A UN-mediated agreement in Geneva signed by Pakistan and the Soviet puppet government of Afghanistan, April 14, 1988, provided for: (a) the withdrawal of Soviet troops from Afghanistan;

(b) establishment of a neutral State of Afghan; and (c) repatriation of millions of Afghan refugees, most of them living in Pakistan. The U.S. and USSR pledged to serve as guarantors of the agreement. Afghan rebels rejected the pact and vowed to continue fighting while the "Soviets and their puppets" remained in Afghanistan. According to Mikhail Gorbachev, Leader of the Soviet Union, the withdrawal of Soviet troops would begin May 15, 1988, and would be completed by February 15, 1989. There were 100,300 Soviet troops in Afghanistan when the withdrawal began. The Soviet government on May 25, 1988 revealed the casualty figures for the 8½-year war: 13,310 Soviet soldiers were killed; 35,478 wounded; and 311 were missing.

In 1981 tension and unrest escalated in the Autonomous Province of Kosova, where ethnic Albanians are the overwhelming majority of the total population, they protested that the Serb-dominated YPA conducted acts of atrocities and used excessive military and police brutality against Albanians. The YPA presence added to local resentment. Demonstrations and civil disobedience in Kosova resumed in 1987 and continued through 1990.

The capital city of Beirut, Lebanon, in 1983 became a civil war battle zone. In order to separate the warring factions, the city was divided by the "Green Line" which created two sectors, one Christian and the other Muslim. Terrorist bombings in Beirut were a way of life. The brutal massacre in the refugee camps prompted international response. U.S. President Ronald W. Reagan sent U.S. Marines to Beirut to augment the contingence of multinational peacekeeping force composed of soldiers from three European nations Britain, France, and Italy. The mandate of the peacekeeping force was to enforce the cease-fire, but they found themselves drawn into the national struggle between Lebanese factions. On April 18 fifty people were killed in an explosion set up by terrorists which destroyed the U.S. embassy. The U.S. people were appalled and horrified, following October 23 when a TNT suicide bomb blew up the U.S. Marine headquarters killing 241 Marines, and in a separate attack the Muslims killed 58 French soldiers. On February 7, 1984, President Reagan ordered U.S. Marines to withdraw from Beirut. Meanwhile, the Lebanese civil war continued among the belligerent groups of Christian, Druze, Palestinian, Shite, and Sunni.

Following Tito's death, the SFRY economy declined due to international oil crises, heavy foreign borrowing, and communist inefficient investment policies. Economy reform was consistently blocked by the diametrically opposed interests in the communist structure. Croatia and Slovenia, culturally different from the rest of the federation, resisted the central government policy of redistributing their wealth. Opening the beaches of Istria and Dalmatia, and the mountains of Slovenia to western tourists, provided a source of hard currency for the two republics of Croatia and Slovenia.

In order to cover-up their culpability of past, present, and future malicious intentions, early October 1986 the Serbian Academy of Sciences and Arts (Srpska akademija nauka i umetnosti - SANU), comprised mostly of members of the communist party, published a secret manifesto accusing their Yugoslav communists of impeding their territorial expansionism and conspiring against Serbia during Tito's regime.

During 1987, the YPA held large scale military maneuvers in Slovenia. The military exercises were used as scare tactics to intimidate the people, but instead made the Slovenes cognizant of Serbia's design for ultimate territorial conquest. Those maneuvers were the prelude of YPA intervention in the republics of Slovenia, Croatia, and later in Bosnia-Herzegovina.

Due to financial irresponsibility, on May 16, 1988, the Yugoslav government imposed price and wage control to comply with the International Monetary Fund (IMF) promise of $430 million in new credit and rescheduling of $21 billion in loans from Western Capitalist creditors. On November 23, 1988, the Serbian government took ruthless action by prohibiting public assemblies and demonstrations of ethnic Albanians, who constitute an overwhelming majority of the population in the autonomous province of Kosova. Units of the Yugoslav Peoples Army (YPA) and Serbian police were dispatched to Kosova in February 1989, to quell the anti-Serbian demonstrations; the province of Kosova remained under Serb occupation.

When the wave of anti-communist political and economic reform swept Eastern Europe in the late 1980's, the new democratic movement in the SFRY challenged the monolithic Yugoslav communist system in place since 1945. At the opening of the Communist Central Committee meeting held from January 30 to February 1, 1989, Admiral Petar Šimić member of the Presidium of the Yugoslav League of Communists, stated "the YPA is ready to crush anyone who dare destroy the great achievements of the communist liberation struggle and the socialist revolution." The Hungarian government announced on February 28, 1989, the security and alarm system along the Austrian frontier would be dismantled. Turkey closed its frontiers with Bulgaria on August 12, 1989, after 300,000 expelled ethnic Turkish refugees arrived from Bulgaria. On August 16, 1989, the Hungarian government set up temporary campsite near Budapest, the capital city of Hungary, to welcome East German citizens seeking freedom and new life in West Germany. Chancellor Helmut Kohl of West Germany expressed his gratitude to the Government of Hungary for this humanitarian gesture.

By striking a note of Serbian national hegemony, Milošević awakened new nationalism and democratic aspiration in the republics of Croatia and Slovenia. The Serbian League of Communists on May 8, 1989 elected

Slobodan Milošević as President of the Socialist Republic of Serbia. From the date he took over the reins of Serbia, he became unbearable and very difficult to deal with in order to maintain a normalcy of relations in Yugoslavia. Milošević imposed the communist tactics by preaching fear and threatened anyone who was unwilling to go along with his policy. On May 15, 1989, Janez Drnovšek of Slovenia succeeded Raif Dizdarević of Bosnia-Herzegovina in the one-year rotary post of President of the Yugoslav Presidency (Chief of State).

An unprecedented conflict developed on July 8, 1989 when a group of fanatic Serbs returning to the town of Knin in Croatia, after commemorating the 600th anniversary of their military defeat at Kosova Polje in Kosova (a battle of Kosova Polje in which the invading Ottoman Turks had defeated the Serbian armies on June 28, 1389, or June 20, 1389 under the old style calendar). The riot fomented by the ruthless demagogic Slobodan Milošević got out of control when the belligerent Serbs attacked the peaceful ethnic Croat residents.

The ever rising levels of inflation and the ensuing falls in standards of living, led to repeated unrest in the country. On September 13, 1989, thousands of Serbs protested in Belgrade, demanding government action to curb inflation. Milošević and fellow communists accused Slovenia of promoting unrest. Under the direct authority of Milošević, on September 26 the Presidency of the SFRY issued a warning to the Republic of Slovenia that any revision to the Constitution of Slovenia must be approved by the Federal Constitutional Court. In keeping with the Serbian perennial biased policy, the same Presidency of the SFRY not only ignored, but never issued a warning to the Republic of Serbia when the Serbs amended the Constitution of Serbia which abolished the legitimate authorities of Kosova and Vojvodina.

The parliament of Slovenia on September 27, 1989 approved three amendments to the republic's constitution, (a) the right to secede from Yugoslavia by means of democratic referendum; (b) right to political and economic sovereignty; and (c) barred the Yugoslav [communist] People's Army from intervening in the political affairs of Slovenia. It became evident that the Yugoslav federation could only survive if it became a genuine community of free nations with equal rights and obligations.

A traditional assertion of Croatian Roman Catholic celebration of the Eucharist (the Christian sacrament commemorating Christ's Last Supper, a.k.a. "Holy Communion") was held in Solin, Croatia, on October 8, 1989 honoring Zvonimir, King of Croatia (1075-1089). Also, annually on October 8th the city of Zadar in Dalmatia celebrates its patron Saint Simon.

During the two-day session October 20-21, 1989, the Central Committee of the LCY approved a policy for the development of political pluralism and the protection of human rights and individual freedom. Thus attesting the well known facts that since 1945 the Yugoslav communist regime was against human rights, individual freedom and a democratic society. Relations between the two protagonist Yugoslav republics of Serbia and Slovenia deteriorated on November 29, 1989, resulting in reciprocal economic sanctions. Relations worsened further, when on December 3 the Serbian Chamber of Commerce in Belgrade responded to a call of the Serbian Socialist Alliance (communist political action) by ordering the major Serbian enterprises to cease all economic ties with Slovenia. In response to the Serbian policy, Slovenia replied by reciprocating the sanctions and sealing off all traffic between the two republics. A clear division of national interest emerged when the Croatian parliament voted on December 4, 1989 to support Slovenia's action against Serbian coersive sanctions whereas the Montenegrin League of Communists declared itself on December 11, 1989 in support of their Serbian cohorts.

Founded in 1842 as Matica Ilirska (Matrix Illyrian), changed its name in 1874 to Matica Hrvatska (Matrix Croatica), is the oldest Croatian cultural organization, at the beginning of 1970 had been denounced by the Yugoslav communist government for encouraging the resurgence of Croatian nationalism in opposition to the communist regime. Matica Hrvatska, banned for the last 18 years, resumed its activities in December 20, 1989.

In December 1989 Slobodan Milošević, head of the Serbian Communist Party (renamed the Serbian Socialist Party), warned that Serbia would insist on territorial concessions from other republics if the SFRY broke up. Milošević believed in his demagogic ability to create dissension, hatred, animosity, and resentment by using the ethnic emotions and prejudices of the Serbian populace. On December 18, 1989, Ante Marković, Yugoslav Premier unveiled an economic austerity program that included a six month wage freeze and a devaluation of Yugoslav currency. The Central Committee of the LCY recommended on December 26, 1989, that the proposal "draft agenda" for instituting economic reform be postponed and scheduled for debate at a party special congress.

The communist republic of Romania on January 12, 1990, became the first Eastern European country to abolish its communist party. Thousands of protesters in the so-called German Democratic Republic (a.k.a. East or communist Germany) stormed the headquarters of East Germany's State Security Service (STASI) in East Berlin on January 15, 1990, which resulted in considerable damage to property. And on that same date, the Republic of Bulgaria rescinded the communist party's monopoly on power.

The fourtenth Extraordinary congress of the LCY held in Belgrade, voted on January 23, 1990, to relinquish its monopoly and stranglehold on the Yugoslav national political power, a position that since 1945 had been the foundation of the communist party's legitimacy. The communist delegation quit the congress in a sign of protest, after demanding greater autonomy for the Yugoslav six republics. As a result the Fourteenth Party Congress, communist parties in the SFRY changed their names, e.g. the League of Communists of Serbia changed its name to the Socialist Party of Serbia.

On January 26, 1990, as rioting spread to several towns in Kosova, the Serbian police units armed with automatic weapons surrounded the key buildings and the university campus of Pristina. Serbian police occupied the mine of Stari Trg at Trepca where a disturbance also took place in 1989. The first deaths occured on January 27, 1990 when nine ethnic Albanians from Kosova were killed by Serbian police in the towns of Orahovac and Đakovica. As expected, the Milošević controlled Serbian media claimed that the Serbian police had acted in self-defense, however, reliable eyewitnesses reported that the demonstrations were peaceful and none of them were armed. In another incident, one demonstrator was killed and eight were hospitalized after the Serbian police had moved in to destroy the barricades erected by demonstrators at Peć. A riot broke out at Podujevo in Kosova, where on January 29, 1990 several thousand ethnic Albanian students demonstrated against Serbian brutality. The riot took a new turn when a confrontation between ethnic Albanians (constituting the overwhelming majority in Kosova) and Serbian police erupted in the village of Kosovska Vitina. Thousands of Serbs outside the Federal Assembly in Belgrade, on January 30-31, 1990, demanded that the YPA be deployed in Kosova to silence the ethnic Albanians, and also to protest against the stance of Croat and Slovene leaderships for voicing their support for the cause of freedom and equality of ethnic Albanians in Kosova. The Montenegrin stooges in Titograd (Podgorica) voiced their support for Serbian tyranny.

At a conference of the Slovenian League of Communists (SLC), held in Ljubljana on February 4, 1990, the SLC declared its independence from the League of Communists of Yugoslavia (LCY), and adopted a new name, the Party of Democratic Reform. The parliament of the Republic of Slovenia on July 3, 1990, declared that its laws and constitution take precedence over those of the SFRY. The two pro-western and economically progressive republics of Slovenia and Croatia were the first to hold democratic multiparty elections, both elected non-communist governments. In Slovenia, former communist Milan Kučan reached the presidency as leader of the diverse anti-communist DEMOS coalition. Before the first republic elections on April 22, 1990 in Croatia, some of the new political parties had formed coalitions. The largest coalition in Croatia was the "Croatian Democratic Union - CDU"

(Hrvatska demokratska zajednica-HDZ) which gained a solid parliamentary majority under the leadership of Franjo Tudjman, who became President of the Republic of Croatia. On the May 19, 1990 election, the CDU/HDZ won 205 votes (seats) out of 349. The communists who had ruled since 1945 received 77 votes. The two republics of Macedonia and Bosnia-Herzegovina followed with their democratic elections, but the two republics of Serbia and Montenegro (Serbia's gullible ally) gave election victories to the communists.

Among Yugoslavia's trouble spots, the province of Kosova was the most enduringly problematic, both economically and politically. Although the Serbs and Montenegrins constituted a small minority in Kosova, they controlled the government of Kosova and suppressed separatist Kosovar movements. The autonomy granted to the provinces of Kosova and Vojvodina in the Yugoslav Constitution of 1974 was revoked on July 1, 1990 by Slobodan Milošević and his henchmen. Ethnic trouble in Kosova, between the Albanian overwhelming majority and Serbian small but vicious minority threatened to spark a war between the two protagonists.

Early in 1990, ethnic Serb terrorists from several Serbian enclaves in Croatia, skirmished with local police and Croatian security forces. Milošević's communists and Serb-četnici gave the "terrorists" substantial moral and political encouragement, including military and financial assistance. Large supplies of illegal arms, stored by the Serb controlled YPA, were distributed to Serb terrorists in multi-ethnic areas of Croatia, sharpening the threat of terrorism and possible war. In accordance with the constitution of the SFRY establishing the annual leadership rotation, Borisav Jović, a fanatic Marxist-Serb, became the President of the Yugoslav Federal Presidency on May 15, 1990. On July 1, 1990 Serbian President Slobodan Milošević's coup' d'état abolished the two autonomous provinces of Kosova and Vojvodina, but retained their rights in the Yugoslav Federal Presidency in order to control the two votes of support. On July 5, 1990, the SR of Serbia dissolved the parliaments and governments of the two autonomous provinces of Kosova and Vojvodina. Moreover, Serbian police seized the Albanian language TV and radio stations in Pristina, the capital city of Kosova.

On July 26, 1990, the Croatian Parliament dropped the attribute "Socialist" from the name Republic of Croatia and ordered the communist red star with its hammer and sickle removed from the state symbols.

In the meantime, East and West Germany signed a reunification treaty on August 11, 1990 to be implemented on October 3, 1990. In Moscow on September 12, 1990 the four Allied powers and the two Germany's officials signed the Treaty of Final Settlement with respect to a reunited Germany as one nation. The former German Democratic Republic (communist East

Germany) became the five eastern states (Länder) of the Federal Republic of Germany (FRG) with a temporary capital at Bonn.

The republics of Slovenia and Croatia proposed that the Republic of Yugoslavia be restructured as a free confederation of states, each with national sovereignty and their own militia, conducting their own foreign policy modeled after the EEC; the formula includes a uniform monetary system, and a common free market economy. Serbia immediately rejected the proposed confederation of states, arguing that the large number of Serbs living in republics other than Serbia would be compelled to become citizens of foreign countries. Amid roadblocks, street fights, and increased tension, on August 18, 1990 the Serbian minority voted on an unofficial referendum for political and administrative autonomy. The unauthorized ballot was declared illegal by the Republic of Croatia.

On October 19, 1990 the U.S. Department of State issued the following statement: "The U.S. Government is concerned about increasing political and ethnic tensions in Yugoslavia and their potential impact on the transition to democracy and free markets which we have encouraged throughout Central and Eastern Europe. The U.S. firmly supports unity, democratic change, respect for human rights, and market reform in Yugoslavia. The U.S. believes that democracy is the only enduring basis for a united, prosperous and voluntary Yugoslav union. Free and fair elections, both at the federal level and it's individual republics and autonomous provinces, are essential to establishing democracy throughout Yugoslavia. The U.S. would strongly oppose any use of force that would block democratic change in Yugoslavia."

Tensions within communist Yugoslavia continued to escalate. On October 23, 1990, Croats and Slovenes adamantly demanded democratic revision of the SFRY government, otherwise the two pro-western republics would secede. The Serbs, on the other hand, expected and insisted that the YPA intercede on behalf of communist Yugoslavia and impose unity of the central communist government of Yugoslavia. In direct response to an ongoing Serbian tariff, on October 30, 1990, Slovenia imposed customs duties on Serbian portable personal property. This action and counteraction ended the unified Yugoslav internal market. In November 1990 Marijana Milošević nee Marković, wife of President Milošević of Serbia and Supreme Chairman of Yugoslavia (Serbia and Montenegro), formed a new LCY, thus salvaged the old-faded organization of the same name. The new LCY comprises mostly of Serbian and Montenegrin retired military and former communist officials who advocate socialism (communism) principles and condemn the republics of Croatia and Slovenia as Western capitalist puppets. The Yugoslav republics were further separated by their reactions to the collapse of communist regimes in Eastern Europe. Pro-Western Croatia and Slovenia were the first republics to hold multiparty elections in early 1990; both elected non-communist governments. Later in 1990, the republics of Macedonia and Bosnia-Herzegovina followed suit, but Serbia and Montenegro gave decisive victories to the communists in their republic elections.

In the Middle East, following a dispute over oil production and financial repayment, Iraq invaded and annexed Kuwait on August 2, 1990. U.S. President George Bush promptly condemned the act of aggression, but used propaganda techniques to disseminate fear and exaggerate about Iraqi's world threat. President Bush visualized his big war based on a line in the shifting and sinking sands, organized a multinational coalition against a relatively weak Iraqi military establishment. As a rich nation, the USA had a large surplus of armament but lacked financial allocation for the manpower. Germany and Italy participated in military operations against Iraqi occupation forces. Japan contributed more than their fair share of financial support for UN member states to use "all necessary means to uphold and implement UN Security Council Resolution 660 of August 2, 1990." Deployment of U.S. troops, "Operation Desert Shield," began on August 7, 1990. Economic sanctions on Iraq were imposed by UN Security Council Resolution 678 of November 8, 1990 and set January 15, 1991 as a deadline for Iraqi forces to withdraw unconditionally from Kuwait. On January 12, 1991, President Bush obtained Congressional approval to use force against Iraq. With deployment of 532,000 U.S. troops (total allied forces of 700,000), about 2,000 aircraft stationed mostly in Saudi Arabia, and 100 warships in the Persian Gulf, the United States led a coalition of 30 nations, under the unified command of U.S. Gen. Norman H. Schwarzkopf (German: "Blackhead"), were ready to expel Iraqi forces from Kuwait. Operation "Desert Storm" commenced at midnight of January 16, 1991 with high-tech air war on Iraq that lasted for six weeks. The ground assault lasted only 100 hours (February 24-28). On February 26, the Allies entered Kuwait City. President Bush ordered a unilateral cease-fire on February 27, which was officially accepted and signed on April 6, 1991. The cease-fire proved to be premature because Saddam Hussein, President of Iraq, remained solidly in power, and defiant as ever. U.S. casualties during the Gulf War were 144 killed in combat, and 122 non-hostile deaths. An estimated 200,000 Iraqis were killed in the war.

The CSCE held the second summit in Paris on November 19-21, 1990, marking the formal end of the Cold War (the first CSCE summit was held in 1975 at Helsinki, Finland). On November 21, the leaders of the 34 participating states, represented by 11 presidents, 22 premiers, one Vatican representative and many foreign ministers who signed a treaty to reduce conventional weapons. They also signed a "Charter of Paris" for Europe, proclaiming an end to "confrontation" and pledging "democracy, peace, and unity." The following is the full text of the signed "Charter of Paris":

~ The Charter of Paris ~

Done at Paris, France   November 21, 1990

We, the Heads of State or Government of the States participating in the Conference on Security and Cooperation in Europe (CSCE) have assembled in Paris at a time of profound change and historic expectations. The era of confrontation and division of Europe has ended. We declare that henceforth our relations will be founded on respect and cooperation. Europe is liberating itself from the legacy of the past. The courage of men and women, the strength of the will of the peoples and the power of the ideas of the Helsinki Final Act have opened a new era of democracy, peace, and unity in Europe. Ours is a time for fulfilling the hopes and expectations our peoples have cherished for decades: steadfast commitment to democracy based on human rights and fundamental freedoms; prosperity through economic liberty and social justice; and equal security for all our countries. The Ten Principles of the Final Act will guide us towards this ambitious future, just as they have lighted our way towards better relations for the past fifteen years. Full implementation of all CSCE commitments must form the basis for the initiatives we are now taking to enable our nations to live in accordance with their aspirations. Wherefore, we, the undersigned High Representatives of the participating States, mindful of the high political significance we attach to the results of the Summit Meeting, and declaring our determination to act in accordance with the provisions we have adopted, have subscribed our signatures below.

[Signatures]

In reply to the YPA threats, on December 3, 1990, President Franjo Tudjman of Croatia, stated "the democratic institution of Croatia is here to stay, regardless of the YPA course of action." The Croatian people were strongly motivated by the belief that the historic uprising of the United Colonies, which culminated in the War of Independence of 1775-1783 against the despotic British tyranny, was similar in all respects to the Croat's conflict with Austro-Hungary until 1918, and with Serbian autocratic rulers, in one form or another, ever since the Versailles Treaty. These struggles for freedom were the sublime efforts by Croats, as an oppressed people, determined to win their rightful place among civilized nations free from tyrannical overlords.

In December 1990, Bosnia-Herzegovina elected a multiparty assembly in which the anti-communist Muslim Party for Democratic Action (PDA) won a plurality of the 240 seats, and PDA president Alija Izetbegović became the first non-communist president of the republic of Bosnia-Herzegovina.

On December 22, 1990, a new Constitution of the Republic of Croatia was promulgated by the Croatian Parliament. Pursuant to Article 140 of the Constitution of the Republic of Croatia, effective June 25, 1991, Croatia proclaimed the right of disassociation from the SFRY. Accepting the principles of the Charter of Paris, the Republic of Croatia guaranteed to all its citizens their national and all other fundamental rights and freedoms.

207

Article 14 of the Constitution read: "Citizens shall enjoy all rights and freedoms, regardless of race, color, sex, language, religion, political or other opinion, national or social origin, property, birth, education, social status or other properties." The Parliament established the official Croatian coat-of-arms (Hrvatski grb), the national flag (zastava), and the anthem (himna) of the Republic. The coat-of-arms is a shield consisting of two main components, comprised of 25 alternating checkered fields (13 red and 12 white or silver) and above it a red premier field with a five-pointed heraldic crown depicting the historical emblems of the ancient geographic regions of Croatia; appearing from left to right are Croatia, the Republic of Dubrovnik, Dalmatia, Istria, and Slavonia. The flag, rectangle in size with a ratio of the width to the length is one-to-two, it consists of three equal horizontal stripes of red (top), white (center), and blue (bottom) with the Croatian coat-of-arms in the center overlaping the three colors of the flag.

The official lyrics of the Croatian National Anthem (Himna Republike Hrvatske) "Lijepa Naša Domovino" by Antun Mihanović is as follows:

LIJEPA NAŠA DOMOVINO
(Our Lovely Homeland)

REPUBLIC OF CROATIA

(REPUBLIKA HRVATSKA)

1990

CHAPTER 6

SERBIAN WAR OF AGGRESSION, 1991-1995

Croatia was built on the dreams and deeds of immigrants. Let the world know that Croatia is one people free and independent, therefore all political connection between Croatia and Yugoslavia is completely dissolved. The ensuing analogy is offered to those who condemn Croatians for the steadfastness and resolute commitment to establish a sovereign republic of Croatia, based on democratic principles; to the creation of an open, free market economy; to the human rights; to an honorable peace and territorial integrity. It must be borne in mind that the United Colonies didn't achieve their independence by peaceful means, dialogue, or compromise. The British crown in its barbaric methods of imposed subjugation compelled the founding people of the United States of America to take up arms and fight for freedom and human dignity, against all forms of tyranny. After a prolonged war against Britain, the people of the thirteen United Colonies demanded a complete break with the British monarchy as an institution and King George III, as a despotic person. On June 7, 1776, delegates from the thirteen United Colonies meeting at the second Continental Congress in Philadelphia, PA heard Richard Henry Lee (1732-1794), introduce the following resolution in behalf of independence: "that these United Colonies are, and of right ought to be free and independent states, that they are absolved from all allegiance to the British crown, and that all political connection between the United Colonies and the state of Great Britain is, and ought to be, totally dissolved." Subsequently, the humiliated British mounted a full-scale military attack to crush the colonial rebellion. Despite the fact that the British were better equipped and trained, the British had to fight against determined and angry colonial patriots. In the beginning the British succeeded in isolating New England, they suffered heavy losses in defeating George Washington's Continental Army at Long Island and New York. The colonial patriots outnumbered and poorly equipped, fought gallantly to ultimately achieve freedom and independence for themselves and their future generation. Then, the colonists got rid of British tyranny. Now, Croatia got rid of the Serbian oppressor and freed themselves from Yugoslav tyranny.

Wars are often inspired and exacerbated by propaganda, innuendo, disinformation and lies, which are employed by dishonest people like Serbian political and military leaders. These incogitant individuals who in their propensity for speaking often forget to interlock their brain with their mouth, thus enabling them to tell the truth, if possible. Consequently, they disseminate misinformation and falsehoods to deceive the gullible populace.

Before 1919 there were wars between warmongering Serbia and other countries, but no war was ever fought between Croatia and Serbia. The bellicose attitude between Croatia and Serbia commenced with the tragic experiment of the tyrannical Serb Karađorđević government (1921-1940) created by the Versailles Peace Treaty. Contrary to Serbian allegations which reflect their ill views and dishonest interests, Serbs base their notion that they are always the victims when in reality they are the perpetrator of wrongs. The Serbian war of aggression (1991-1995) is the most tangible evidence on how overbearingly proud are the Serbs.

On January 8, 1991, a corrupted "Serbiangate" was discovered when the Serbian National Bank in Belgrade had covertly obtained 18,300 billion Yugoslav dinars ($1.4 billion) from the Serbian controlled Yugoslav Federal Bank in Belgrade. The Serbian government of Slobodan Milošević used the misappropriated money to pay the elite Serb communists, to provide for their increase in higher pensions and benefits, and reward them with advance payment for having supported the reelection of Milošević's Serbian Socialist Party (formerly known as the Serbian Communist Party). Furthermore, the Yugoslav Defense Minister Veljko Kadijević, a Serb tyrant, threatened to use the purportedly invincible Yugoslav People's Army-YPA (Jugoslavenska Narodna Armija-JNA) against Croatia if the Republic of Croatia went ahead with organizing their own defensive military organization.

The Serb-controlled Yugoslav Federal Presidency on January 9, 1991, authorized the Serbian dominated YPA to impose a crackdown and to disarm all Territorial Defense Force organizations. The obvious aim was to prevent the law abiding Croatians and Slovenians from being in possession of arms, therefore, unable to defend and protect their homes and families against Serb terrorists. Appropriately, Croatia and Slovenia defied the Serbian warnings and refused to disarm their forces. To create maximum fear upon the Serbs everywhere, on January 10, 1991 the despotic Slobodan Milošević declared that "if Yugoslavia became a confederation of independent states, the power of the military forces of the Republic of Serbia would unite all Serbs in a single state." Like so many other Serb propagandists, Milošević proceeded to ignore or twists the facts in an attempt to justify and support his prejudices.

In a common cause, the republics of Croatia and Slovenia concluded an agreement on January 20, 1991, whereby in the event of armed invasion by the Serbian dominated YPA against either republic, they pledged to intervene on behalf of each other and fight side by side against the invaders.

Municipalities along the old military frontier of Vojna Krajina comprised of majority ethnic Serbs on February 18, 1991, declared unilaterally a self-governing body of Krajina with the town of Knin as it's capital. The following background information should be useful for understanding the Vojna Krajina (Military Frontier or in German "Militärgrenze") commissioned by Rudolf II, Emperor of Habsburg (1576-1612). The name Krajina is extracted from the "Vojna Krajina." The Military Zone was constructed as military fortification along the dividing border, in the sparsely populated southern land of Croatia and Slavonia, between the two main protagonists and belligerant empires, Austria on one side and the Ottoman Turks on the other. Although administered by Austrian military authority and the official language was German, the territory was always an integral part of Croatia, never Serbia. The Vojna Krajina was abolished at the end of the nineteenth century and the territory was rightfully returned to Croatian administration. Contrary to Serbian propaganda and deliberate falsehood designed to deceive the ignorant and the gullible, the town of Knin from 1522 to 1688 was a Turkish military installation and never a part of Vojna Krajina. In fact according to the official census, the majority of ethnic Serbs domiciliated in the Republic of Croatia live outside Krajina. Moreover, Krajina was never a compact Serbian enclave comparable to the ethnic Albanian population of Kosova where the Albanians represent the overwhelming majority, and the Serbs represent a small minority. Nevertheless, the Albanians of Kosova are subjugated under the tyrannical Serbian government of Slobodan Milošević.

The Slovene Assembly in Ljubljana on February 20, 1991, adopted a resolution on the disassociation of Slovenia from the SFRY. After the overwhelming vote in favor of the resolution, Milan Kučan, President of Slovenia stated that Slovenia was willing to negotiate in good faith on the future constitution of a Yugoslav confederation. The next day, the Croatian Assembly in Zagreb approved a resolution asserting the primacy of Croatia's Constitution and laws over those of the communist SFRY regime.

The President of the Yugoslav Federal Presidency Borisav Jović, a fanatic Serb-Marxist, on March 2, 1991 ordered YPA units to the town of Pakrac to protect only ethnic Serbs and expel the Croatian police who were compelled to withdraw from the area on March 3. President Milošević of Serbia announced on March 18 that the Republic of Serbia no longer recognized the authority of the SFRY. The next day, Milosević expelled the delegate of Kosova from the Yugoslav Federal Presidency. A designated working group which included members from each of the six republics, began drafting political and economic issues for eventual incorporation to the future national constitution. Two of the most volatile issues were: (a) outline of a new federal structure, and (b) procedure for a republic to secede from the federation. In March 1991 U.S. President George Bush assured the Yugoslav Premier Ante Marković that the U. S. Government would not encourage or reward those who would break up and destroy the [communist] government of the SFRY.

On March 31 Serb terrorists attacked a Croatian police unit at the Plitvice National Park. The Croatian police took control of the park, but the YPA armored units arrived with instructions to eject the Croatians and transfer the park to the Serb terrorists. This unlawful action was strong evidence and acknowledgment that the YPA was directly and unequivocally supporting the Serb terrorists. On April 2 President Franjo Tudjman of Croatia declared, "we won't let a single centimeter of Croatian territory be taken from Croatia."

On April 11, during the summit at Brdo-kod-Kranja in Slovenia, the presidents of the six Yugoslav republics agreed to hold a referendum by the end of May 1991 to determine the future structure of Yugoslavia, namely a community of independent and sovereign states, as advocated by Croatia and Slovenia, and supported by Bosnia-Herzegovina and Macedonia or, a central federal state controlled by Serbia as advocated by Serbia and Montenegro.

The Croatian National Guard was created in April 1991, to replace the Territorial Defense Force which had been under the direct jurisdiction of the Serb dominated YPA. The Serb terrorists in Krajina demanded on April 29, the closing of the police station and the ouster of Croatian police officers from the village of Kijevo southeast of Knin. Again, the Serb controlled YPA intervened on behalf of Serb terrorists, and expelled the Croatian officials from Kijevo. On May 2, 1991, Croatian police units were ambushed by Serb terrorists in the Croatian village of Borovo Selo near Vukovar; the brutal attack resulted in the death of 13 police officers and four civilians. In the village of Polaca in southern Croatia, one Croat policeman was assassinated by Serb terrorists. In response to these atrocities, President Franjo Tudjman of Croatia characterized the brutalities as the beginning of Serbian terrorist activities against the Croatian people. Tudjman blamed Serb extremists (a.k.a. Serb-četnici) for acts of terrorism in the name of Serboslavia, also known as greater Serbia.

According to U.S. Senate Amendment to the Foreign Operation Appropriations Act of FY-1991, the United States assistance to SFRY was cut off effective May 5, 1991. This action was invoked to condemn the Serbian severe repression of human rights and for failure to conduct free elections in Kosova where the ethnic Albanians are the majority of the population. Hereupon, the provision required the U.S. Secretary of State to certify to Congress that Human Rights are in full compliance in the SFRY.

On May 6, 1991, thousands of Croats demonstrated outside the YPA headquarters in the Dalmatian city of Split, to protest against the YPA blockade of the village of Kijevo. In response to increasing unrest in Croatia, on May 7, 1991 the YPA stepped-up the military mobilization of Serb and Montenegrin reserve organizations for deployment against Croatia.

Amusingly, on May 12, 1991 Serb terrorists in Krajina held an unauthorized referendum to secede from the pro-western republic of Croatia and join in territorial unification with Milošević's Serbia. Promptly, the Government of Croatia declared that the referendum by Serb outlaws was fraudulent, illegal, and the results were declared null and void.

Under the system of annual rotating leadership of the collective Yugoslav Federal Presidency, the current Vice-President of the Presidency Stjepan Mesić (a Croat) on May 15, 1991 was scheduled to become the President of the Yugoslav Federal Presidency, but Milošević et al., filibustered the process and blocked Mesić from becoming the Yugoslav head of state, since at least five votes, or the simple majority was required. The eight members of the collective Yugoslav Federal Presidency (six republics and two autonomous provinces) voted as follows: four members (Croatia, Slovenia, Bosnia-Herzegovina, and Macedonia) voted in favor of Mesić, three others (Serbia, Kosova, and Vojvodina) voted against; and one (Montenegro) abstained.

In a statewide referendum held on May 19, 1991, the citizens of Croatia left no doubt of their strong belief in democratic government. The results of the referendum were: 83 percent of the total 3,652,225 registered voters went to the polls and 93.2 percent of them voted in favor of a "sovereign and independent Republic of Croatia."

The U.S. Ambassador to Yugoslavia, Warren Zimmermann, on May 21, 1991 asserted that Secretary of State James Baker would resume economic assistance to Yugoslavia if the issue of Yugoslav president was resolved and Stjepan Mesić was allowed to assume his role as President of the Yugoslav Federal Presidency. On May 24, 1991, U.S. Secretary Baker invoked the discretionary waiver authority of the U.S. Senate Amendment and so informed the U.S. Congress. In addition to the requisite certification, Secretary Baker also provided Members of Congress with the following statement on US policy toward Yugoslavia, on violations of human rights in the Republic of Yugoslavia (Serbia and Montenegro) and on new US policy steps: "The provisions of the U.S. Senate Amendment, which entered into effect on May 5, 1991, established certain conditions for United States assistance to Yugoslavia, as well as discretionary waiver authority for the Administration in implementing the Amendment. The Administration has examined its response to the provisions of the Amendment against the background of the ongoing crisis in Yugoslavia. US policy toward Yugoslavia is based on support for the interrelated objectives of democracy, dialogue, human rights, market reform, and unity."

The YPA augmented by battle-ready 25,000 infantry troops and supported by aircraft, armored vehicles, tanks, and artillery weapons arrived in Slovenia where military and political tension appeared to be mounting as the Republic of Slovenia edged toward independence which was strongly opposed by the Republic of Serbia. In preparation of a defensive strategy, on May 24, 1991 Slovene authorities responded by cutting off the water supply, electric power, and communications to YPA installations in Slovenia. On May 29, 1991, the leader of Serb-terrorists in Krajina, Milan Babić announced that in Krajina only the laws of the republic of Serbia were applicable.

Executing the will of the people as expressed by the referendum of May 19, 1991, the Republic of Croatia declared its "disassociation" from the despotic SFRY and proclaimed its independence on May 30, 1991. Hereafter, May 30th is celebrated as the "Statehood Day" and the National Holiday of Croatia. The constitutional decision on the sovereignty and independence of the Republic of Croatia became effective June 25, 1991 and formally seceded from the SFRY on October 8, 1991 (Saint Simon's day/Sveti Šimun dan). To protect and defend the territorial integrity of Croatia, the Government of Croatia announced the establishment of a Croatian armed forces to safeguard its sovereignty. On the same date, Slobodan Milošević, the demagogue of Serbia and promoter of "Serboslavia," warned that Croatia will never become independent unless the Krajina of Croatia becomes part of Serbia. Therefore, Milošević conceded that Croatia has the right to secede from the morally corrupt and despicable Yugoslav regime. The ethnic Serb minority, comprising 12.2% of the total population in the Republic of Croatia, were against the legitimate democratic government of Croatia because they vehemently opposed, and intensely resented being deprived of their privileges as an elite class, and hereafter to be considered just like any other citizen of Croatia, with all the rights and full equality. These irrational Serbs insisted in a permanent affirmative action and the continuation of their accustomed "status quo" (insisting in numerically better jobs and higher salary, preferential treatment, and special tax exemption), similar to those conferred to them during the Serbian Karađorđevic monarchy (1921-1941), later extended to them by Tito's communist tyranny (1945-1990). The paranoid Milošević and his Serbian clique continued to practice trickery against Croatia, hoping to provoke and create incidents that would justify the YPA to intervene on behalf of Serbia, occupy and destroy Croatia. On June 6, 1991 the leaders of the Yugoslav six constitutent republics met in Zagreb, Croatia. They agreed to consider a compromise plan as basis for future negotiation to transform the Yugoslav republic into a loose confederation, united for a common purpose. In reality, this was another Milošević gimmick intended to deceive the international community. A public demonstration took place in Kosova on June 13, 1991. The leader of ethnic Albanians in Kosova, Veton Suroj was arrested by the Serbian police and sentenced to sixty days imprisonment for organizing a peaceful demonstration in the form of a funeral procession, symbolizing the "internment of Serbian brutality."

After the CSCE foreign minister meeting at Berlin where the membership discussed the political situation in Yugoslavia and Albania, U.S. Secretary of State James Baker visited Yugoslavia on June 21 and Albania on June 22, 1991. In Belgrade, during a news conference, Secretary Baker stated that the United States has had a longstanding, close, and friendly relationship with the Republic of Yugoslavia. During the Cold War era, the United States firmly supported the unity, territorial integrity, and independence of [communist] Yugoslavia. In the post Cold War era, the United States had strongly supported Yugoslavia's transition to democracy and a free market. Yugoslavia has long enjoyed most-favored-nation (MFN) trade status with the United States and was the ninth largest user of the Generalized System of Preference (GSP), which gives duty free access for many exports to the United States of America.

* * * * *

~ US Secretary of State in Belgrade ~

June 21, 1991

Secretary James Addison Baker III, during his one day visit to Belgrade, met with Yugoslav Premier Ante Marković and the presidents of the six Yugoslav constituent republics. Concerning the future of the Socialist Federal Republic of Yugoslavia (SFRY), here are excerpts from remarks by Secretary Baker at the Federation Palace in Belgrade, Yugoslavia, on the same day:

"Let me say that we came to Yugoslavia because of our concern about the crisis, really, our concern about the dangers of a disintegration of this country. Instability and break-up of Yugoslavia, we think, could have some very tragic consequences, not only here [in Yugoslavia], but more broadly, in Europe as well. We're obviously not alone in having these concerns. The 34 other countries of the Conference on Security and Cooperation in Europe (CSCE) have all expressed, along with us, our collective concern when we were at our meeting in Berlin. My discussions with Yugoslavia's neighbors and with members of the European Community (EC) also indicated the depths of these concerns. And I have today conveyed these very serious concerns in the meetings that I have been privileged to have. In all candor, ladies and gentlemen, what I heard today has not allayed my concerns, or our concerns. Nor, I suspect, will it allay the concerns of others when we give them a readout of these meetings. Now having said that, I do have to say that we did see and find some common ground here today. First of all, everyone I spoke to stressed the fact that they were prepared to continue a dialogue on the future of Yugoslavia. Secondly, all of them indicated a wish to avoid violence and all of them indicated strong opposition to any use of force. Thirdly, they all recognized the legitimate interest of the international community, and, I think, welcomed its continued effort to promote dialogue and promote a peaceful resolution of these problems through negotiations. In all of these meetings, I stressed the importance of respecting human and minority rights, of continuing the process of democratization, and of continuing a dialogue to create a new basis for unity. In particular, I emphasized the need to move ahead on the constitutional rotation of the federal presidency, as well as the need to avoid unilateral acts that could preempt the negotiating process."

* * * * *

As a follow-up to the above remarks by U.S. Secretary Baker, and in reply to a question from a member of the newsmedia, should any of the Yugoslav constituent republics break away, Secretary Baker stated: "I was asked the question this morning whether or not the United States would recognize the forthcoming declaration of independence by Slovenia, a declaration that is expected, I think, in a day or so. I said that it would not be the policy of the United States to recognize that declaration, because we want to see this problem resolved through negotiation and through dialogue and not through preemptive unilateral actions." After the conversation between Secretary Baker and Serbia's President Slobodan Milošević, it appeared that Milošević perceived that the U.S. would look the other way and ignore Serbia's hostile aim with regard to territorial conquests, whence, Milošević decided to seize lands from the other Yugoslav constituent republics and merge them into Serboslavia.

Four of the six constituent republics, which once comprised communist Yugoslavia, unilaterally declared their "independence" during 1991: the Republic of Croatia on June 25; the Republic of Slovenia on June 25; the Republic of Macedonia on September 8; and the Republic of Bosnia-Herzegovina on October 15.

At an emergency session on June 25, 1991, the Serb-controlled Yugoslav Federal parliament in Belgrade called on the YPA to intervene and protect Yugoslavia's borders. However, the post of President of the Yugoslav Federal Presidency and the Commander-in-Chief of the YPA, was still vacant since the May 15, 1991 deadlock, and therefore the YPA lacked the constitutional authority to comply with the parliamentary request. The proclamation of independence on June 25, 1991 by the Republic of Croatia from the Yugoslav communist regime was followed by an ignominious conflict "Serbian War of Aggression" orchestrated and promoted by Serb extremists, such as the notorious paramilitary and political group "četnik" (plural, četnici), and directed by Serb and Montenegrin communists under the duet leadership of the ruthlessly fanatic Slobodan Milošević and his spouse, Mirjana Marković-Milošević an ardent Serb-Marxist. By their complete control of the rump government of Yugoslavia (Serbia and it's puppet Montenegro), the YPA was ordered to attack and occupy the Republic of Slovenia on the laughable pretense of defending the Yugoslav territory from Martian invasion.

In the town of Glina, Croatia, on June 26, 1991, four people were killed during fighting initiated by Serb terrorists when they attempted unsuccessfully to take control of the local police station. Also, a Croat policeman was killed during a clash with Serb terrorists in the village of Bršadin. An ambush by Serb-bands involving the Croatian police in the Krajina resulted in two policemen and three civilians killed. In the face of Serbia's war of aggression and escalating terrorist activities, the EC assumed a negotiating role to end the cessation of hostilities. EC's declarations, brought to the United Nations Security Council by three of its members Belgium, Britain, and France, included the following: (a) dispatch of monitors, (b) implementation of cease-fire, (c) return of all forces to their previous positions, (d) a three-month suspension of the declarations of independence by the republics of Croatia and Slovenia, and (e) embargo on armaments and military equipment to the whole of Yugoslavia.

After Slovenia seized their territorial border custom facilities on June 26, 1991, trucks and various construction equipment were used to place road-blocks, thus impeding YPA units from reaching custom posts along the Slovenian borders with Italy, Austria, and Hungary. The YPA under Gen. Konrad Kolsek, a Slovene, commander of the YPA Fifth Army bombed and then closed down the airport of Ljubljana, capital of Slovenia. Fierce fighting erupted throughout Slovenia, resulting in at least 100 Slovenes killed and wounded, and hundreds of YPA soldiers killed, wounded and captured. Yugoslav Premier Ante Marković, on June 27-28, 1991 denied responsibility for the YPA intervention in Slovenia. Marković declared that "the federal government of Yugoslavia never ordered, nor could order, any military action in Slovenia."

In the meantime, on June 28, 1991, German Foreign Minister Hans Dietrich Genscher, announced that the 35-nations of the CSCE had reached a consensus on the Yugoslav crisis, specifically, the Serbian war of aggression. The cease-fire was mediated by three foreign ministers representing the EC; the so-called "troika" included Jacques Poos of Luxembourg, Gianni De Michelis of Italy, and Hans van den Broek of the Netherlands. The terms of agreements were: (a) three months postponement of Croatia and Slovenia declarations of independence; (b) allow the ascension of Stjepan Mesić, a Croat, to President of the Yugoslav Federal Presidency on June 30; and (c) withdrawal to their barracks of all YPA units deployed in Slovenia. General Blagoje Adžić, a Serb-Marxist and YPA Chief-of-Staff, on July 2, 1991 vowed to establish full control with his overwhelming military power and crush all democratic and anti-communist resistances.

Meanwhile the EC members differed whether to recognize Croatia and Slovenia, as advocated by Belgium and Denmark. In keeping with established democratic tradition, German Chancellor Helmut Kohl stated, "the peoples of Europe must be free to choose their own future." In reiterating the German government policy, Foreign Minister Hans-Dietrich Genscher warned that Germany would insist on severe political and economic sanctions against Yugoslavia if the YPA continued to defy the legal authority of the federal government.

* * * * *

~ President Bush's Report on Implementation of the CSCE ~

Washington, DC, July 1, 1991

The following is the U.S. President's report to Congress on implementation of the Helsinki Final Act of the Conference on Security and Cooperation in Europe (CSCE) for the period from April 1, 1990 to March 1, 1991:

"During the reporting period, Yugoslavia suffered a deepening political crisis significantly affecting its performance under the Helsinki principles. In many parts of the country, there was a significant broadening of the democratic process. At the same time, rising ethnic tensions, most notably in Serbian-dominated Kosova, led to repression and violence. Yugoslavia's adherence to Helsinki principles expanded during the reporting period, but in Kosova the reverse was true, leading fellow CSCE states to invoke the Human Dimension Mechanism. The one-party communist system that ruled Yugoslavia since World War II largely disappeared in 1990. For the first time since before World War II, Yugoslavia experienced multi-party elections in all six constituent republics. Balloting procedures in most republics were generally fair, but in Serbia, the ruling communist party used its control of the media and financial resources to the detriment of the opposition parties. The federal government, under Prime Minister Ante Markovic, attempted a sweeping program of political and economic reforms. After initial progress, this program fell afoul of inter-republican differences, which have, for example, blocked a number of proposed amendments to the federal constitution intended to eliminate remnants of the one-party system and allow multi-party elections at the federal level.

Rising ethnic tensions and the persistence of old anti-democratic structures in Yugoslavia reached the point where they threatened the existence of a unified federal state. Conflict deepened, especially in parts of Croatia and Bosnia. Ethnic conflict in Kosova between majority Albanians and minority Serbs, who consider the province the 'heart of Serbia,' led to massive violations of human rights, including scores of deaths at the hands of police, thousands of arrests for the expression of political opinions, and the firing of tens of thousands for political strikes. Serbian/Croat tension also reached dangerous levels. The Yugoslav military is highly secretive and provides little information about its activities to the Yugoslav people, let alone to the CSCE partners. As the Yugoslav crisis worsened, the Yugoslav military played an increasingly assertive political role, acting essentially outside the control of civilian authorities and in an anti-democratic fashion."

* * * * *
* * * * *

~ Conflict in Yugoslavia ~

Washington, DC, July 2, 1991

Statement by White House Press Secretary Marlin Fitzwater:

"The President of the United States deeply regrets the resumption of violent conflict in Yugoslavia and urges all parties to observe the cease-fire agreement worked out with representatives of the European Community (EC). President Bush also urges Yugoslav authorities to accept an EC offer of international cease-fire observers. The United States is prepared to endorse such a plan at tomorrow's emergency meeting of the CSCE in Prague, Czechoslovakia. President Bush has written a letter to President Stjepan Mesić of Yugoslavia expressing his grave concern over the situation in Yugoslavia and urging him to ensure that civilian control over the military is reestablished and peace restored. He also expressed the hope that all parties in Yugoslavia would seek a dialogue toward a new and democratic basis for Yugoslavia's future, in which the aspirations of all the Yugoslav peoples can be realized. The President reiterated US support for the EC's ongoing efforts to help resolve the Yugoslav crisis and urged President Mesić to continue cooperating with the United States, the EC, and others in the interest of a peaceful transition to a new Yugoslavia."

* * * * *

To celebrate the happiest "4th of July," thousands of Croatian and Slovenian conscripts disclaimed their affiliation with the Serb-dominated YPA, returned home to volunteer in their local militia, defend their loved ones and fight against the Serb-fomented aggression. Fighting broke out in Ljubljana between the YPA and the independent Slovenian defense forces. In Zagreb, capital of Croatia, thousands of unarmed Croatians joined their fellow citizens in installing barricades to obstruct passage of YPA convoys.

At the EC meeting in The Hague, Netherlands, on July 5, 1991, the CSCE imposed an arms embargo and freezing of financial and economic aid to Yugoslavia. The EC declared that it would approve diplomatic recognition to Croatia and Slovenia if Yugoslavia does not accept EC binding mediation. On July 7 the EC delegation and representatives from Croatia, Slovenia, and the SFRY government held peace talks on the Island of Brijuni (Brijoni). The terms of the Brijuni agreement called for (a) three-month delay of implementation by Croatia and Slovenia their independence declarations; (b) immediate cessation of hostilities, YPA troops would retreat to their bases, Slovenian militia would be demobilized, and all prisoners would be released; (c) Slovenian police would be allowed to control the customs posts on the republic's borders with Italy, Austria, and Hungary. Customs revenues would be placed under a special account and shared jointly by Slovenia and the SFRY government; and (d) the EC would station observers in Slovenia and Croatia. While the EC mediated the truce talks, a group of Serb thugs began fighting in the northern Croatian village of Tenja. The fighting temporarily ended when YPA tanks interposed themselves between the combatants, thus allowing the Serbian forces more time to reorganize and renew their terrorist attacks.

After encountering unexpectedly stiff resistance from the Slovenian defense force, the YPA in frustation and near defeat decided to save face and withdrew from Slovenian territory. On July 18, 1991, the Serb-controlled Yugoslav communist regime in Belgrade announced the withdrawal of its YPA from the Republic of Slovenia. The embarrassment and humiliation for the YPA military failure was averted by a three month cease-fire arranged by the EC. At the end of the cease-fire Slovenia reasserted its independence, but Serbia and YPA in order to prevent their own disaster chose not intervene militarily. Therefore, the YPA and the Serbian resistance to Slovenian independence ended. Meanwhile, the Republic of Slovenia had already strengthened cultural and economic relations with western European nations, especially Austria and Germany, shed the remnants of the communist centralized economic system, and proceeded with the rapid integration into western market systems.

While the fighting in Slovenia abated, heavy fighting had persisted throughout Croatia, between the well-armed YPA supplementary units and Serb irregular forces on the one side, and the outnumbered and poorly equipped Croatian National Guard forces on the other. The Croatian forces blockaded waterways, encircled the YPA military barracks and facilities, closed airspace, and disrupted communications and services within the Croatian territory. Nevertheless, Croatian territory had been persistently subjected to YPA and Serb-četnici direct fire from artillery, rocket batteries, armored vehicles, naval and air units, causing high civilian casualties and property destructions. There had been forced evacuations of large numbers of Croatian civilian refugees from Serbian occupied territories of Croatia, thus altering the demographic composition of Serbian controlled areas.

In the Croatian village of Mirkovci, fighting erupted when Serb-četnici attacked the Croatian militia and killed 20 people. YPA tanks positioned inside the territory of the republic of Serbia shelled the Slavonian village of Erdut killing nine Croatian guardsmen in their military barracks, and three Croatian guardsmen in nearby Dalj, Slavonia, on July 25, 1991. Units of Serb-četnici on July 26, used Croat civilians as human shields when they seized the town of Struga, about 60 mi/95 km south of Zagreb. The EC troika that had mediated the cease-fire in Slovenia - Hans van den Broek of the Netherlands, Jacques Poos of Luxembourg, and Joao de Deus Pinheiro of Portugal - arrived in Belgrade on July 31 to stem the newest bloodshed. The negotiation had collapsed on August 4 when Serbian representatives abruptly decided to boycott the meetings chaired by the EC mediator.

Under YPA and terrorist attack, on July 31, 1991 Croatian forces retreated from the town of Kostajnica, a mountain town located on the Croatia-Bosnia border 55 mi/88 km south of the city of Zagreb. A major government reorganization approved on August 1 by the Croatian Parliament (Sabor) was implemented on August 3, 1991. President Tudjman included in his cabinet members of the political opposition in a "government of democratic unity" which continued to be dominated by the Croatian Democratic Union-CDU (Hrvatska demokratska zajednica-HDZ). For the record, the new democratic cabinet had two communists, two social democrats, seven Independents, and five members of smaller parties.

221

An estimated 50,000 Croatians fled from their homes to escape air and ground attacks by YPA and Serb outlaws. As many as 80 Croatian militiamen were killed fighting the Serbian terrorists and YPA forces in the town of Dalj, in northeastern Slavonia. Croatian forces on August 2, 1991, recaptured the town of Kostajnica in the Banija region, but lost the village of Erdut, Dalj, and Aljmas near Osijek. Envoys of the WEU meeting in London, England, on August 7, 1991 failed to reach a decision on a proposal to send a military peacekeeping force to Croatia. German Chancellor Helmut Kohl threatened Serbia with economic sanctions, and with German diplomatic recognition of Croatia and Slovenia, if truce violations by Serbs continued. The President of the Yugoslav Federal Presidency, Stjepan Mesić on August 8, 1991 stated that Croatia would not negotiate any change to its borders or allow Serb-terrorists to keep Croatian territory they had seized during the Serbian war of aggression. The CSCE meeting in Prague, Czechoslavakia, offered their "good office" for a mediation of the crisis in Yugoslavia. While the world's attention was focused on the fighting in Croatia and Slovenia, the YPA and the government of Serbia had tightened their grip on the two provinces of Kosova and Vojvodina. The Serbian parliament approved the Serb military takeover of the television and radio stations in Pristina and Novi Sad, capitals of the provinces of Kosova and Vojvodina respectively.

The President of Croatia, Franjo Tudjman set August 31, 1991 as the deadline for YPA to withdraw their troops from Croatia or risk being treated as an occupation force and "all necessary steps" would be taken to defend the territory of Croatia. Although the mandated truce that began August 7, 1991 still existed in Croatia, as of August 23, 1991 there had been hundreds of documented violations committed by the Serbs, and more than 100 Croatians killed by the Serbs during the so-called ceasefire.

Fighting between Serb terrorists and Croatian National Guard erupted after the German Foreign Minister, Hans Dietrich-Genscher reminded the Yugoslav Ambassador to Germany, Boris Frlec, that Germany would recognize Croatia and Slovenia as separate states if the YPA continued to ally itself with the Serb terrorists in Croatia. The government of Austria declared that it would recognize Croatia and Slovenia if other European nations did the same. Meanwhile, fierce fighting was reported in the city of Vukovar, where Croatian forces were besieged by Serb-četnici supported by YPA forces. The fighting also continued around Osijek, Vinkovci and several other communities in eastern Slavonia. The YPA forces launched a full-scale offensive in support of Serb terrorists fighting in the Republic of Croatia. Yugoslav armored units, planes and gunboats shelled and bombed Croat military installations throughout Croatia. More than 100,000 Croats had fled from the Slavonia and Dalmatia regions. Thousands of refugees had crossed the border into Croatia and Hungary to escape Serbian mercenaries. The cities of Vukovar and Vinkovci in the northeastern Slavonia region of Croatia, were bombarded on an unprecedented scale. Fighting also continued around the town of Knin in northern Dalmatia where Serb outlaws ordered the general mobilization of every male between the age of 18 and 60.

Expressing dismay at the increased Serbian brutality, destruction of properties, complete disregard for humanity, and the active YPA support for terrorist Serbs, the EC, on August 27, 1991, convened a special conference to establish an arbitration procedure to resolve the explosive crisis. On the same day, President Franjo Tudjman of Croatia met with two YPA officials, Defense Minister Veljko Kadijević and his chief of staff Blagoje Adzić on the island of Brijuni in the northern Adriatic Sea, and concluded a cease-fire agreement. Needless to say, the cease-fire fell through almost immediately as the untrustworthy Serbs kept killing and destroying throughout Croatia. Austrian Foreign Minister Alois Mock urged the western government to consider military intervention to bring an end to the YPA's violence in Croatia. Serb irregulars assisted by YPA seized the important Beničanci (45 38' N; 18° 11' E) oil field located in eastern Slavonia. Until 1990, Beničanci's refinery accounted for one-third of SFRY oil production. On August 29, 1991, Henri Wijnaendts, a Dutch diplomat who headed a team of EC observers in Croatia, said that his team had gathered conclusive evidence that the YPA was directly involved in fighting against Croatia. Serb terrorists assisted by YPA launched their attacks on Croatian forces throughout Dalmatia. Violent clashes took place in and around the towns of Gospić, Knin, Kruševo and other locations. On September 2, 1991, the Yugoslav Federal Presidency voted 7 to 1, to approve an EC plan to end the conflict in Croatia, but clashes fomented by Serb-terrorists and their staunch YPA sponsor continued in spite of the peace accord. Serbs bombarded Vukovar and Osijek, also launched an offensive near Petrinja in south central Croatia.

The EC foreign ministers met at The Hague, Netherlands, on September 3, 1991, and decided to hold a peace conference on the crisis beginning September 7. The EC nominated three constitutional law scholars - Robert Badinter of France, Aldo Corrasaniti of Italy, and Roman Herzog of Germany - to the arbitration panel. British diplomat Peter Alexander Rupert Carrington, former foreign minister who had negotiated an end to the civil war in Zimbabwe in 1979, was named the chairman of the conference. The foreign ministers of 12 EC nations and the presidents of Croatia, Serbia, and Yugoslavia were in attendance at the peace conference. Before adjourning on September 7, 1991, the conference adopted a formal statement: "The declaration established as a basic for negotiation that (a) internal borders could not be changed by force; (b) the rights of minorities must be guaranteed; and (c) full account must be taken of all legitimate concerns and aspirations. Any differences which could not be resolved through negotiation would be submitted to an EC arbitration commission." Repeatedly and sarcastically, the SFRY welcomed the EC and UN sponsored peace agreements, but in distinctive Serbian demagoguery they broke every promise, thus displaying their arrogant way of life.

Two Muslims were killed in fighting with Serb rebels on September 4, 1991 near the town of Bratunac northwest of Srebrenica. These hostile confrontations marked the first instance in which violence had spread in Bosnia-Herzegovina. The YPA and Serbian forces stepped up their attacks on the besieged cities of Vukovar and Osijek. The government of Germany warned that it would unilaterally grant formal recognition to Croatia and Slovenia, if the YPA and Serb terrorists persisted in their war path of aggression.

September 8, 1991 the Republic of Macedonia by a referendum became the third republic to vote for secession from the rump FRY (Serbia and Montenegro). In the referendum, 75% of the registered electorate of 1,400,000 voters had cast ballots in favor of secession. Three-fourths of Macedonia's 1.3 million eligible voters had participated in the referendum (Macedonia's ethnic Albanian minority, which made up about 25% of the population had boycotted the referendum). The results showed that 95% had voted in favor of a "sovereign and independent Macedonia."

Fierce fighting in various towns, particularly in Okućani and Pakrac in central Croatia, erupted as Croatian forces fought against the YPA and Serb irregulars, and converged toward the control of highways linking eastern Croatia with the capital city of Zagreb. Serb-četnici backed by the YPA seized the important Maslenica bridge span over the Novigrad Channel (Novigradsko Zdrilo) located on the main highway linking Zagreb with the port city of Zadar on the Dalmatian coast.

The YPA forces involved in the Croatian fighting had ignored orders issued by Stjepan Mesić, President of the Yugoslav Federal Presidency, to withdraw to their barracks. Yugoslav Defense Minister Veljko Kadijević on September 12, 1991 rejected the legal order issued by Mesić (the commander in chief of the YPA) to withdraw the YPA troops to their barracks. The insubordination of Kadijević was tantamount to sedition, therefore, he should have been arrested, court-martialled, and punished like a traitor. The President of the Yugoslav Federal Presidency, Stjepan Mesić accused the YPA of staging what amounted to a military coup by ignoring his Presidential Directives. On September 12, 1991 at the CSCE during a human rights conference in Moscow, James A. Baker III, U.S. Secretary of State, appealed to Serbia and the YPA to halt their offensives in Croatia or risk complete isolation.

The Yugoslav crisis was part of the turmoil besetting former communist Europe and the former Soviet Union. The most tragic events occurred in Croatia, where Croatians paid a heavy toll in human life, a paralyzed economy, buildings and homes ruined, hospitals and churches destroyed, historical monuments destroyed and damaged, and the infrastructure devastated. The conflict perpetrated by the Serbian war of aggression resulted in one-third of the territory of Croatia being occupied by militant Serb and Montenegro forces helped and encouraged by Serb dominated YPA.

On September 19, 1991, the EC declared that it would accept any results negotiated and conducted in good faith, provided the outcome was based on EC enunciated principles: (a) the unacceptability of the use of force; (b) the change of borders by force which EC was determined not to recognize; and (c) respect for human rights of all peoples. Australia, informed the UN Secretary General that the situation had deteriorated to the point that the Security Council should consider the issue as a matter of urgency.

U.S. Deputy Secretary of State Lawrence Eagleburger met on October 1, 1991 with Serbian Deputy Premier Kosutić. The Deputy Secretary referred to the Secretary's statement on Yugoslavia at the September 25, 1991, meeting of the UN Security Council. The Deputy Secretary reiterated to Kosutić that the USA assesses actions by the Serbian leadership and the Yugoslav People's Army aimed at redrawing by force the internal borders of Yugoslavia as a grave challenge to the basic values and principles which underlie the CSCE. The Deputy Secretary emphasized to Kosutić that while the United States appreciates the concerns of Serbs inside and outside Serbia in the present context, the United States does not and will not accept repression and aggression in the name of those concerns. The Deputy Secretary underscored to Kosutić the United States, like the European Community (EC), is determined never to recognize any outcome of the Yugoslav crisis that would be based on the use of force to change Yugoslavia's internal borders. The Deputy Secretary underscored to Kosutić that continued use of aggressive force by the Serbian leadership in tandem with the YPA will only ensure their exile from the new Europe. Eagleburger urged that the Serbian government take clear and concrete steps to demonstrate its commitment to the EC-sponsored peace conference chaired by Peter Carrington of Britain, and to renounce any intention of seeking internal border changes through the use of force. The USA has repeatedly called upon all republics in Yugoslavia to respect the rights of all national groups living within their boundaries. In this regard, Serbian violations of the human rights of ethnic Albanians in Kosova continue to be a major concern in the CSCE context. The United States will accept any future political arrangements that are decided on peacefully and democratically by the peoples of Yugoslavia through dialogue and negotiation.

The Security Council convened on September 25, 1991, in response to requests from Austria, Canada, and Hungary that it urgently consider the deteriorating situation in communist Yugoslavia, which they feared could endanger international peace and security. The UN became actively involved in the situation when the Security Council, meeting at the ministerial level, unanimously adopted its Resolution 713 expressing deep concern at the fighting in Yugoslavia and calling on all States to implement immediately a "general and complete embargo on all deliveries of weapons and military equipment to Yugoslavia".

On October 8, 1991, the UN Secretary General (January I, 1982 - December 31, 1991) Javier Pérez de Cuéllar of Peru appointed Cyrus Robert Vance, former U.S. Secretary of State, as his Personal Envoy for Yugoslavia. Thereafter, the Secretary-General and his Personal Envoy maintained constant contact with all the parties to the conflict, with the Presidency of the EC, with the Chairman of the CSCE - participating States, with Peter Carrington of Britain, Chairman of the ECCY, and with other interested parties in their efforts to find a solution to the crisis. As part of the collective effort to stop the fighting and to find a peaceful solution to the conflict, the UN Secretary General's Personal Envoy undertook several missions to Yugoslavia from 11 to 18 October 1991, during which time he discussed with all concerned the feasibility of deploying a UN peacekeeping operation. At the sixth plenary meeting on October 18, 1991, the Chairman of the EC Conference on Yugoslavia presented a draft paper for a settlement: (a) sovereign and independent republics; (b) comprehensive arrangements for the protection of human rights; and (c) recognition of the original establised international borders.

The main conflict took place in Slavonia, in eastern Croatia, although Serbia, Montenegro, and the YPA concentrated their naval blockades and fierce air strikes on the seaport-city of Zadar in northern Dalmatian. Also, the YPA attacked and besieged the city of Dubrovnik in southern Dalmatia, despite the fact that it contained no military installations and less than five percent of the population were ethnic Serb minorities.

* * * * *

~ **U.S. Promotes Peace in Yugoslavia** ~

Washington, DC, October 17, 1991

Statement by Ralph Johnson, Principal Deputy Assistant Secretary of State for European and Canadian Affairs before the Senate Foreign Relations Committee:

"The events we are witnessing today in Yugoslavia are nothing less than a tragedy: a tragedy for the peoples of Yugoslavia, a tragedy for Europe, and a tragedy for the entire world community. Forty-six years after the killing ended the bloodiest war that human civilization has known (a war that was particularly devastating to Yugoslavia) today Yugoslavia is poised on the brink of massive violence. The nearly continuous fighting between Croatian forces and those of the federal Yugoslav military and forces of the Serbian republic, with the accompanying naval blockades and air strikes, is the worst aspect of this crisis. It has led to death, destruction, and suffering in much of Croatia and has prompted tens of thousands of people to flee their towns and villages, in some cases for the safety of other countries. It has reintroduced in Europe a level of violence and cruelty that has not been seen since the Second World War. The aggressive expansionism of the Serbian regime of Slobodan Milošević, with the support of the Yugoslav People's Army (YPA), has intimidated the governments of Bosnia-Herzegovina and Macedonia, both of which fear that the fighting could at any day spill over into their republics and ignite an even worse explosion. The Serbian government has repressed dissent at home and has revoked the autonomy of the Provinces of Vojvodina and Kosova. The Hungarian minority in Vojvodina is fearful for its future, but for the ethnic Albanians of Kosova, their worst nightmares have already come true: Serbia has closed down Kosova's schools, fired ethnic Albanians from the civil service, schools, and universities; arrested hundreds of Albanians on trumped-up charges; embarked on a campaign to Serbianize the province; and blocked the free exercise of democracy during the recent vote on independence.

The US Government was the first to condemn these actions and, along with 16 other CSCE states, invoked the CSCE human dimension mechanism in August 1990 to underscore our concern over the repression by Serbia. Since then, the situation has worsened. USA again raised the issue of Serbian actions at the Moscow human rights conference last month. But Serbia's intentions have become increasingly clear, and increasingly more disturbing. United States public position on this has been unambiguous. I also want to stress that no one is blameless in this conflict. The policies of the Croatian government toward the Serbian minority does not justify Serbia's action, but they have contributed to the atmosphere of tension and recrimination that led to violence.There are also sensitivities related to the historic experience of Croatian-Serbian conflict in the Second World War, during which the Croatian puppet government allied with Nazi Germany, run by the Ustasha movement, massacred hundreds of thousands of people, mainly Serbs, Jews, and Gypsies. And there are, unfortunately a sizable number of people in Croatia today - not the current government but of more extreme elements of the nationalist movement - who are proud to call themselves the heirs of the Ustasha. I certainly do not associate all Croatian nationalists with that tendency, but to Serbs this is a real and understandable concern.

With the departure this month of most YPA units from Slovenia, the republic has traveled far down the road to independence. United States position on the future of Slovenia is identical to that toward Yugoslavia as a whole. We will accept any future political arrangements that are decided on peacefully and democratically by the Yugoslav people, through dialogue and negotiation, but we do not believe that partial solutions, unilateral actions or outcomes achieved by force and intimidation are conducive to achieving comprehensive settlement. Here are the five principles that Secretary Baker enunciated in his address to the CSCE meeting in Moscow last month that are also central to our policy toward Yugoslavia as a whole and its individual republics. We have made this position very clear in response to requests from Croatia and Slovenia for United States recognition of their independence. To reiterate, the five points are: (a) determining the future of the country peacefully and democratically, consistant with CSCE principles; (b) respect for all existing borders, both internal and external, and change to those borders only through peaceful and consensual means; (c) support for democracy and the rule of law, emphasizing the key role of elections in the democratic process; (d) safeguarding of human rights, based on full respect for the individual and including equal treatment of minorities; and (e) respect for international law and obligations, especially adherence to the Helsinki Final Act and the Charter of Paris."

* * * * *

227

The above statement of October 17, 1991 by Assistant Secretary of State Ralph Johnson wrongly depicted the Serbians as anti-Axis. In reality, the Serbian puppet government under Gen. Milan Nedić, collaborated with Nazi Germany. Furthermore, the Serb-četnici of Draža Mihajlović and other extremist groups collaborated with Nazi Germany and Fascist Italy. Although, the Croatian puppet government under Ante Pavelić allied with Axis forces, the Independent Republic of Croatia was divided by a demarcation line which designated the boundary "sphere of influence" of the Axis power, Germany in the northeastern area and Italy in the southwestern area. Perhaps, Tito's communist partisans were the only ones who fought during the Second World War on the Allied side and were declared victorious. Ralph Johnson and others speaking in diplomatic gobbledegook should know better than to disseminate misinformation and tell half-truths since doing so is tantamount to cover-up. The actual problem between Croatia and Serbia started after the First World War when the Serbian autocracy reneged on a commitment agreed and signed on July 20, 1917 at Corfu (Kérkyra), and proceeded in establishing an arrogant, domineering, and undemocratic regime.

It is imperative that the truth always be known; therefore, it is morally unjust and historically wrong to state that Croatians killed Serbians without continuing the sentence and asserting that Serbians killed Croatians, etc. Throughout the Second World War several foreign armies and numerous military and paramilitary elements in support of nationalist or internationalist causes, like pro or anti-Axis, and pro or anti-communists, operated inside the Yugoslav territory and committed crimes against humanity. According to the most reliable data available and contrary to Serbian propaganda, a total of 321,000 Croats, Slovenes, Muslims, Macedonians, Serbs, and Montenegrins were killed during the war. Today, fifty years since the end of the war, no comprehensive casualty figures have been published which listed the number of people slaughtered within each belligerent, political, and ethnic group by their antagonists. Undoubtedly, wilful killing and reprisals had been committed by all sides against civilians, belligerents, and suspected or known collaborators. Numerically, some murderers may have committed fewer crimes, but all were horrible, heinous, and inexcusable acts of barbarism.

On October 31, 1991, Serb-četnici in cooperation with YPA forces kept advancing into Croatian territory and bombarded the Croatian strongholds in Vukovar, Vinkovci, Osijek, Zadar, Dubrovnik, and other locations.

In November 1991 the recently established Croatian Supreme Council (War Cabinet) chaired by the President of the Republic of Croatia, Franjo Tudjman, ordered all Croatian officials to vacate any Yugoslav federal posts that they held. The Yugoslav Federal Presidency lost its last vestige of ethnic balance when Stjepan Mesić on December 5, 1991, resigned his post as

President of the Yugoslav Federal Presidency. Although opposed to the proposed war budget for 1992, whereby 80% of the military appropriation was earmarked for the Serbian-led YPA, Ante Marković the Yugoslav Federal Premier resigned on December 19, 1991.

The city of Vukovar, in eastern Slavonia was designated for all-out defense by the Croats; however, after intense bombardment and almost complete destruction by Serbian and YPA forces, Vukovar surrendered on November 18, 1991 after the cease-fire was arranged by the EC, which supervised the subsequent evacuation of Croatian civilians. The medieval city of Dubrovnik was threatened by heavy Serbian bombardment, which aroused international protest. Croatian blockade of YPA garrisons were in response to continued Serb, Montenegrin, and YPA ostensible atrocities, at the same time that Croatia requested that the EC and the UN intervene and negotiate a settlement. The YPA and Serb attacks continued against civilian population and disruptive deployment of troops, ships, and aircraft in coefficient maneuvers against Croatian hospitals, schools, museums, churches, and other institutions, prevented such an international force from being deployed.

Following the UN Secretary General concerning the feasibility of deploying UN peacekeeping in Yugoslavia, his Personal Envoy on November 23, 1991, convened in Geneva, Switzerland, a meeting which was attended by the presidents of Croatia, Serbia, and the Yugoslav Defense Minister, as well as Carrington. During the meeting, the Croat, the Serb, and the Yugoslav parties reached agreement on an immediate cease-fire and on a number of other issues, such as the lifting by the Government of Croatia of its blockade of YPA trapped inside the territory of Croatia. Each of the parties expressed the wish to see the speedy establishment of a UN peacekeeping operation. However, while progress was made on the other issue, the cease-fire broke down almost immediately. While the agreement of November 23 was proceeding, the unconditional cease-fire remained unimplemented. Yugoslav forces committed numerous provocative cease-fire violations. A number of artillery and other attacks took place in Croatia during of November 25 and December 6, 1991. The civilian population in the historic center of Dubrovnik, was attacked by artillery. Also, YPA units and Serbian irregular armed groups attacked Osijek in eastern Slavonia. The situation in Croatia continued to worsen, particularly concerning the humanitarian area.

At the request of France and Germany, the Security Council met on November 27, 1991 to consider the establishment of UN peacekeeping in Yugoslavia. In the light of the urgency of the matter, on the same date the Security Council unanimously adopted Resolution 721, and approved the efforts of the UN Secretary General and his Personal Envoy, also endorsed the statement made by the Personal Envoy to the parties that the deployment of a UN peacekeeping operation in Yugoslavia could not be envisaged without full compliance by all parties with the Geneva agreement of November 23, 1991. Following weeks of intensive negotiations with all parties concerned, the implementation of the Geneva agreement was pursued and the general principles were defined for a UN peacekeeping operation. In Croatia, the mission to monitor the release of prisoners in cooperation with the ICRC was set up by EC and CSCE, governed by memoranda of understanding of July 13, and September 1, 1991, and extended indefinitely on December 14, 1991,

The UN has been providing humanitarian relief assistance to the refugees and displaced persons since the beginning of the conflict in the former Yugoslavia. The UN relief effort has been coordinated by UNHCR, which was designated a lead humanitarian agency for the former Yugoslavia. In December 1991, it was estimated that there were approximately 500,000 refugees, displaced persons and other victims of the conflict requiring assistance and protection. As the conflict intensified, the humanitarian problems increased dramatically with widespread violations of basic human rights and international humanitarian law. Under such difficult circumstances, the UNHCR, UNICEF, WHO, other United Nations agencies concerned, ICRC and many NGOs have continued their work.

On December 15, 1991, the Security Council, by its Resolution 724, approved the UN Secretary General report which contained a plan for a possible peacekeeping operation. A small group of military officers, civilian police and UN Secretariat staff travelled to Yugoslavia to prepare for the implementation of this plan. Thereafter the UN Secretary General and his Personal Envoy focused their efforts on consolidating the cease-fire and securing unconditional acceptance of the UN plan by all parties to the conflict, including assurances of their readiness to cooperate fully in its implementation.

At the end of 1991, Milošević sought to consolidate the advantages gained by the Serb-četnici by settling Serbs in areas vacated by Croat inhabitants, and covertly supporting the plan to make the Serbs in Krajina an integral part of Serboslavia. As the authority of the rump Yugoslav government in Belgrade dwindled and arbitration of disputes faltered, the unpredictability of Serb-četnici and YPA forces became a major obstacle for the UN diplomats seeking an effective cease-fire between Serbian and Croatian forces.

Western European support was especially important for Bosnia-Herzegovina where an uneasy peace among Muslims, Serbs, and Croats was threatened by a commitment made by Milošević, to unite all Serbs in a single nation and to create Serboslavia. It appeared that the strategy of the YPA, under

Serbia's design, was to attack Croatia in force and from all sides; spread the engagement by using the YPA numerical superiority and military capability; destroy Croatian towns and cities; kill non-Serb children, men, and women at the place of contact; and turnover the administrative and military control to the dictator Milošević to achieve his dream of creating the Serboslavian tyranny. The initial successes by YPA, and četnici (Serbs and Montenegrins) were attributed to a lack of organized strong Croatian resistance. However, when the Croats adopted a coordinated tactic of defending their territorial integrity they succeeded in mobilizing the spirit of "Patriotic War" against the invaders. Unequivocally, the YPA was not a modern fighting organization like they depicted themselves to those who believed in their Serbian propaganda. Alone, without outside help, both Yugoslavia like Russia are unable to defeat anyone. History proves that the Yugoslav and the Russian military institutions are fundamentally chicken-hearted.

In 1991, the Serbian war of aggression against Croatia was established through a series of coverted premeditated military operations by the YPA with the support of local Serbian paramilitary and terrorist organizations. The Serbian communist government in Belgrade dreaded the break up of the communist Yugoslav regime which would result in a significant loss of status and wealth for their Serbian leadership. The Yugoslav government employed Serbian police forces and common criminals in Knin and other Serb-held territory to maintain road blocks and obstruct commercial traffic to the Dalmatian littoral. This was done under the rubric of keeping the communist Yugoslav regime together. In addition to supplying arms and provisions to the radical Serbs, the Yugoslav regime also used its monopoly of the media to instigate and disseminate falsehoods, distort facts with lies, innuendoes, and half-truths in order to cover-up the inefficiency, corruption, and incompetency of Milošević's government. Gullible Serbs everywhere were subjected to intense propaganda with a series of documentaries and reports that exaggerated war atrocities committed unilaterally by non-Serbs against the Serbian population. This revived campaign had a significant imprint on Serbs and fomented concern and fear such as: "The Croatian government killed millions of Serbs during the Second World War - there is hardly a Serbian family in Croatia and Bosnia who did not suffer at the hands of the Croats." Hypocritically, the Serbian controlled media and friends of Serbia never mention that initially two-thirds of Tito's Partisans fighting against the Axis were Croats and not Serbs. The same insincere people cleverly refer to the Croatian government as the Nazi puppet regime, and attempt to identify the whole Croatian people with the quisling regime. Conversely, the arrogant Serbs and their marionettes conceal the facts that the Serb-četnici collaborated during the Second World War with the Axis (Nazi and Fascist), and under the war criminal Mihajlović, Nedić, et al., the Serb-četnici killed more people inside and outside Serbia than anybody else. Now the Serb assassins are repeating and multiplying their heinous crime against humanity in their genocidal war in Croatia and Bosnia-Herzegovina.

After months of indecisiveness and bickering within the European Community, the German Foreign Minister Hans Dietrich-Genscher on December 1, 1991 renewed international initiative for diplomatic recognition of the republics of Croatia and Slovenia. On December 5, during a meeting in Bonn, German Chancellor Helmut Kohl, assured President Tudjman of Croatia that Germany was ready to recognize Croatia. This diplomatic move would be a first step to isolate and stop Yugoslavia (Serbia and Montenegro) from pursuing the war of aggression.After all was said and done, Serbia and Montenegro were solely responsible for provoking and escalating the conflict. On the other side of the argument, members of the European Community, e.g., the USA, France, and England opposed recognition of the two breakaway republics because they contended that de jure Croatian and Slovenian independence would further inflame the situation, contribute not only to political instability in the region but also widen the ethnic rifts and encourage ethnic separatism in Europe. The EC plan was based on the framework of economic and political union signed at Maastricht, Netherlands, on December 9-10, 1991. Recognizing the importance of international understanding, the Republic of Ukraine on December 12, 1991 announced in favor to recognize Croatia and Slovenia as independent nations. At the meeting of foreign ministers in Brussels, Belgium, on December 15-16 German Chancellor Kohl rejected any notion of retreat. His argument was that the fighting was a result of Serbian war of aggression and conquest, against Croatia's territory and Croatia had the right to self-determination. A determined German leadership, firm in their assertiveness and commitment for what's right, on December 23, 1991 announced that Germany formally recognized the independence of Croatia and Slovenia.

In the meantime, the Badimer Commission in evaluating the applications of Croatia concluded that Croatia, just like any other invaded nation in the world, lacked in commitments toward the protection for the ethnic Serbs. The foreign ministers, Genscher of Germany, and Alois Mock of Austria suggested to the Croatian government to amend its laws to address the commission's reservations which was centered on CSCE principles concerning human rights and democratic rule. The Croatian Parliament (Sabor), on May 8, 1992 adopted the controversial human rights legislation, guaranteeing special status to ethnic Serbs in Knin and Glina, the two districts in Croatia where Serbs are in majority. On January 15, 1992, Germany established diplomatic relations with Croatia and Slovenia. On the same day, the European Community announced their decision to formally recognize Croatia and Slovenia as independent nations. Also, the following countries recognized the two republics: Albania, Australia, Austria, Bulgaria, Canada,

Czechoslovakia, Estonia, Hungary, Iceland, Latvia, Lithuania, New Zealand, Norway, Poland, Romania, Switzerland, and Ukraine, followed by Italy on January 17; South Africa, April 3; the USA on April 7 recognized also Bosnia-Herzegovina; and Israel on April 16. France established diplomatic relations with Slovenia on April 23, and with Croatia on April 24, 1992. Ultimately, most members of the United Nations welcomed the the Republic of Croatia in the family of nations.

The Serb-četnici in cahoots with the Serb-dominated YPA started killing non-Serbian people shortly after their failed attempt to stop Slovenes from declaring their non-Yugoslav status, and to take advantage of the lack of preparedness and almost non-existent Croatian force. The Serb-dominated YPA and Serb-četnici captured one-third of Croatian territory. In the process, 10,000 Croats were killed and over 300,000 ousted from their homes in a war of ethnic cleansing.

The international community responded compassionately to two appeals launched, in December 1991 and May 1992 by UNHCR, also on behalf of UNICEF and WHO. However, in view of the continued and alarming deterioration of the humanitarian situation, particularly in Bosnia-Herzegovina, it became evident that further assistance was required. Consequently, the International Meeting on Humanitarian Assistance to the Victims of Conflict in the former Yugoslavia, held on July 29, 1992 in Geneva, endorsed a seven-point humanitarian response plan proposed by the UNHCR. The elements of the plan were: (a) respect for human rights and humanitarian law; (b) preventive protection; (c) access to those in need; (d) measures to meet special humanitarian needs; (e) temporary protection measures; (f) material assistance; and (g) rehabilitation.

In January 1992, after more than a dozen failed cease-fire agreements, a new cease-fire negotiated by former U.S. Secretary of State Vance went into effect. The Vance plan promised to disarm paramilitary groups, demilitarize the Serbian occupied territories of Croatia, ensure the departure of the YPA and allow the return of all displaced persons (DPs) to their former place of residence. The plan called for an end of the war and the deployment of UN troops and police. It established a UNPROFOR in the Serbian occupied areas. The UN divided the occupied zone into four separate sectors (north, south, east, and west) and sent separate battalion commanders and headquarters staff to each sector. The troops were charged with ending the activities of all paramilitary groups and enforcing a demilitarization zone. The police were to ensure that local police forces were doing their jobs without ethnic prejudice. Withdrawal of the YPA was supposed to be complete by the end of the summer of 1992. However, many Serbian soldiers in the units occupying Croatian territory continued to stay in the area and were absorbed by the special police units to conceal their identity. Moreover, in violation to the agreement Serbian units near the city of Dubrovnik remained in the region long after they agreed to depart.

The UN did not do the job it was sent to do in Croatia. On almost every account the UN effort was a failure. Serbian armed forces controlled most of the territory under UN protection and were consistently involved in major violations of human rights after the Vance plan was signed. The occupied areas of Croatia were still militarized and ruled by Serbian paramilitary bands and noted war criminals. Rather than open the path for a peaceful political settlement which recognized the integrity of Croatia's territory, the UN peacekeepers legitimized the Serbian occupation. In fact, the UN role in the occupied territories of Croatia actually made the security situation worse. Not only did the UN troops fail to disarm the paramilitary groups, they stood by passively as the Serbs and Montenegrins improved their tactical positions. The UN presence solidified Serbian and Montenegrin territorial gains in Croatia. In addition to monitoring the tactical improvement of Serbian forces in occupied Croatia, the UN witnessed, but did nothing to stop the Serb četnici from expelling non-Serbs from their homes.

Since early fall 1992, Serbs in the occupied territories were on a lunatic binge of violence and hatred against non-Serb population right under the nose of UN protection forces, The UN peacekeepers monitored and documented thousands of cases of non-Serbs being expelled from the Serb occupied areas. The UN also made it clear that it would not use force to stop the Serb terrorists from violating International Law. In effect, the UN provided Serb terrorists with the environment necessary to commit war crimes. U.S. State Department Human Rights Reports to the U.S. Congress consistently documented the direct involvement of Serb-četnici, Serb paramilitary groups, and special Serb police forces in major human rights abuses against non-Serbs in the UNPAs. In 1992, a UN Russian Battalion Commander in Sector East accepted expensive gifts from the Serbian terrorist leader Željko Ražnjatović (a.k.a. "Arkan"). It was not suprising since the Russians had chosen to set up their base camp next door to "Arkan's" terrorist training camp in Erdut, Slavonia (west of Osijek and north of Vukovar), where the untrustworthy Russian soldiers regularly socialized. It's important to notice that "Arkan" is wanted by Interpol for a series of armed robberies in Europe. He is also a documented war criminal.

With the Security Council's concurrence, on January 1, 1992 the newly elected UN Secretary General, Boutros Ghali, former Egyptian Deputy Prime Minister, sent to Yugoslavia a group of 50 military liason officers, with the task of using their good offices to promote the cease-fire. On January 2, 1992, Cyrus Vance, the Personal Envoy convened in Sarajevo a meeting between military representatives of the Republic of Croatia and representatives of the YPA, in order to implement the cease-fire. Meanwhile, the YPA and Serbian forces had secured control of virtually all ethnic Serbian areas in Croatia.

On February 15, 1992, the UN Secretary General recommended to the Security Council the establishment of the United Nations Protection Force (UNPROFOR). The Security Council, by its Resolution 743 of February 21, 1992, approved the report and established UNPROFOR for an initial period of 12 months. The Security Council confirmed that the Force should be an interim arrangement to create the conditions of peace and security required for the negotiation of an overall settlement of the Yugoslav crisis within the framework of the European Community Commission on Yugoslavia (ECCY). It requested the UN Secretary General to deploy immediately those elements of UNPROFOR which could assist in developing an implementation plan for the earliest possible full deployment of the Force.

The Government of Croatia claimed there was no longer any overall political solution to negotiate with Serb outlaws. The only issue was the return of the UNPAs and the pink zones to Croatian control. The Serb leadership refused to consider these territories to be a part of the Republic of Croatia and rejected talks on this basis, recalling that the plan was explicitly not intended to prejudge a political solution to the Yugoslav crisis. Further, the Serbs argued that two parties to the original plan, the Republic of Serbia under Milošević and the FRY controlled by Milošević no longer recognized the legal status of peacekeeping operation in the areas where UNPROFOR was deployed. In these circumstances, the UN Secretary-General saw three options with regard to UNPROFOR's mandate in the Republic of Croatia: (1) to renew the mandate entrusted to UNPROFOR by Resolution 743 dated February 21, 1992, with no change; (2) to modify that mandate; and (3) to give UNPROFOR no mandate in the Republic of Croatia and confine its operations to the republics of Bosnia-Herzegovina and to Macedonia.

Referring to option one, the UN Secretary General stated that the Government of Croatia made it clear that it could agree to a renewal of UNPROFOR's present mandate only if certain conditions were met, including (a) the complete disarmament of all paramilitary forces and terrorist organizations in the UNPAs and the pink zones with a destruction of their heavy weapons, voluntary and unconditional return of all refugees and (DPs) to their homes in the UNPAs; (b) maintenance of tight controls by the Force in those border areas where the boundaries of the UNPAs coincide with internationally recognized frontiers of the Republic of Croatia; and (c) restoration of Croatian authority in the pink zones. The Croatian Government's position, in effect, required UNPROFOR either to negotiate results which - as a peacekeeping force relying on the cooperation of the parties - it had no power to compel the other side to accept, or to risk unilateral military action by the government.

On the second option, the UN Secretary General warned against any modification resulting in enforcement action, saying that such action would involve the danger of placing UNPROFOR in direct conflict with the Serb terrorists. Enforcement would also require additional military forces and equipment which could not be deployed immediately upon the passage of an enforcement resolution by the Security Council. The mere passage of an enforcement resolution risked threatening the safety and security of UN peacekeeping personnel currently deployed in the UNPAs and some, perhaps most, troop-contributing countries might in these circumstances review their participation in UNPROFOR. Enforcement, the UN Secretary General stated, "would be a fundamental contradiction of the nature and purpose of UNPROFOR's deployment in the Republic of Croatia, as a peacekeeping force entrusted with the implementation of a plan agreed by all parties". As to an alternative modification of the mandate which would convert UNPROFOR into a buffer force deployed along the present front lines in order to prevent recurrence of hostilities, the UN Secretary General did not believe that such an approach would receive the consent of the Government of Croatia.

Speaking of option three, the UN Secretary General believed that the withdrawal of UNPROFOR from the UNPAs would result in the resumption of large-scale hostilities in the areas of its deployment, nullifying the political effort and the material resources invested in ending the conflict that had raged for nearly a year before the deployment of UNPROFOR. In the UN Secretary General's judgement, the difficulties which UNPROFOR and the Security Council faced with regard to the Force's mandate in the Republic of Croatia were attributed to two principal factors: (a) the inability to implement the peacekeeping plan; and (b) the lack of an agreed settlement to the conflict between the Republic of Croatia and the Serb populations living in the UNPAs and the pink zones. Unless these two factors were addressed, a sound basis would not exist for renewing UNPROFOR's mandate in the Republic of Croatia. Urgent efforts were needed to resolve the problems arising from the Croatian offensive, to establish a basis for completing the implementation of the UN peacekeeping plan and to agree on a framework for negotiating, within the principles of the International Conference on Yugoslavia (ICY), a settlement of the underlying dispute.

After receiving a report from the UN Secretary -General dated April 2, 1992, that all the Force Commander's interlocutors had emphasized the need for the earliest possible deployment of UNPROFOR. Therefore, by its Resolution 749 of April 7, 1992 the Security Council authorized the full deployment of the Force. The operational mandate of UNPROFOR extended to the following republics: Croatia, Bosnia-Herzegovina, Macedonia, Yugoslavia and a liaison presence in Slovenia.

On April 7, 1992 the United States recognized Croatia, Slovenia, and Bosnia-Herzegovina as sovereign and independent states and began immediate consultations to establish full diplomatic relations. The United States accepted the pre-crisis republic borders as the legitimate international borders of Croatia, Slovenia, and Bosnia-Herzegovina.

UNPROFOR deployed in Croatia, designated as UNPAs, in which the Security Council judged that special interim arrangements were required to ensure that a lasting cease-fire was maintained. For identification purposes, the UNPAs were those areas in which ethnic Serbs constitute the majority or a substantial minority of the population and where intercommunal tensions have led to armed conflict in the recent past. There were three UNPAs: Eastern Slavonia, Western Slavonia, and Krajina region. For UN purposes, they were divided into four sectors: (a) East-Eastern Slavonia, which includes the areas known as Baranja and Western Srem; (b) North-the northern part of the Krajina; (c) West-Western Slavonia; and (d) South-the southern part of the Krajina. The original UN plan in the Republic of Croatia was based on two central elements: (a) the withdrawal of the YPA from all of Croatia and the demilitarization of the UNPAs; and (b) the continuing functioning, on an interim basis, of the existing local authorities and police, under UN supervision, pending the achievement of an overall political solution to the crisis. UNPROFOR's mandate was to ensure that the UNPAs were demilitarized, through the withdrawal or disbandment of all armed forces in them, and that all persons residing in them were protected from fear of armed attack. To this end, UNPROFOR was authorized to control access to the UNPAs, to ensure that the UNPAs remain demilitarized, and to monitor the functioning of the local police there to help ensure non-discrimination and the protection of human rights. Outside the UNPAs, UNPROFOR military observers were to verify the withdrawal of all the YPA and Serb-Montenegrin irregular forces from the territory of Croatia, other than those disbanded and demobilized there. In support of the work of the humanitarian agencies of the United Nations, UNPROFOR was also to facilitate the return, in conditions of safety and security, of civilian DPs to their homes in the UNPAs.

UNPROFOR under the command of the UN Secretary General and members of the Force were not permitted to receive orders from national authorities. Command in the field was exercised by the Force Commander, Lt. Gen. Lars-Eric Wahlgren of Sweden (Lt. Gen. Wahlgren succeeded Lt. Gen. Satish Nambiar of India in March 1993), who was assisted in his duties by the Deputy Chief of Mission and Director of Civil Affairs, Cedric Thornberry of Ireland. UNPROFOR initially established its headquarters in Sarajevo; and later headquartered in Zagreb. UNPROFOR established in each of the four sectors a Civil Affairs office whose head works alongside, and in close coordination with, the military commander of the sector, performing a wide range of political, legal, informational and administrative functions.

Alarmed by the rapid deterioration of the situation in Bosnia-Herzegovina, the Security Council, in its Resolution 749 of April 7, 1992, appealed to all parties and others concerned to cooperate with the efforts of the EC to bring about a cease-fire and a negotiated political solution. On April 10 the Security Council invited the UN Secretary General to dispatch urgently to the area his Personal Envoy to act in close cooperation with the EC representatives. Vance undertook his mission from April 14 to 18, 1992. Despite all efforts aimed at stopping the fighting, the situation continued to deteriorate.

To rescue whatever was salvageable of the "fragmented Yugoslavia," Serbia and Montenegro on April 27, 1992 proclaimed the dissolution of the Socialist Federal Republic of Yugoslavia (SFRY) and the establishment of a new state, the Federal Republic of Yugoslavia (FRY). Thus acknowledging the existence of the declared independent republics of Croatia, Slovenia, Bosnia-Herzegovina, and Macedonia. Because the SFRY was dissolved and no successor state represents its continuation, the new designated entity has not been formally recognized by the United States or the European Community.

On April 29 the UN Secretary General informed the Security Council of his decision to dispatch Marrack Irvine Goulding of Britain, Under Secretary General for Peacekeeping Operations, to examine the situation in Bosnia-Herzegovina and to look into the feasibility of a UN peacekeeping operation. Following Goulding's mission from May 4-10, 1992, the UN Secretary General reported to the Security Council that it was not feasible to undertake peacekeeping activities in Bosnia-Herzegovina beyond the existing limited involvement of UNPROFOR in Sarajevo and in Mostar.

The Security Council under Chapter VII of the UN Charter, unanimously adopted Resolution 824 dated May 6, 1993, which designated six Muslim enclaves in Bosnia-Herzegovina as "safe areas": Bihać, Goražde, Sarajevo, Srebrenica, Tuzla, as well as Zepa, and their surroundings.

The US strongly endorsed the EC foreign ministers' May 11 declaration on Bosnia-Herzegovina, including the demand for the full withdrawal of the YPA from Bosnia-Herzegovina and the reopening of Sarajevo airport under safe conditions. US Ambassador Warren Zimmermann on May 12, 1992 was recalled from FRY for consultations. The US took this action in coordination with the EC and in light of the aggression carried out against Bosnia-

Herzegovina by Serbian authorities and military in clear and continuing violation of all CSCE principles. On May 16, on instruction from U.S. Secretary Baker, Ambassador Zimmermann sought assurances from the government of Serbia that relief convoys would be allowed free passage into Sarajevo and that the Sarajevo airport would be reopened immediately for humanitarian flights. Ambassador Zimmermann informed President Milošević of Serbia that failure to take these steps would result in immediate termination of Jugoslav Airline Transport (JAT) landing rights in the United States. On May 17 to confirm the Serbian government intransigence and brutality, Serbian forces took hostage a convoy of women and children fleeing the city of Sarajevo. Two days later, Serbia made another uncivilized response when Serbian forces attacked a Red Cross relief convoy heading into Sarajevo, killing an ICRC delegate and destroying the desperately needed humanitarian supplies. The U.S. Government took prompt action - the Department of State ordered the Department of Transportation to terminate the authority of the Serbian national carrier (Yugoslav Airlines) to fly to and from the United States. This meant that their three weekly flights from Belgrade to New York City and on to Chicago ended immediately.

Although the mandate of UNPROFOR originally related only to the Republic of Croatia, it was envisaged that after the demilitarization of the UNPAs, 100 UNPROFOR military observers would be redeployed from Croatia to certain parts of the Republic of Bosnia-Herzegovina. In the light of the deteriorating situation in Bosnia-Herzegovina, the UN Secretary General decided to accelerate this deployment by sending 40 military observers to Mostar on April 30, 1992. Despite efforts by the EC representatives and UNPROFOR to negotiate a lasting cease-fire, the conflict in Bosnia-Herzegovina between the Muslims and Croats on the one side and the Serbs on the other - intensified. On May 14 when risks to their lives reached an unacceptable level, the observers were withdrawn from the area and redeployed in the UNPAs within the Republic of Croatia. About two thirds of UNPROFOR headquarters personnel were also relocated from Sarajevo on May 16-17, 1992. However, approximately 100 military personnel and civilian staff remaining in Sarajevo continued arranging, hosting and sometimes chairing meetings between the hostile parties; accompanying delegations to such meetings; arranging and witnessing exchanges of prisoners, sick, wounded, and war dead; and performing other humanitarian tasks.

The Security Council, in its Resolution 752 of May 15, 1992, demanded, among other things, that all forms of interference from outside Bosnia-Herzegovina, including by units of the YPA as well as elements of the Croatian Army, cease immediately. The Security Council also demanded that those units of the YPA, all Serbian forces, and elements of the Croatian Army in Bosnia-Herzegovina must either be withdrawn, become subject to the authority of the Government of Bosnia-Herzegovina, or be disbanded and disarmed.

The Security Council having examined the application of the Republic of Croatia for admission to the United Nations, adopted Resolution 753 on May 18, 1992 which recommended to the General Assembly that the Republic of Croatia be admitted to membership in the United Nations. The General Assembly having reviewed the recommendation of the Security Council, adopted Resolution 46/638 on May 22, 1992 to admit the Republic of Croatia to membership in the UN. By SCR 754 of May 18, 1992, and the General Assembly Resolution 46/236 on May 22, 1992, the Republic of Slovenia was admitted to membership in the United Nations. Also, by SCR 755 of May 20, 1992, and General Assembly Resolution 46/237 on May 22, 1992, admitted the Republic of Bosnia-Herzegovina to membership in the United Nations.

In accordance with the UN demilitarization of Serb occupied areas, in mid-May 1992 the YPA began to withdraw from Croatian territory, and the 238-day seige of Dubrovnik ended on May 28. However, sporadic shelling by Serbian forces continued along eastern Slavonia and the UNPROFOR proved unable to prevent Serbian forces from expelling thousands of non-Serbs from eastern Slavonia.

On May 26, 1992, the UN Secretary General submitted a further report to the Security Council summarizing the humanitarian situation in Bosnia-Herzegovina and describing various options for providing assistance and protection for humanitarian convoys. On May 30, 1992, the Security Council, in its Resolution 757, condemned the failure of the authorities in the FRY including the YPA, to take effective measures to fulfill the requirements of Resolution 752 dated May 15, 1992. The Security Council instituted an embargo on FRY of products and commodities, financial and economic contacts, and suspended sports contacts as well as scientific, technical and cultural exchanges. The Resolution 757 dated May 30, 1992 also imposed an air embargo and the reduction of staff levels at FRY diplomatic missions. Exempt from the sanctions included foodstuffs and medical supplies, as well as UNPROFOR-related goods and services. The sanctions were to remain in effect until the Security Council decided that the authorities in the FRY including the YPA, had taken effective steps to fulfill the requirements of Resolution 752 dated May 15, 1992. Subsequently, by Resolution 760 dated June 18, 1992, the Security Council decided that sanctions should not apply to those items essential for humanitarian need.

Serbian shells killed 20 civilians in the bread-line massacre in Sarajevo. The U.S. Defense Secretary, Dick Cheney, said military intervention was not an option; the Western allies settled for some economic sanctions against FRY.

Later in the summer, when the press revealed that the Serbs were running concentration camps for ethnic cleansing, the Western diplomats facitiously claimed that they were outraged for lack of military response.

* * * * *

~ **Aggression by the Serbian Regime** ~

New York City, May 30, 1992

Excerpts from a statement by Edward J. Perkins, U.S. Representative to the UN concerning the SCR 757 on sanctions against the former Yugoslavia:

"The Aggression of the Serbian regime and the armed forces it has unleashed against Bosnia-Herzegovina represent a clear threat to internatioal peace and security - and a grave challenge to the values and principles which underlie the Helsinki Final Act, the Charter of Paris, and the UN Charter. The US, the EC, the CSCE community, and the UN Security Council, by the action it is taking today, are sending a clear message to the Serbian regime and to the forces it sponsors in Croatia and Bosnia-Herzegovina. By its aggression against Croatia and Bosnia-Herzegovina and by its repression with Serbia - Kosova, Vojvodina, and the Sandzak, - the Serbian regime can only condemn itself to increasingly severe treatment by a world united in its opposition to Serbian aggression.

The US is determined to see the UN Chapter VII (Action with Respect to Threats to the Peace, Breaches of the Peace, and Acts of Aggression) measures implemented and, if necessary, to seek further measures until the Serbian regime changes course. Serbia must reverse its brutal aggression. Serbia must cease and desist from the campaign of terror it is conducting against the civilian population of Croatia and Bosnia-Herzegovina. The Serbian and Montenegrin leadership must disband, disarm, and withdraw the Yugoslav People's Army (YPA) and armed četnici from Croatia and from Bosnia-Herzegovina immediately. The Serbian regime and its armed surrogates must cease inflicting suffering on the civilian populations of those two sovereigh states, creating a humanitarian crisis of nightmare proportions, and applying force to block international humanitarian relief to its victims. Belgrade and Serbian hard-line leaders in Bosnia must instead cooperate in good faith with international humanitarian relief to those two states. Belgrade must clearly and unequivocally demonstrate respect for the independence, and legitimate sovereign governments of Croatia and Bosnia-Herzegovina, and other former Yugoslav republics.

The US will not have normal relations with Belgrade until it ends its occupation of neighboring states and implements guarantees of rights for members of all national minorities within Serbia and Montenegro, as stipulated by the EC conference on Yugoslavia. Down the road of continued conflict lies ruin. The people of the former Yugoslavia have suffered enough. The US looks forward to the restoration of peace and stability and reason and to the time when people who had lived together peacefully in the past do so again. Reason, compromise, and respect for international principles embodied in the CSCE accords and the UN Chapter must supplant aggression, hatred, and intolerance."

* * * * *

On June 6, 1992, the UN Secretary General reported to the Security Council that UNPROFOR had negotiated, on June 5 an agreement for the handing over of Sarajevo airport to the Force, so that facilities could be made available for humanitarian purposes. Under the agreement, UNPROFOR would ensure the immediate security of the Sarajevo airport and its installations, supervise the operation of the airport, control its facilities and organization, facilitate the unloading of humanitarian cargo and ensure the safe movement of humanitarian aid and related personnel. UNPROFOR would also verify the withdrawal of YPA and Serbian anti-aircraft weapons systems from within range of the airport and its approaches and monitor the concentration of artillery, mortar, and ground-to-ground missile systems in specified areas. By Resolution 758 of June 8, 1992, the Security Council decided to enlarge the mandate and strength of UNPROFOR in accordance with the UN Secretary-General's recommendations. The Force Commander of UNPROFOR decided on June 10, 1992, to dispatch his Chief of Staff to Sarajevo as Commander-designate of UNPROFOR.

Croatian forces on June 21, 1992, launched a limited shelling and attack against Serbian occupation forces in Knin and the surrounding area. In conjunction with this development, the Security Council demanded the Croats withdraw to the positions held prior to the attack and to refrain from entering Croatian territory occupied by Serbs. Therefore, relations between the Republic of Croatia and the UN remained under extreme tension, and Croatia's President Franjo Tudjman threatened to refuse the renewal of UNPROFOR's mandate schedule in March 1993.

SCR 761 of June 29, 1992, authorized the UN Secretary General to deploy additional elements of UNPROFOR to ensure the security of Sarajevo airport and the delivery of humanitarian assistance. Despite continuous fighting, there was a gradual build-up of UNPROFOR personnel in the Sarajevo sector. The first group of 30 UNPROFOR personnel was deployed at the airport on June 29. French troops began to arrive on July 1 and the Canadian battalion was redeployed on July 2 to Sarajevo from Croatia. By July 3, 1992, UN observers and troops were deployed at the airport and at other locations in Sarajevo, and the airport was reopened for the humanitarian airlift.

On the recommendation of the UN Secretary General, the Security Council, by Resolution 762 of June 30, 1992, authorized UNPROFOR to undertake monitoring functions in the pink zones. The Security Council approved the addition of some 60 military observers and 120 United Nations civilian police monitors to carry out these tasks. It also recommended the establishment of a Joint Commission chaired by UNPROFOR and consisting of representatives of the Government of Croatia and of the local authorities, with the participation of the ECMM, to oversee and monitor the restoration of authority by the Croatian Government in the pink zones. The tasks assigned to UNPROFOR included verifying the immediate withdrawal of the Croatian Army, territorial defense forces and any irregular units from the pink zones, supervising the restoration of authority by the Croatian police and the reestablishment of the local police in proportion to the demographic structure of the areas prior to the conflict and monitoring the maintenance of law and order by the existing police forces, with particular regard to the well-being of minorities without discriminating against the Croatian majority.

President Dobrica Cosić of the FRY, on July 1, 1992 nominated Serbian-born Milan Panic as Premier. On July 14 both chambers of the FRY elected Panic as Premier of the FRY. U.S. Secretary of State James Baker on July 8, 1992 met at the Helsinki, Finland, with Milan Panic in his capacity as Premier-designate of the Federal Republic of Yugoslavia (FRY) which consists of the rump republics of Serbia and Montenegro. The Secretary agreed to meet with Panic in the interest of making absolutely sure, that no one in the FRY misunderstood United State's position. The message that the Secretary gave Panic was very clear, and that was that the growing humanitarian nightmare in the former Yugoslavia, for which the Serbian political and military authorities were overwhelmingly responsible, must end, and Serbia-Montenegro must abide by the UN Security Council Resolutions. These requirements include the need to allow the unhindered delivery of humanitarian assistance to all who needed it; to end interference in Bosnia-Herzegovina and respect the territorial integrity and legitimate government of the state; to withdraw, disband, and disarm all Serbian forces in Bosnia-Hezegovina and place their weapons under effective international monitoring; and to cease immediately all forcible expulsions and any attempts to change the ethnic composition of the population. Secretary Baker told Panic quite bluntly that the United States does not question in any way his motives or aims, which the Secretary thought were noble - Panic expressed them as a desire to act in the best interest of both his country of origin [Serbia] and of his adopted country [USA], and to bring peace to that region - but that the world would now demand deeds from rump Yugoslavia [Serbia-Montenegro], not just words. We [USA] have heard words before. The Secretary made it clear to Panic that the U.S. supports a free and democratic Serbia that lives in peace with its neighbors and its own people. Secretary Baker made it very clear that Panic was not a representative of the U.S. Government, and that Panic as Premier-designate of the FRY was not going to Belgrade as a special emissary from the United States. There were no special deals or arrangements made. Panic as a United States citizen, was given a 30-day exemption from the sanctions under U.S. law in order to travel to Serbia.

The Security Council, by its Resolution 764 of July 13, 1992 authorized the UN Secretary General to further strengthen UNPROFOR in accordance with his request of July 10 adding an air traffic element, a helicopter unit, and artillery-locating radar, signal and medical platoons. At the end of July 1992, the Canadian battalion was replaced by three smaller battalions contributed by Egypt, France and the Ukraine. Throughout the conflict, there were massive and systematic violations of human rights, as well as grave violations of humanitarian law in most of the territory of the former Yugoslavia. Ethnic cleansing - by the ethnic group exercising control over a given territory, of members of other ethnic groups - is the direct cause of the vast majority of human rights violations. The practice of ethnic cleansing by Serbs involved a variety of methods, including harassment, discrimination, beatings, torture, rape, summary executions, expulsions, shelling of civilian population centers, relocation of populations by force, confiscation of property, destruction of homes, places of worship, and cultural institutions. In a series of resolutions, the Security Council condemned the practice of ethnic cleansing and other violations of human rights and international humanitarian law. On July 13, 1992, the Security Council, in its Resolution 764 reaffirmed that all parties were bound to comply with the obligations under international humanitarian law and in particular the Geneva Conventions of August 12, 1949 for the protection of war victims, and that persons who commit or order the commission of grave breaches of the Conventions were individually responsible in respect of such breaches.

On July 17, 1992, the parties to the conflict in Bosnia-Herzegovina signed in London, an agreement in which they asked the Security Council to make arrangements for international supervision of all their heavy weapons. The agreement had been negotiated within the framework of the ECCY. Meanwhile, in mid-July 1992, the Government of Croatia called attention to the refugee crisis and declared that Croatia was unable to accept additional refugees. Overwhelmed by the heavy burden of caring for approximately 560,000 DPs, the majority of whom were from Serbian occupied territory within Croatia and from Bosnia-Herzegovina.

In late July 1992, a military court in Split convicted 19 Serb terrorists from Krajina for "threatening the territorial integrity" of the Republic of Croatia. As a precondition of Serbian participation in the EC/UN at the London peace conference on Yugoslavia scheduled for August 1992, the Serb leaders of Krajina renounced their preposterous claims to independence. The UN Secretary General recommended that UNPROFOR should be given authority to control the entry of civilians into the UNPAs and that it should have powers to perform immigration and customs functions of certain areas in Croatia where the UNPA boundaries coincided with international frontiers. The UN Secretary General estimated that additional civilian police and some 350 international personnel would be required to perform these functions. On August 7, 1992, the Security Council, by its Resolution 769, approved the UN Secretary General report and authorized the enlargements of UNPROFOR's strength and mandate recommended therein. On August 10, 1992, Canadian Gen. Lewis MacKenzie, commander of UNPROFOR in Sarajevo was replaced by Egyptian Gen. Hussein Ali Abdebrasik.

Presidential and legislative elections were held in Croatia on August 2, 1992. These were the first nationwide elections to be held under the Croatian Constitution (promulgated on December 22, 1990), which provided for a bicameral legislature composed of a Chamber of Representatives and a Chamber of Municipalities. The elections to the Chamber of Municipalities were postponed, pending the adoption of legislation on the redistribution of municipalities. The elections were contested by eight presidential candidates and numerous political parties. On August 6, 1992 the Chairman of the Election Commission announced the final election results. Of 3,575,032 registered voters, a total 2,677,764 or 74.9 percent of eligible voters had voted. President Franjo Tudjman, member of the HDZ/CDU party, was re-elected with 1,519,100 or 56.7% of the votes; Dražen Budisa (HSLS/CSLP) received 161,242 votes or 6%; and Dobroslav Paraga (HSP/CPR) received 144,695 votes or 5.4%; all other parties received a small percentage of votes. The new Government, under Premier Hrvoje Šarinic (replaced Franjo Greguric), was officially sworn in on September 8, 1992.

On August 6, 1992 President George W. Bush announced that the United States was establishing full diplomatic relations with Croatia, Slovenia, and Bosnia-Herzegovina. The United States will open embassies in Zagreb and Ljubljana. The new embassy in Zagreb will be housed in the former U.S. Consulate General building. The embassy in Ljubljana will be in temporary quarters at the U.S. Information Service cultural center at a local hotel.

The world community was appalled by the continuing deterioration of the situation in the former communist Yugoslavia (SFRY). The destruction of villages, executions, rapes, and indiscriminate killings continue apace. Serbs' vile policy of ethnic cleansing (ethnic extermination) was only intensifying. The world was witnessing some of the most egregious abuses of human rights that Europe has seen since the Second World War, if ever. The television presentation and press media reported of detention centers, which shocked civilized people everywhere. Moreover, the detention of such persons was part of a policy of forced population transfers carried out on a massive scale and marked by the systematic use of Serbian brutality. Among the long list of methods used were harassment, murder, rape, confiscation of property, deportation and the taking of hostages - which reduce individuals to the level of bargaining counters - all in violation of international humanitarian law. The ICRC delegates have had only limited access to the republic's various regions and, despite repeated approaches made in this respect, they were denied to receive comprehensive lists of places of detention controlled by the various parties to the conflict or notified of persons captured, and were thus unable to bring help to all the victims. Finally, after repeated requests, the ICRC has had access to only a very limited number of POWs.

An occurrence notable for such incongruity, on August 13, 1992, the regime of the FRY recognized Slovenia as an independent republic. President Milan Kučan of Slovenia promptly replied by stating, "this diplomatic recognition is worthless, until the FRY itself obtains international recognition."

In separate developments, the Security Council, disturbed by the situation prevailing in Sarajevo, which severely complicated UNPROFOR's efforts to ensure the security and functioning of Sarajevo airport and the delivery of humanitarian assistance, adopted Resolution 770 on August 13, 1992. The Security Council, acting under Chapter VII of the UN Charter, called on States to "take nationally or through regional agencies or arrangements all measures necessary" to facilitate, in coordination with the UN, the delivery of humanitarian assistance to Sarajevo and wherever needed in other parts of Bosnia-Herzegovina. The SCR 771 of August 13, 1992 reaffirmed that all parties to the conflict were bound to comply with their obligations under international humanitarian law, and strongly condemned violations, including ethnic cleansing. With this, the Security Council again demanded that relevant international humanitarian organizations, in particular ICRC, be granted immediate, unimpeded and continued access to all camps, prisons and detention centers within the territory of the former Yugoslavia.

* * * * *

~ Unspeakable Savagery in Yugoslavia ~

Geneva, August 13, 1992

Excerpts from an address by John R. Bolton, Assistant Secretary for International Organization Affairs, before a special session of the UN Human Rights Commission, Geneva, Switzerland:

"The United States of America requested this unprecedented extraordinary session of the UN Human Rights Commission because, along with many others, we are appalled at the unspeakable, immoral savagery being unleashed upon the citizens of what used to be Yugoslavia. Under the UN Charter, this Commission has a critical moral responsibility to turn the spotlight of international scrutiny upon the darkness in that land. We are making use of a new mechanism to convene the Commission on an emergency basis so that it can address a human rights crisis as it unfolds.

That there are ongoing abuses of human rights in direct violation of international law is not in doubt. The deliberate targeting of civilians is a violation of one of the most basic tenets governing the conduct of war, set forth in a host of international treaties, covenants, and declarations which condemn - if not criminalize - these vicious acts. We have seen the carnage being wreaked upon the innocent civilian population of Bosnia as military forces vie for control in the name of ethnic supremacy. The neighbors of former Yugoslavia, as well as its several constituent republics, know all too well the campaign of expulsion being waged in wide swatches of territory, which has created the largest refugee crisis in Europe since the end of Second World War. The policy which its perpetrators chillingly call "ethnic cleansing" is an abhorrent breach of international human rights standards, as well as the norms of civilized behavior.

In recent days, we have begun to receive yet even more ominous, profoundly disturbing reports of camps where people are being systematically abused, tortured, and even executed. In

246

the name of humanity, we must now exercise every effort to ensure that the truth sets them free.

I wish to make a direct appeal to the parties in the conflict and to those who control the weapons. Nothing can come of this violence except more violence. Political gains obtained through violence can only be maintained through further violence and repression. Unquestionably, such political gains and violent territorial changes will never be recognized or sanctified by civilized persons. Any state enlarged through the bloodshed of innocent civilians is an international pariah, an outlaw state. The international community will never accept the redrawing of boundaries by force in Yugoslavia; the sooner the parties accept this fundamental fact, the sooner we can turn to peacefully resolving this crisis.

To the perpetrators of the appalling acts now alleged, I say that the international community took a vow when it realized what had been committed by Nazism in Europe during the Second World War: 'Never again.' The Nuremberg [and Tokyo] tribunal reaffirmed the principle of individual accountability for crimes against humanity committed in the name of national or ethnic groups. The United States is fully prepared to join with others to see that individuals guilty of violations of international law and human rights principles are held strictly accountable. We have proposed in the United Nations a 'war crimes' resolution to ensure this accountability; we want to see it adopted as soon as possible.

Our century has already borne witness to the most ferocious and horrible violations of human rights. We do not now wish to see this grievous record augmented as the century draws to a close. We ask the people of Serbia-Montenegro this simple question: Do they wish to go down in history as citizens of the last fascist [Nazi or communist] state in Europe? The men of violence must be shown that there is no real, lasting alternative to peaceful negotiation to solve their differences. Nothing can excuse or justify the slaughter and misery being heaped upon the innocent people of the former Yugoslavia."

* * * * *

In 1992, the UNHCR held two special sessions at Geneva (August 13 and 14; November 30 and December 1), to consider the situation of human rights in the former Yugoslavia. On August 13-14, 1992, the Commission convened a special session - the first ever in its history - on the human rights situation in the former Yugoslavia. The Commission, in its Resolution 1992/S-1/1, condemned in the strongest terms "ethnic cleansing" and human rights violations in the former Yugoslavia. The Commission requested its Chairman to appoint a Special Rapporteur to investigate first hand the human rights situation in the former Yugoslavia, and to make recommendations for ending human rights violations as well as for preventing future occurences, and to gather systematically information on possible human rights violations which may constitute war crimes. The Commission condemned the abhorrent practices of ethnic cleansing (ethnic extermination) and called on all parties to ensure the protection of the rights of persons belonging to national or ethnic, religious and linguistic minorities. Subsequently, Tadeusz Mazowiecki, former Premier of Poland, was appointed Special Rapporteur. Since then, Mazowiecki conducted several missions to the former Yugoslavia, accompanied by the Chairman of the Working Group on Arbitrary Detention, submitted regular reports to the Commission, which were also made

247

available to the General Assembly and the Security Council. The Special Rapporteur concluded, in his first report of August 28, 1992 and reconfirmed in his second report of October 27, 1992, the following: "Human rights violations are being perpetrated by all parties to the conflicts. There are also victims on all sides."

The UN General Assembly on August 25, 1992, adopted its Resolution 46/242 condemning the massive violations of human rights and international humanitarian law, in particular the abhorrent practice of ethnic cleansing (ethnic extermination), and demanded that the heinous practice be brought to an end immediately. It called for further steps to stop the massive and forcible displacement of population from and within Bosnia-Herzegovina, as well as all other forms of violation of human rights in the former Yugoslavia. It also affirmed the accountability of States for human rights violations committed by their agents upon the territory of another State and called upon all States and international organizations not to recognize the consequences of the acquisition of territory by force and of ethnic cleansing. The General Assembly also demanded the safe, unconditional and honorable repatriation of the refugees and deportees to their homes in Croatia and in Bosnia-Herzegovina and recognized their right to receive reparation for their losses.

The London Conference on former Yugoslavia was held on August 26-28, 1992, in London, England. The conference was co-chaired by British Premier John Major as the Head of State/Government of the Presidency of the EC and by UN Secretary General Boutros-Ghali. The conference endorsed certain principles as the basis for a negotiated settlement of the problems of former Yugoslavia. The conference has given to all concerned a better foundation to defuse, contain, and bring to an end the conflict in former Yugoslavia. It has established a new, permanent negotiating forum, co-chaired by the UN and the EC, in Geneva. The conference developed an international plan of action to deal with this crisis.

* * * * *

~ **London Conference on Yugoslavia** ~

London, August 26, 1992

Excerpts from an address of Acting U.S. Secretary of State Lawrence Eagleburger:

"We have gathered here today because, as members of the family of nations - East and West, Muslim, Christian or Jew - we are compelled to help the peoples of the former Yugoslavia in their hour of suffering and need. Just 3 years ago, mankind began anew its long-interrupted march toward freedom, enlightenment, and the rule of law. We have every reason then to hope that all nations liberated from communism would join not only the Western circle of democracy, but also the circle of peace created by the reconciliation of historical enemies. I call upon the Serbian forces to lift the sieges of Sarajevo, Goražde, Tuzla, Bihać, Mostar, and other Bosnian cities. Toward this end, we must create a durable international negotiating mechanism, one that will operate permanently with all the relevant parties present to achieve a just and lasting settlement. Only by agreeing to a peace process on the basis of principles enshrined in the UN Charter and CSCE can we ensure that negotiations do not become a vehicle for consolidating the fruits of aggression. Successful negotiations will require us, above all, to raise the costs now for those who perpetuate the violence and continue to hold territory acquired by force. Thus, we believe the third task of this conference is to reaffirm the international community's resolve to tighten comprehensive economic sanctions against the vicious Yugoslavia (Serbia-Montenegro) and to maintain its political isolation until they comply with relevant UN Security Council Resolutions (UNSCR). We must resolve no longer to tolerate continuing and flagrant violations of the sanctions regime. The UN Sanctions Committee transshipment guidelines must be strengthened to include strict documentation and inspection procedures. Arrangements for Sanctions Monitors should also be established in areas bordering Yugoslavia (Serbia-Montenegro), such as Hungary, Romania, Bulgaria, Macedonia and Albania, and implement new measures to eliminate violations occurring via the Danube River and in the Adriatic.

In conclusion, I began by describing the tragedy in the former Yugoslavia in terms of the seemingly endless cycle of violence and vengence which has characterized the Balkans for so many centuries. But in truth, there is nothing fatalistic about what is going on in those lands. The fact of the matter is that the conflict was willed by men seeking to perpetuate Europe's last communist regime by manipulating age-old hatreds and fears. Nevertheless, the peoples of the former Yugoslavia can still refuse to drink the lethal brew which their leaders have put before them. If they should so refuse, they will be able to join a democratic Europe in a process of integration which is rendering obsolete traditional notions of sovereignty, and which is enhancing the interests of minorities across the continent. The world's democracies will welcome the Serbs and Montenegrins to their midst, and offer them greater security than they could ever hope to enjoy under the law of the jungle now prevailing. But those peoples who choose the irrational path of hatred and aggression cannot expect membership in the newly enlarged community of democratic nations. We will simply not allow them to make a mockery of the more humane and rational future that the collapse of communism and the end of the threat of nuclear holocaust promises."

* * * * *

The US Department of State on September 1, 1992 announced that, in order to follow up quickly on the results of the London Conference on former Yugoslavia and to participate actively in the Geneva talks beginning September 3, Acting Secretary of State Lawrence Eagleburger has appointed the former Ambassador to Yugoslavia Warren Zimmermann as US coordinator and US representative on the steering committee of the conference. Ambassador Zimmermann will retain his position as Director of the Bureau of Refugee Programs.

On September 10, 1992, following consultations with a number of Governments, the UN Secretary General submitted a report to the Security Council recommending the expansion of UNPROFOR's mandate and strength in Bosnia-Herzegovina. Resolution 776, which was adopted on September 14, 1992 made no reference to Chapter VII of the UN Charter, the Security Council approved the UN Secretary General report and authorized the enlargement of UNPROFOR's mandate and strength in Bosnia-Herzegovina for these purposes.

The Security Council, by its Resolution 777 of September 19, 1992, considered whether or not the FRY could continue to retain the membership of the former SFRY in the United Nations. The Security Council by a vote of 12-0, with China, India, and Zimbabwe abstaining, recommended to the General Assembly the ouster of Yugoslavia from the UN. On September 22, 1992 the General Assembly, by its Resolution 47/1, and vote of 127-6, with 26 abstentions, agreed with the Security Council's recommendations to expel Yugoslavia from the UN membership for its war of aggression..

The third enlargement of UNPROFOR's mandate in the Republic of Croatia came about in October 1992, when the UN Secretary General reported to the Security Council on an agreement reached regarding the Prevlaka Peninsula/Prevlaka Poluotok (42°24'N; 18°31'E) located south of Dubrovnik. Under this agreement, the YPA would withdraw completely from the territory of the sovereign Republic of Croatia, the Prevlaka Peninsula would be demilitarized, and heavy weapons would be removed from neighboring areas of Croatia and Montenegro. On October 6, 1992, the Security Council, by its Resolution 779, authorized UNPROFOR to assume responsibility for monitoring the agreed arrangements. By the same resolution, the Security Council approved the UN Secretary General's action to ensure the control by UNPROFOR of the vitally important Peručka Dam/Peručko Nasip (43°50'N; 16°32'E), located in the hinterland of central Dalmatia, situated in one of the pink zones in the Republic of Croatia.

The international community has continued its efforts to facilitate the release of prisoners and detainees within the territory of the former Yugoslavia. It was widely believed that only a very small percentage of detainees were genuine prisoners of war, with most prisoners being innocent civilians. After ICRC visited camps and detention centers in August 1992, the three major groups in Bosnia-Herzegovina (Croats, Muslims, and Serbs) agreed on August 27, 1992 on the release of all civilians who had been illegally detained and on the evacuation of the sick and wounded from the camps and detention centers. On October 1, 1992, the parties signed, an Agreement on the Release and Transfer of Prisoners, thereby committing themselves to liberate all detainees including the small percentage of combatants detained, except those who were accused of committing grave breaches of international humanitarian law.

Resolution 780 was adopted by the Security Council on October 6, 1992, expressing its grave alarm at the continuing reports of widespread violations of international humanitarian law in the territory of the former Yugoslavia. The Security Council requested the UN Secretary General to establish an impartial Commission of Experts to examine and analyze the information submitted pursuant to Resolution 771 dated August 13, 1992 and the present

Resolution 780, together with such information as the Commission may obtain through its own investigations or efforts, with a view to providing the UN Secretary General with its conclusions on the evidence of grave breaches of the 1949 Geneva Conventions and other violations of humanitarian law committed in the territory of the former Yugoslavia. In a further development, the Security Council, on October 9, 1992, adopted its Resolution 781 banning all military flights in the airspace of Bosnia-Herzegovina, except for those of UNPROFOR and other flights in support of UN operations, including humanitarian assistance. The Security Council requested UNPROFOR to monitor compliance with the ban, and that it place observers, where necessary, at airfields in the former Yugoslavia.

In a report dated October 14, 1992 to the Security Council, the UN Secretary General announced his decision to establish a Commission of Experts. On October 23, 1992, the UN Secretary General informed the Security Council that he had appointed the following five persons as the members of the Commission: Fritz Kalshoven of the Netherlands (Chairman), Cherif Bassiouni of Egypt, William Fenrick of Canada, Keba Mbaye of Senegal, and Torkel Opsahl of Norway. On October 24, 1992, one of the co-chairmen of the SCICY, David Harold Owen, a British politician, threatened to impose sanctions on Croatia if it did not stop supporting the Croatian Union of Herceg-Bosna with headquarters in Mostar. Croatia continued its involvement in Bosnia-Herzegovina to protect its citizens and ethnic Croats from Serb-četnici and other terrorist elements.

On November 10, 1992, the Security Council adopted its Resolution 786 authorizing the expansion of UNPROFOR's strength by 75 military observers to enable it to monitor airfields in the Republic of Bosnia-Herzegovina, the Republic of Croatia, and the FRY. On November 11, 1992, the President of the Republic of Macedonia conveyed to the UN Secretary General a request for the deployment of UN observers in Macedonia in view of his concern about the possible impact on it of fighting elsewhere in Yugoslavia. Such deployment was also recommended by Vance and Owen, Co-Chairmen of the SCICY.

On November 16, 1992, the Security Council adopted its Resolution 787, in which it considered that in order to facilitate the implementation of the relevant Security Council resolutions, observers should be deployed on the borders of the Republic of Bosnia-Herzegovina, and requested the UN Secretary General to present his recommendations on this matter. The Resolutions in question were: Resolution 713 dated September 25, 1991, which established a complete embargo on all deliveries of weapons and military equipment to Yugoslavia; Resolution 752 dated May 15, 1992, which demanded that all forms of interference from outside Bosnia-Herzegovina,

251

including by units of the YPA as well as elements of the Croatian Army, cease immediately; Resolution 757 dated May 30, 1992, which imposed comprehensive mandatory economic sanctions against the FRY, and Resolution 787 dated November 16, 1992, which demanded that all forms of interference from outside Bosnia-Herzegovina, including infiltration into the country of irregular units and personnel, cease immediately.

The Commission of Experts commenced its work early in November 1992. Since then, it carried out four main tasks: (a) the examination and analysis of information obtained from various sources; (b) identification of cases warranting in-depth investigation; (c) verification of facts; and (d) consideration of issues of law. Following its third session in Geneva on January 25-26, 1993, the Commission of Experts transmitted to the UN Secretary-General, in February 1993, its first interim report, together with a number of ancillary documents, including a report of a preliminary site exploration of a mass grave near the city of Vukovar in Croatia.

In late November 1992, the Croatian Chamber of Representatives (Zastupnički Dom) approved legislation providing for the internal administrative redivision of Croatia, for electoral purposes, into 21 counties, 420 municipalities and 61 towns. At the beginning of January 1993, proportional representation was introduced to replace the former plurality electoral system. Elections to the Chamber of Counties (Županijški Dom) were held on February 7 and 21, 1993. The CDU/HDZ won with 37 seats, while the Croatian Social-Liberal Party (CSLP), together with allied parties, obtained 16 seats, the Croatian Farmers' Party (CFP) won five seats, the Istrian Democratic Assembly (IDA) three seats and the Social Democratic Party (SDP), the Party of Democratic Reform of Croatia (PDRC), and the Croatian People's Party (CPP) gained one seat each.

The Special Rapporteur, Tadeusz Mazowiecki's, second and third reports were considered at the second special session of the Commission on Human Rights from November 30 thru December 1, 1992. The second report concentrated primarily on Bosnia-Herzegovina, especially on the practice of ethnic cleansing, and also gave attention to the human rights situations in Croatia and the FRY. The third report indicated that ethnic cleansing not only continued, but in some regions intensified, with the primary responsibility falling on the Serbian authorities in de facto control of certain territories in Bosnia-Herzegovina and in the UNPAs in Croatia. The Serbian command of the YPA and the political leadership of the Republic of Serbia were identified as sharing responsibility. According to this report, Albanians, Croats, Hungarians, Muslims and other minority groups were discriminated against in Kosova, Vojvodina and Sandzak (Muslim denominated region located partly in Serbia and partly in Montenegro). Discrimination and violations of the human rights occurred in territories controlled by the Government of Bosnia-Herzegovina, and to some extent in Bosnia-Herzegovina territory under the control of Croats. Discrimination and other human rights abuses also occurred in Croatia, in particular against those cutthroat Serb-četnici. Reminiscense of past experiences when Serb-četnici of Mihajlović instituted the act of cutthroat "Zaklati," (abbreviated by the code letter "Z"), as the trademark of Serbian brutality.

On November 30, 1992, the Commission on Human Rights adopted Resolution 1992/S-2/1, condemning all human rights violations and ethnic cleansing in the territory of the former Yugoslavia. The Commission demanded that all parties extend full cooperation and protection to the Office of the UNHCR and other international humanitarian organizations and relief agencies assisting refugees and DPs. Calling for the release of all persons arbitrarily arrested or detained, it demanded that the ICRC be granted access to all camps, prisons and places of detention and that all parties ensure safety and freedom of movement for ICRC. On December 18, 1992, the General Assembly, in its Resolution 47/147 commended the Special Rapporteur for his reports and urged all States and organizations to consider implementing the recommendations contained in those reports. The UN Secretary General submitted to the Security Council on December 9, 1992, a report recommending an expansion of UNPROFOR to establish a UN presence on Macedonia's borders. The UN Secretary General indicated that the Force's mandate would be essentially preventive and recommended that the UNPROFOR comprise an estimated battalion of up to 700 all ranks, 35 military observers, 26 civilian police monitors, 10 civil affairs staff, 45 administrative staff and local interpreters. This contingent is to operate under UNPROFOR's "Macedonia Command" with headquarters in Skopje, the capital of Macedonia. The Security Council, by its Resolution 795 adopted December 11, 1992, approved the UN Secretary General's report and authorized the establishment of UNPROFOR's presence in Macedonia.

* * * * *

~ War Crimes in Yugoslavia ~

Geneva, Switzerland, December 16, 1992

Statement made by Secretary of State Lawrence Eagleburger at the International Conference on the former Yugoslavia: "It is clear in reviewing the record since the London International Conference on the former Yugoslavia that the promises broken have been largely Serbia promises broken. It is the Serbs who continue to besiege the cities of Bosnia; Serb heavy weapons which continue to pound the civilian populations in those cities; the Serb air forces which continue to fly in defiance of the London agreements; and Serbs who impede the delivery of humanitarian assistance and continue the odious practice of "ethnic cleansing." It is now clear, that Milošević and Karadžić have systematically flouted agreements to which they had solemnly and yet cyncically, given their assent.

The United States Government believes it is time for the international community to begin identifying individuals who may have to answer for having committed crimes against humanity. We have, on the one hand, a moral and historical obligation not to stand back a second time in the century while a people faces obliteration. But we have also, a political obligation to the people of Serbia to signal clearly the risk they currently run of sharing the inevitable fate of those who practice ethnic cleansing in their name. Let's begin with the crimes themselves, the facts of which are indisputable: (a) The siege of Sarajevo, ongoing since April 1992, with scores of innocent civilians killed nearly every day by Serb artillery shelling; (b) The continuing blockade of humanitarian assistance, which is producing thousands upon thousands of unseen innocent victims; (c) The destruction of Vukovar in the fall of 1991, and the forced expulsion of the majority of its population; (d) The terrorizing of Banja Luka's 30,000 Muslims, which has included bombings, beatings, and killings; (e) The forcible imprisonment, inhuman mistreatment, and willful killing of civilians at detention camps, including Banja Luka/Manjaca, Brčko/Luka, Krajina/Prnjavor, Omarska, Prijedor/Karatern, and Trnopolje/Kozarac; (f) The August 21 massacre of more than 200 Muslim men and boys by Serb police in the Vlasica Mountains near Varjanta; (g) The May-June murders of between 2,000 and 3,000 Muslim men, women, and children by Serb-četnici at a brick factory and a pig farm near Brčko; (h) The June mass execution of about 100 Muslim men at Brod; and (i) The May 18 mass killing of at least 56 Muslim family members by Serb-četnici in Grbavci near Zvornik.

We know that Serbs have not alone been responsible for the massacres and crimes against humanity which have taken place. For example, in late October Croatian fighters killed or wounded up to 300 Muslims in Prozor, and between September 24-26, Muslims from Kamenica killed more that 60 Serb civiliams and soldiers.

We can do more than enumrate crimes; we can also identify individuals who committed them. For example: Borislav Herak a Serb from Bosnia who has confessed to killing over 230 civilians; and "Adil and Arif" are two members of a Croatian paramilitary force which in August attacked a convoy of buses carrying more than 100 Serbian women and children, killing over half of them.

We also know the names of leaders who directly supervised persons accused of war crimes, and who may have ordered those crimes. These include: (a) Željko Raznjatović, (a.k.a. 'Arkan') whose paramilitary forces, [the tigers], have been linked to brutal ethnic cleansing in Zvornik, Srebrenica, Bratunac, and Grobnica; and who were also linked to the mass murders of up to 3,000 civilians near Brčko; (b) Vojislav Šešelj, whose [white eagles] forces has been linked to atrocities in a number of Bosnian cities, including the infamous incident at Brčko; (c) Dragoljub Prcac, commander of the Omarska Detention Camp, where mass murder and torture occurred; and (d) Aden Delic, the camp commander at Cebebici where in August at least 15 Serbs were beaten to death.

Finally, there is another category of fact which is beyond dispute - namely, the fact of political and command responsibility for the crimes against humanity. Leaders such as Slobodan Milošević, the President of the Republic of Serbia, Radovan Karadžić, the self-declared President of the Serbian Republic in Bosnia, and General Ratko Mladić, commander of Serbian military forces in Bosnia, must eventually explain whether and how they sought to ensure, as they must under international law, that their forces complied with international law. They ought, if charged, to have the opportunity of defending themselves by demonstrating whether and how they took responsible action to prevent and punish the atrocities which were undertaken by their subordinates."

* * * * *

The North Atlantic Treaty Organization (NATO) was formed against the backdrop of emerging post-war tensions engendered by the threat of Soviet expansionism and concern over political and economic instability in Western Europe. On April 4, 1949, in Washington, D.C., the Foreign Ministers of Belgium, Canada, Denmark, England, France, Iceland, Italy, Luxembourg, Netherlands, Norway, Portugal, and United States signed the North Atlantic Treaty, the political framework for an international alliance designed to prevent aggression, or, if necessary, to resist attack against any alliance member. In 1952 Greece and Turkey were admitted to the treaty, followed by the Federal Republic of Germany in 1955 and by Spain in 1982. The collapse of the Soviet Union, the dissolution of the Warsaw Pact, and the progress of European integration have not ended the need for NATO's essential commitment to safeguard freedom and security of all its members by political and military means in accordance with UN principles. The Rome Declaration on Peace and Cooperation in November 1991 further underlined NATO's intention to redefine its objective in light of changed circumstances. In June 1992, NATO Foreign Ministers expressed concern over continuing violence similiar to the Serbian war of aggression. On July 10, 1992, the North Atlantic Council agreed on a NATO maritime operation in the Adriatic, in coordination with the WEU, to monitor compliance with the UN embargo against Serbia and Montenegro. On September 2, 1992, the Security Council approved UN humanitarian relief efforts in Bosnia-Herzegovina. On November 18, 1992, in coordination with the WEU, NATO agreed to enforce a naval blockade against Serbia and Montenegro. On December 17, 1992, the Security Council ordered the enforcement of its Resolution 781 of October 9, 1992 declaring a ban on military flights over Bosnia-Herzegovina.

In response to the grave human rights violations, the General Assembly on December 18, 1992, adopted two Resolutions, 47/147 on the situation of human rights in the territory of the former Yugoslavia, and 47/121 dealing with the situation in Bosnia-Herzegovina. The General Assembly, concerned about the human tragedy in the territory of the former Yugoslavia, and at the continuing massive and systematic violations of human rights occurring in most of that territory, particularly in the area of Bosnia-Herzegovina under Serbian occupation forces: (a) condemned unreservedly the abhorrent and odious practice of ethnic cleansing and recognized that the Serbian leadership in territories under its occupation and control in Bosnia-Herzegovina, the YPA and the political leadership of the Republic of Serbia bear primary responsibility for this reprehensible practice, which flagrantly violates the most fundamental principles of human rights; (b) condemns also the specific violations identified by the Special Rapporteur, most of which are caused by ethnic cleansing [ethnic extermination], and which include killings, torture, beatings, rape, disappearances, destruction of houses, and acts or threats of violence aimed at forcing individuals to leave their homes, as well as reports of violations of human rights in connection with detention; (c) condemns further the indiscriminate shelling of cities and civilian areas, the systematic terrorization and murder of non-combatants, the destruction of vital services, the besieging of cities and the use of military force against civilian populations and relief operations by all sides, recognizing that the main responsibility lies with Serbian forces.

(d) Condemns in particular the violations of human rights and humanitarian law in connection with detention, including killings, torture, and the systematic practice of rape, and calls upon all parties in the former Yugoslavia to close immediately all detention centers not in compliance with the Geneva Conventions and to release immediately all persons detained; and (e) draws the attention of the Commission of Experts established by SCR 780, dated October 6, 1992, to the need for an immediate and urgent investigation by qualified experts of a mass grave near the city of Vukovar in eastern Croatia and other mass grave sites and places where mass killings are reported to have taken place.

Appalled by reports of the massive, organized and systematic detention and rape of women, the Security Council, by its Resolution 798 on December 18, 1992, strongly condemned these acts of unspeakable brutality, expressed support for the initiative of the EC to dispatch a delegation to investigate the situation, and requested the UN Secretary General to provide all necessary support to enable the EC delegation to have free and secure access to the places of detention. The EC delegation conducted its investigative mission by making two visits to the former Yugoslavia, from December 18-24, 1992 and from January 19-26, 1993. Its final report was circulated as a document of the Security Council on February 3, 1993.

On December 21, 1992, the UN Secretary General submitted to the Security Council his recommendations concerning free and secure means of access to detention locations. In the report, he indicated that in order to ensure compliance with the relevant Security Council resolutions, it would be necessary to give UNPROFOR a mandate which would include the right not only to search but also to turn back or detain military personnel, or confiscate weapons, or sanctioned goods whose passage into or out of Bosnia-Herzegovina would be contrary to the decisions of the Security Council. He proposed an enlargement of UNPROFOR with approximately 10,000 additional troops to provide for a 24-hour observation and search operation at one hundred twenty-three crossing points on Bosnia-Herzegovina's border with neighboring countries.

From July 1992 until the end of December 1992, ICRC registered approximately 10,800 detainees in more than twenty-five known places of detention throughout Bosnia-Herzegovina. During that period, a total of 5,534 prisoners were released under ICRC auspices. The ICRC estimates that there are still a considerable number of prisoners, mostly civilians, who have not been visited or registered. According to ICRC, the Agreement of October 1, 1992 had not been implemented because the belligerents did not fully respect their obligations under the Agreement, and also because of difficulties in finding third countries willing to accept the prisoners.

On January 4, 1993, during the Geneva round of talks, the Co-Chairmen of the SCICY put to the parties concerned, Croats, Muslims, and Serbs, a comprehensive package as the basis for a purported fair, just and lasting peace. The Co-Chairmen included a set of constitutional principles along with a map setting out the organization of Bosnia-Herzegovina divided into 10 provinces, and augmented by an agreement for peace. The Co-Chairmen explained that all three elements of the package were inextricably linked and could not be implemented separately. Mate Boban, the leader of the Croats of Bosnia, accepted all three documents. The other two parties (Muslims and Serbs) asked for further discussions on parts of the two documents and on the proposed map.

After proved failure of the UN to restore to Croatian control the Maslenica bridge (43°24'N; 16°12'E) located in a pink zone, a strategically vital communications link between northern Croatia and the Coast of Dalmatia in the Adriatic Sea, the Croatian Army on January 22, 1993, launched a successful and limited offensive in a number of locations in the southern part of UNPROFOR's Sector South and the adjacent pink zones. The attack was centered on the strategic Maslenica bridge which links central Croatia with the Adriatic coast, and the Zemunik airport near the city of Zadar. On January 26, the warmonger president of the FRY, Dobrica Ćosić, a Serb-Marxist warned the UN that, if UNPROFOR did not intervene, FRY would dispatch troops to defend the ethnic Serbs residing in the Republic of Croatia. Croat forces achieved their objectives, but Serb-četnici stole the heavy weapons from UNPROFOR control. The Government of Croatia explained that it took this action out of impatience with the unjustifiable slow progress of negotiations in respect of various economic situations in and adjacent to the UNPAs and pink zones. Although the Government of Croatia had adopted the general amnesty required as a condition for a reinstatement of Croatian authority in the pink zones, neither the process of reintegrating those zones in Croatia's legal, economic and social system had begun, nor had Croatian authority in those zones been restored and local police force re-established in proportion to the zones' demographic structure prior to the conflict, in accordance with the UN peacekeeping plan. Two UN-French peacekeepers were killed and eight were wounded by Serb terrorists in fighting near Zadar on January 27, 1993; consequently, the French Government dispatched an aircraft carrier to the Adriatic Sea. Meantime, the Croatian forces regained control of the Maslenica bridge and the Zemunik airport near Zadar.

The Security Council on January 25, 1993, adopted its Resolution 802, in which it demanded an immediate cessation of hostile activities by Croatian armed forces within or adjacent to the UNPAs and their withdrawal from these areas, return of all heavy weapons seized by Serb forces from UNPROFOR-controlled storage areas, and strict compliance by all parties with the terms of cease-fire arrangements. It further demanded that all parties comply fully and immediately with all provisions of relevant SCR, and to refrain from any actions which might undermine efforts aimed at reaching a political settlement. As to the implementation of Resolution 802, the Government of Croatia on January 26, 1993 informed the Force Commander of UNPROFOR that, upon compliance by the Serb outlaws with the various provisions of the resolution, Croatia would remove their military, but not their police, from the areas they had liberated. For its part, Serbia demanded that Croatian forces return to their positions before the implementation of the resolution could be considered. Eventually, after several rounds of talks held under the auspices of Vance and Owen, the Co-Chairmen of the SCICY, the Government of Croatia and the Serb authorities signed an agreement regarding the implementation of Resolution 802.

On January 27, 1993, the Croatian Army attacked and captured the Perucka Dam/Peručko Nasip. The Serbian responded to the Croatian offensive by using acts of terrorism and breaking into a number of storage areas, which were under joint control and under a double-lock system in the UNPAs, and in a typical Serbian-style committed theft by misappropriating the UN weapons. In analyzing the situation in the Republic of Croatia, the UN Secretary General described UNPROFOR's experience there as a mixed one. Its principal success has been in ensuring the complete withdrawal of the YPA from the sovereign territory of the Republic of Croatia, including the Prevlaka Peninsula. UNPROFOR's presence had helped prevent a recurrence of hostilities in the UNPAs and pink zones. However, non-cooperation by the defiant Serb authorities had prevented UNPROFOR from demilitarization of the UNPAs and disarming the četnici of Serbia and Montenegro, including their irregular forces. As a result, UNPROFOR had not been able to establish the conditions of peace and security that would have permitted the voluntary and peaceful return of refugees and DP to their homes. Nor had UNPROFOR been able to establish the border controls called for in Resolution 769 dated August 7, 1992.

On January 30, 1993 after further intense negotiations in Geneva, President Alija Izetbegović of Bosnia-Herzegovina, Radovan Karadžić the leader of the Serb terrorists, and Mate Boban representing the Croats of Bosnia, signed the nine constitutional principles on the basis of which a new constitution for Bosnia-Herzegovina was to be drafted. Also, the Croats of Bosnia and the Serbs of Bosnia signed the agreement for peace dealing with the cessation of hostilities, the restoration of infrastructure, the opening of routes, the separation of forces, the demilitarization of Sarajevo, the monitoring of borders, and the return of forces to designated provinces. The government of Bosnia-Herzegovina stated that it would not sign the agreement for peace because it felt that the arrangements relating to the control of heavy weapons were not strong enough. As to the provincial boundaries, only Mate Boban confirmed his acceptance of the proposed map and signed it.

Fighting between Serbs and Croats continued into February of 1993 in "Sector South" of the Serb-held Krajina, centering around Obrovac, Benkovac, and Skradin (near Knin), the coastal town of Zadar, Šibenik, Biograd, and Vodice, and Karlovac south-west of Zagreb. After Western negotiators had painstakingly drawn up a peace plan that divided Bosnia into a patchwork of Serb, Croat, and Muslim territories, the European allies supported it, but the Clinton Administration advised the Bosnian government to reject the peace plan as constituted. As already noted, the UNPROFOR was established on February 21, 1992 by SCR 743 for an initial period of 12 months. On February 10, 1993, before the mandate of the UN Force expired, the UN Secretary General submitted to the Security Council a report in which he summarized the activities of UNPROFOR and presented his recommendations on its future.

In his report to the 49th session of the Commission on Human Rights, which was submitted through the UN Secretary General to the General Assembly and the Security Council on February 10, 1993, the Special Rapporteur described the human rights situation in the territory of the former Yugoslavia. The Special Rapporteur stated that evidence was mounting of war crimes committed mostly by Serbs during the conflicts in both Croatia and in Bosnia-Herzegovina. Numerous cases had been documented of summary executions and death threats, disappearances, torture and ill-treatment of detainees and destruction of property including religious sites. Rape of women was widespread in both Croatia and Bosnia-Herzegovina conflicts. There were victims among all ethnic groups and there were rapists among the armed forces of all parties. In addition, the Special Rapporteur sent a team of medical experts to the area to investigate reports of widespread occurrence of rape. According to the experts' report, the overwhelming majority of the rapes that they have documented had been committed by ethnic Serbs against Muslim women and girls from Bosnia-Herzegovina.

The operation to protect humanitarian convoys throughout the Republic of Bosnia-Herzegovina has been persistently thwarted by obstruction, mines, hostile fire and the refusal of the parties on the ground, particularly, but not exclusively, the Serb terrorists to cooperate with UNPROFOR. Nevertheless, from the deployment of additional UNPROFOR battalions for this purpose from November 1992 until January 1993, a total of 34,600 tons of relief supplies had been delivered to an estimated 800,000 beneficiaries in 110 locations throughout Bosnia-Herzegovina.

The Co-Chairmen of the SCICY decided to hold a further round of peace talks in New York so that the good offices of the Security Council could be used in helping the three sides to overcome their outstanding difficulties. The first round of New York talks, held from February 3 to 8, 1993, did not produce concrete results. Meaningless progress was achieved during the resumed round of the talks from March 1 to 6; on March 3, 1993 only President Alija Izetbegović of Bosnia-Herzegovina, signed the agreement for peace after having been assured by the Force Commander of UNPROFOR that physical control of heavy weapons could be undertaken.

The UN Secretary General Boutros Ghali on February 9, 1993 had forwarded to the Security Council an interim report prepared by a Commission of Experts on war crimes in the former Yugoslavia. The Commission of Experts' report had endorsed the creation of a War Crimes Tribunal by the Security Council, and had also urged the completion of its database on human rights violations in the former Yugoslavia "to provide the foundation for the formulation of conclusions on the evidence of war crimes." On February 19, 1993, having considered the UN Secretary General's report, the Security Council adopted Resolution 807, by which it extended the UNPROFOR mandate for an interim period until March 31, 1993. The Security Council demanded, inter alia, that the parties and others concerned comply fully with the UN peacekeeping plan in Croatia and their other commitments, and refrain from positioning their forces near the UNPAs and in the pink zones. The Security Council urged the parties and others concerned to cooperate fully with the Co-Chairmen of the SCICY in the discussions under their auspices in order to ensure full implementation of the UN peacekeeping mandate in the Republic of Croatia. In accordance with SCR 807 dated February 19, 1993, the Co-Chairmen of the SCICY held several rounds of talks in New York City, NY and Geneva, Switzerland, with representatives of the Government of Croatia and the representative of Serb populations living in the UNPAs and the pink zones.

In a historic decision, the SCR 808 was adopted on February 22, 1993, for the establishment of an ad hoc war crimes tribunal for the prosecution of persons responsible for serious violations of international humanitarian law committed in the territory of the former Yugoslavia since 1991. The resolution asked the UN Secretary General to submit within 60 days proposals for creating such tribunal. The Security Commission adopted two resolutions on February 23, 1993. Resolution 1993/7, requested the UN Secretary General to provide for the appointment of human rights field officers in the former

Yugoslavia. By Resolution 1993/8 the Commission condemned the abhorrent practice of rape and abuse of women and girls in the territory of the former Yugoslavia which was being used as an instrument of ethnic cleansing.

In a follow-up to the recommendations made by the Special Rapporteur, subsequently reflected in Commission on Human Rights Resolutions 1992/S-2/1 of November 30, 1992 and 1993/7 of February 23, 1993, human rights field officers were being deployed in the territory of the former Yugoslavia. In the meantime, the UN Secretary General recommended that the Security Council decide to extend UNPROFOR's existing mandate for an interim period up to March 31, 1993, in order to give the Co-Chairman of the SCICY the necessary time. Concerning UNPROFOR activities in Bosnia-Herzegovina, where it had a more limited mandate, the UN Secretary General noted in his February 1993 report that the Force had succeeded in keeping Sarajevo airport open, despite interruptions as a result of hostile Serbian military action against humanitarian aircraft. In the period from July 3, 1992 to March 18, 1993, the humanitarian airlift organized by UNHCR under UNPROFOR protection brought in approximately 3,000 aircraft carrying a total of 33,000 tons of food, medicines and other relief goods.

At its fourth session, held in Geneva from March 1-3, 1993, the Commission of Experts decided to send a reconnaissance mission to facilitate the investigation into mass killings in the Vukovar area. The team was authorized to visit other sites if deemed necessary. From April 18-29, 1993, a delegation of the Commission of Experts visited the cities of Belgrade, Ljubljana, Sarajevo and Zagreb, and conducted talks with senior government officials in those four capitals. The purpose of the mission was to obtain the cooperation of those involved with war crime documentation or investigation in the respective countries. The UN Secretary General established the Trust Fund to support the activities of the Commission in carrying out its mandate.

On March 11, 1993, Sadako Ogata reported to the Security Council that 3.8 million people were receiving assistance in the whole of the former Yugoslavia. In Bosnia-Herzegovina alone, some 2.28 million people, or half of the original population, were beneficiaries of humanitarian assistance from UNHCR, and the situation there was still deteriorating and that UNHCR's biggest concern remained gaining humanitarian access to the victims, especially those enclaves in eastern Bosnia-Herzegovina where access had in many instances been denied altogether. The enormous suffering and devastation in Bosnia-Herzegovina underscored the critical importance of an immediate cessation of hostilities. The UN on March 17, 1993, issued a revised Consolidated Inter-Agency Appeal for the period from April 1 to December 31, 1993. The Appeal calls for $840 million as new funding requirements in addition to the $496 million already spent or committed by

UN and associated agencies in the former Yugoslavia since the beginning of the emergency operation in November 1991.

The next round of New York talks lasted from March 16 to 25, 1993. After further intensive discussions of the working paper on interim governmental arrangements, the government of Bosnia-Herzegovina and the Croats of Bosnia signed an agreement on March 25, 1993. As part of that agreement, they also signed a revised map of provincial boundaries. The interim arrangements paper thus formally became the fourth element of the overall peace agreement. The Serbs of Bosnia declined to sign the two documents, becoming the only side lagging behind in signature of all four documents.

Although the ban on military flights in the airspace of Bosnia-Herzegovina had been violated by all three parties on nearly 400 occasions since its imposition, it had achieved its principal purpose of preventing the use of air power in military combat in the Republic of Bosnia-Herzgovina. UNPROFOR observers, using Airborne Warning and Control System (AWACS) information made available by the NATO, had found no evidence to suggest that any party had flown combat air missions, or conducted hostilities from the air since the interdiction regime was established by the Security Council. UNPROFOR's efforts in Bosnia-Herzegovina, the UN Secretary General pointed out, had been characterized by a regrettable tendency on the part of the host Government of Bosnia-Herzegovina to blame it for a variety of shortcomings, whether real or imagined. Criticism of UNPROFOR's performance in Bosnia-Herzegovina had largely been directed at its failure to fulfill tasks that the Force had not been mandated, authorized, equipped, staffed or financed to fulfill. There had been a number of criticisms on the Force by the Government of Bosnia-Herzegovina and by elements answerable to it, both in public statements and declarations.

The UN Secretary General reported on March 16, 1993, that three aircraft dropped bombs on two villages east of Srebrenica on March 13 before leaving in the direction of the FRY. It was the first time since the Security Council instituted the no-fly zone in Bosnia-Herzegovina that aircraft were used in combat activity in that country. On March 17, 1993, the Security Council demanded from the Serbs an immediate explanation of the violations and particularly of the aerial bombardment of the two villages, and requested the UN Secretary General to ensure that an investigation was made of the reported possible use of the territory of the FRY to launch air strikes against Bosnia-Herzegovina. On April 27, 1993, the UN Secretary General reported to the Security Council that on March 24, 1993 the FRY had been requested to provide information relevant to the incidents. The only response received from the Milošević controlled FRY was a verbal note conveying a statement by the government of the FRY in which it stated that airplanes and helicopters belonging to the Air Forces and to the Army of the FRY have not violated the airspace of Bosnia-Herzegovina since the no-fly zone came into effect.

On March 20, 1993 the government of Bosnia-Herzegovina instituted proceedings against the FRY for alleged violations of the 1948 Convention on the Prevention and Punishment of the Crime of Genocide. Bosnia-Herzegovina requested the International Court of Justice (ICJ) to adjudge and declare that FRY had violated and was continuing to violate several provisions of the Genocide Convention as well as the UN Charter, the 1949 Geneva Conventions for the protection of war victims and their 1977 Additional Protocol I, the 1907 Hague Regulations on Land Warfare and the Universal Declaration of Human Rights; that FRY was using force and the threat of force against Bosnia-Herzegovina, violating its sovereignty and intervening in its internal affairs, as well as encouraging and supporting military and paramilitary actions in and against Bosnia-Herzegovina; that Bosnia-Herzegovina had the sovereign right under the UN Charter and customary international law to defend itself and to request assistance of any State in doing so, which was not to be impaired by SCR 713 dated September 25, 1991, and subsequent resolutions imposing and reaffirming an arms embargo upon the former Yugoslavia; that those consequent resolutions should not be construed as imposing an arms embargo upon Bosnia-Herzegovina; that, pursuant to the right to collective self-defense, other States had the right to come to the immediate defense of Bosnia-Herzegovina at its request; that FRY should cease and desist immediately from its breaches of the foregoing legal obligations; and that FRY should pay reparations for damages sustained by Bosnia-Herzegovina. On the same day, Bosnia-Herzegovina requested the ICJ to indicate provisional measures to the effect the FRY should cease and desist immediately from all acts of genocide, from military or paramilitary actions and support for such actions in or against Bosnia-Herzegovina and from any other use or threat of force against it; that Bosnia-Herzegovina had the right to seek support and assistance from other States in defending itself; and that other States had the right to come to its immediate defense.

In response to a suit initiated by the Government of Bosnia-Herzegovina on March 20, 1993; the ICJ found that it had prima facie jurisdiction to issue its Order under the Convention on the Prevention and Punishment of the Crime of Genocide concluded by the UN in 1948, to which the FRY and Bosnia-Herzegovina are parties. The Convention describes as genocide acts committed with the intent to destroy, in whole or in part, a national, ethnical, racial or religious group. While the ICJ acted speedily to issue its provisional measures, a judgment on the merits of the case will be handed down only after the parties fully brief and argue it. The Court's Order emphasized that the facts and law of the dispute meanwhile remain unsettled. Under its

Statute, the Court has the power to indicate provisional measures for preserving the rights of either party, pending judgment on the merits of the case. The ICJ noted it was unable to indicate measures for the protection of any disputed rights which fall outside the scope of the Genocide Convention.

On March 25, 1993, Sadako Ogata of Japan, in her capacity as the Chairwoman of the Working Group on Humanitarian Issues of the International Conference on Yugoslavia, convened a high-level intergovernmental meeting in Geneva to discuss needs in the war-torn region. More than 55 nations and international organizations participated in the meeting. According to the findings by the UNHCR, over 2.7 million people were directly affected by the crisis and were in need of emergency humanitarian assistance - particularly in the areas of food, shelter and health care. On the basis of those findings, the UNHCR, and other concerned UN agencies and NGOs, formulated a Consolidated Inter-Agency Program of Action and Appeal for the period September 1992 to March 1993. The overall requirements identified by the Assessment Mission amounted to over $1 billion. Subsequently, it was established that $434 million would be required for addressing life-threatening priority needs to be channelled through the UN system. The areas targeted for immediate relief were food, health services and shelter.

Throughout recent months Croatia was confronted with a period of political and economic uneasiness, culminating in nationwide strikes in protest against low wages and high inflation. In an attempt of partial appeasement, on March 29, 1993, Premier Hrvoje Šarinin (who was sworn in on September 8, 1992) resigned. A former executive of the Croatian Industrija Nafte, Nikica Valentić was appointed by President Tudjman as Premier of the Republic of Croatia. In the February 1993 elections in Istria, the political party of Istrian Democratic Assembly (IDA) advocating Istrian autonomy received 72% of the total votes cast. The IDA proposed that the historic territory of Istria, mostly of Croatian, Slovenian, and Italian speaking people be allowed to become an autonomous region within Croatia. The Croatian government strongly objected to any self-governing authority in Istria.

On March 30, 1993, the Security Council, by adopting its Resolution 815, extended the mandate of UNPROFOR for an additional interim period until June 30, 1993. It also decided to reconsider within one month, or at any time at the request of the UN Secretary General, UNPROFOR's mandate in the light of developments of the SCICY and the situation on the ground. The Security Council requested the UN Secretary General to report to it on how the UN peace plan for Croatia could be effectively implemented. On March 31, 1993, the Security Council adopted its Resolution 816, by which it extended the ban on military flights to cover flights by all fixed-wing and

264

rotary-wing aircraft in the airspace of Bosnia-Herzegovina. Acting under Chapter VII of the UN Charter, the Council authorized Member States to take, under the authority of the Security Council and subject to close coordination with the UN Secretary General and UNPROFOR, all necessary measures in the airspace of Bosnia-Herzegovina to ensure full compliance with the ban on flights, and proportionate to the specific circumstances and the nature of flights. It also requested the Member States concerned, the UN Secretary General and UNPROFOR to coordinate closely on those measures and on the starting date of the implementation, and to report on the starting date to the Security Council.

The UN Secretary General, on April 8, 1993 reported to the Security Council that representatives of the Government of Croatia and the Serb authorities had signed, on April 6, 1993, an agreement regarding SCR 802 dated January 25, 1993. According to one of the provisions of the agreement, it shall enter into force when the Co-Chairmen of the SCICY have received from both parties assurances regarding the stationing of police in the areas from which the Croatian Government's armed forces are withdrawn, and that UNPROFOR shall exclusively fulfill all police functions in those areas during an interim period. The agreement provides, for the cessation of hostilities and strict compliance with the cease-fire arrangements. Within five days from the cessation of hostilities, the Croatian forces were to commence their withdrawal to the line of confrontation existing before the outbreak of hostilities on January 22, 1993, and to complete their withdrawal within a further five days. No Serb armed forces were to enter the areas from which the Croatian forces withdrew. In parallel with that, over a maximum period of 10 days, all Serb heavy weapons in the area were to be returned to UNPROFOR supervision. The Force Commander of UNPROFOR has assessed the additional resources required to implement the agreement and has recommended that UNPROFOR be augmented by two mechanized infantry battalions of some 900 all ranks each, one engineer company of up to 150 troops all ranks, and 50 additional military observers. The UN Secretary General recommended that, once the agreement enters into force, the Security Council approve the recommended changes to UNPROFOR's strength and mandate.

The Security Council, on April 7, 1993, recommended to the General Assembly that the Macedonia Republic of former Yugoslavia be admitted to UN membership. In adopting its Resolution 817 of April 7, 1993, the Security Council, after having noted that the difference which had arisen over the name of that State needed to be resolved in the interests of maintaining peaceful relations in the region, welcomed the readiness of the Co-Chairmen of the SCICY to use their good offices to settle the matter and promote confidence-building measures among the parties. On April 8, 1993, the

General Assembly decided to admit to membership in the UN the State being provisionally referred to for all purposes within the UN as the former Yugoslav Republic of Macedonia pending settlement of the difference that had arisen over the name of the State.

By an Order of April 8, 1993, the ICJ indicated that the FRY should immediately take all measures within its power to prevent commission of the crime of genocide. The Court stated that the government of the FRY should in particular ensure that any military, paramilitary or irregular armed units which may be directed or supported by it, as well as any organizations and persons which may be subject to its control, direction or influence, do not commit any acts of genocide, of conspiracy to commit genocide, of direct and public incitement to commit genocide, or of complicity in genocide, whether directed against the Muslim population of Bosnia-Herzegovina or against any other national, ethnical, racial or religious group. The ICJ also held that neither party should in any way aggravate or extend the dispute. Judge Tarasson of the ICJ appended a declaration to the Order. On April 9, the UN Secretary General transmitted to the Security Council a letter from the UN Secretary General of NATO, Manfred Wörner of Germany, informing him that the North Atlantic Council had adopted the "necessary arrangements" to ensure compliance with the ban on military flights and that it was prepared to begin the operation at noon Greenwich Mean Time (GMT) on April 12, 1993. Wörner also reported that so far Britain, France, the Netherlands, Turkey, and the USA had offered to make aircraft available for the operation. To commence the enforcement on time, aircraft from France, the Netherlands and the United States were initially deployed in the region and liaison cells were established at UNPROFOR's headquarters in the capital city of Zagreb, Croatia, and in Kiseljak, Bosnia-Herzegovina.

The operations authorized by Resolution 816 dated March 31, 1993 started, as scheduled, on April 12, 1993 at 12:00 GMT. The UN Secretary General was informed by NATO that all the countries offering to make aircraft available for the operation would participate fully in it.

On April 16, 1993, the Security Council, acting under Chapter VII of the UN Charter, adopted Resolution 819, in which it demanded that all parties treat the town of Srebrenica and its surroundings as a safe area which should be free from any armed attack or any other hostile act. It demanded the immediate withdrawal of Serb paramilitary units from areas surrounding Srebrenica and the cessation of armed attacks against that town. The Security Council requested the UN Secretary General to take steps to increase the presence of UNPROFOR in Srebrenica and to arrange for the safe transfer of sick and wounded, and demanded the unimpeded delivery of humanitarian assistance to all parts of Bosnia-Herzegovina, in particular to the civilian population of Srebrenica. By other provisions of the Resolution 819, the Security Council condemned and rejected the deliberate actions of the barbaric Serbs to force the evacuation of civilians from Srebrenica and other parts of Bosnia-Herzegovina in its campaign of ethnic cleansing. Following the adoption of Resolution 819, the UNPROFOR's Force Commander, the Commander of the Serb-četnik forces and the Commander of the Muslim forces signed, on April 17, an agreement for the demilitarization of the town of Srebrenica and its surroundings. The UNPROFOR's Force Commander reported that 170 UNPROFOR troops, civilian police and military observers had been deployed in Srebrenica to collect weapons, ammunition, mines, explosives and combat supplies and that by noon on April 21, they had successfully demilitarized the town of Srebrenica which has remained calm since April 18, 1993. As requested in Resolution 819, the Security Council's fact-finding mission, composed of representatives of France, Hungary, New Zealand, Pakistan, the Russian Federation, and Venezuela, visited the region from April 22 to 27, 1993. Having considered the mission's report and recommendations, on May 6, 1993 the Security Council adopted Resolution 824 in which it declared that, in addition to Srebrenica, Sarajevo and other such threatened areas, in particular the towns of Tuzla, Žepa, Goražde, Bihać and their surroundings, should be treated as safe areas by all the parties concerned.

On April 17, 1993 the Security Council adopted its Resolution 820, by which it commended the peace plan for Bosnia-Herzegovina and welcomed the fact that the plan had been accepted in full by two of the parties in Bosnia. The Security Council decided to strengthen the sanctions regime imposed against the FRY effective nine days after the date of adoption of the resolution, unless the Serbs signed the peace plan and ceased its military attacks in Bosnia-Herzegovina. The stronger sanctions would prevent diversion to the country of commodities and products, by land and sea, and freeze all its funds held in other Member States. Further sanctions against FRY included: preventing the diversion to it of commodities and products said to be destined for other places; authorization for the transshipment of commodities and products through that country on the Danube; forbidding any vessels registered in that country, owned by it, operated by it or suspected of violating Security Council resolutions to pass through installations within the territory of Member States; authorizing Member States to freeze any funds in their territory belonging to that country, to ensure that they were not made available for the benefit of the Yugoslav authorities. The Security Council expressed its readiness, after all three parties in Bosnia-Herzegovina have accepted the peace plan and on the basis of verified evidence, provided by the UN Secretary General, that the Serbs were cooperating in implementing it, to review all the measures and other relevant resolutions with a view to gradually lifting them.

Despite the efforts of the Co-Chairmen of the SCICY and the intensive round of talks from April 21 to 25, 1993 the Serbs continued to reject any peace plan. The deadline established by SCR 820 dated April 17, 1993 passed and the new sanctions regime against the FRY came into force at midnight on April 26, 1993. In its Resolution 820 the Security Council requested the UN Secretary General to report on the implementation of the peace plan once it had been accepted by all the parties. The peace plan included a wide range of measures requiring the deployment of additional peacekeeping troops in Bosnia-Herzegovina. These measures included the cessation of hostilities throughout Bosnia-Herzegovina, the restoration of infrastructure, the opening of routes, the separation of forces, the demilitarization of Sarajevo, the monitoring of the borders of Bosnia-Herzegovina, and the return of forces to designated provinces.

The UN Secretary General on April 26, 1993 reported that the multitude of tasks envisaged in the peace plan would exceed the planning capability of the UN Secretariat and that of UNPROFOR. Therefore, consultations were initiated with NATO which indicated that it would consider a formal request to undertake detailed planning for the implementation of the plan and make available a core headquarters structure into which other potential troop contributors could be incorporated. On the basis of preliminary studies, NATO experts estimated that 60,000 troops would be required for the implementation of the various military tasks envisaged in the peace plan. The UN Secretary General indicated that the implementation of the plan would involve a UN operation conducted under the authority of the Security Council and financed collectively by Member States under the peacekeeping scale of assessments. The UN would have overall political and strategic control which would be exercised by the UN Secretary General under the authority of the Security Council. As to the principal civilian tasks of the peace plan, they included the restoration of law, order and civil authority throughout Bosnia-Herzegovina in conformity with the following six constitutional principles: (a) the preparation of a constitution in accordance with the six principles; (b) the resolution of problems concerning provincial borders, and related political issues; (c) the preparation of internationally supervised, free and fair elections to be held for the central government as well as the provincial governments; (d) the provision of arrangements for the highest level of internationally recognized human rights through domestic and international mechanisms; (e) the reversal of ethnic cleansing and the establishment of conditions in which those refugees and DPs who wished to return to their homes may do so; and (f) the provision of humanitarian aid and appropriate levels of relief and rehabilitation assistance.

On April 29, 1993, the General Assembly, on the recommendation by the SCR 821 of April 28, decided that the FRY shall not participate in the work of the Economic and Social Council. The UN Secretary General submitted to the Council on May 3, 1993 a detailed report covering such issues as the legal basis for the establishment of the International Tribunal, its competence and organization, investigation and pre-trial proceedings, trial and post-trial proceedings, cooperation and judicial assistance, and general provisions. The Statute of the Tribunal was annexed to the report.

The Co-Chairmen of the SCICY Vance and Owen, together with Co-Chairman-designate Thorvald Stoltenberg (Foreign Minister of Norway appointed to succeed Vance effective May 1, 1993), convened a meeting of the three parties to the conflict in Bosnia-Herzegovina. The meeting took place during May 1 and 2, 1993 in Athens, Greece. The main attendees were President Alija Izetbegović of Bosnia, Mate Boban representing Croats of Bosnia, and Radovan Karadžić representing the Serbs of Bosnia. The meeting was also attended by President Franjo Tudjman of Croatia, President Dobrica Čosić of the FRY, President Slobodan Milošević of Serbia, and President Momir Bulatović of Montenegro. The two day meeting resulted in Karadžic's signing, on May 2, the two documents of the peace plan - the map of provisional provincial boundaries and the agreement on interim arrangements. Karadžić indicated, however, that the documents would have to be approved by the so-called "Assembly" at Pale representing the Serbs of Bosnia. Hereupon, the peace process suffered a reversal when, on May 5, 1993 notwithstanding Karadžic's signature and the strong pressure from the international community, the Serbian Assembly at Pale rejected the peace plan and voted to hold a referendum on the subject.

Fighting intensified in eastern Bosnia-Herzegovina, with Serb paramilitary units attacking several cities in the area, including Srebrenica. The military attacks resulted in a heavy loss of life among the civilian population and severely impeded UN humanitarian relief efforts in the area. The UNHCR reported that thousands of Muslims were seeking refuge in Srebrenica from surrounding areas which were being attacked and occupied by Serb forces, and that hundreds of persons were dying weekly from military action, starvation, exposure to cold or lack of medical treatment. In April 1993, despite the strong political pressure from the international community and the Security Council, and the efforts by UNPROFOR and UNHCR in the field, the fighting persisted and the humanitarian situation in Bosnia-Herzegovina continued to deteriorate.

The government of Croatia proceeded unrelenting and unwavering to reconstruct the Maslanica bridge which was reopened for traffic in July 1993. During the rebuilding and after the opening of the bridge, the Serbs became so irritant and frustrated by the ever present Croatian forces in the vicinity, launched an attack on Croatian positions. In mid-July, the UN negotiated an agreement "the Erdut Agreement" whereby, Croatian forces were to give up the Maslenica area, to be returned under the UNPROFOR control, and revert certain villages to the Serbs; in exchange, President Milošević of Serbia, to demonstrate his supreme political and military authority, promised to issue an order whereby the Serbian troops would cease attacking the Maslenica bridge and surrounding area and return the stolen weapons and ammunition to UNPROFOR. Because the untrustworthy Serbian paramilitary reneged on a commitment to return to UNPROFOR the surreptitiously acquired weapons from UN storage, Croatian forces renounced their withdrawal from the important highway leading to the Maslenica bridge across the Novigrad Sea/Novigradsko More (44°12'N; 15°33'E) by July 31, 1993 deadline for final implementation of the accord. In June 1993 fighting intensified between Croatian and Serbian forces. On June 14-15, Biograd and Zadar on the Dalmatian coast came under heavy YPA and Serb shelling. In August 1993, Croatian Foreign Minister Mate Granić declared the so-called Erdut Agreement superfluous. Therefore, the Serbs put into action a full-scale mobilization in the Serbian occupation territory of Baranja, Slavonia, and Western Srem. In the meantime most of the YPA units had withdrawn from Croatian territory but the Serbian irregular forces still occupied approximately 30% of the territory of Croatia.

In late September 1993, the UN Secretary General recommended the extension of the UNPROFOR mandate in the former Yugoslavia for a further six months; the Croatians, however, rejected the recommendation, claiming that it ignored certain issues vital to Croatian interests. On October 5, 1993, the SCR 871 by unanimous vote extended UNPROFOR's mandate in Croatia. This Resolution also required the return to Croatian sovereignty all pink zones (areas outside the official UNPA's), the restoration of all communication links between those regions and the remainder of Croatia, and the disarmament of Serb paramilitary groups. The Croat administration accepted Resolution 871, but it was rejected by the Serbs.

Following a request by Bosnia-Herzegovina and after the views of FRY had been ascertained, the Vice-President of the ICJ, by an Order of October 7, 1993, extended the time-limits for a Memorial (a written statement of facts or a petition presented to the ICJ) by Bosnia-Herzegovina and a Counter-Memorial by FRY to April 15, 1994 and April 15, 1995, respectively. The Memorial was filed within the prescribed time-limit.

Brutal Serb shelling prevented humanitarian assistance from entering Sarajevo. On November 9, 1993, the Serbs shelled the Sarajevo school yard, killing four children, wounding forty others. The White House press secretary Dee Dee Myers response to the attack, "We are not going to allow the city of Sarajevo to be strangled, to be cut off, to be relentlessly attacked."

The resignation of the Commander of UN forces in the former Yugoslavia, General Jean Cot, was announced on January 18, 1994. Cot had reportedly angered the UN Secretary General by publicly demanding the right to launch air strikes on his own authority against Serb terrorists. Meanwhile, General Francis Briquemont who resigned for "personal reasons" was replaced as Commander of UN forces in Bosnia-Herzegovina on January 24, 1994 by a British officer, Gen. Michael Rose.

* * * * *

~ Croatian and Serbian Joint Declaration ~

Geneva, January 19, 1994

The Republic of Croatia and the Federal Republic of Yugoslavia:

"Proceeding from positive experience in joint endeavors to promote peace processes in the solution of the crisis in the territory of the former Yugoslavia, guided by the United Nations Charter and basic CSCE documents, aspiring to establish good neighborly relations and wishing to contribute in a resolute way to the just and lasting solution of the crisis in the former Yugoslavia, and to re-establish stability in this part of Europe, have agreed to start the process of normalization of their mutual relations.

As the first step in that direction, they have decided to open official representations of the two governments in Zagreb and Belgrade - The Office of the Republic of Croatia in Belgrade and Office of the Federal Republic of Yugoslavia in Zagreb. The opening of these offices should facilitate the relations and contacts between the two States, contribute to the development of mutual confidence, including the process of normalization of Croat-Serbian relations, in the interest of peace, cooperation and stability in the region. The governments of the Republic of Croatia and the Federal Republic of Yugoslavia will provide the technical and other facilities for the work of the offices to begin operating on February 15, 1994."

Signed by: Mate Granić, Minister of Foreign Affairs
Republic of Croatia

Vladislav Jovanović, Minister of Foreign Affairs
Fedeal Republic of Yugoslavia

* * * * *

The first normalization of relations between the Republic of Croatia and the FRY occurred in Geneva on January 19, 1994, Croatia's Foreign Minister Mate Granić signed a joint declaration with his FRY counterpart Vladislav Jovanović. This declaration called for the establishment of representative offices in the respective capitals by February 15, as part of the dual-track peace approach to normalize relations. The foreign ministers' joint declaration was an important first step which may lead to full reciprocal recognition of the two countries within their internationally recognized borders, consistent with the SCR 871 of October 5, 1993 which called for confidence building measures. On February 5, 1994, Serb terrorists shelled

271

Sarajevo marketplace, killing 68 people and wounding 107 others. US President Clinton's response was, "We rule nothing out in the way of reprisals."

* * * * *

~ Sarajevo Marketplace Shelling ~

Washington, DC, February 7, 1994

Statement released by U.S. Secretary of State Christopher:

"The civilized world is outraged by the savage bombing of the Sarajevo market-place on Saturday, February 5, 1994. The death toll from this shelling is not only the worst since this tragic conflict began, it is also a part of a pattern of shelling of civilian areas by Serb artillery that has continued despite NATO's repeated warnings. I have been in touch with several of my NATO counterparts over the weekend to discuss how the alliance and the international community should respond to Saturday's tragedy.

UN Secretary General Boutros-Ghali has requested that the North Atlantic Council take the necessary decisions to enable NATO military forces to be prepared to respond to a UN request for air strikes. Under Boutros-Ghali's proposal, air strikes would be directed against artillery and mortar positions in and around Sarajevo when UNPROFOR determines that they are responsible for attacks against civilian targets. The proposal made by Boutros-Ghali would expand on NATO's current policy of being ready to respond to UN requests for close air support to assist UNPROFOR if it is attacked in carrying out its humanitarian missions in Bosnia-Herzegovina.

We welcome Boutros-Ghali's proposal and will support it when we and our allies take it up at the North Atlantic Council later this week. His request indicates that the United Nations and NATO are and will continue to be working closely together on this terrible problem. At NATO, we are also looking at other possible steps to respond to Saturday's attack, and we are also looking at the larger problem of the Serbs' unacceptable actions against the civilian population in Bosnia's capital. We expect that the North Atlantic Council will decide on a course of action - an overall strategy - within the next few days. While attention has been properly focused on Saturday's tragic events, we are continuing the search for ways to reinvigorate the diplomatic efforts aimed at achieving a political settlement of the conflict in Bosnia. We welcome the statement of the Bosnian Government leaders that, despite what happened Saturday, they remain committed to the negotiating process. We are looking for ways to bring additional support to these efforts to obtain a viable settlement."

* * * * *

Macedonia declared its independence from the Socialist Federal Republic of Yugoslavia (SFRY) on September 8, 1991. Macedonia was admitted to the United Nations under a provisional name in 1993. A United Nations force which included 300 United States troops, was deployed in Macedonia in 1993 to deter the warmongering Serbians from carrying out their expansionistic design for establishing Serboslavia. Better late than never, on Feb. 9, 1994, the U.S. officially recognized of the Republic of Macedonia.

The North Atlantic Council, the highest executive body of NATO, at a meeting on February 9, 1994 agreed with UN Secretary General Boutros Ghali's request to implement any future UN request for air strikes, issued an ultimatum authorizing air strikes against Serb artillery and mortar positions in or around the besieged Bosnian capital of Sarajevo. The ultimatum, in line with a decision adopted by NATO leaders at a summit meeting in January led to NATO's first military action since its foundation in 1949. Only Greece, among NATO's 16 member states, failed to support air strikes against Serbs. NATO issued an ultimatum to the Serbs, to the effect that if heavy weapons in an exclusive zone comprising a 12.4 mi./20 km belt of land around Sarajevo are not removed by February 21, then air strikes would commence. Russia, Romania, and Greece criticized the NATO ultimatum. After the Hungarian Foreign Minister Geza Jeszenszky's visit to Belgrade on January 28-29, Hungarian Premier Peter Boross said on February 11 that NATO surveillance aircraft would be denied access to Hungarian air space in the event of NATO air attack on Serb artillery and mortar.

On February 13, 1994, Dusan "Dusko" Tadić, a Serb from Bosnia, accused of war crimes, was arrested in Munich, Germany. Tadić who was hiding in Germany was suspected of committing atrocities against Muslims in Bosnia-Herzegovina's Omarska Prison camp in 1992. The arrest was made under German law which provides for the trial of people suspected of war crimes, even if the crimes were committed in another country.

A Spanish aircraft, part of the NATO task force enforcing the air exclusion zone over Bosnia-Herzegovina, was forced to make an emergency landing after sustaining slight damage from ground fire over Croatia on March 8. Four people aboard the CASA-212 logistics aircraft were slightly injured. A series of incidents on March 10-12, 1994 including the killing of a French soldier by sniper fire on March 11 and the bombardment of French positions by Serb heavy weapons on March 12, prompted French peacekeepers in Bihac to request air support. However, some three hours elapsed before the request was granted, at which time strikes had been ruled out due to poor weather. This episode confirmed doubts as to the capacity of the UN ineptness to provide effective air support to the UNPROFOR. The UN chain of command required the approval first of the commander of UN forces in Bosnia-Herzegovina, Gen. Rose, then of the Commander of UN Forces in former Yugoslavia, Gen. Jean Cot, and finally of Yasushi Akashi of Japan, the Special Envoy to former Yugoslavia.

UN Secretary General Boutros Ghali's mistaken view of the Serbian war of aggression and the lack of understanding by western nations concerned with not displeasing Russia, contributed to the savagery. If there had been the will to stop the war, NATO powers would have imposed their thrust and crushed the aggressor Serbs and their equally guilty surrogates.

273

* * * * *

~ Bosnia and Croatia: Peace Agreement ~

Washington, DC, March 18, 1994

Opening statement by U.S. President Clinton at signing of federation agreement between the Muslims and Croats of Bosnia [Croat-Bosniac Federation]. "We have come to bear witness to a moment of hope. For twenty-three months, the flames of war have raged through the nations of the former Yugoslavia. By signing these agreements today, Bosnian and Croatian leaders have acted to turn back those flames and to begin the difficult process of reconciliation.

Around the globe the tension between ethnic identity and statehood presents one of the great problems of our time. But nowhere have the consequences been more tragic than in the former Yugoslavia. There nationalists and religious factions, aggravated by Serbian aggression, have erupted in a fury of ethnic cleansing and brutal atrocities.

The agreements signed today offer one of the first clear signals that parties to this conflict are willing to end the violence and to begin a process of reconstruction. The accord calls for a federation between the Muslims and Croats of Bosnia. The Muslim-Croat entity has agreed on the principles of a confederation with Croatia. Together, these steps can help support the ideal of a multiethnic Bosnia and provide a basis for Muslims and Croats to live again in peace as neighbors and compatriots.

The agreements are as important for Croatia's future as they are for Bosnia's. And it is the hope of all present today that the Serbs will join in this process toward peace as well. These agreements are a testament to the perseverance and to the resolve of many people: the Croatian and Bosnian diplomats who kept probing for openings toward peace; the UN soldiers from many nations represented here today who have worked to bring both stability and humanitarian supplies; and the NATO pilots who have helped put air power at the service of diplomacy.

We have engaged in this work because the United States has clear interests at stake: an interest in helping to prevent the spread of a wider war in Europe; an interest in showing that NATO remains a credible force for peace; an interest in helping to stem the terrible, destabilizing flows of refugees this struggle is generating; and, perhaps most clearly, a humanitarian interest we all share in stopping the continuing slaughter of innocents in Bosnia.

The documents signed here are only first steps, but they are clearly steps in the right direction. For while documents like these can define the parameters of peace, the people of the region themselves must create that peace. Economic, political, and security arrangements for the new federation must be given a chance to work. The cease-fire between Croats and Bosnian Government forces must hold. Croats and Muslims, who have fought with such intensity, must now apply that same intensity to restoring habits of tolerance and co-existence.

The issue of the Petrinja region of Croatia must be resolved. Serbia and the Serbs of Bosnia cannot sidestep their own responsibility to achieve an enduring peace. Neither the United States nor the international community can guarantee the success of this initiative. But the U.S. has stood by the parties as they have taken risks for peace, and we will continue to do so.

I have told Presidents Izetbegović and Tudjman that the U.S. is prepared to contribute to the economic reconstruction that will bolster these agreements. If an acceptable, enforceable settlement can be reached, the U.S. is prepared, through NATO, to help implement it."

* * * * *

274

The Constitution for the proposed Croat-Bosniac Federation was drafted during nine days of intensive negotiations in Vienna, Austria, ending on March 13, 1994. U.S. Special Envoy for Yugoslavia, Ambassador Charles Redman, mediated the negotiations. Agreement to draft the constitution had been reached as part of the Framework Agreement establishing the new federation that was concluded in Washington, DC on March 1. As in the Framework Agreement, the constitution provides for the appointment of a human rights Ombudsperson by the CSCE (renamed "OSCE") during the first three years of the new federation's existence. There is also a provision for the International Court of Justice (ICJ) to appoint foreign judges to fill one-third of the seats on the Constitutional Court during the first five years of the federation. The constitution strikes a balance between the rights of the federal government and the regional cantons, and contains safeguards guaranteeing significant representation for both communities in executive, legislative, and judicial bodies at each level of government. The preliminary agreement on confederation between the new federation and Croatia establishes a series of progressive steps in the economic cooperation of the federation and Croatia, aimed at eventually establishing a confederation.

On March 18, 1994, Bosnian and Croatian leaders arrived at the White House in Washington, DC (USA), to sign agreements to create a federation between the Muslims and Croats of Bosnia. This Muslim-Croatian entity will then enter into a confederation with Croatia. The agreement between the Muslims and Croats is of strategic consequence. It changes the power equation in the area and places greater pressure on the Serbs to join negotiations on their future status in Bosnia and on territorial issues. At a ceremony at the White House hosted by U.S. President Clinton on March 18, 1994, representatives from Bosnia-Herzegovina and Croatia signed an accord on the creation of a Croat-Bosniac Federation, and a further preliminary agreement on the establishment of a confederation linking the new Bosnian federation to Croatia in a loose confederation.

The federation agreement with Bosnia-Herzegovina was signed by Premier Haris Silajdžić of Bosnia, and by Kresimir Zubak, the leader of the Croats in Bosnia. The Croat-Bosniac Federation accord, signed by Presidents Franjo Tudjman of Croatia and Alija Izetbegović of Bosnia-Herzegovina, envisaged the creation of a Confederation Council.

In accordance with the Croatian-Yugoslav pact of January 19, 1994, the Republic of Croatia opened a bureau in Belgrade, the capital of Yugoslavia, on March 18, 1995, with Zvonomir Marković as the Bureau Chief-in-Charge.

The U.S. Ambassador to Croatia, Peter Galbraith, in talks on March 27 with Serb-held Krajina President Milan Martić, had ruled out independence for the

Serb-held Krajina. Moreover, Galbraith asserted, there is no possibility of a political arrangement under which the Krajina territory would either be independent or become part of Yugoslavia.

Serbian artillery bombardment of Goražde, a UN safe area in eastern Bosnia-Herzegovina, on March 28-31, 1994, claimed the lives of 30 people and wounded 132. Other safe areas, such as Srebrenica, were also shelled by Serbian forces during the month of March.

On April 2, 1994, the Commander of UN forces in Bosnia, Michael Rose claimed that none of the belligerants seek to make major strategic changes in the Goražde area. Nevertheless, the U.S. State Department was not about to rule out the use of air strikes to protect UN safe areas, but. U.S. Defense Secretary William Perry said on April 3 that military force would not be used to halt the Serb assault on Goražde. Despite U.S. President Clinton's insistence on April 4 that there was no green light for the Serb advance, there was criticism that the U.S. position had precisely this effect.

Croatia's governing party, the Croatian Democratic Union (HDZ), split on April 5, 1994, when certain elements, led by the Croatian Assembly's two chairmen, Stjepan Mesić, Chamber of Representatives (Zastupnički Dom) and Josip Manolić, Chamber of Counties (Županijski Dom) broke away to form the Croatian Independent Democrats (Hrvatski nezavisni demokrati - HND). The HND was formally established at a founding conference on April 30, 1994 at which Mesić was elected chairman of the HND and Manolić as one of the deputy chairpersons. Purportedly, the origins of the split began after a policy disagreement concerning the military alliance with the Bosnian government and the support of the Croatian Defense Council (HVO) campaign to seize territory in southern Bosnia-Herzegovina.

* * * * *

~ President Clinton's Letter to U.S. Congress ~

April 12, 1994

To: The Speaker of the House of Representatives
         (The President Pro Tempore of the Senate)

Dear Mr. Speaker:
(Dear Mr. President:)

"One year ago, I provided you with my initial report on the deployment of U.S. combat-equipped aircraft to support the NATO enforcement of the no-fly zone in Bosnia-Herzegovina. I provided you with follow-on reports on October 13, 1993, February 17, 1994, and March 1, 1994. I am reporting today on the use of U.S. combat-equipped aircraft on April 10-11 to provide protection for U.N. personnel who came under attack in Goražde, Bosnia-Herzegovima. Since the adoption of SCR 713 on September 25, 1991, the UN has actively sought solutions to the conflict

276

in the former Yugoslavia. Under SCR 824 of May 6, 1993, certain parts of Bosnia-Herzegovina have been established 'safe areas.' Goražde is specifically included as a location that should be treated as a safe area 'by all the parties concerned and should be free from armed attacks and from any other hostile acts.' In addition, SCR 836 and 844 of June 4 and 18, 1993 respectively, authorize Member States, acting nationally or through regional organizatioons, to use air power in the safe areas to help protect the UNPROFOR.

Recent heavy weapons (tank and artillery) fire in the Goražde area has resulted in a serious threat to the citizens remaining in Goražde and to UNPROFOR and UNHCR personnel operating there. On April 10, the city was subjected to sustained Serbian tank and artillery fire. The UNPROFOR and UNHCR personnel in Goražde were placed in great danger. Based on the threat to UNPROFOR, as reported by UN observers in the city, the UNPROFOR commander requested the UN Special Representative for Bosnia-Herzegovina to authorize close air support (CAS) strikes on the Serbian firing positions. The UN Special Representative approved the request. Consistent with approved procedures and rules of engagement, two U.S. aircraft from NATO Allied Force Southern Europe (AFSOUTH) engaged Serbian targets after receiving targeting orders from the Commander in Chief, AFSOUTH.

On April 11, 1994, UN personnel in Goražde requested NATO air support after again coming under attack by Serbian gunners. United States F/A-18 aircraft from AFSOUTH were successful in neutralizing Bosnian-Serb targets that had been firing on the city. There were no NATO or UN casualties as a result of the operations on April 10 and 11, 1994.

It is my hope that the clear resolve of the UN and NATO as shown by these actions will encourage the parties to the conflict in the former Yugoslavia to respect the decisions of the Security Council concerning the protection of UN personnal and of the declared safe areas. United States forces will continue to serve as part of this important NATO enforcement effort and will remain prepared to respond to UN and NATO requests for further action against those who violate these decisions. These actions are being taken in Bosnia-Herzegovina in conjunction with our allies to implement the decision of the Security Council and the North Atlantic Council and to assist the parties to reach a negotiated settlement to the conflict. It is not now possible to determine the duration of this operation. I have directed the participation of U.S. Armed Forces in this effort pursuant to my constitutional authority to conduct U.S. foreign relations and as Commander in Chief.

I am providing this report as part of my effort to keep the Congress fully informed, consistent with the War Powers Resolution. I remain grateful for the continued cooperation with you in this endeavor. I shall communicate with you further regarding our efforts for peace and stability in the former Yugoslavia."

Sincerely, William Jefferson Clinton
President, United States of America

* * * * *

On April 10, 1994 responding to the new Serb assault, Gen. Rose rapidly requested NATO aircraft to bomb Serbian targets on the ground, in the first such action by NATO in its history. Yasushi Akashi of Japan, UN Special Envoy to former Yugoslavia, gave final approval to the request. Later that day two U.S. F-16 jets dropped three bombs on a Serbian artillery command post (CP) near Goražde. In a renewed Serb bombardment of Goražde on April 11, two F/A-18 jets dropped only three bombs, destroying one Serb armored personnel carrier. A British Sea Harrier Jet on reconnaissance mission over Bosnian territory was shot down by Serbs ground-to-air missiles. Despite the strike, the Serb bombardment of Goražde continued for a further 90 minutes that day. The UN declared the safe area of Goražde was attacked anew by Serbs on April 15, 1994, pledging not to advance on the town. Russian President Boris N. Yeltsin, portraying himself as an international leader, reminded the Serbs to stop attacking Goražde.

On April 20, 1994 a meeting of the North Atlantic Council of the 16 NATO member states agreed to the proposal of UN Secretary General to permit air strikes to defend the UN safe areas, even in instances where UN personnel were not directly threatened. The Serb assault on Goražde continued. NATO issued an ultimatum on April 22 when U.S. President Clinton warned that the Serbs should not doubt NATO's willingness to act.

Per order of Milošević, the Serbian Radical Party (SRS), on April 28, 1994 abolished its paramilitary wing, the Serbian četnik movement. The četnik movement, which had revived the Second World War nationalist army of the same name in July 1990, had been responsible for committing war crimes during the Serbian war of aggression in Croatia beginning in 1991. The movement had been abolished to avoid accusations of terrorist activity. Nevertheless, the četnik (plural četnici) as a fanatical movement and anti-democratic organization, is alive in many countries, including Serbia and places in the USA.

The UN Special Envoy to the former Yugoslavia, Yasushi Akashi, criticized U.S. policy in Bosnia-Herzegovina as afraid, timid, and tentative. The USA's permanent representative at the UN, Madeleine Korbel Albright, responded by sharply criticizing Akashi in a letter to the UN Secretary General Boutros Ghali on April 30, 1994. Boutros Ghali agreed on May 2 that criticism of U.S. policy by his staff was completely unacceptable.

The U.S. Senate on May 11, 1994, voted in favor of the USA's unilateral breaching of the arms embargo imposed on Yugoslavia by the UN Security Council. Senator Bob Dole, the Republican leader in the Senate, argued that the embargo violated Article 51 of the UN Charter which guaranteed the right of member nations, including Bosnia, to self defense. U.S. President Clinton repudiated the Senate vote on May 25, 1994, arguing that a unilateral U.S. decision to ignore the embargo would kill the peace process, sour U.S. relationships with European Allies in NATO and the UN, and undermine the partnership that the USA was trying to build with Russia.

On May 30, 1994, Croatia introduced a new currency called "kuna." The kuna is a Croatian name for a marten, a small ferretlike mammal found in the forests of Croatia. During the years between 1260 and 1384, a silver coin with the likeness of a marten engraved on one side was minted for the governor of Croatia. Also, above the marten was engraved a Jerusalem cross, while a six-pointed star was engraved below. Surrounding these three distinct symbols were engraved the words "Monetarecis Sclavonia" (meaning "Currency of Slavonia"). The importance of the marten as a symbol of Croatia is demonstrated by the adoption of the marten as one of the five elements of the Croatian coat-of-arms. The marten (kuna) has had a long and legitimate history in Croatia. Merely because the marten was used by others during the Second World War, does not disqualify it from further use. If this absurd criterion is used to judge history, many international symbols, e.g. eagle, lion, etc. would be disqualified. Symbols do play a certain role in the minds of the some people, if these people are not open minded and unaffected by prejudice or bias. In spite of some perception based on ignorance and lack of fundamental knowledge, the symbol of marten (Croatian: "kuna") remains an attractive, legitimate, and unique name for a monetary system, because of its Croatian origins and its firm historical grounding. Today, Croatia is a sovereign nation, member of the international community, in the same legitimate tradition as Germany, Japan, Italy etc., which kept the names of their own currencies regardless of world opinion, including that of Serbia. Those who condemn Croatia for its righteous prerogative should perform a thoughtful self-analysis.

Gen. Michael Rose, the commander of the UNPROFOR, on June 9, 1994, hailed the one-month ceasefire accord as the beginning of the end of the war in Bosnia-Herzegovina. Proving Gen. Rose was militarily wrong, by the end of the month there had been repeated ceasefire violations; on June 29, 1994, Gen. Andrew Ridgway, who commanded UNPROFOR in Gornji Vakuf, Bosnia, said there was no peace in Bosnia-Herzegovina and no ceasefire. Croatian President Tudjman visited Sarajevo to open Croatia's embassy, hailing this as a decisive implementation of the Washington agreement signed on March 18, 1994 which may pave the way for ending the war.

The town of Mostar in southern Bosnia-Herzegovina, which was the scene of fierce fighting between Muslims and Croats earlier in the war, formally came under EU administration on June 23, 1994, at a ceremony attended by German Foreign Minister Klaus Kinkel, President Tudjman of Croatia, Kresimir Zubak, leader of Croatians in Bosnia, and the EU Administrator, Hans Koschnick.

The Serbian troops in Bosnia seized five heavy weapons, including one T-55 tank, from a depot guarded by Ukrainian UN peacekeepers at Ilidža, well within the heavy weapons exclusion zone around Sarajevo. In response to the Serbian harassment in Bosnia, NATO bombers on August 5, launched air strikes against Serbian targets for the first time since April 1994, after receiving a request to that effect from Gen. Rose, the commander of UNPROFOR. The strikes, by French, Netherlands, and U.S. aircraft, reportedly destroyed an anti-tank vehicle. The weapons seized by the Serb forces on August 5, were returned to a UN depot on the next day.

U.S. President Clinton on August 11, 1994 warned that if the Serbs had not accepted the Contact Group plan by October 15, the United States government would urge the UN Security Council to lift the arms embargo on the Bosnia-Herzegovina government. Meanwhile, thousands of people reportedly fled from the Muslim enclave of Bihać in northwestern Bosnia-Herzegovina as the enclave was overrun by Bosnian government forces on August 21. Fikret Abdić, a wealthy entrepreneur and former member of the Bosnian collective presidency who had led the rebellion in Bihać in October 1993, also fled on August 21 as his stronghold in the town of Velika Kladusa fell to the Bosnian Army's Fifth Corps.

Pope John Paul II visited Zagreb on September 10-11, 1994. In an address to a crowd of approximately 500,000 people attending an open-air mass on September 11, the Pope on his first official visit to Croatia welcomed Croatian independence, encouraged Croats to seek reconciliation with the Muslims and Serbs, and urged the warring people of the region to seek forgiveness and atonement.

The UN Security Council approved on September 14, 1994 a selective suspension of international sanctions against FRY for 100 days. The suspension was to commence on confirmation by UN observers that the FRY blockade on Serbian occupied territory of Bosnia was genuine. Passenger flights and cultural and sporting links were to resume. Bosnian President Alija Izetbegović and Croatian President Franjo Tudjman met on September 14, in Zagreb, reached agreement on key points in establishing the Croat-Bosniac Federation: (a) Interim municipal governments were to be established by September 30; (b) cantonal authorities, the next highest tier of government, were to be set up by October 31; (c) key roads between Muslim and Croat areas were to be opened up; (d) a program for the return of refugees was to be drafted; (e) the establishment of a joint command of the Bosnian army and the Croatian Defense Council, HVO was to be hastened; and (f) Croats were to be fairly represented in the government of Bosnia-Herzegovina.

NATO warplanes strafed and bombed an unmanned Serbian T-55 tank near northwest Sarajevo on September 22. The strike followed an attack by Serb forces on a French UNPROFOR vehicle north of Sarajevo. The commander of Serbian forces in Bosnia, Gen. Ratko Mladić, claimed with proving his case that on September 23, 1994 the UNPROFOR strike had targeted civilians. Mladić accused UNPROFOR of siding with the Muslims.

Croatia's Chamber of Representatives (Zastupnički Dom) resolved on September 23, 1994 that the existing mandate in Croatia of the UNPROFOR should be terminated. In a second resolution, the deputies demanded that a new mandate be drawn up, requiring UNPROFOR (a) to disarm Serb terrorists, (b) to guarantee the return of Croatian refugees and displaced persons to their homes in the Serb-held territory of Krajina; and (c) to protect Croatia's internationally recognized external border. President Tudjman on September 26 backed the Chamber's stance, and on addressing the UN General Assembly in New York, NY urged the international organization to redefine the UNPROFOR mandate.

In a speech to the UN General Assembly on September 27, 1994, President Izetbegović announced that his government would not request the immediate cancellation of the UN arms embargo on Bosnia-Herzegovina, but would defer such a request for six months. U.S. President Clinton, who had played on all sides of the subject for and against the lifting of the embargo, warmly welcomed Izetbegović's initiative which he claimed to have averted a split between the USA and its European allies over the issue.

The Croatian government on September 30 reversed its opposition to a renewal of the mandate in Croatia of the UNPROFOR in exchange for assurances from the international community that a high priority would be given to the reintegration of the Serb-held territory in Croatia. The UN Security Council Resolution 947 of September 30, 1994, renewing the UNPROFOR mandate for six months from January 1995, retaining the UN's determination that Croat refugees and displaced persons should return to UN-Protected Areas in Serb-held Krajina.

A border dispute between Slovenia and Croatia flared up after the State Chamber (the lower house of the Slovene National Assembly) on October 3, 1994 overwhelming approved a reorganization of local government which assigned territory claimed by both Slovenia and Croatia to a Slovenia municipality. This dispute concerned claims with Italy over compensation for ethnic Italians dispossessed after the Second World War. The territory which had been under dispute since 1945, is located in the northwestern Istrian Peninsula and the Slovene seaport of Koper (a.k.a. Capodistria) south of the Italian seaport city of Trieste.

Some of the international sanctions against Yugoslavia imposed in 1992 were suspended on October 5, 1994, after UN observers accepted the authenticity of Yugoslavia's economic blockade of Serbian occupation forces in Bosnia-Herzegovina. International flights to the Yugoslav and Serbian capital of Belgrade were to resume, the Montenegro port of Bar was to reopen, and sporting and cultural links were to be restored.

UN officials disclosed on October 18 that Gen. Rose was to be replaced as UNPROFOR commander in Bosnia-Herzegovina on completion in January 1995 of his one-year term. Another British officer, Gen. Rupert Smith, would succeed Rose who had been persistently criticized by the Bosnian government and others for being insufficiently tough in his response to Serb aggression. The Bosnian Assembly (legislature) on October 25, 1994 denounced Rose for having allegedly done everything to water down the decisiveness of the free world in punishing Serb crimes.

Early in November 1994, Bosnian government forces, backed by the Croatian Defense Council (HVO), advanced on three fronts in central Bosnia, in the Bihać area, and around the capital Sarajevo. In the first major gain for Bosnian government forces since the outbreak of war in the spring of 1992, the strategic town of Kupres in central Bosnia fell to Muslim and Croatian troops on November 3, 1994. The victory was also the first major success for military cooperation between Croat and Muslim armies. Serbian forces counterattacked in the Bihać area on November 9, 1994 using infantry, tanks, artillery and air power. Consequently, Bosnian government forces were rapidly driven back. By November 12 Serb forces had re-crossed the River Una, and by November 14 the Serbs had regained some 80% of all the territory lost in the two-week Bosnian government offensive. Bihać was an important strategic center, which if controlled by Serbs would improve communications between the various Serb-held territories, thus lessen the likelihood that Croatian sovereignty would be restored in the Krajina region. The Croatian government warned on November 4 that it would intervene militarily to prevent the fall of Bihać to Serb forces.

The USA announced on November 11, 1994, that it would no longer enforce the arms embargo against the former Yugoslavia. The decision, which applied to U.S. naval vessels in the Adriatic sea, caused dismay among USA's European allies. British Foreign Secretary Douglas Hurd and French Foreign Minister Alain Juppé both described the U.S. decision as worrying. Nevertheless, Hurd pledged that British troops would remain in Bosnia-Herzegovina throughout the winter. The French troops in Bosnia-Herzegovina were put on alert for a possible withdrawal. NATO Secretary General Willy Claes pledged on November 12 to continue to enforce fully and totally all UN Security Council resolutions which form the basis of NATO involvement in former Yugoslavia. Members of the Western European Union (WEU), meeting in the Dutch town of Noordwijk on November 14, 1994, pledged to continue to observe the UN embargo.

The Republican leader in the U.S. Senate, Robert Dole, on November 11, 1994, criticized the UN role in former Yugoslavia arguing that the United Nations should get off NATO's back and let NATO take care of Serbian war of aggression. Reviewing his attack on November 27, Dole accused UN officials of having helped the Serbian war of aggression, and claimed that the UN had become almost irrelevant.

Serb aircraft bombed the Muslim enclave of Bihać on November 9, 18 (when napalm and cluster bombs were dropped), and 19, 1994. The planes were based at the Udbina airfield in Serb-held Krajina; punitive air strikes against the airfield were beyond the existing remnant of NATO's air strike authority, which covered only Bosnia-Herzegovina. The UN Security Council meeting on November 19, 1994 unanimously adopted Resolution 958 authorizing air strikes on Serbian forces inside the Croatian territory held by Serbs. NATO aircraft struck the Udbina airbase under Serb-held occupation on November 21, damaging the base's runway and anti-aircraft installations. NATO struck again on November 23, destroying three Serb surface-to-air missile sites at the town of Dvor in the Serb-held Krajina and between Otaka and Bosanska Krupa in north-western Bosnia. Ridiculously, the Russian foreign ministry warned that the air strikes would lead to nothing but prolonged bloodshed. Despite the NATO air strike, Serbian forces advanced within the periphery of Bihać on November 24, and consolidated their gains around the town, but a strong and decisive counterattack by Croatian and Bosnian government troops prevented the Serbs from occupying the town of Bihać.

Croatian officials signed a landmark economic agreement on December 2, with officials of the Serb-held Krajina. The agreement envisaged the re-establishment of key services between Croatia and the Serb-held Krajina including the reintegration of water, oil, electricity, supplies and the opening of key roads. The first tangible benefit of the agreement was the limited reopening on December 21, 1994, of the motorway from the Croatian capital of Zagreb to Lipovac in eastern Croatia, which had been closed since 1991.

The U.S. Administration faced mounting criticism for its vacillating Bosnian policy, especially from leading members of the Republican Party in the United States following their success in the mid-term elections for U.S. Congress in November 1994. Senator Bob Dole (R-Kansas) and Representative Newt Gingrich (R-Georgia) who would become leaders respectively of the Senate and the House of Representatives in January 1995, both argued strongly on December 4, 1994, for an aggressive bombing campaign against Serbian and Yugoslav targets, to paralyze Serbian military and civil authority. Gingrich derided the UN as totally incompetent. However, U.S. Secretary of State Warren Christopher responded by defending the wavering U.S. policy with the preposterous assertion that a bombing campaign against the heartland of Serbia was unworkable and that only a diplomatic solution was possible. According to diplomatic sources, Secretary Christopher will continue to oscillate with his policies, which will be proven wrong since a strong military power against Serbia is the only action that the barbaric Serbs understand.

French Foreign Minister Alain Juppé criticized the U.S. commitment to assist UNPROFOR in a contemplated withdrawal from Bosnia-Herzegovina. Juppé on December 7, 1994, condemned the U.S. government which teaches daily lessons to other governments but have not lifted a little finger to put even one man on the ground. Juppé had formally requested NATO to draw up plans for the withdrawal of the 23,000 UNPROFOR troops from Bosnia. U.S. President Clinton had issued an order on the same day that in the event of such a withdrawal, the U.S. would deploy 20,000 ground troops in Bosnia-Herzegovina to secure safe passage for the departing UN troops.

Former U.S. President Jimmy Carter visited Bosnia-Herzegovina on December 18-20, 1994, in a private capacity, to mediate between Serbs and Muslims. Radovan Karadžić, leader of Serb terrorists, agreed to a memorandum of understanding following talks with Carter: (a) the division of Sarajevo into two cities; (b) natural and defensible frontiers for the Serb and Muslim sectors of the reconstituted Bosnia; (c) equal distribution of natural resources and infrastructure between the two sectors; (d) economic viability for the two sectors; and (e) Serb access to the sea. Apparently, Carter in his enthusiastic desire to please the arrogant Serbs failed to remember the lessons in history and geography. Today, rump Yugoslavia consists of Serbia and Montenegro. The seaport of Bar in southwest Montenegro connects with the interior of Yugoslavia by means of the Belgrade-Bar railroad, built by Tito's communist brigades to give Serbia access to the sea. Also, the Gulf of Kotor with the spectacular fjord and the strategic seaport of Kotor is another of Serbia's outlets to the sea.

The CSCE began during the Cold War as a way to promote dialogue and decrease tensions between East and West. In August 1975, 35 nations signed the Helsinki Final Act, which outlines democratic principles governing relations among nations. The act contained a provision to continue regular discussions on a broad range of concerns in what became known as the Helsinki process. The CSCE, by law, monitors and encourages progress in implementing the provisions of the Helsinki Accords. With the end of the Cold War, all CSCE states for the first time accepted the principles of pluralism and free markets as the basis for their cooperation. In December 1994, at the Budapest Summit meeting the CSCE was renamed the OSCE to reflect its increased role in European security and cooperation by defining and protecting human rights.

* * * * *

~ War Crimes Tribunal ~

Washington, DC, December 28, 1994

Statement by U.S. Department of State spokesman Michael McCurry in support of the War Crimes Tribunal for the former Yugoslavia.

"The UN has established an international war crimes tribunal for the former Yugoslavia - the first international war crimes tribunal since those convened in Nuremberg and Tokyo at the conclusion of World War II. In creating this tribunal - and the one recently established for Rwanda - the UN Security Council has reaffirmed a fundamental principle that binds civilized societies: Those who commit crimes of genocide and crimes against humanity must be held accountable for their actions.

Efforts by Serbs to rid Bosnia of its non-Serb, mainly Muslim, population are continuing. As indicated in a recently issed UNHCR report, the Muslim population of northern Bosnia has been reduced by a factor of 10 - from over 500,000 inhabitants to about 50,000, in just two years. Overall, UNHCR estimates that since the Bosnian tragedy began, Serbs have expelled, killed, or imprisoned over 90% of the 1,730,000 non-Serbs who, before the war, lived throughout the territory now held by the Serbs.

The latest round in this campaign of ethnic cleansing - begun last summer - has accelerated in recent months, especially in the Bijeljina area in northeast Bosnia, in Banja Luka in northwest Bosnia, and in Rogatica, north of the Goražde enclave. Within the last 10 days, we have received reports that Serbs expelled more than 100 Muslims from Bijeljina. The refugees claimed that before they left, Serbs locked them in unlit rooms and abused them. Brutal and heinous methods have been employed to force the Muslim population from their homes. There have been numerous incidents of Serbs bursting into Muslim homes at night to evict, rob, and rape the residents. Women, children, and elderly people have been forced to flee during such evictions, regardless of their health or physical condition. Men of military age have been taken prisoner and made to perform forced labor in detention camps and on the front lines.

These crimes did not arise spontaneously or by happenstance. Unless those responsible are held accountable, there can be no lasting peace and reconciliation in Bosnia. That is why the tribunal established by the UN is so important. For its successful functioning, the tribunal will need the support - both moral and material - of the international community. Since the tribunal's creation, this Administration has voluntarily contributed nearly $13 million, including cash contribution of $3 million; the services, at a cost of up to $6 million, of over 20 experienced prosecutors, investigators, and other experts to assist the investigation of atrocities; and our assessed contribution to the tribunal budget. Much more will be needed. The tribunal cannot undo the atrocities that have taken place, but it can hold accountable those who committed them and send an unmistakable signal that henceforth violations of international humanitarian law - including any acts of genocide - will be met with justice."

* * * * *

In a letter to UN Secretary General on January 12, 1995, Croatian President Franjo Tudjman stressed that Croatia found the present situation in the Serb occupied territories of Croatia wholly unacceptable, and added that the continued UNPROFOR presence was significantly counterproductive to the peace process. The Serb-held areas, which comprised approximately 30%

of internationally recognized Croatian territory, had been seized by Serb rebels in mid-1991. UNPROFOR which had first arrived in Croatia in March 1992, patrolled four UNPA's or buffer zones between Croatian and Serb forces. Under the terms of the peace plan of January 1992, which had formed the basis of the UNPROFOR mandate in Croatia, Serb-held areas were to have been demilitarized.

A nine-point accord was signed in Munich, Germany, on February 5, 1995 by the Bosnian Federation President and Bosnian Croat leader Krešimir Zubak and Bosnian Premier Haris Silajdžić, chaired by U.S. Assistant Secretary of State for European and Canadian Affairs Richard Holbrooke. The intent of the accord was to address disagreements over the implementation of the Croat-Bosniac Federation, which included an agreement to submit grievances to an international mediator for binding arbitration. On the same day, the so-called legislature of the Serb-held Krajina voted to suspend implementation of its December 1994 economic agreement with Croatia.The suspension of the agreement followed the Croatian termination in January of the mandate of UN peacekeepers in Croatia which was later extended.

Heavy fighting continued in February in the Bihać enclave, a UN declared "safe area." On February 12, 1995, U.S. officials claimed that more than 1,100 Serb terrorists had entered the Bihać area from the neighboring Serb-held territory in Croatia. Timely, a UN convoy carrying one hundred tons of food reached Bihać on February 22 to assist an estimated 200,000 civilians in the area.

Tension in the Krajina rose with reports from mid-February that the Serb terrorists were making military preparations for a possible assault by Croatian government forces. Krajina military officials claimed on February 20 that Croatian warplanes had made reconnaissance sorties over the Serb-held territory of Krajina. Rajko Lezajić, the fanatic self-styled speaker of the so-called legislature of Serb-held Krajina showed his deep ignorance in basic international affairs when he declared on February 27, 1995 that the Serb-held and occupied territory of Krajina would never be returned to Croatia. Evidently Lezajić had imbibed a dangerous quantity of locally produced stimulants, "rakija and slivovitz" (spirits, alcoholic beverages), enough to cause him to become an increasingly more feeble-minded person.

An offensive by Bosnian government forces began on March 9, 1995, against Serb forces in the Majevica mountains northeast of Tuzla in northern Bosnia, and in the Mount Vlašić area around Travnik in central Bosnia. Some 2,000 Bosnian government troops advanced into the Majevica mountains, from where Serb gunners retaliated by bombarding Tuzla with at least 500 shells. At least 30 Bosnian troops were killed and 80 injured in a direct hit on the

Bosnian government barracks in Tuzla. Bosnian government forces on March 24 seized the communications tower at Solice, 9.3 mi./15 km east of Tuzla, and surrounded a large underground Serb ammunition dump some 7.5 mi./12 km north-east of Tuzla. Bosnian government forces on April 7 gained ground on Mount Vlašić (44°17′N; 17°40′E).

The situation in Croatia has been at a virtual stalemate since 1992, when UNPROFOR was established to restore peace in the region. President Franjo Tudjman of Croat had given notice in January 1995 of the termination of the UNPROFOR mandate in Croatia. The U.S. supported the goal of Croatian reintegration, but expelling the UN peacekeepers would create a very dangerous situation. To avoid the possible restarting of the war and the likelihood of fighting over the "buffer zone," the UN would have to vacate the area. To prevent the escalation of tensions, President Tudjman agreed on March 12, 1995, to permit the continued presence of UN peacekeepers. The agreement followed talks between Tudjman and U.S. Vice President Albert Gore, Jr. in the Danish capital of Copenhagen. The continued UN presence in Croatia ensured considerable inflows of hard curency to Croatia, since the withdrawal of the peacekeepers and of UN bureaucrats based in Croatia would have constituted a major economic blow.

Slovene and Croatian officials agreed during talks in Zagreb on March 23, 1995 to divide equally ownership of the Krsko (45°58′N; 15°30′E) Slovenia, nuclear power station between the two countries.

On March 31, 1995, the Security Council unanimously passed three resolutions: (a) Resolution 981, establishing UNCRO mission for Croatia; (b) Resolution 982, establishing UNPROFOR mandate until November 30, 1995, but only for Bosnia-Herzegovina; and (c) Resolution 983, establishing UNPREDEP mission for Macedonia. The reconfigured force in Croatia, the mandate for which will be in effect until the end of 1995, will monitor Croatia's international border, help implement the cease-fire and economic agreements, and facilitate the passage of humanitarian supplies.

A Russian UN commander in eastern Croatia, the corrupt Gen. Aleksander Perelyakin, was dismissed on April 11, 1995, and ordered to leave the area and go home. According to a UN spokesman, it was revealed that Perelyakin was suspected of having tolerated or participated in the sale of arms to the Serb terrorists in Krajina and having turned a blind eye to the sale and transfer of heavy weaponry to the Serbs in occupied territory.

Serbian forces on April 13, 1995 shelled the suburbs and airport of the historic southern Adriatic port of Dubrovnik, killing one person. In a letter of April 13 to the U.S. Security Council, the Croatian Deputy Premier and

Foreign Minister Mate Granić protested about the shelling, which he described as a serious deterioration of the security situation in southern Croatia. The Croat forces captured several mountain peaks on the Croatian-Bosnian border, bringing Knin, the so-called capital of the Serb-held Krajina within artillery range. In late April, Bosnian government forces made gains south of the Bihać enclave.

The UN Security Council on April 21, 1995, approved Resolution 988 extending for 75 days the selective retention of international sanctions against Yugoslavia imposed to discourage Yugoslav support for the Serbian campaign in Bosnia-Herzegovina.

Croatian forces recaptured a small but significant portion of territory held by Serbian forces since 1991, in an operation executed rapidly on May 1-2, 1995. The clash represented the heaviest fighting between Croatia and Serbia since September 1993. The seized enclave, located in western Slavonia was the most vulnerable of the territory which comprised the Serb-held Krajina. The seizure was justified by Croatia as limited but necessary to restore the vital E-70 highway link from Zagreb to Belgrade via Lipovac. A force of some 7,200 Croatian soldiers entered the enclave on May 1, backed by tanks, helicopters and rocket launchers. Serbian troops fled the Croatian advance in panic. Croatian forces on May 2 had taken full control of the E-70 and liberated the town of Okučani. The Serbian forces in the town of Pakrac surrendered on the evening of May 2. The despicable Serbs retaliated by launching two rocket attacks at Zagreb. Eleven rocket-propelled shrapnel-spraying Orkan cluster bombs, fired from Serb-held territory only 40 km/25 miles south of Zagreb, struck the capital city on May 2, killing five people. In a second attack on May 3, one person was killed when six Orkan rockets struck Zagreb. A total of 175 people were injured in the attacks. The towns of Karlovac and Sisak were also shelled on May 2 by Serb forces using conventional artillery. The U.S. Ambassador to Croatia, Peter Galbraith, condemned the first attack on May 2, 1995 as a repugnant act clearly intended to kill many people. Serb officials claimed that the rockets had been intended only for military targets, although Serb forces had consistently used similar tactics during the conflict.

Thousands of Serbs fled south toward the town of Bosanka Gradiška in Serb-held territory of Bosnia-Herzegovina. Despite the Croatian claims to have respected the human rights of Serbs, there was controversy over conflicting reports regarding the extent of casualties during the operation. The Croatian Defense Minister Gojko Susak claimed on May 4, 1995, that 400 Serbs and 33 Croatian soldiers had been killed. However, Serbian propaganda claimed that hundreds of thousands of Serbs had lost their lives. Multi-national journalists who actually visited the described scene following the military operation found no evidence that such atrocities were committed. One EU Monitor, Gunter Baron, on May 4 praised the Croatian military operation as excellent, professional, competent, and correct.

Evidently the Serbs cannot see, cannot smell, cannot speak the truth, and cannot tell the difference between right and wrong. Perhaps, because they received the same specialized training on falsehoods as those who disseminated lies and exaggerated about having counted millions of Serbs killed by Croats (uštasi and partisans) during the Second World War. Before making false and unsubstantiated allegations against anyone, and especially against Croatian people, the Serb intelligentsia, under equal opportunity provisions and affirmative action ought to contemplate declassifying their secret files and, without obfuscating the issues, consider only the facts; that is, Croatian military forces never carried on a military campaign inside Serbia proper during the Second World War. Obviously, the Serbs must have been killed by friendly fire or members of their own Serb organizations, e.g., Mihajlović, Nedić, Ljotić, etc., who collaborated with the Axis Powers and were assisted by occupation forces of Bulgaria, Hungary, and Romania. In addition, Serbian terrorists and assassins operated both inside and outside Serbia, including in the sovereign territory of Croatia.

In the name of their monarchy, Serbians committed wilful killing, raping, mutilating, torturing, wantonly destroying villages, plundering and pillaging property. By preponderance of evidence every ethnic group suffered during the war and was subjected to reprehensible acts and died from various causes, related or unrelated to war activities. Moreover, since not all Serbians were killed by non-Serbs, members of the Serb intelligentsia should release documents detailing how many Serbians were killed in Croatia by: (a) Serb-četnici; (b) Serb-fascists and/or nazis; (c) Serb-communists; and (d) Serbs not included in items "a" thru "d" above.

Serbian propaganda disseminated absurd information, overloaded with the usual recycled Serb garbage, ornamented with half-truths and ludicrous innuendo trying to depict the Serbs for what they are not, innocent people. Serbian unsubstantiated data revealed that in Yugoslavia at least 700,000 and up to 1,700,000 Serbs (between April 6, 1941 and May 15, 1945) were murdered by Croatians. Everybody knows that's untrue and grossly overestimated when compared with factual reported casualties. Similar counterproductive propaganda techniques were used unsuccessfully by others to create a deliberate false impression, influence, deceive, and manipulate gullible people. It is imperative that the world knows what really happened and continues to occur. The truth hurts but only the truth makes people free. Much has been said in distorted truths about the Croatian people. For example, "It is morally unjust and historically incorrect to state that only Croatians killed Serbians, Jews, Gypsies, etc., without continuing the sentence and emphasizing that Serbians also killed Croatian, Jews, Gypsies, etc. Moreover, Serbians killed Croatians and others long ago in order to establish their ethnic pure imperialist state of Serboslavia. Megalomaniacal Serbs claim that any territory inhabited by a Serb is the land of mother Serbia. If this is translated from "Mein Kampf" and embellished by Dante's "Inferno," people everywhere will recognize the echoes of "one people, one Serbia, one Milošević" on their way straight down to hell. Throughout the Second World War several foreign armies and various pro or anti-Axis and pro or anti-communist forces operated within the territory of Yugoslavia. Most of the "native" belligerant groups fought against each other, although on different occasions they collaborated with the Axis occupation armies. In summary, according to data obtained from an independent and highly respected international source, among the four major "native" combatant groups, a total of 321,000 were killed during the Second World War in Yugoslavia from causes directly associated with the war. Data are for the period April 6, 1941 through May 8, 1945 when hostilities were officially terminated. The following is the breakdown of total deaths:

a. 96,300 (or 30% of the total) Croatians were killed by Serbs, Germans, Italians, and Communist partisans (comprised of Croats, Serbs, Slovenes, Bosnians, Montenegrins, Macedonians, etc.)

b. 86,670 (or 27% of the total) Comunist partisans (comprised of Croats, Serbs, Slovenes, Bosnians, Montenegrins, Macedonians, etc.) were killed by Germans, Italians, Croats, Serbs, Slovenes, Bosnians, Montenegrins, Macedonians, etc.

c. 70,620 (or 22% of the total) Bosnians were killed by Serbs, Germans, Italians, Montenegrins, and Communist partisans (comprised of Bosnians, Croats, Serbs, Slovenes, Montenegrins, Macedonians, etc).

d. 67,410 (or 21% of the total) Serbians were killed by Croats, Slovenes, Germans, Italians, Bosnians, and Communist partisans (comprised of Serbs, Croats, Slovenes, Bosnians, Montenegrins, Macedonians, etc.).

Undoubtedly, mass reprisals were committed against civilians, belligerants and collaborators. Numerically, some murderers may have committed fewer crimes, but all crimes were horrible, heinous, and inexcusable acts of barbarism. Any person, however highly placed, who commits an act which constitutes a crime under international law is individually responsible and must be treated as a war criminal.

The International War Crimes Tribunal, on May 15, 1995 charged 59 people with war crimes alledgedly committed in the Bosnian town of Tuzla in May 1992. Those charged included Tuzla's mayor Izet Hadžić and several Muslim officers of the former Tuzla garrison of the Yugoslav People's Army (YPA). On May 18, 1995, Serbs bombarded Orašje.

In Serb-held Krajina of Croatia, the make-believe assembly on May 21, 1995 voted for the unification with Serb-held territory in Bosnia. The so-called president of Serb-held Krajina, Milan Martić favored the unification, but the so-called premier of the Serb-held Krajina, Borislav Mikelić opposed it.

May 25, 1995, U.S. President Clinton released the following statement regarding UN-NATO airstrikes against Serbs:

"I welcome the decision of the UN and NATO to launch airstrikes today against a Serb ammunition site in Bosnia following the violence of the past several days in and around Sarajevo. This action was taken in response to Serbian defiance of yesterday's UNPROFOR demand for the return of heavy weapons to designated weapons' collection points in accord with existing agreements. This action should help UN and the NATO sustain their ability to ease suffering in the region. I hope that today's airstrikes will convince the Serbian leadership to end their violations of the exclusion zone and comply with their other agreements with the UN. I appreciate the courage and dedication of the UN forces in the former Yugoslavia and trust that this evidence of UN and NATO determination will serve to enhance the ability of these forces to remain and perform their missions."

NATO aircraft on May 25, 1995, struck an ammunition dump near Pale, destroying two weapons bunkers. The NATO strike and support aircraft were drawn from the air forces of the USA, France, the Netherlands, and Spain. A second round of air strikes was launched against nearby Pale target on the morning of May 26 destroying six weapons bunkers. In retaliation, the Serbs launched a massive bombardment of Tuzla on the evening of May 26, killing 48 people and injuring 150. The city of Sarajevo was also shelled and it's water and electricity supplies were cut off.

On May 26, 1995, the Serbs took 200 UN peacekeepers hostage and used them as human shields against NATO air strikes. NATO Secretary General Willy Claes stated, "the international community cannot accept any longer to be humiliated." Serbian outlaws on May 26 captured and held hostage UNPROFOR personnel. One captive, Canadian Capt. Patrick Rechner, was shown on Serb TV warning that he and his colleagues had been threatened with death if there was a resumption of NATO bombing. As of May 30, a total of 222 UN peacekeepers had been disarmed and captured by Serb terrorists and 131 had been surrounded. Among those detained were 10 French soldiers captured on May 27 as Serbian irregulars seized two UN observation posts at Vrbanja bridge in Sarajevo. The seizure prompted the first combat operation by UN troops, when 30 French soldiers backed by light tanks stormed the Serbian posts later the same day, which resulted in freeing the two French soldiers who had been held hostage by the Serb terrorists. Two French soldiers and four Serbian irregulars were killed during the operation. On May 28, 1995, Serb forces near the town of Cetingrad, inside the Serb held territory, shot down a helicopter carrying the foreign minister of Bosnia-Herzegovina, Irfan Ljubijankić, killing him and five others. Ljubijankić, was a native of Bihac. On June 1, the government of Bosnia-Herzegovina chose Muhamed Šaćirbey (a.k.a. Šaćirbegović), a U.S. citizen, who served as Bosnia's envoy to the UN, to be the new foreign minister.

The Contact Group Ministeral meeting at The Hague on May 29, 1995 issued the following statement:

"The foreign ministers of France, Spain, Germany, and the EU Commissioner for external affairs (representing the Troika of the EU), the foreign ministers of Britain and of Russia and the US Secretary of State, together with the co-chairmen of the international conference on the former Yugoslavia, met in The Hague, Netherlands, on May 29, 1955. They condemned the escalation of violence by the parties and any hostile act against UN personnel. They most strongly condemned the Serbs in Bosnia for the shelling of the safe areas, in particular in Tuzla on May 25, 1995. They consider that the outrageous acts against UNPROFOR members and UN observers are unacceptable. They hold Pale leaders accountable for the security of UN personnel taken hostage and warn them that they will bear the consequences if these personnel are not correctly treated and returned unharmed to their units. The ministers once again strongly urged the Serb authorities in Pale, Bosnia, to accept the Contact Group plan as a starting point for negotiations. The ministers agreed on the need to reinforce UNPROFOR. To this effect, they have decided on the need to secure UNPROFOR's right of freedom of movement, in general, and the right of access to safe areas in particular and to provide the UN with a capacity for rapid reaction. They requested the UN commanders to urgently consider the modalities of these measures. They stress the importance of a renewal of the cessation of hostilities agreement. The ministers agreed to give a new impetus to the diplomatic process in order to reach a political settlement of the conflict, which they consider as the only possible solution. They support mutual recognition among the states of the former Yugoslavia. In that respect, they agreed to make a new effort with a view to the earliest possible FRY (Serbia-Montenegro) recognition of Bosnia-Herzegovina and the strengthening of the borders closure. A resolution on sanctions suspension should be finalized in the United Nations Security Council. Ministers will meet again in the near future in order to examine UNPROFOR's situation in the light of progress made by then in the above mentioned military and political fields."

U.S. Defense Secretary William J. Perry announced on May 30, 1995 that a contingency force of approximately 2,000 U.S. marines, supported by Hawker Harrier jets and Cobra attack helicopters, was to be deployed off the Dalmatian coast in the eastern Adriatic sea. Secretary Perry stressed and emphasized that before any action was to be taken to deploy the troops on the ground, the U.S. Congress would be consulted. U.S. President Clinton on May 31 declared his willingness to deploy U.S. ground troops to assist NATO in any reconfiguration of UNPROFOR personnel, i.e. in operations to extract UNPROFOR troops from dangerous situations in Bosnia. Hitherto such assistance would be provided in the event of a full-scale UN forces withdrawal from the region. David Owen of England resigned on May 31, 1995 as EU mediator in the former Yugoslavia, and was replaced on June 12 by former Swedish Premier Carl Bildt.

The first of twelve 105-mm light guns arrived in the Croatian port of Split on May 31, as part of the equipment for the Rapid Reaction Force (RRF), thus augmenting UNPROFOR with fire-power capability to defend itself against Serb terrorist attacks, enforce compliance of UN mandate, and punish those who disregard law and order. In an astounding report submitted to the Security Council on June 1, 1995, UN Secretary General Boutros Ghali argued by stating that aggressive military action by RRF was incompatible with UN peacekeeping mandate. Boutros Ghali concluded that "UNPROFOR should not attempt to protect civilians or to punish aggressors," but should return to conventional peacekeeping activities. UN Secretary General's foolish and ill-advised conclusions raised deep doubt over the continued existence of the UN-designated safe areas of Bihać, Goražde, Sarajevo, Srebrenica, Tuzla, and Zepa.

The first U.S. aircraft to be lost over Bosnia, a U.S. F-16C fighter, stationed at Aviano Air Force Base in northern Italy, was hit by a Russian-made SA-6 (SAM) surface-to-air missile fired by Serb forces near Banja Luka in northern Bosnia on June 2, 1995 and crashed. The F-16's pilot, Captain Scott F. O'Grady, ejected from the plane and eluded capture by Serb forces for six days. The second F-16C jet on the same mission returned safely to it's home base. Upon receiving a voice radio message "this is Basher-52" a rescue team comprised of two CH-53 helicopters and 20 U.S. marines from "Kearsarge," an amphibious assault ship stationed in the Adriatic Sea, landed near O'Grady's hiding place in a wooded area southwest of Banja Luka and rescued him from Serb-held territory on June 8, 1995.

On June 4, 1995, Croatian forces had recaptured and liberated from Serb-held territory the strategic Mount Dinara (44°04'N; 16°23'E), located in southcentral Croatia and northwestern Bosnia-Herzegovina.

* * * * *

~ U.S. Policy on Bosnia-Herzegovina ~

Washington, DC, June 8, 1995

Excerpts of Statement by Peter Tarnoff, Under Secretary of State for Political Affairs, before the Senate Foreign Relations Committee and the House Committee on International Relations:

"Our principal goals in the Balkans remain to contain and help bring to an end the ongoing conflicts which threaten U.S. interests in European stability and integration. From the outset of these conflicts, we have sought to preserve Bosnia-Herzegovina as a multi-ethnic state, support the peaceful restoration of Croatian sovereignty throughout the country, assist the peacekeeping and other activities of our NATO allies and the UN, and relieve the human suffering. We have led efforts to achieve negotiated settlements , led by NATO military responses to calls by the Un for assistance in protection of its forces and safe areas for the people of Bosnia, deployed peacekeeping troops in the Former Yugoslav Republic of Macedonia, and conducted the longest humanitarian airlift in history. Despite many disappointments and frustations, the international community's efforts have yielded significant benefits. UNPROFOR'S presence has diminished the level of killing. NATO's operation "Deny Flight", which enforces the 'No-Fly Zone' has ended serial bombardment of cities. UNPROFOR provides essential support to the UNHCR in the delivery of relief to 2.2 million people throughout the former Yugoslavia, including 787,000 refugees and displaced persons. The war between the Croats and the Muslims was brought to an end in March 1994 with the formation of the Federation, which has sharply reduced the need for humanitarian relief. UNPROFOR has also performed well in monitoring the peaceful implementation of the Washington accords between the Muslims and Croats. The monitors that we and other members of the ICFY deployed on the border between Bosnia and Serbia-Montenegro have reduced the Serb army's ability to wage war over the past year. Without these UN and national programs, the situation would have been much worse in Bosnia.

Our diplomatic goal in Bosnia remains to end the war consistent with the internationally agreed Contact Group effort. Several weeks ago, the Contact Group decided to explore an initiative, backed by Bosnian President Izetbegović, that would tie Milošev´c's recognition of Bosnia and acceptance of tighter control over his country's borders with Bosnia and Croatia to sanctions suspension for Serbia. For the past several months, Belgrade has distanced itself from the policies of the Pale leadership, both by closing its border with Serb-held Bosnia and, most recently, by Milošević's condemnation of the hostage-taking by Pale and efforts to secure their release. By recognizing Bosnia, Milošević would frustrate the dreams held by many in Pale of merging the territory under their control to greater Serbia, thus enhancing the chances that Pale would negotiate seriously with the Bosnian Government. We do expect Milošević to 'deliver' the Serbs in Bosnia to the negotiating table single-handedly. The Serbs in Pale have a large measure of political independence from Belgrade, so much so that Milošević views Karadžić more as a rival than a partner. However, Belgrade exercises substantial persuasive influence with Serbs in Bosnia, as witnessed in Belgrade's partially successful efforts to win release of the UN hostages. Should Belgrade agree to the recognition package under discussion, this influence would fall squarely behind the Contact Group efforts to bring the parties back into negotiations.

In recent days, the Administration has worked closely with Contact Group partners and the UN to secure both release of UN personnel held by the Serbs and further information on the U.S. F-16 pilot, Captain Scott F. O'Grady shot down June 2, 1995 near Banja Luka. We have endeavored to ensure the immediate and unconditional release of all UN personnel. As of June 7, Serb forces released 229 of the detainees; another 149 UN personnel are still being detained or blocked in their positions. Efforts to secure their release are ongoing.

We have always felt the UN arms embargo unfairly penalizes the Government of Bosnia, which is the victim of Serb aggression. In 1993 and 1994, we advocated multilateral action to end the embargo but lacked sufficient support in the UN Security Council. In compliance with the Nunn-Mitchell Amendment, we have ended our participation in enforcement efforts against the Government of Bosnia but continue to honor the arms embargo. We still firmly oppose unilateral lifting of the arms embargo. It would lead to a wider and bloodier conflict, with a very uncertain outcome, for which the U.S. would have ultimate responsibility. Such a conflict would cause major strains in NATO and the UN and risk direct confrontation with Russia which, along with Serbia, might choose to provide military assistance to the Serbs in Bosnia. It would undermine other Security Council Resolutions and sanctions regimes, such as Iraq and Libya, that serve critical U.S. interests. I know Under Secretary Slocombe wants to address this issue further.

Our efforts to stabilize the situation in Bosnia are complemented by several other initiatives. In Croatia we are working with the parties and the UN to prevent escalation of fighting in the aftermath of the Croatian action to regain full control of UN Sector West and the Knin Serb retaliation on Zagreb and other areas. Ongoing clashes in Croatia and violations of agreements on cease-fires, separation zones, and economic cooperation demonstrate the need for an effective UN peacekeeping presence. These clashes could trigger a widening of the conflict and threaten the maintenance of UN peacekeeping operations throughout the region. Having helped persuade President Tudjman to maintain a new UN force of peacekeepers and border monitors in Croatia, we are working with Contact Group partners and others to minimize the danger of renewed hostilities and advance the cause of a negotiated settlement. This includes encouraging the parties to agree to the UN force's expeditious implementation of a new mandate.

We have also redoubled our efforts in the last few months to support the Bosnian Federation, which remains the best hope for building democracy and ethnic tolerance in the region. To date, our efforts have helped end the fighting and reopen humanitarian convoy routes in parts of central Bosnia, thereby improving the prospects for long-term reconciliation between the Muslim and Croat communities. We have been working with the 21 other governments who form the Friends of the Federation to expand international economic and political support to ensure that the Bosnian Federation becomes a durable entity and a model of ethnic harmony and tolerance in this troubled region. Withdrawal of UNPROFOR would gravely damage our efforts to bolster the Bosnian Federation."

* * * * *

In order to compel the Serbs to return UN weapons stolen during May and June 1995, NATO recommended prompt airstrikes. To protect their loot, the Serb terrorists responded by taking hundreds of UN peacekeepers hostage. The UN command in Bosnia circulated a memorandum predicting the Serbian attack to safe areas. The hostage crisis which began with the seizure of 377 UN personnel by Serbian forces in May was resolved in June. Serb leader Radovan Karadžić declared on June 13, 1995, that the crisis was over, but warned that hostages would once again be seized if the UN used air strikes against Serb targets. President Tudjman of Croatia on June 15 appointed his son, Miroslav Tudjman, deputy head of the National Security Department and Director of the Croatian Intelligence Service (CIS).

The SCR 998 dated June 16, 1995 approved the expansion of the peacekeeping force by up to 12,500 soldiers, including the Rapid Reaction Force. The German Bundestag on June 30, 1995 voted to deploy aircraft and 1,000 service personnel to support the Rapid Reaction Force.

The German Air Force were to be based at Piacenza, Italy, while at least 600 military personnel were to establish a field hospital near the Croatian port of Split. The German deployment was to be the first by German forces since 1945, and followed a German Constitutional Court ruling of July 1994 permitting the dispatch of German troops to foreign countries.

On July 6 when the Serbs attacked Srebrenica a garrison of 70 Dutch UN peacekeepers were stationed in that town, while 330 Dutch forces were based at Potocari, north of the town. On July 8, Serb forces overran the Dutch troops based in Srebrenica and a number of Dutch troops were taken hostage. The Serbs dressed in stolen UN uniforms committed all types of crimes against humanity. Dutch and U.S. military aircraft under NATO carried out two air strikes on Serb sites near Srebrenica. On July 11, 1995, Serbian troops overran the town of Srebrenica, a Muslim enclave and UN-designated safe area, later killing, raping and robbing thousands of civilian refugees. U.S. Defense Secretary Perry commented by saying, "this raises the question as to whether the UN force will be able to continue to stay in Bosnia." Once Srebrenica was under Serbian control they began shelling Potocari and only stopped the barrage when NATO complied with Serbian demands to halt all air activity.

The Serb military commander, Ratko Mladić, on July 12, 1995 supervised the loading of Muslim women and children on to trucks and buses for transport to Tuzla. However, draft-age Muslim men were detained and transported to concentration camps in Serb-held territory. By July 13, thousands of Muslim women and children from Srebrenica had been crowded into unsanitary makeshift camps around the Tuzla airport. Following their invasion on Srebrenica, the Serb forces turned their attention towards the nearby safe area of Zepa. Serbian assault on Zepa began on July 14 and the town itself was eventually taken on July 25, after Bosnian government troops abandoned the town and fled into the surrounding hills.

Gen. Janko Bobetko retired as Chief of General Staff of the Croatian Army, was replaced on July 15, 1995, by Gen. Zvonimir Cervenko, hitherto head of President Tudjman's military office, who also became a member of the Presidential Council on Defense and National Security.

On July 16, 1995 U.S. Gen. John Shalikashvili, Chairman, Joint Chiefs of Staff Admiral Jacques Lanxade of France, and Marshal Peter Inge of Britain met in London England, but failed to agree on a response to the Serbian assaults on the designated "safe areas" of Bosnia-Herzegovina. On July 21, 1995, Serb forces released the Dutch soldiers whom they had been holding since the capture of Srebrenica. Once released, the Dutch soldiers confirmed some of the Serbian atrocities recounted by the Muslim refugees in Tuzla. The ambivalence of the Dutch towards the refugees was also revealed. Many Muslims of Srebrenica surrendered to the Dutch, seeking UN protection, only to be handed over to the Serb occupation troops.

On August 23, 1995, Mazowiecki released a fact finding report on Srebrenica that found significant, direct and circumstantial evidences of summary executions of Muslim individuals and groups of people by the Serb forces. On the question of mass executions, Mazowiecki said, "evidence so far obtained leads to the chilling conclusion that mass executions had occurred."

The International War Crimes Tribunal at the Hague on July 25 formally indicted Radovan Karadžić of Pale (43°48′N; 18°35′E)and Ratko Mladić of Han Pijesak (44°05′N; 18°58′E) on charges of genocide and crimes against humanity. At the same time, the Tribunal had issued warrants for the arrests of both Serbs. The Tribunal also indicted 22 other Serbs for war crimes, including Milan Martić, the so-called president of the Serb-held Krajina, for attacks on Croatian cities and crimes against humanity.

The U.S. Senate on July 26, 1995, by a vote of 69 to 29, passed a bill on ending the arms embargo unilaterally. Proposed by the Republican Majority Leader, Senator Bob Dole (R-Kansas) and sponsored by Senator Joseph Lieberman (R-CT), with broad bipartisan support, the bill would require the U.S. government to lift the embargo after a complete withdrawal of UN peacekeeping forces from Bosnia-Herzegovina, or within 12 weeks of a request by the Bosnian government. In addition, an amendment to the bill would require the U.S. President to seek a multilateral lifting of the arms embargo from the UN Security Council before the USA acted unilaterally.

On July 27, 1995, NATO Secretary General Willy Claes warned that lifting the embargo could fuel a full-scale Balkan War. However, the Bosnian Muslims acclaimed the passage of the bill through the U.S. Senate. The Bosnian Premier Haris Silajdžić described on July 27 the lifting of the embargo as a victory of the principle of justice.

The U.S. House of Representatives on August 1, 1995, by a vote of 298 to 128, approved a bill on ending the arms embargo unilaterally; but on August 11, U.S. President Clinton vetoed the bill, and Clinton argued that ending the arms embargo would intensify the fighting, jeopardize diplomacy and make the outcome of the war in Bosnia a USA responsibility.

Following the Croatian operation "Storm" many condemned the military action and suggested that it would have been better if Croatian blitzkrieg had not been undertaken, thus saving the lives of terrorist Serbs. Evidently, these same people conveniently ignored that the Serbs as the culprit of aggression are responsible for most of the atrocities and inflicted human casualties. In addition the media de-emphasized the brutal expulsion by Serbs of 500,000 ethnic Croats, Hungarians, Germans, Ukrainians, and Ruthenians from Croatia during the Serbian war of aggression and occupation. In the summer of 1995, Croatia, with a military ranking probably in the bottom half of the world nations, liberated most of the Serb-occupied land in less than 48 hours. The superinflated mighty army of Serbia tucked its collective tail and ran faster than the bullets, with hardly a fight. Military operation "Storm" successfully launched by Croatia on August 4, 1995, liberated the Krajina territory, which had been held hostage by Serbians since 1991.

The liberation of the Krajina effected the military situation around Bihać and precipitated a large-scale exodus of Serbs into areas of Bosnia under Serb-held territory. While the USA, German, and other governments were supportive of the Croatian liberation offensive, England, France, and Russia were displeased by the events as demonstrated by their wishy-washy policy. On August 7, 1995, U.S. President Clinton issued a statement that he was hopeful the Croatian offensive would turn out to be an avenue to a quicker diplomatic resolution and not a road to a longer war.

On August 6-7, 1995 Bosnian government forces and Croatian troops carried out a successful push against Serb positions in the Bihać enclave. Towns in Croatia, which were occupied in 1991 by Serb terrorists were finally liberated by Croatian troops on August 8, 1995. Now, the towns and territories are back where they belong, under Croatia's tricolor (red-white-blue) checkered flag. In the aftermath of Croatia's liberation of Krajina, the U.S. Administration on August 9 unveiled a new peace initiative for former Yugoslavia. In an intensive round of diplomacy, the proposal was introduced to the Contact Group's five members and to the warring parties by U.S. Assistant Secretary of State for European and Canadian Affairs, Richard Holbrooke, and the U.S. National Security Advisor Anthony Lake. On August 10, the U.S. representative at the UN Security Council released a series of satellite photographs, which showed fresh mass graves on the outskirts of Srebrenica, and charged that the Serbs had carried out mass executions of draft-age Muslim men following the capture of the town.

To commemorate the liberation of the Croatian town of Knin on August 5, 1995, the Croatian National Bank (NBH) on September 5, 1995 issued a gold coin valued at 700 Kuna (approximately U.S. $140). All proceeds from the sale were to benefit the children of fallen Croatian soldiers.

* * * * *

~ U.S. Statement on UNSCR 1009 ~

New York City, August 10, 1995

Statement by Madeleine Korbel Albright, U.S. Representative to the United Nations, before the United Nations Security Council:

"The United States Government supports this resolution as an expression of continued commitment by this UN Security Council to peace and to the relief of human suffering in the former Yugoslavia. We regret the decision by the Government of Croatia to launch an offensive against the Krajina region. We also urge all parties to refrain from further attacks, whether within Croatia or Bosnia-Herzegovina.

The latest round of violence has produced yet another flow of civilian refugees within the former Yugoslavia. By tractor, truck, car, and cart, tens of thousands have fled the current military operations. The protection of those civilians must be a priority for all parties concerned. The rights of Serbs who choose to remain in Croatia must also be respected. History warns us that the failure to safeguard innocent lives leads only to more hatred, killing, and destruction. For this reason, it is essential that international agencies have unimpeded access to observe conditions in Krajina and to provide humanitarian relief where needed.

Mr. President, the turbulence of the past week's events coupled with restrictive policies imposed by the Government of Croatia have made it difficult to assess the extent to which Croatian forces or their Bosnian allies may have been guilty of violations of international humanitarian law. My government expects the war crimes tribunal to investigate allegations of abuse against unarmed civilians, including reports that five elderly Serbs were killed and refugees were bombed in the village of Dvor - and we will fully support the tribunal's work.

We join as well in condemning in strong terms the wrongful acts committed against UN peacekeeping forces and in the Council's extension of condolences to the families of the Czech and Danish peacekeepers who were killed. In this regard, let me welcome the statement of the representative of Croatia accepting responsibility for attacks on UN peacekeepers, committing to investigating these incidents, and promising cooperation with United Nations Confidence Restoration Operations (UNCRO) and other international organizations.

Many in Croatia have hailed the recent military actions as a great victory. But it is difficult to see how any society can derive real satisfaction from the defeat and flight of hundreds of thousands of its own citizens. This resolution reminds Croatia of its obligation to create conditions conducive to the safe return of those persons who have left their homes. And it stresses the importance of granting access by the ICRC to those who have been taken prisoner or detained. At the same time, while we regret the means used, we must also recognize that the safe area of Bihać is now open to humanitarian relief. For the citizens of Bihać, the long siege is over. Let it remain so. The events of this past week have not changed the overriding imperative for all parties in the former Yugoslavia, which is to cease the conduct of war and explore instead - with seriousness and good faith - the options that exist for achieving peace. That is the one path toward real security; that is the only way to bring to an end the cycle of disruption and tragedy that has affected all the people of the region."

* * * * *

~ Bosnia-Herzegovina Arms Embargo ~

Washington, DC, August 11, 1995

Statement by U.S. President William Jefferson Clinton released by the White House, Office of the Press Secretary:

"I am announcing today my decision to veto legislation that would unilaterally lift the arms embargo against Bosnia-Herzegovina. I know that Members of Congress share my goals of reducing the violence in Bosnia and working to end the war. But their vote to unilaterally lift the arms embargo is the wrong step at the wrong time. The people of the United States should understand the consequences of such action for our nation and for the prople of Bosnia.

First, our allies have made clear that they will withdraw their troops from Bosnia if the United States unilaterally lifts the arms embargo.The United States, as the leader of the NATO alliance, would be obliged to send thousands of United States ground troops to assist in that difficult operation.

Second, lifting the emgargo now could cause the fighting in Bosnia to escalate. The Serbs will not delay their assaults while the Bosnian Government receives new arms and training. Getting humanitarian aid to civilians will only get harder.

Third, unilaterally lifting the embargo will lead to unilateral United States responsibility. If the Bosnian Government suffered reverses on the battlefield, we - not the Europeans - would be expected to fill the void with military and humanitarian aid.

Fourth, intensified fighting in Bosnia would risk provoking a wider war in Europe.

Fifth, for this bill to become law now would undercut the new diplomatic effort we are currently engaged in, and withdrawal of the UN mission would virtually eliminate chances for a peaceful, negotiated settlement in the foreseeable future.

Finally, unilateral lift would create serious divisions between the United States and its key allies, with potential long-lasting damage to the NATO alliance.

This is an important moment in Bosnia. Events in the past few weeks have opened new possibilities for negotiations. We will test these new realities, and we are now engaged with our allies and others in using these opportunities to settle this terrible war by agreement. This is not the time for the United States to pull the plug on the UN mission. There is no question that we must take strong action in Bosnia. In recent weeks, the war has intensified. The Serbs have brutally assaulted three of the UN safe areas. Witnesses report widespread atrocities - summary executions, systematic rape, and renewed ethnic cleansing in Bosnia. Tens of thousands of innocent women and children have fled their homes. Now the Croatian Army offensive has created new dangers and dramatically increased the need for humanitarian aid to deal with displaced persons in the region. But these events also create opportunities.

Along with our allies, we have taken a series of strong steps to strengthen the UN mission, to prevent further attacks on safe areas, and to protect innocent civilians.

NATO has decided it will counter an assault on the remaining safe areas with sustained and decisive use of air power. Our response will be broad, swift, and severe, going far beyond the narrow attacks of the past;

For the first time, military commanders on the ground in Bosnia have been given operational control over such actions, paving the way for fast and effective NATO response; and

Well-armed British and French troops are working to ensure access to Sarajevo for convoys carrying food, medicine, and other vital supplies.

Despite these actions, many in Congress are ready to close the books on the UN mission. But I am not - not as long as that mission is willing and able to be a force for peace once again. I recognize that there is no risk-free way ahead in Bosnia. But unilaterally lifting the arms embargo will have the opposite effect of what its supporters intend. It would intensify the fighting, jeopardize diplomacy, and make the outcome of the war in Bosnia a United States responsibility. Instead, we must work with our allies to protect innocent civilians, to strengthen the UN mission, to bring NATO's military power to bear if our warnings are defied, and to aggressively pursue the only path that will end the conflict - one that leads to a negotiated peace."

Signed: William Jefferson Clinton
            President, United States of America

* * * * *

Bosnian government forces, supported by Croats of Bosnia, on August 12, launched an intense offensive around the Serb-held town of Donji Vakuf, in central Bosnia. Also on the same day Croatian forces attacked and silenced the positions from which Serbian-Montenegrin terrorists had been able to shell the southern Croatian port city of Dubrovnik.

On August 19, 1995 three dedicated U.S. Diplomats lost their lives in the pursuit of peace near Sarajevo. Deputy Assistant Secretary of State Robert C. Frasure, Deputy Assistant Secretary of Defense for European and NATO Affairs Joseph J. Kruzel and Air Force Col. Samuel Nelson Drew a member of the National Security Council, were killed in a crash when their armored personnel carrier traveling on Mount Igman on the way to Sarajevo ran off the road and skidded over the edge, as it precipitated downward the mountain the vehicle hit a landmine and exploded. Two other members of the delegation were injured. These men were part of the U.S. team searching for an end to the tragic conflict in Bosnia-Herzegovina. In addition, one French soldier was killed, and two were injured. The three were part of the UN team escorting the delegation.

The main railway linking the Croatian capital city of Zagreb to the city of Split in Dalmatia (a distance of 264mi./425 km) reopened on August 26, 1995. It's opening marked the reestablishment of railway traffic between northern and southern Croatia. President Franjo Tudjman, government and public officials, and foreign diplomats were among 500 passengers who traveled on the commemorative train named the "Train of Freedom." The regular rail service Zagreb-Gospić-Knin-Split resumed on August 27 when the train Marjan Express left Zagreb for Split. Since July 1991, this route was interrupted as 73 mi./118 km of railway lines were within the Serb-held territory. The opening of this railway line made it possible to restore, after the necessary repairs, the railway links with Šibenik and Zadar on the Adriatic Sea. For Croatia, the restoration of traffic between the inland of Croatia and the Adriatic ports of Zadar, Šibenik, Split, and Ploče are vitally important to the economic and tourist developments in Dalmatia.

On the morning of August 28, 1995 a single mortar shell landed near the market place in central Sarajevo, killing 37 people and wounding 40 others. The next day the UN announced their investigations had proved beyond any reasonable doubt that the shell had been fired from a Serbian position. This premeditated carnage provoked international outrage against the Serbs who accused the Bosnian government forces of bombarding the market place. As in the case of previous shelling of the same market in February 5, 1994, the Serbs on the eve of important events in the negotiations, perpetrated a massacre to sabotage the peace process. Conveniently, without any remorse Serbs always deny any involvement by "blaming the victim(s)."

On August 30, NATO responded to the Sarajevo market bombing by launching operation "Deliberate Force" (DF), a series of devastating air attacks on Serbian targets across Bosnia-Herzegovina. The attacks, which continued on August 31, amounted to the most ferocious outside intervention in the war in former Yugoslavia, and the largest military operation mounted by NATO since its formation in 1949. Operation "DF" was launched at around 2 A.M. local time on August 30. Over a 12-hour period, aircraft from five NATO countries -France, the Netherlands, Spain, England, and USA- flew some 300 sorties from bases in Italy and from the U.S. aircraft carrier Theodore Roosevelt stationed in the Adriatic Sea. The aircraft targeted radar, communication, missile and artillery sites in 23 target areas across Serb-held territory in Bosnia, mainly around Sarajevo, Tuzla, Pale, Goražde, Banja Luka, and Mostar. In coordination with NATO, the UN Rapid Reaction Force, comprising Dutch, French, and British units, fired hundreds of artillery rounds on Serbian artillery, mortar emplacements, and ammunition dumps around Sarajevo. In what was regarded as a significant policy shift, it was announced at the end of the first day of NATO attacks, that the Serbs were ready to conduct peace negotiations as part of a team headed by Milošević, a demagogic scum who has pledged to rule wherever there is a Serb and establish Serboslavia, even at the risk of killing its own Serbs. The world must realize that Milošević, a fanatic Serb-Marxist, is a dangerous man, acting like a wolf in sheep's clothing, and at times like a sheep in wolf's clothing, has never shed his Serbian primitive civilization.

* * * * *

~ Principles Endorsed by the Contact Group ~

September 8, 1995

Text of the Agreed Basic Principles endorsed by the Contact Group (Britain, France, Germany, Russia, United States, and EU negotiator) and signed by the Foreign Ministers:

1. Bosnia-Herzegovina will continue its legal existence with its present borders and continuing international recognition.

2. Bosnia-Herzegovina will consist of two entities, the Federation of Bosnia-Herzegovina and established by the Washington Agreements, and the Republika Srpska.

3. The 51:49 parameter of the territorial proposal of the Contact Group is the basis for a settlement. This territorial proposed is open for adjustment by mutual agreement.

4. Each entity will continue to exist under its present constitution (amended to accommodate these basic principles).

5. Both entities will have the right to establish parallel special relationship with neighboring countries, consistent with the sovereignty and territorial integrity of Bosnia-Herzegovina.

6. The two entities will enter into reciprocal commitments (a) to hold complete elections under international auspices; (b) to adopt and adhere to normal international human rights standards and obligations, including the obligation to allow freedom of movement and enable DP to repossess their home or receive just compensation; (c) to engage in binding arbitration to resolve disputes between them.

7. The entities have agreed in principle to the following: (a) the appointment of a Commission for DP authorized to enforce (with assistance from international organizations) the obligations of both entities to enable DP to repossess their homes or receive just compensation; (b) the establishment of a Bosnia-Herzegovina Human Rights Commission, to enforce the entities human rights obligations. The two entities will bide by the Commission's decisions; (c) the establishment of joint Bosnia-Herzegovina public corporations, financed by the two entities, to own and operate transportation and other facilities for the benefit of both entities; (d) the appointment of a Commission to Preserve National Monuments; and (e) the design and implementation of a system of arbitration for the solution of disputes between the two entities.

Signed: Muhamed Šaćirbey
Foreign Minister of Bosnia-Herzegovina

Mate Granić
Foreign Minister of Croatia

Milan Milutinović
Foreign Minister of Serbia and Montenegro

* * * * *

303

In Geneva, Switzerland, on September 8, 1995 the foreign ministers of the republics of Bosnia-Herzegovina, Croatia, and the FRY tentatively agreed to take an important step toward the path to peace in the former communist Yugoslavia. As a result of intensive mediation by Richard Holbrooke and his team - supported by the Contact Group partners of the European Union (EU) and the Russian Federation - the three foreign ministers have endorsed a set of Agreed Basic Principles that should serve as the framework for a political settlement to the conflict in the territory of Bosnia-Herzegovina. Moreover, the foreign ministers of Croatia and the FRY also have agreed to work actively toward a peaceful solution concerning the territory in Eastern Slavonia, the Serb-held area within the recognized boundary of the Republic of Croatia, also known as UN Sector East.

During the news conference at the White House on September 15, 1995, U.S. President Clinton issued the following statement:

"I welcome the agreement for the Serbs in Bosnia to comply with a condition set by NATO and the United Nations for ending the NATO air strikes. United States pilots and crews and their NATO colleagues have been carrying out those strikes to prevent further slaughter of innocent civilians in the Sarajevo area and in the other safe areas of Bosnia. Now the Serbs have stated that they will end all offensive operations within the Sarajevo exclusion zone, withdraw their heavy weapons from the zone within six days, and allow road and air access to Sarajevo within 12 hours. NATO and the UN, therefore, have suspended air operations temporarily and will carefully monitor the Serb compliance with these commitments. That suspension is appropriate. But let me emphasize that if the Serbs in Bosnia do not comply with their commitments, the air strikes will resume. Today's developments are a direct result of NATO's steadfastness in protecting the safe areas and the close cooperation between the UN and NATO. They also reflect the intense diplomatic efforts by Assistant Secretary of State Richard Holbrooke and the U.S. negotiating team, as well as those of our European and Russian partners. Now the Serbs must carry out their commitments and then turn their energies toward a political settlement that will end this terrible conflict for good. They should have no doubt that NATO will resume the air strikes if they fail to keep their commitments. - if they strike again at Sarajevo or the other safe areas. Today's actions, however, following last week's successful meeting in Geneva of the Foreign Ministers of Bosnia, Croatia, and Serbia, are important steps along the path to peace in Bosnia. A lot of work remains to be done, but we are absolutely determined to press forward to reach a settlement to this conflict - not on the battlefield, but at the negotiating table. We can and we must end Bosnia's long nightmare."

In Denver, Colorado, on September 20, 1995 U.S. President Clinton stated, "The UN and NATO commanders are in agreement that the Serbs have completed the required withdrawal of heavy weapons from the exclusion zone. The Sarajevo airport has been opened. UN and humanitarian traffic is moving along the main routes into the city. Therefore, the commanders have concluded that the NATO airstrikes can be discontinued."

The Croatian Parliament (Sabor) in September 1995 passed an election law that allowed Croatians living outside Croatia to vote in the election. International monitors criticized the government of Croatian for allowing Croatians in diaspora (dispersed in foreign countries) to vote. It just happened that U.S. citizens are permitted to vote in the United States election regardless of their residence abroad. On October 29, 1995 the Republic of Croatia held new elections for the House of Representatives (Zastupnički Dom), one of two Chambers of the Croatian Parliament (Sabor). President Tudjman's political party, the Croatian Democratic Union-CDU (HDZ) won 45.23% of the votes. The coalition led by the Peasant Party won 18.26%, the Social Liberal received 11.55%, the Social Democrat (former communist party) got 8.93%, the Party of Rights won 5.01%, and all others got 11.02%. The OSCE reported that the elections were conducted in an "orderly and free manner," but that flaws "marred the overall fairness of the elections." Criticism was leveled at the reduction from 13 to 3 seats for the Serbs (based on an estimated number of Serbs still living in Croatia following the exodus from the Krajina in August 1995), and the designation of 12 international seats for Croatians in diaspora where voting took place in 42 countries around the world. A new government was formed by Zlatko Matesa, chosen by President Tudjman to be the new Premier of Croatia. In Croatia where democratic institutions had been hindered by Serb terrorists committed to obstruct the political and economic developments, Croatia is slowly but surely advancing toward a democratic system and free market economy.

The presidents of Croatia, Bosnia, and Serbia on November 1, 1995 gathered at Wright-Patterson Air Force Base (WPAFB) outside Dayton, Ohio (USA) for the beginning of peace talks on Bosnia-Herzegovina and Croatia to end the Serbian war of aggression that has left five-hundred-thousand people homeless and sparked atrocities unmatched in Europe since the Nazis and communists killed tens of millions of people. U.S. Secretary of State Warren Christopher welcomed the three presidents (setting across a conference table from his left to right, Alija Izetbegović of Bosnia, Franjo Tudjman of Croatia, and Slobodan Milošević of Serbia) and said, "Europe could be plunged into a wider war requiring U.S. military intervention. Future generations would surely hold us accountable for the consequences." The peace talks were built on two sets of principles that would divide Bosnia into two entities, (a) Croat-Muslim Federation would control 51% of the territory,

305

and (b) a Republika Srpska would control 49%. The agreements established a joint government to be set up with representatives from both the Croat-Muslim and the Serb sides. The Bosnian peace agreement initialled in Dayton, Ohio, on November 21, 1995 was formally signed in Paris, France, on December 14, 1995 by the presidents of Croatia, Bosnia, and Serbia.

The foreign and defense ministers of NATO on December 1, 1995 chose Javier Madariaga Solana, the foreign minister of Spain's socialist government, as NATO's new Secretary General. Solana will succeed Willy Claes, who had resigned in October 1995. NATO's ministers on December 5 formally elected Solana, a one-time opponent of Spain's membership in NATO, to the top post at a meeting at NATO's headquarters in Brussels, Belgium. After a 29-year boycott, France returned to the military institution of NATO on December 5, 1995, strengthening the unity of the alliance as it prepared to lead a peace mission in Bosnia. In 1966, President Charles de Gaulle pulled France out of NATO's military committees and requested the departure of U.S. soldiers from France to distance his country from the U.S. dominated alliance. In the first such step, French Defense Minister Charles Millon attended the alliance military committee and attended meetings of NATO defense ministers. At NATO meeting all 16 members comprised of each countries' foreign and defense ministers approved the peace Implementation Force (IFOR) plan and endorsed the agreement on Bosnia-Herzegovina.

Representatives of 50 nations and international organizations met in London, England, on December 8-9, 1995 to discuss non-military issues relating to the Bosnia-Herzegovina peace plan. On December 8 the participants agreed to elect former Premier Carl Bildt of Sweden (Sverige), the European Union's chief mediator in the Bosnia-Herzegovina peace talks, to head the newly created Peace Implementation Council (PIC). The PIC was established to oversee civilian efforts and supervise the elections in Bosnia-Herzegovina and the rebuilding of its infrastructure.

A review and analysis of the UN performance during the past years, especially in connection with all the wishy-washy policies and indecisions regarding Bosnia-Herzegovina, reveals that Boutros Ghali as UN Secretary General displayed poor judgment and lack of leadership. Therefore, his tenure for a second term at the helm of the United Nations must be denied.

Two French pilots, Captain Frédéric Chiffot and Lieutenant José Souvignet, were filmed alive with their Serb captors after the French Mirage-2000 was shot down on August 30, 1995 during a NATO raid near Pale. Recalcitrant Serbs ignored the ultimatum issued by the French Foreign Minister, Hervé de Charette, who stated that the two French pilots must be released or the

Serbs would face multiple consequences. President Jacques Chirac of France called President Milošević of Serbia to demand in no uncertain terms the release of the two pilots or the signing of the peace treaty on December 14 will be postponed. The Serbs released the two pilots to the French authorities on December 12, 1995 in the town of Zvornik, Bosnia.

Concerning the military operations in Bosnia-Herzegovina on December 13, 1995 after hours of rancorous debate, the U.S. Senate voted 69 to 30 to support the deployment of U.S. troops, and voted 52 to 47 against a resolution to oppose the deployment, and rejected by vote of 77 to 22 a previously U.S. House-approved bill to block funding the deployment of U.S. troops if the Clinton administration did so without approval from U.S. Congress. The same night, the U.S. House voted 287 to 141 for a resolution opposing the President's policy, but supporting the deployment of U.S. troops, and defeated by a vote of 218 to 210 legislation prohibiting funds for the deployment of U.S. troops in Bosnia-Herzegovina.

The accord signed on December 14, 1995 will last longer than Munich's agreement of September 29, 1938 when Chamberlain declared "peace in our time," which resulted in the partition of Czech territory. Then as now, the arrangement was imposed upon the people, but the partition of Bosnia-Herzegovina is much more complex than the Sudenten in 1938. The new concord ended a state of hostility; Croatia would regain its territory; and Bosnia-Herzegovina was redefined with its territory partitioned into two entities (the Croat-Bosniac Federation and the recognized Republika Srpska) with 51:49 parameter. The entities will have the right to establish relationships with neighboring states, but these must be consistent with the sovereignty of Bosnia-Herzegovina. Hopefully, the peculiar structure of the Bosnia-Herzegovina government will not be an obstruction in achieving a lasting peace. Remember, the Serbian war of aggression is still on, as attested by the territories of eastern Slavonia, Baranja, and western Sirmium, particularly the oil fields of Beničanci (45°38′N; 18°11′E) and Đeletovci (45°11′N; 19°01′E), not yet reunited into Croatia. One thing is certain, by denying to Croatia the important military and political victory over the Serbian aggressor and oppressor, the situation will remain fragile and the healing process will take a long time. Peace without victory imposes a burden on NATO to provide security for UN teams investigating war crimes and apprehending indicted war criminals by all means available. NATO must take an aggressive role in establishing law and order. Before celebrating the agreement of Dayton/Paris appeasement, Croatia must remain vigilant of the rocky intrigues and deceptions that will be introduced from time to time by Serbia, its surrogates or proxies. Prompt and firm action must be taken to respond and deal with every deficiency resulting from the fragile agreement. Holbrooke must share the blame of obtruding and replicating past wrongs by insisting on a deadline, practicing a coercive diplomacy, and compelling the stamp of approval without discerning the consequences. Holbrooke, with all his diplomatic wheelings and dealings, never understood that he was doing business with Milošević, a master of deceit.

A multinational force of 60,000 troops (Implementation Force-IFOR) to be deployed in Bosnia-Herzegovina should maintain peace and enforce a 2.5 mi/4 km wide "zone of separation" (ZOS) between Muslim-Croat and Serb territorial entities. Meanwhile, the OSCE accepted the most challenging tasks: (a) establish a legal framework for holding and monitoring elections by September 1996; (b) reporting on the human rights situation; and (c) limiting armament and troop levels in Bosnia-Herzegovina. The OSCE continues to insist on the IFOR redeployment for long-term missions to Macedonia, Kosova, the Sandzak, and Vojvodina.

History tells us that U.S. President Abraham Lincoln (1809-1865) responded to the siege of Ft. Sumter in Charleston Harbor, SC (USA), where a small force of U.S. soldiers, having scant provisions and being greatly outnumbered, were subjected to a relentless Confederate bombardment. Henceforth, the U.S. Civil War (1861-1865), also called "War of Secession" or "War Between the States," started as a consequence of political and economic rivalry between an agrarian South (the Confederacy) and an industrial North (the Union), the controversial abolition of slavery, and the debate on the constitutional right of states to secede from the Union. The civil war resulted in a total of 498,332 dead (365,511 Union forces and 133,821 Confederate forces). An analogy in conjunction with the above historical event which occurred one hundred thirty years later, President Franjo Tudjman of Croatia responded to the siege of Croatia (1991-1995) created by the scoundrel Slobodan Milošević, who set into motion the operations and activities which commenced the Serbian war of aggression. There were those who disagreed with Croatia's resoluteness and called Tudjman "evil," just because he did everything possible to defend and preserve the sovereignty and independence of the Republic of Croatia. Remember, Tudjman did not start the war. It was thrust upon him, and few could have shouldered the responsibility considering the alternative. The Republic of Croatia had the inherent right under the United Nations Charter and international law to defend itself and repel the aggressor. Pursuant to the right to collective self-defense, other states had the right to come to the defense of the Republic of Croatia at its request. The territorial conquest by the vicious Serbs and Montenegrins, aided and abetted by the despicable YPA under the leadership of the megalomaniac Milošević et al., turned out to be a fitting failure, thus ending their dream of establishing a repulsive Serboslavian empire. Serbia must rid itelf of the damned clique of hatemongers and demogogues who give rise to anarchy and disaster.

* * * * *

~ Croatia and Bosnia Joint Council ~

Paris, France, December 14, 1995

The entire text of the "Agreement on the Establishment of the Joint Cooperation Council" is printed below.

"Determined to contribute to the establishment and maintenance of just and lasting peace in the region; aware that mutual cooperation is in their interest and of a broader importance; prepared to take every necessary step, in their countries and internationally, focused on association with European integrations; interested in cooperating with the international community in the reconstruction and development of their countries; the Republic of Croatia and the Republic of Bosnia -Herzegovina and the Federation of Bosnia -Herzegovina have agreed as follows:

Article I. The Joint Cooperation Council of the Republic of Croatia and the Republic and Federation of Bosnia-Herzegovina (hereinafter referred to as Joint Council) will be established.

Article II. The Joint Council will deal with the promotion, strategic planning and coordination of cooperation as follows: (a) In relations between the Republic of Croatia and the Federation of Bosnia-Herzegovina, particularly in the following fields: education, science and technology, information, tourism, sports and protection of environment, welfare, economic relations, and promotion of cooperation between non-governmental organizations. (b) In relations between the Republic of Croatia and the Republic of Bosnia-Herzegovina, particularly in the following fields: coordination of foreign policy and of appearance with respect to third countries and international organizations, coordination of activities related to association with the European Union, the Council of Europe, Partnership for Peace with NATO, and association with other regional, European and broader associations, coordination of development and of cooperation with the international community in reconstruction and development, military cooperation, dealing with issues related to the succession of the former SFRY, and other matters of common interest to the two States.

Article III. The Joint Council will consist of ten members, five from the Republic of Croatia and five from the Republic and the Federation of Bosnia-Herzegovina. The President of the Joint Council will be the President of the Republic of Croatia Franjo Tudjman, and the Vice-President will be President of the Presidency of the Republic of Bosnia-Herzegovina, Alija Izetbegović. The parties hereto will appoint the members of the Joint Council within 15 days of the signing of the Agreement.

Article IV. This Agreement has been concluded in six identical copies with the official English translation.

Article V. The Agreement will enter into force on the day of its signing."

Signed: Franjo Tudjman
President of the Republic of Croatia

Alija Izetbegović
President of the Republic of Bosnia-Herzegovina

* * * * *

The UN Security Council by adopting Resolution 1031 on December 15, 1995, welcomed the signing of the Bosnia-Herzegovina Peace Agreement; approved the withdrawal of UN forces and agreed to the transfer of UNPROFOR to the Implementation Force (IFOR) under NATO command.

Robert Frowick, an official of the U.S. State Department, on December 19, was appointed by OSCE (formerly CSCE) to oversee the non-military activities in Bosnia-Herzegovina. Frowick would head a civilian task force responsible for monitoring the political elections, ascertain compliance with human rights and ensure the fulfillment of disarmament control. On December 20, 1995 the United Nations forces in Yugoslavia, under the command of Gen. Bernard Janvier of France, formally relinquished control of the military operations to NATO under the command of Admiral Leighton W. Smith, Jr. of USA, with headquarters in Naples, Italy.On December 28, 1995, French Defense Minister Charles Millon divulged that the two French pilots shot down on August 30, 1995 and captured during a NATO mission against Serbs in Bosnia were brutally treated by their Serb captors.

If those culpable for the Serbian War of Aggression remain unpunished, justice will never be achieved since the aggressors will be perceived as having been rewarded for their war crime atrocities and crimes against peace. Hereafter, the hot pursuit of war criminals will be one of the most sensitive issues, there will be no peace without justice. War criminals must be brought to justice and held accountable for their crimes. The fact that a person who committed an act which constitutes a war crime acted as the head of a State or as a government official does not relieve that person from responsibility for the illegal act. When military or paramilitary personnel commit massacres and atrocities against the civilian population of occupied territory or against prisoners of war, the responsibility may rest not only with the actual perpetrators but also with their leaders. Milošević, the infamous parasite of Serbia and possibly of the whole world, had a dream to implement ethnic extermination, thus aggrandize Serboslavia. Documentary evidence attests that aggressive wars were planned and conducted in the most barbaric way by the evil Milošević, in cahoots with his protégé, thugs, and accomplices such as Radovan Karadžić, Ratko Mladić, and others. The international community, must resolve not to succumb to political or military pressure, but exert every effort to bring all war criminals to justice. Commencing with individual and collective atonement, Serbians and Montenegrins must change and improve their culture, behave in a civilized manner, quit bad-mouthing others, clean up their act, apply common sense, get aboard and genuinely contribute to make the world a better place to live. In conclusion, to create a harmonious civilization, people ought to repent for past wrongs by affirming their mea culpa, and instill wholehearted understanding in the pursuit of a peaceful world.

310

APPENDIX A

BASIC FACTS ABOUT CROATIA

(Osnovni Podaci o Hrvatske)

Location of the Republic of Croatia: Southeastern Europe

Geography: Croatia's terrain is geographically diverse with enchanting scenery; flat plains along northeastern territory, low mountains and highlands near Adriatic coast, coastline, and islands. It can be divided into three main geographic regions:

•Mediterranean/Adriatic - This region consists primarily of the highly indented coastline (1,104 miles/1,778 km) of the Adriatic littoral, stretches from the northern outskirts of Savudrija (45 30'N; 13 30'E) in NW Istria to Prevlaka Peninsula/Prevlaka Poluotok (42 24'N; 18 31'E) southern tip of Dubrovnik in Dalmatia. Known as the coast of thousand islands because it is compriosed of 1,185 islands and islets.

•Mountain/Dinaric - This region is the mountain belt, which joins Mediterranean and Pannonian regions, is the smallest in area and the most sparsely populated, has three main plateaus with areas of forests and grazing land.

•Pannonian - This region is located in the north and northeastern Croatia and is comprised by the Pannonian plain. This region is the largest and the most densely populated area, has a moderate continental climate with extensive arable land and is traversed by three important rivers, Drava, Sava, and Danube.

Area (Površina):

		Sq. km	Sq. mi	Percentage
Total	(Ukupno)	56,538	21,829	100.0
Land	(Kopno)	56,410	21,780	99.8
Water	(Vodu)	128	49	0.2

Geographic Coordinates (Geografske Koordinate):

Point (Krajnjh Točaka)	Place (Mjesto)	Commune (Općina)	Latitude (Sjeverna Širina)	Longitude (Istočna Dužina)
North (Sjever)	Žabnik	Čakovec	46° N 32' E	16° N 21' E
South (Jug)	Oštra	Dubrovnik	42° N 23' E	18° N 32' E
East (Istok)	Radevac	Vukovar	45° N 11' E	19° N 26' E
West (Zapad)	Savudrija	Buje	45° N 18' E	13° N 30' E

Land Boundaries (Dužina Kopnenih Granica):

		km	miles	Percentage
Total	(Ukupno)	2,028	1,260.0	100.0
Slovenia	(Northwest)	501	311.0	24.7
Hungary	(North)	329	204.0	16.2
Serbia	(East)	241	150.0	11.9
Bosnia-Herzegovina	(East)	932	579.0	46.0
Montenegro	(South)	24	15.5	1.2

Coastline (Dužina Morske Obale s Otocima):

		km	miles	Percentage
Total	(Ukupno)	5,790	3,598	100.0
Land	(Kopno)	1,778	1,105	30.7
Island and Isle	(Otok i Otoci)	4,012	2,493	69.3

Maritime Claims (Pomorsko Pravo):

Continental shelf	- 200 meter (656 ft) depth;
Exclusive economic zone	- 12 nautical miles - nm / 22.2 kilometers;
Exclusive fishing zone	- 12 nautical miles - nm / 22.2 kilometers;
Territorial sea	- 12 nautical miles - nm / 22.2 kilometers.

Climate (Klima):

Mediterranean and continental; inland a continental type of climate, with cold winters and hot summers; but along the Adriatic coast and the islands a Mediterranean climate is prevalent, with mild winters, hot dry sunny summers, less than average rainfall.

Terrain (Teritorija):

Geographically diverse; flat plains along northeastern territory, low mountains and highlands near Adriatic coast, coastline, and islands.

Natural Resources (Prirodna Bogatstva):

Oil, coal, bauxite, low-grade iron ore, calcium, natural asphalt, silica (also called "silicon dioxide"), mica (mineral silicates containing hydroxyl, alkali, and aluminum), clays, salt, fruit (grapes, sweet and sour cherries, apples, plums, pears, corn, wheat, figs), and livestock.

Land Use (Zemlja Upotrebi):

32% arable land; 20% permanent crops; 18% meadows and pastures; 15% forest and woodland; and 15% other.

Population (Stanovništvo):

Year (Popis)	Male (Musko)	Female (Zensko)	Total (Ukupno)	Density (Prosječan) km²	mi²	Average Annual Rate
1948	1,769,730	2,010,128	3,779,858	66.9	173	-
1953	1,861,229	2,074,793	3,936,022	69.6	176	8.1
1961	1,986,204	2,173,492	4,159,696	73.6	191	7.4
1971	2,139,048	2,287,173	4,426,221	78.3	203	6.2
1981	2,226,890	2,374,579	4,601,469	81.4	210	3.8
1991	2,346,067	2,438,198	4,784,265	84.6	220	3.9

Nationality (Narodnost):

Noun: Croat(s); adjective: Croatian.

Ethnic Composition (Etnički Sastav):

		1971		1991	
		Total	%	Total	%
Croats	(Hrvati)	3,513,647	79.4	3,736,356	78.1
Serbs	(Srbi)	626,789	14.2	581,663	12.2
Muslims	(Muslimani)	18,457	0.4	43,469	0.9
Slovenes	(Slovenci)	32,497	0.7	22,376	0.5
Hungarians	(Mađari)	35,488	0.8	22,355	0.5
Italians	(Talijani)	17,433	0.4	21,303	0.4
Yugoslavs	(Jugoslaveni)	84,118	1.9	106,041	2.2
Others *	(Ostali)	63,368	1.4	114,400	2.4

* Includes 18 ethnic groups, and those who refused to reply.

Religion (Vjeroispovijesti):

	1991	
	Total	%
Roman Catholics (Rimokatolika)	3,659,963	76.5
Eastern Orthodox Christians (Pravoslavnika)	531,031	11.1
Protestants (Protestanta)	66,968	1.4
Muslims (Muslimana)	57,411	1.2
Atheists (Bezbožnik)	186,586	3.9
Others (Ostali)	282,306	5.9

Language (Jezik):

The Croatian language and the Latin script is in official use in the Republic of Croatia.

Literacy (Piemenost):

96.5% (male 98.6%, female 94.5%) age 10 and over.

APPENDIX B

BOSNIA PEACE AGREEMENT

The Agreement, initialed at Wright-Patterson Air Force Base, Dayton, Ohio (USA) on November 21, 1995, was signed at the Elysée Palace in Paris, France, on December 14, 1995. Presidents Franjo Tudjman of Croatia, Alija Izetbegović of Bosnia, and Slobodan Milošecić of Serbia signed the document for their respective governments. Also, U.S. President William J. Clinton, German Chancellor Helmut Kohl, French President Jacques Chirac, British Premier John Major, Russian Premier Viktor S. Chernomyrdin, and for the European Union Carl Bildt of Sweden signed the document as witnesses to the Agreement. The abstracts from the Agreement are as follows:

General Framework Agreement

The Republic of Bosnia and Herzegovina, the Republic of Croatia, and the Federal Republic of Yugoslavia (hereinafter the "Parties"), recognized the need for a comprehensive settlement to bring an end to the tragic conflict in the region; desiring to contribute toward that end and to promote an enduring peace and stability; affirming their commitment to the Agreed Basic Principles issued on September 8, 1995, the Further Agreed Basic Principles issued on September 26, 1995, and the cease-fire agreements of September 14 and October 5, 1995; noting the agreement of August 29, 1995, which authorized the delegation of the Federal Republic of Yugoslavia (FRY) to sign, on behalf of the Republika Srpska, the parts of the peace plan concerning it, with the obligation to implement the agreement that is reached strictly and consequently, have agreed as follows:

Article I - The parties shall conduct their relations in accordance with the principles set forth in the United Nations Charter, as well as the Helsinki Final Act and other documents of the Organization for Security and Cooperation in Europe. In particular, the Parties shall fully respect the sovereign equality of one another, shall settle disputes by peaceful means, and shall refrain from any action, by threat or use of force or otherwise, against the territorial integrity or political independence of Bosnia-Herzegovina or any other State.

Article II - The parties welcome and endorse the arrangements that have been made concerning the military aspects of the peace settlement and aspects of regional stabilization, as set forth in the Agreements at Annex 1-A and Annex 1-B. The Parties shall fully respect and promote fulfillment of the commitments made in Annex 1-A, and shall comply fully with their commitments as set forth in Annex 1-B.

Article III - The Parties welcome and endorse the arrangements that have been made concerning the boundary demarcation between the two Entities, the Federation of Bosnia-Herzegovina and Republika Srpska, as set forth in the Agreement at Annex 2. The Parties shall fully respect and promote fulfillment of the commitments made therein.

Article IV - The Parties welcome and endorse the elections program for Bosnia-Herzegovina as set forth in Annex 3. The Parties shall fully respect and promote fulfillment of that program.

Article V - The Parties welcome and endorse the arrangements that have been made concerning the Constitution of Bosnia-Herzegovina, as set forth in Annex 4. The Parties shall fully respect and promote fulfillment of the commitments made therein.

Article VI - The Parties welcome and endorse the arrangements that have been made concerning the establishment of an arbitration tribunal, a Commission on Human Rights, a Commission on Refugees and Displaced Persons, a Commission to Preserve National Monuments, and Bosnia-Herzegovina Public Corporations, as set forth in the Agreements at Annexes 5-9. The Parties shall fully respect and promote fulfillment of the commitments made therein.

Article VII - Recognizing that the observance of human rights and the protection of refugees and displaced persons are of vital importance in achieving a lasting peace, the Parties agree to and shall comply fully with the provisions concerning human rights set forth in Chapter One of the Agreement at Annex 6, as well as the provisions concerning refugees and displaced persons set forth in Chapter One of the Agreement at Annex 7.

Article VIII - The Parties welcome and endorse the arrangements that have been made concerning the implementation of this peace settlement, including in particular those pertaining to the civilian (non-military) implementation, as set forth in the Agreement at Annex 10, and the international police task force, as set forth in the Agreement at Annex 11. The Parties shall fully respect and promote fulfillment of the commitments made therein.

Article IX - The Parties shall cooperate fully with all entities involved in implementation of this peace settlement, as described in the Annexes to this Agreement, or which are otherwise authorized by the United Nations Security Council, pursuant to the obligation of all Parties to cooperate in the investigation and prosecution of war crimes and other violations of international humanitarian law.

Article X - The Federal Republic of Yugoslavia and the Republic of Bosnia-Herzegovina recognizes each other as sovereign independent States within their international borders. Further aspects of their mutual recognition will be subject to subsequent discussions.

Article XI - This Agreement became effective December 14, 1995.

[Signatures]

Annexes to Bosnia Peace Agreement

1-A   Agreement of Military Aspects of the Peace Settlement

1-B   Agreement of Regional Stabilization

2   Agreement on Inter-Entity Boundary Line and Related Issues

3   Agreement on Elections

4   Constitution of Bosnia-Herzegovina

5   Agreement on Arbitration

6   Agreement on Human Rights

7   Agreement on Refugees and Displaced Persons

8   Agreement on the Commission to Preserve National Monuments

9   Agreement on Bosnia-Herzegovina Public Corporations

10   Agreement on Civilian Implementation

11   Agreement on International Police Task Force

APPENDIX C

U.N. SECURITY COUNCIL RESOLUTIONS

No.	Date	Area	Purpose
713	9/25/91	Y	Weapons embargo against all former Yugoslavia
721	11/27/91	Y	Preliminaries to establishing UNPROFOR
724	12/15/91	Y	Establishes sanctions Committee
727	1/8/92	C	Deployment of 50 liaison officers
740	2/7/92	C	Increases in liaison officers
743	2/21/92	C	Establishes UNPROFOR
749	4/7/92	C	Authorizes full deployment of UNPROFOR
752	5/15/92	B	Demands all cease fighting in Bosnia
753	5/18/92	C	Admits Croatia to the U.N.
754	5/18/92	Y	Admits Slovenia to the U.N.
755	5/20/92	B	Admits Bosnia to the U.N.
757	5/30/92	Y	Imposes sanctions on Serbia and Montenegro
758	6/8/92	B	Authorizes UNPROFOR deployment to Sarajevo
760	6/18/92	Y	Exempts humanitarian aid from sanctions
761	6/29/92	B	Additional UNPROFOR deployment to Sarajevo; mandate to ensure security of airport
762	6/30/92	C	Additional UNPROFOR mandate in Croatia "pink zones"
764	7/13/92	B	UNPROFOR reinforcements in Sarajevo
769	8/7/92	C	Enlarges UNPROFOR mandate in Croatia to perform customs functions
770	8/13/92	B	Asks member states to facilitate delivery of humanitarian aid in Bosnia
771	8/13/92	B	Demands unimpeded access for humanitarian organizations
776	9/14/92	B	Enlarges UNPROFOR mandate to protect humanitarian convoys in Bosnia
777	9/19/92	Y	Federal Republic of Yugoslavia (Serbia and Montenegro) expelled from U.N. membership
779	10/6/92	C	Enlarges UNPROFOR mandate in Croatia - Prevlaka peninsula
780	10/6/92	Y	Establishes war crimes commission
781	10/9/92	B	Bosnia no-fly zone

No.	Date	Area	Purpose
786	11/10/92	B	Enlarges UNPROFOR mandate to authorize and monitor flights into Bosnia
787	11/16/92	Y	Restricts transshipments
795	12/11/92	M	UNPROFOR deployment to Macedonia
798	12/18/92	B	Condemnation of war crimes
802	1/15/93	C	Demands cessation of attacks on UNPROFOR and end of cease-fire violations
807	2/19/93	Y	Demands respect for UNPROFOR's security and extends mandate until 3/3/93
808	2/22/93	Y	Establishes war crimes tribunal
815	3/30/93	Y	Extends UNPROFOR mandate until 6/30/93
816	3/31/93	B	Authorization to enforce no-fly zone
817	4/7/93	M	Admits Macedonia to the U.N.
819	4/16/93	B	Designates Srebrenica as safe area
820	4/17/93	Y	Strengthens embargo on Serbia and Montenegro
821	4/28/93	Y	Excludes Serbia and Montenegro from ECOSOC
824	5/6/93	B	Designates six safe areas in Bosnia
827	5/25/93	Y	Establishes international War Crimes Tribunal
836	6/4/93	B	Enlarges UNPROFOR mandate to deter attacks on safe areas
838	6/10/93	B	Requests report on deploying monitors on Bosnia's borders
842	6/18/93	M	Authorizes U.S. to deploy in Macedonia
843	6/18/93	Y	Requests to examine financial impact of sanctions
844	6/18/93	Y	Authorizes reinforcement of UNPROFOR
845	6/18/93	M	Urges Greece and Macedonia reach settlement
847	6/30/93	Y	Extends UNPROFOR mandate until 9/30/93
855	8/9/93	Y	Calls for continuation of CSCE missions in Serbia and Montenegro
857	8/20/93	Y	Candidates for judges of War Crimes Tribunal
859	8/24/93	B	Calls for cease-fire
869	9/30/93	Y	Extends UNPROFOR mandate until 10/1/93
870	10/I/93	Y	Extends UNPROFOR mandate until 10/5/93
871	10/5/93	Y	Extends UNPROFOR mandate until 3/31/94
877	10/21/93	Y	Appoints international tribunal prosecutor
900	3/4/94	B	Appoints Special Coordinator for Sarajevo
908	3/31/94	Y	Extends UNPROFOR mandate until 9/30/94
913	4/22/94	Y	Demands immediate release of U.N. personnel
914	4/27/94	Y	Increases UNPROFOR personnel by 6,550

No.	Date	Area	Purpose
936	7/8/94	Y	Appoints prosecutor of International War Crimes Tribunal
941	9/23/94	B	Condemns Bosnian Serb ethnic cleansing
942	9/23/94	B	Imposes economic sanctions on Bosnian Serbs
943	9/29/94	Y	Lifts some sanctions against Serbia and Montenegro
947	9/30/94	Y	Extends UNPROFOR mandate until 3/31/95
958	11/19/94	C	Extends air strike authority to Croatia
959	11/19/94	C	Clarifies safe area regime
967	12/14/94	Y	Permits Serbs to export diphtheria serum
970	1/12/95	Y	Continues suspensions of some sanctions against Serbia and Montenegro
981	3/31/95	C	Establishes UNCRO mission for Croatia
982	3/31/95	B	Extends UNPROFOR mandate until 11/30/95 but only for Bosnia
983	3/31/95	M	Establishes UNPREDEP mission for Macedonia
988	4/21/95	Y	Extending selective retention of sanctions
990	4/28/95	C	Call for Croatia to cooperate with UNCRO
994	5/17/95	C	Ensure the safety and security of the Zagreb-Belgrade highway
998	6/16/95	C	Expansion of the peacekeeping force
1009	8/10/95	C	Protection of refugees and displaced persons
1031	12/15/95	Y	Welcome the signing of the Peace Agreement in Bosnia-Herzegovina, approved the withdrawal of UNPROFOR, and transfer its authority to IFOR under NATO unified command

Legend: B = Bosnia
C = Croatia
M = Macedonia
Y = Former Yugoslavia Areas

APPENDIX D

(MARCH 1995)

Country	Croatia	Bosnia	Macedonia	Total
Argentina	862			862
Bangladesh		1,238		1,238
Belgium	769	100		869
Canada	1,218	820		2,038
Czech Republic	957			957
Denmark	953	280		1,233
Egypt		418		418
Finland	43			43
France	843	3,781		4,624
Indonesia	220			220
Jordan	3,283	100		3,383
Kenya	974			974
Malaysia		1,545		1,545
Nepal	898			898
Netherlands	148	1,482		1,630
New Zealand		249		249
Nordic			556	556
Norway	111	636		747
Pakistan		2,983		2,983
Poland	1,141			1,141
Russia	856	472		1,328
Slovakia	567			567
Spain		1,372		1,372
Sweden	128	1,030		1,158
Turkey		1,469		1,469
Ukraine	555	460		1,015
United Kingdom		3,155		3,155
United States	299		540	839
Subtotal	**14,825**	**21,590**	**1,096**	**37,511**
Headquarters Units				404
Total troop strength			**3**	**5**

APPENDIX E

ABBREVIATIONS

ACNL/AVNOJ	Anti-Fascist Council for the Liberation of Yugoslavia /Antifasčisticko vijece narodnog oslobođenije Jugoslavije
CSCE	Conference on Security & Cooperation in Europe (OSCE)
DP	Displaced Persons
EC	European Community
ECCY	European Community Commission on Yugoslavia
EEC	European Economic Community
FRY	Federal Republic of Yugoslavia (Serbia and Montenegro)
GDP	Gross Domestic Product
GNP	Gross National Product
GSP	Generalized System of Preference
HVO	Croatian Defense Council
ICJ	International Court of Justice
ICRC	International Committee of the Red Cross
IMF	International Monetary Fund
IMO	International Maritime Organization
IMT	International Military Tribunal
MFN	Most Favored Nation
NATO	North Atlantic Treaty Organization
NGO	Non-Governmental Organization
NLA	National Liberation Army of Yugoslavia
OKW	Oberkommand der Wehrmacht (Armed Forces High Cmd.)
OSCE	Organization on Security & Cooperation in Europe (CSCE)
OSS	U.S. Office of Strategic Services
OZNA	Dept. for the Protection of the People
SACMED	Supreme Allied Commander-Mediterranean
SCICY	Steering Committee of the Int'l. Conference on Yugoslavia
SCR	UN Security Council Resolution
SDB	State Security Service
SFRY	Socialist Federal Republic of Yugoslavia
UN	United Nations
UNCRO	UN Confidence Restoration Operations
UNESCO	UN Educational, Scientific and Cultural Organization
UNHCR	United Nations Humanitarian Commission for Refugees
UNICEF	United Nations Children's Fund
UNPA	United Nations Protection Area
UNPROFOR	United Nations Protection Force
WEU	Western European Union
WHO	World Health Organization
YPA	Yugoslav People's Army

INDEX

A

Abdebrasik, Hussein Ali: 244
Abdić, Fikret: 280
Academy of Science at Zagreb: 15
Acre (Galilee): 12
Adrianople (Adrianopolis/Edirne):
Adriatic Region (Dalmatia): 7, 11
Adžić, Blagoje: 218, 223
Aetolian League: 3
Afghan/Afghanistan: 198, 199
Agmts./Pacts/Treaties/Declarations:
   Agreement "Sporazum" of 1939: 71
   Aix-la-Chapelle (Aachen) of 802: 8
   Allied Powers: 31, 32, 140, 177
   Anschluss Germany-Austria of 1938: 65
   Anti-Comintern: 62
   Atlantic Charter: 168
   Ausgleich (Compromise) of 1867): 22
   Axis "Berlin-Rome" of 1936: 62, 80
   Axis "Berlin-Rome-Tokyo" of 1940: 80
   Axis-Powers/Forces: 228, 289
   Balfour Declaration of 1917: 37, 69
   Balkan Entente of 1934: 57
   Balkan League Treaty of 1912: 28, 29
   Brest-Litovsk of 1918: 37
   Britain-Poland Treaty of 1939: 71
   Central Powers: 31, 33
   Charter of Paris (1990): 206
   Congress of Vienna (1815): 19
   Corfu (Kérkyra) Declaration: 34, 228
   Dayton Agreement on Bosnia(1995): 306
   Franco-Yugoslav Treaty: 64
   French-USA Non-Aggression (1928): 46
   Friendship & Non-Aggression Pact: 96
   German-Soviet Economic Agmt: 69
   German-Soviet Nonaggression Pact of
   1939: 69
   German-Yugoslavia Trade Pact: 74
   Greco-British Agreement: 75
   International Non-Aggression: 8
   Japan-Soviet Neutrality Treaty: 101
   Kellogg-Briand Peace Treaty of 1929: 46
   Little Entente of 1933: 45, 53
   London Charter of 1945: 178
   Munich (München) Agreement: 66, 307
   Nagodba (Compromise) of 1868: 22, 26
   Naval Conference at London of 1936: 61
   Pact of Friendship/Non-Aggression: 96
   Pact of Steel (1939): 69, 80
   Peace of Tilsit/Sovetsk of 1807: 19
   Personal Union: (Pacta Conventa): 12

   Quadruple Alliance of 1815: 19
   Soviet-Romanian Agreement: 162
   Treaty of Alliance-Italy & Croatia: 109
   Treaty of Bucharest (1913): 29
   Treaty of Campo Formio (1797): 18
   Treaty of Commerce & Navigation: 76
   Treaty of Final Settlement (1990): 204
   Treaty of Friendship (1924): 44
   Treaty of Friendship (1925): 46
   Treaty of Friendship (1927): 45
   Treaty of Friendship (1937): 46
   Treaty of Karlowitz (1699): 16
   Treaty of London (1913): 29
   Treaty of London (1915): 32, 40
   Treaty of Ouchy (Switzerland): 28
   Treaty of Passarowitz (Požarevac): 17
   Treaty of Portsmouth, NH(USA): 27
   Treaty of Požum (1805): 18
   Treaty of Prague (1866): 22
   Treaty of Pressburg (Bratislava): 18
   Treaty of Rapallo (1920): 41
   Treaty of Saint Germain (1919): 40, 65
   Treaty of San Stefano (1878): 23, 24
   Treaty of Schönbrunn (1809): 19
   Treaty of Sistova/Svištov (1791): 18
   Treaty of Trianon (1920): 42
   Treaty of Versailles (1919): 40, 42, 61
   Tripartite Pact of 1940: 80, 82, 85-88,
   94, 116, 138
   Triple Alliance of 1882: 32
   Vis Agreement of 1944: 162, 166, 168
   Warsaw Pact (1955-1991): 190, 192
   Yugoslav-Bulgaria Pact of 1937: 62
Agram (see Zagreb)
Agron, King of Illyria: 3
Akashi, Yasushi: 273, 277, 278
Alamannic: 4
Alamogordo, NM (USA): 175
Albania/Albanians (Shqipni): 29, 60, 63,
82, 84, 99, 104, 109, 151, 153, 178, 252
Albright, Madeleine Korbel: 278
Alexander, Harold: 147, 164, 165, 166
Alfieri, Dino: 118
Algiers (Algeria/Algerie): 146
Aljmas (near Osijek): 222
Ambrosio, Vittorio: 122
Amphitheater (Colosseum): 3
Andrew II (Arpad Dynasty):12
Andrianople: 5
Anfa (Casablanca), Morocco: 118
Anfuso, Filippo: 85

Anjou Dynasty: 12
Antić, Milan: 86
Antonescu, Ion M. (1882-1946): 80, 94
Anzio (Italy): 157, 158
Aquileia (Aquileja/Aglar): 6
Arabian/Arabs: 6
Arcadius, East. Rom. Emp. (395-408): 6
Arnautović, Damian: 61
Arpad: 12
Ashkenazic Jews: 41
Asia Minor: 14
Atlantic Security System: 76
Atomic Bomb (A-bombs): 69, 177
Attila (the Hun): 6
Attlee, Clement Richard (1883-1967): 176
Aurelian, Rom. Emp. (270-275): 4
Austerlitz/Slavkov (Czech Rep.): 18
Australia: 46, 71, 182, 225
Austria (Österreich) /Austrian: 52, 60, 65-66, 91, 164, 166, 174, 212, 218, 221-222, 226
   Austro-Hungarian: 7, 14, 17-19, 22, 27-28, 30-32, 38-41, 55, 63
   Fuerstenburg: 100
   Salzburg: 19, 172
   Vienna/Congress of Vienna: 16
AVNOJ/ACNLY (see Yugoslavia)
Avars: 6, 7, 8
Aviano Air Force Base, Italy: 293
Azana, Manuel: 62

B

Babić, Milan: 215
Bader, Paul: 142
Badinter, Robert: 223, 232
Badoglio, Pietro (1871-1956): 84, 151-153, 155
Bakar: 17
Baker, James A.: 214-216, 224, 239, 243
Balkan (Balkans): 7, 13, 146, 151, 154
Balbo, Italo (1896-1940): 66
Baltic Sea: 74
Banat: 17, 40
Banja Luka: 159, 293, 302
Bar (Antivari): 284
Baranja: 270, 307
Bari (Italy): 156, 159
Baron, Gunter: 288
Barthou, Jean Louis (1862-1934): 57:
Basariček, Đuro: 46
Bassiouni, Cherif: 251
Bastico, Ettore: 84
Battles:

Battle of Austerlitz (Slavkov): 18
Battle of Dunkerque (Dunkirk): 77
Battle of Lepanto: 14
Battle of Milvian Bridge (Saxa Rubra): 5
Battle of Neretva: 149
Battle of Sutjeska: 149, 150
Bauer, Antun of Zagreb: 184
Baumbach, Norbert: 94
Bavaria (Bayern): 11, 53
Bayazet I, Sultan (1389-1402): 13
Beirut (Lebanon): 199
Belgium (Belgique):18, 31, 44, 76, 167, 218, 232
Belgrade/Beograd: 18, 99, 101, 161-163
Belluno, Italy: 172
Benedictine Abby of Nursia: 157
Benedictine Monastery (Solin): 9
Bengasi (Libya): 151
Beničanci Oil Fields: 223, 307
Benkovac: 259
Benzler, Felix: 122, 127, 134, 135, 138
Benzon, Branko: 135
Berchtold, Leopold von (1863-1942): 32
Berlin: 160, 169, 174, 196
Berlusconi, Silvio:
Besserabia: 69, 78, 139
Bianci (Bijance): 10
Biddle, Anthony J. Drexel: 147
Bihać: 101, 159, 238, 267, 282-283, 286, 288, 293, 298
Bildt, Carl: 293, 306
Biograd (Biograd na Moru): 12, 259, 270
Bircanin: 142
Biševo (Busi): 32
Bismarck, Otto Christian von: 110
Bleiburg-Maribor Massacres: 175
Blum, Leon (1872-1950): 61
Boban, Mate: 257, 258, 259, 269
Bobetko, Janko: 296
Bohemia: 40, 66, 68, 71, 139
Böhme, Franz: 129, 134
Bonfatti: 103, 124
Bormann, Martin: 118
Bor Mining Area: 128
Borna (810-821): 9
Borovo Selo: 213
Bosanka Gradiška: 288
Bošković, Ruđer Josip (1711-1787): 17
Bosnia-Herzegovina: 13, 24, 27, 39-40, 113, 120, 132, 204, 207, 213, 217, 233, 237-238, 244, 249, 256, 262-263, 267-268, 270, 276, 278, 282, 284, 297, 304-307, 310
   Moslem/Muslem/Muslim/Muslimani: 13-14, 71, 113, 228, 230, 238-240, 250-253, 257, 259-261, 267, 269, 279-280,

284, 291, 296-298
ZOS (Zone of Separation): 308
Boutros, Ghali: 234, 248, 260, 273, 278, 293, 306
Brač (Brazza) Island: 18, 19, 32
Braići (Ravna Gora): 132
Branimir, Croatian Duke (879-892):10
Bratunac (Bosnia): 224
Brauchitsch, Walther von: 83-84, 97, 116
Braun nee Hitler, Eva (1910-1945): 172
Brazil (Recife Naval Station): 145
Brdo kod Kranja (Slovenia): 213
Bretton Woods, NH (USA): 161
Briand, Aristide (1882-1932): 46
Brijuni (Brioni): 1, 192, 220, 223
Brindisi (Italy): 155, 157
Briquemont, Francis: 271
Britain/British/England: 19, 28, 31, 33, 40, 46, 61, 66, 68, 70, 77, 80, 82-83, 87-88, 97, 114, 121, 138, 151, 153, 157-158, 161, 164, 168-169, 175, 178, 182, 199, 218, 232, 266, 298, 302
  Somaliland: 80
  Monarchy/Crown: 210
  RAF: 80
  Special Operations Exec.: 158
  Tyranny: 210
Broek, Hans van den: 221
Broz, Josip (see Tito)
Bronze Age: 1
Brsadin: 217
Bucharest (Bucureşti): 99
Budak, Mile: 58
Budapest (Buda-Pest): 99
Budisavljević, Srđan: 170
Bukovina: 78, 139
Bulgaria/Bulgarians/Bulgars: 6, 28-31, 46, 54-55, 57, 60, 62, 80, 82-83, 85, 91, 99, 103, 109, 139, 142-143, 148, 156, 162-163, 166-167, 202, 289
Bush, George H. W.: 206, 212, 245
Byzantine/Byzantium (see Istanbul)

C

Caesar Augustus (27 BC-14 AD): 3
Cairo (Egypt): 155
Calabria (Italy): 152, 153
Canada/Canadians: 46, 56, 73, 138, 142, 144, 158, 182, 226, 242
  Japanese Civilian Internment: 142
Candian Doge/Candian Sea: 10, 15
Carinthia: 2, 19

Carnegie Commission (1913): 29
Carniola: 2
Carpathian Mountain (anc. Carpates): 7
Carrington, Peter A. R.: 223, 225, 226
Carter, James Earl, Jr.: 284
Casablanca (French Morocco): 146
Caserta (Italy): 161
Cassino (Italy): 157
Castellano, Giuseppe: 153
Cathedral of St. Stephen (Zagreb): 185
Cavagnari, Domenico: 84
Cavallero, Ugo (1880-1943): 84, 86
Cavtat (Epidaurum): 2, 7
Celts: 2
Cervenko, Zvonimir: 296
Česky: 63, 139
Cetin (Cetingrad): 13, 18, 292
Cetina River: 2, 9
Chamberlain, Neville A. (1869-1940): 307
Channel Islands (a.k.a. Norman Isles): 78
Chapter "77": 197
Charette, De Hervé: 306
Charlemagne, Charles I (742-814): 8
Charles I, Emperor (1916-1918): 33, 38
Charles VI, Emperor (1711-1740): 17
Chemnitz (Germany): 163
Cheney, Richard (Dick): 240
Chiffot, Frédéric: 306
China/Chinese: 66, 182, 250
Chirac, Jacques: 307
Chotek, Countess Sofie: 31
Christian/Christianity: 14
Christopher, Warren: 283, 305
Churchill, Winston L. S. (1874-1965): 76, 120, 142, 148, 156, 161, 164-166, 168, 176
Ciano, Galeazzo (1903-1943): 64, 134
Cieszyn: 66, 139
Cincar-Marković, Aleks.: 78, 85, 86, 101
Čiovo (Bua) Island: 32
Cisleithan Territory: 30
Claes, Willy: 282, 291, 297
Claudius II, Rom. Emp. (268-270): 4
Clinton, William J.: 272-273, 276, 278, 280-281, 284, 291, 293, 297-298
Clodius, Carl: 110
Colombia: 138
Compiègne Forest (June 22, 1940): 77
Congress of Oppress. Nationalities: 38
Consmelli, Giuseppe: 85
Constantine I (King of Greece): 32
Constantine I, Rom. Emp. (306-337): 5
Constantinople (See Istanbul)
Continental Congress (1776): 210
Copenhagen, Denmark: 287
Corrasanti, Aldo: 223

325

Ćosić, Dobrica: 243, 257, 269
Costa Rica: 138
Cot, Jean: 271, 273
Cres (Cherso) Island: 8, 20, 32
Croat/Croatian (Hrvatska): 8-10, 14, 16-20, 22, 30, 38-39, 44, 52, 54, 71, 104, 110-111, 113, 122, 126, 131-132, 135, 140, 148, 167-168, 173, 199- 205, 207, 210-212, 218, 220, 225, 228, 230-240, 242, 245, 250-253, 257, 259, 269-271, 279, 281, 286-289, 294, 298, 301, 304-305, 308
Banovina Hrvatska (1939): 71
Bašćanska Ploća: 11
Constitution of 1990: 207, 212, 245
Constitutional Law (Državno Pravo): 12
Converted to Christianity: 8
Cravat or "Kravata" (Necktie): 24
Croatian Anthem: 20, 208
Croat-Bosniac Federation: 275, 280, 286, 305, 307
Croatian Coat-of-Arms: 208
Croatian Defense Council (HVO): 276, 280, 282
Croatian Flag: 57, 208, 298
Croat (Hrvati) Tribes: 7
Currency "Kuna" (Marten): 278
Dalmatian Dog: 24
Dalmatic Garment: 24
Democratic Union (CDU): 203, 221, 305
Eagle (Hrvatski Orao): 50
Elections: 42, 47, 66, 214, 252, 305
Émigrés: 58
Extraordinary Decree & Order: 116
German Frontier: 107
German "Legion": 100
Grammar Published in 1650: 15
Independent Croatian State (1941-1945): 55, 100, 143
Independence Day (June 25, 1991): 217
Kings of Croatia: 10
Language Newspapers:
  "Croatia Press": 55, 59
  "Croatian Rights": 58
  "Dalmatin": 19
  "Danica" (Morning Star): 20
  "Dom" (Home): 25
  "Independent Croatian State": 59
  "Novine Hrvatske": 20
  "Zora Dalmatinska": 21
Matica Hrvatska (Matrix Croatia): 21, 202
Matica Ilirska (Matrix Illyrian): 21
Military Operation "Storm": 298
National Bank (NBH): 298
National Guards: 213, 221, 223
Parliament (Sabor): 12, 17, 21-23, 38, 46, 71, 143, 204, 221, 232, 305
Party of Rights (Frankists/Frankovci): 26
Peasants Party: 26, 39, 42, 45, 50, 60, 63, 71, 93, 305
Republicans: 44
Republican Peasant Party: 42
Serb Coalition: 26
Social Democrats of Croatia: 305
Statehood Day (May 30, 1991): 215
Supreme Council: 228
Territorial Defense Force: 213
Train of Freedom: 302
Triune Kingdom (1848): 21
Ustaše/Ustaša: 47, 59, 100, 120, 170, 173
Crystal Night (Kristallnacht): 66
CSCE/OSCE: 206, 215, 220, 222, 224-226, 232, 239, 275, 284, 308, 310
Cuba: 138
Čubrilović, Vaso: 63
Cuéllar, Javier Pérez de: 226
Custozza, near Verona (Italy): 22
Cvetković, Dragiša: 67, 70, 85, 86, 87
Czartoryski, Adam Juraj (1770-1861): 21
Czechs/Czechoslovakia: 30, 38, 45-46, 53, 66, 68, 71, 139, 174, 192, 197

D

Đakovica: 203
Đakovo: 23
Dalj (near Osijek): 1, 221, 222
Dalmatae (Illyrian tribe): 2
Dalmatia/Dalmatian (Dalmacija): 2, 4, 6-11, 14, 16-19, 32, 40, 101, 153, 164- 165, 222, 223
Dalmatin (1806-1810): 19
Dandolo, Vinko: 19
D'Annunzio, Gabriele (1863-1938): 41
Danilo (near Šibenik): 1
Danube (Dunav) River: 6, 92, 126
Danzig (Gdańsk): 55, 71, 73
Davidović, "Ljubo" Ljubomir: 63, 67
Dayton, Ohio (USA): 305
Debrecen (Hungary): 160, 165
DeGaulle, Charles A. J. (1890-1970): 78, 79, 147, 162
Degrelle, Leon (Rexists): 76
Deletovci: 307
Delnice: 101
De Michelis, Gianni: 218
Demitrius II (King of Macedonia): 3
Denmark: 75, 167, 218

Deutschland (see Germany)
DeVecchi, Cesare: 84
Dictatorships in Europe (1922-1936): 60
Dimitrijević, Dragutin T.: 26, 28, 31, 33
Dinara Mount: 294
Diocletian, Rom. Emp./ (284-305): 4
Dizdarević, Raif: 201
Djilas, Milovan: 82
Dobrunja (Dobrogea): 80, 139
Documents/Exhibits/Readings:
Aggression by the Serbian Regime: 241
Pres. Clinton's Ltr. to Congress: 276
Atlantic Charter (1941): 121, 168
Berlin-Rome-Tokyo Axis "Tripartite": 81
Bosnia & Croatia Peace Agmt: 274
Bosnia-Herzegovina Arms Embargo: 300
Charter of Paris (1990): 207
Circular of the Reich Foreign Ministry: 58
Conference on Resettlement: 130
Confiscation of Eccl. Property: 119
Conflict in Yugoslavia: 219
Contact Gp. Ministerial Statement: 292
Conversation: Hitler & Mussolini: 123
Conversation with King Alexander: 53
Corfu Declaration (1917): 34
Croatia and Bosnia Joint Council: 309
Croatian-Serbian Joint Declaration: 271
Discussions on Resettlement: 115
German-Soviet Nonaggression Pact: 69
Guidlines in Religious Activities: 119
Hitler's Directive No. 25: 89, 91, 93
Hitler's Directive No. 26: 95
Imminent Action in the Balkans: 97
London Conference on Yugoslavia: 248
Meetings bet. Ribbentrop & Ciano: 105
Memo by Reich State Secretary: 77
Memo from Franz Rademacher to Martin Luther: 133
Memo from Grew to Truman: 172
Memo of Situation in Yugoslavia: 64
Message by Franklin D. Roosevelt: 138
Order of Reich Chancellor: 56
Political Report from Yugoslavia: 67
Political Position of Yugoslavia: 83
Principles Endorsed by Contact Gp.: 303
Reich Foreign Minister Circular: 111
Reich Fgn. Minister for the Führer: 110
Resettlement of Serbs from Croatia: 125
Resettlement of Slovenes: 108
Sarajevo Marketplace Shelling: 272
Serb-četnici of Mihajlović: 148
Situation in Serbia: 135
Telegram to Reich Foreign Minister: 131
United Nations Declaration: 140
United States Forces in Iceland: 117

US Policy on Bosnia-Herzegovina: 294
US Policy Toward Yugoslavia (Feb 1954): 187
US Policy Toward Yugoslavia (Apr 1955): 189
US Policy Toward Yugoslavia (Nov 1955): 193
US Policy Toward Yugoslavia (Apr 1957): 194
President Bush's Report on CSCE: 219
President Clinton's Statement on UN-NATO Airstrikes: 291
President Clinton's Welcome Ending UN-NATO Airstrikes: 304
US Promotes Peace in Yugoslavia: 226
US Sec. State Baker in Belgrade: 216
US Statement on UNSCR 1009: 299
War Crimes in Yugoslavia: 253
War Crimes Tribunal: 285
White House Conf. Statement: 304
Yugoslavia Adhesion to the Tripartite Pact (Axis): 88
Yugoslavia and the USSR: 79
Yugoslavia's International Position: 190
Yugoslavia's Unspeakable Savagery 246
Dodecanese Islands (Greece): 84
Dole, Robert (Sen. R-KS): 278, 283, 297
Domagoj, Gov. of Dalmatia (864-876): 9
Domenican Republic: 138
Dondolo, Vinko: 19
Dönitz, Karl: 173
Đorđević, Milorad: 76
Drasković, Milorad: 34
Drava River: 7, 100
Drew, Samuel Nelson: 301
Drežnik: 18
Drina River: 6
Drnovšek, Janez: 201
Drvar (Bosnia): 159
Drvenik (Zirona) Is.: 32
Državno Pravo: 12
Držislav, King Stjepan (969-997): 10
Dubrava: 82
Dubrovnik (Ragusa): 8, 10, 12, 16-18, 165, 226, 228-229, 234, 287, 301
Dufour, Albert: 52, 54
Duisburg (Germany): 42
Đukanović, Blasi: 142
Duke of Spoleto: 109
Dulles, John Foster (1888-1959): 192
Đuričić, Marko: 34
Đurišić, Pavle: 169
Dusseldorf: 42
Duvno Polje (Bosnia): 11
Dvor (Bosnia): 283

E

Eagleburger, Lawrence: 225, 249
Eastern Orthodox: 29
Eastern Roman Empire: 6, 11
ECCY: 226, 235
ECMM: 242
Edirne (Adrianople): 29
Egypt/Egyptian: 4, 83, 243
Eichmann, Adolph (1906-1962): 126
Einstein, Albert (1879-1955): 51, 69, 144
Eisenhower, Dwight D. (1890-1969): 145, 147, 153, 155-156, 173
Elections: 42, 47, 66, 203-204, 214, 245, 305
El Salvador: 138
Emmanuele III, Vittorio (1900-1948): 69, 119, 151
Encyclical (Encyclicus): 63
England (See Britain/British)
Enola Gay (B-29 Superfortress): 177
Epiru/Epeiros: 2
Erdut: 221, 222, 234, 270
Eritrea (Ethiopia): 60
Estonia: 38, 60, 69, 74, 78, 84, 139
Ethiopia (Abyssinia): 60
Europe/European:
    European Community (EC): 218, 220-226, 229-232, 238-239, 244, 248, 304
    European Congress of 1878: 24
    V-E Day (Victory in Europe): 174

F

Faeroe Island & Iceland: 76
Falange Party: 62
Feine, Gerhard: 94, 96
Fenrick, William: 251
Ferdinand, Franz (1863-1914): 31
Ferdinand I (1558-1564) Rom. Emp.: 14
Ferdinand I, Emp. (1835-1848): 21
Ferdinand I of Bulgaria (1887-1918): 27
Ferdinand II (1619-1637): 15
Feudalism: 11, 20
Finland: 38, 69, 75, 139, 167
Fiume (see Rijeka)
Flavius, Rom. Emp. (475-476): 6
Foggia (Italy): 155
Foscani (Romania): 160
Fotić, Constantin: 147
France/French: 14, 18-19, 28, 33, 40, 46, 52, 61-62, 66, 68, 70-71, 77, 79, 97, 167, 178, 182, 199, 218, 229, 232, 242-243, 266-267, 280, 291, 298, 301-302

Free French Force: 116, 140, 157
French Indochina: 119
French Third Republic: 79
Maquis (France Force): 79
Marseilles: 57
Francis Duke of Lorraine (1706-1765): 17
Francis I, Emp. (1804-1835): 19
Franco, Francisco B. (1892-1975): 62, 82
Frank, Josip (1844-1911): 26
Frankfurt (Germany): 42
Frankish Missionaries: 8
Frankopan, Krsto Franjo (1643-1671): 16
Franks/Frankish: 4, 9
Frasure, Robert C.: 301
Franz Josif, Emperor (1848-1916): 17, 22, 24, 33
Freundt, Alfred: 91, 93, 94, 96
Freyberg: 114
Friederburg, Hans G.: 174
Frlec, Boris: 222
Frowick, Robert: 310

G

Gacka: 11
Gaj, Ljudevit: 20
Galatz (Romania): 160
Galbraith, Peter: 275, 276, 288
Galicia (Halicz/Galich): 19, 40
Garašanin, Ilija (1812-1874): 21
Gaul (France): 4
Gavin, James Maurice (1907-1990): 151
Gavrilović, Milan: 77, 93, 96
General System of Preference: 216
Geneva/Geneve (Switzerland):
    Geneva Peace Conference, 1918: 39
    Geneva Conventions: 104, 244, 251, 256, 263
Genocide Convention: 263
Genoese/Genoa (Italy): 12
Genscher, Hans Dietrich: 218, 222, 232
Genthius, Illyrian King: 3
George II (King of Greece): 107, 114
Gepidae: 6
Germany (Deutschland): 28, 30-32, 46, 55, 60-62, 66, 69-71, 73, 75, 85-86, 97, 101, 104-105, 107, 111, 114, 118, 134, 138-141, 143, 154, 156-158, 163, 167-168, 174, 221, 229, 232, 298
    Berlin "Walls": 196
    Democratic Republic (GDR): 190, 202
    East Prussia (Ostpreussen): 71
    Fed. Republic of Germany (FRG): 190
    Final Solution "Endlösung:" 141

German-Italian Frontier: 118
German Language (1784): 18
German Ranger Commando: 155
German Reich (1938-1945): 65
German East-West Reunif. (1990): 204
Gestapo: 56, 180
Gustav Line: 157, 158
Lightning War (Blitzkrieg): 70, 99
Nazi/Nazism: 62, 228
Nuremburg/Nürnberg Laws (1935): 60
Nuremburg/Nürnberg Trial: 178-180,182
Schutzstaffel-SS: 28, 53, 180
V-1 (Vergeltenungswaffe Ein): 160
V-2 (Vergeltenungswaffe Zwein): 160
Volksdeutsche (German nationals): 74,
89, 118, 120, 126, 131
West Germany joined NATO: 190
Gdynia/Gdingen (Poland): 161
Gheorghieff, Vlatko: 57
Gibraltar (British Colony): 82
Gingrich, Newt (Rep. R-GA): 283
Glagolitic (Old Slavonic): 11, 17
Glina: 217, 232
Goebbels, Josef Paul (1897-1945): 179
Goražde: 238, 267, 276-278, 293, 302
Gorbachev, Mikhail: 199
Gore, Albert Jr.: 287
Göring, Hermann W. (1893-1946): 60, 69,
100
Gorizia/Gorica/Görz: 19, 32, 172
Gornji Milanovac: 134
Gornji Vakuf (Bosnia): 279
Gorski Kotari: 18
Gospić: 223, 302
Goths/Gothic: 6
Goulding, Marrack Irvine: 238
Gradisca: 32
Grandja, Ivan: 46
Granić, Mate: 270, 271, 288
Gran Sasso, Monte (Italy): 152
Gratian, Rom. Emp. (375-383): 5
Greece/Greeks (Ella/Hellas): 2, 28, 30-31,
57, 60, 82, 84, 86, 93, 97, 99, 103-104,
107, 109, 114, 129, 153, 158, 162, 165-
167, 273
    Canea: 114
    Crete (Kriti/Candia) Island: 29, 82, 114
    Epirus (Epeiros):
    George II, King: 107, 114
    Heraklion: 114
    Logothetopulos, George: 107
    Maleme: 114
    Maliakós (Maliacur) Gulf: 106
    Peloponnese: 158
    Piraeus (Piraiéus): 83

Salonika (Thessaloniki): 29, 32, 33, 86,
99, 103, 109, 166
Sitia Bay: 114
Suda Bay: 114
Thessaly: 158
Tsolakoglou, George: 107
Tsouderos, Emmanuel: 107
Greenland (Grønland): 75
Green Line (Beirut, Lebanon): 199
Gregorić, Danilo: 85
Grgur (Bishop of Nin): 11
Grosskoff, George Wilhelm: 120
Groves, Leslie R.: 144
Grujica (Gruica): 32
Guam Island (USA Possession): 137, 140
Guatemala: 138
Gubec, Matija (1573): 14, 15
Gundulić, Ivan Franjo (1589-1638): 15
Gustav Line: 158
Gypsies: 41, 290

H

Habsburg (see Austria)
Hadžič, Izet: 291
Haiti (Haïti): 138
Hague, (Netherlands): 220, 223
Hague Convention/Regs.: 99, 104, 105
Hanford, WA (USA): 145
Harriman, Averill William (1891-1986): 159
Heeren, Viktor von: 64, 74, 78, 83, 85, 86
Hektorović, Petar (1487-1571): 13
Helsinki (Finland): 206, 243, 284
Hendaye, France: 82
Henderson, George: 178
Heraclius, Byzantine Emp. (610-641): 8
Herceg (Duke): 12
Herzegovina (See Bosnia-Herzegovina)
Herzog, Roman: 223
Heydrich, Reinhard (1904-1942): 131, 144
Himmler, Heinrich (1900-1945): 53, 67,
118, 120, 126, 179
Hindenburg, Paul von (1847-1934): 52
Hinković, Hinko: 34
Histria/Histri (see Istra/Istria)
Hitler, Adolph "Führer" (1889-1945): 52,
61, 63, 66, 69, 71, 73, 82-83, 85-89, 93,
100, 109, 116, 118-120, 128, 131, 134,
141, 152, 172, 176, 179
    Hitler's Directive (Weisung):128
    No. 18: 83
    No. 20 "Marita": 84
    No. 21 "Barbarossa": 84, 116
    No. 28 "Merkur": 114

Hitler's Speech to Reichstag: 73, 74
Holbrooke, Richard: 286, 298, 304, 307-308
Holloman AFB, NM (USA): 175
Holy Bible: 15
Homo Crapiniensis: 1
Honduras: 138
Honorius I, W. Rom. Emp. (395-423): 6
Horstenau, Edmund G. von: 101, 116
Hoxha, Enver: 178
Hrvatska (see Croatia)
Hungary/Magyars: 10, 13-14, 18, 20, 26, 40, 54-55, 68, 80, 82, 87, 99, 101, 103, 139, 160, 165, 167-168, 192, 200, 218, 222, 226, 252, 267, 289, 298
Huns: 6
Hurd, Douglas: 282
Hvar (Lessina/Pharos) Island: 2, 32, 157

I

Igman, Mount (Sarajevo): 301
Iguandon Dinosaur: 1
Ilić, Bogoljub: 93
Illyria/Illyrians/Illyricum: 2-4, 6-8, 18-21
  Illyrian Movement: 21
Ilovik (Asinello): 32
IMRO (Int. Macedonian Rev. Org.): 57
India: 46, 182, 250
Inferno (Dante's): 290
Inge, Peter: 296
Innsbruck (Austria): 172
Int'l Commissions/Committees:
  Bank (World Bank): 161
  Commit. Red Cross (ICRC): 230, 245-246, 250, 253, 256-257
  Monetary Fund (IMF): 161
  Peace Implementation Council: 306
  Trident Conference (1943): 150
Iran (Persia): 5, 6, 7, 12, 123
Iraq/Irak: 206
Ireland (Hibernia): 46
  Irish Free State: 46
Iron Age: 1
Issa (see Vis)
Istra/Istria/Histria/Istrian: 1, 2, 7, 14, 18, 30, 32, 40, 164, 264
Italian/Italy: 6, 28, 30-32, 38, 46, 54, 60, 62, 66, 77, 83-84, 86, 101, 104-105, 118, 135, 138, 140-142, 153-154, 157-158, 161-162, 218
  Albania: 68, 82
  Armistice (1943): 153
  East Africa (1936-1941): 60

Fascism/Fascists: 62, 228
  Italian Socialist Republic (1943): 152
  Somaliland (1936-1941): 60
Istanbul (Constantinople/Byzantium): 6, 7
Iwo Jima Island (Western Pacific): 170
Izetbegović, Alija: 258, 260, 269, 275, 280-281, 305

J

Jajce (Bosnia): 101
Janković, Milojko: 103
Janvier, Bernard: 310
Japan (Nippon) Japanese: 27, 31, 46, 61, 66, 101, 104, 119, 137-138, 140, 144, 176
  Hiroshima: 177
  Jawata (Kyushu Island): 160
  Nagasaki: 177
Jasenovac: 132
Jeftić, Bogoljub: 60, 94
Jelačić, Josep (1801-1859): 21
Jelić, Branimir: 55, 59
Jemissaries: 13
Jesuit Monastery in Dubrovnik: 15
Jesuit Order (1534): 15, 17
Jeszenszky, Geza: 273
Jevđevic: 142
Jew/Jewish: 28, 41, 79, 126-127, 129, 132, 134, 137-138, 141, 150, 190
  Ashkenazic Jews: 41
  Sephardic Jews: 41
Jodl, Wilhelm (1890-1946): 109, 174
Johnson, Lyndon Baines (1908-1973): 196
Johnson, Ralph: 228
Jokšimović, Dragić: 182
Joseph I (1678-1711), Emp.(1705-1711): 16, 17
Joseph II, Emperor (1765-1790): 16, 17
Jovanović, Dragoljub: 63
Jovanović, Ivan: 63
Jovanović, J. M.: 67
Jovanović, Slobodan: 94, 147
Jovanović, Vladislav: 271
Jovian, Rom. Emp. (363-364): 5
Jović, Borisav: 204, 212
Julian, Rom. Emp. (361-363): 5
Juppé, Alán: 282, 284
Justinian I, Rom. Emp. (527-565)): 6, 7
  Justinian Code: 5
Jurandvor (Krk island): 11

K

Kadijević, Veljko: 211, 223, 224

Kálmán, King of Hungary (1095-1116): 12
Kalnik, Mount: 17
Kamphoevener von: 107
Karađorđević Dynasty:40, 41
Karadžić, Radovan: 258, 269, 284, 295, 297, 310
Karadžić, Vuk Stefanović (1787-1864): 20
Kardelj, Edvard: 82, 178
Karlobag: 17
Karlovac (Karlstadt): 17, 18, 19, 259, 288
Karlsbad (Austria): 172
Kasche, Siegfried: 101, 109-110, 120, 122, 131, 135
Kašić, Bartul (1575-1650): 15
Katyn Forest: 150
Kavala: 29
Keitel, Wilhelm: 174
Kellogg, Frank B. (1856-1937): 46
Kennedy, John F. (1917-1963): 196
Kesselring, Albert: 152, 153, 164
Kidnapped Christians: 14
Kijevo: 213
Kinkel, Klaus: 279
Kirk, Alexander C.: 174
Kleist, Ewald von (1881-1954): 99, 101
Klis: 9
Knin: 12, 15, 201, 212, 223, 231-232, 242, 298, 302
Kočevje: 120, 126, 131
Kohl, Helmut: 200, 218, 222, 232
Kolsek, Konrad: 218
Končar, Rade: 82
Kopaćina (Brač island): 1
Korçë (Albania): 83
Korčula (Curzola/Corcyra Nigra): 2, 12, 32
Kordun: 132
Korea (Tae Han Minguk): 27, 169
Korfanty, Adalbert: 42
Korošec, Anton: 34, 38
Koschnick, Hans: 279
Kosova: 63, 113, 197. 199, 204, 212, 215, 222, 252, 308
Kosova Polje (Blackbirds Plain): 13, 201
Kosovska Vitina: 203
Kostajnica: 221, 222
Kostec, Josip: 123
Koštio (Brać Island): 1
Košutić, August: 93, 94, 225
Kotor (Cattaro): 8, 18, 92, 103, 284
Kragujevac: 134
Krajina (Military Frontier/Militärgrenze): 15-17, 19, 24, 211-215, 217, 237, 244, 259, 276, 282-283, 286, 288, 291, 297-298
Krakow (Cracow/Kraukau): 7
Kraljevica: 17

Kraljevo: 134
Kranj: 19
Krbava: 11
Krešimir I, King (935-945): 10
Krešimir, Mihajlo II, King (949-969): 10
Krešimir III, King (1000-1030): 10, 12
Krešimir, Petar IV, King (1058-1074): 10
Krk (Curicum/Veglia) Island: 2, 8, 20
Krsko Nuclear Power Station: 287
Krupanj: 127
Kruševo: 26, 223
Kruščica (Dalmatia, Croatia): 14
Kruzel, Joseph J.: 301
Kublai Khan: 12
Kućan, Milan: 203, 212, 246
Kulovec, Antun: 86
Kumanovo: 167
Kupa (Kulpa) River: 101
Kupres (Bosnia): 282
Kupreško Polje (Bosnia): 159
Kuribayachi, Tadamichi: 170
Kurile Island: 169, 177
Kurland: 38
Kustenland: 2
Kuwait: 206
Kvarner (Quarnero) Island: 2, 22
Kvaternik, Eugene (1825-1871): 22
Kvaternik, Slavko (1878-1947): 58-59, 100, 116, 118

L

Labin (Albona): 2
Ladislas I (László I): 12
Laganja, Ante: 34
Lake, Anthony: 298
Lanxade, Jacques: 296
Lastovo (Lagosta) island: 32
Latvia (Latvija): 60, 69, 74, 78, 84, 139
Laval, Pierre (1883-1945): 79, 122
Law and Order: 24, 66
Lazar, Czar of Serbia: 13
League of Nations (1920-1946): 42, 50, 55-56, 75, 139
Lebanon (Liban): 116, 199
Lechfeld (near Augsburg): 11
Lemnos Island (Greece): 82
Lenin (Uljanov, Vladimir Ilych): 140, 158
Leningrad (see Petersburg/Petrograd)
Lepoglava: 12
Leopold I (b. 1640), Emp. (1658-1705): 16
Leopold II, Emp. (1790-1792): 18
Leopold III, King of Belg. (1934-1951): 76
Leskošek, Franc: 82

Leuters, Rudolph: 145
Lezajić, Rajko: 286
Liaotung Peninsula: 27
Liburnia/Liburni:Liburnian: 2
Libya (Jamahiriya): 28, 66
Lidice (Czech Republic): 144
Lieberman, Joseph (Sen. R-CT): 297
Lijevče Polje: 170
Lika: 11, 132
Lincoln, Abraham (1809-1865): 308
Lincoln "Red Brigade": 62
List, Wilhelm: 99, 128
Lithuania (Lietuva): 60, 68-69, 73-74, 78, 84, 139
Livno (Bosnia): 101, 159
Livonia (Latvian-Estonian): 38
Ljotić, Dimitrije: 64, 122, 173, 289
Ljubijankić, Irfan: 292
Ljubljana (Laibach/Emona): 18-19, 101, 126, 153, 164, 218, 220, 245, 261
Logothetopulos, George (see Greece)
Löhr, Alexander (1885-1947): 114, 151
Lombards/Lombardy: 6-8, 18-19
London Charter: 178
Lorković, Mladen: 58, 110
Lošinj (Lussino) Island: 20, 32
Ludovik II (King): 13
Lučić, Hanibal (1485-1553): 13
Lunjević, Nikodije: 26
Lunjević, Nikola: 26
Luther, Martin: 118, 127, 138
Luzon Island (Philippines): 140

M

Maastricht (Netherlands): 232
MacArthur, Douglas (1880-1964): 176-177, 182
Macedonia/Macedonians: 24, 26, 29, 39, 83, 109, 117, 148, 158, 166, 204, 206, 213, 217, 224, 228, 235, 237-238, 251, 265-266, 272, 308
Maček, Vladko (1879-1964): 50, 59, 62-63, 66, 70, 86, 91, 93-94, 96-97
MacKenzie, Lewis: 244
MacVeigh, Lincoln: 155
Maddalena Island (Sardinia, Italy): 152
Maginot Line (France): 77
Magyars/Magyrization (see Hungary):
Majevica Mountains (Bosnia): 286
Major, John: 248
Malletke, Walter: 96
Malo Grašće (Brać Island): 1
Mamoru, Shigemitsu: 177

Manchuria (Manchukuo): 52, 177
Mandić, Ante: 170
Mann, Henrich (1871-1950): 51
Manolić, Josip: 276
Maps:
Banovina of Croatia, 1939: 72
Banovine of the Kingdom of Yugo.: 49
Ind. State of Croatia, 1941-1945: 102
Kingdom of Serbs, Croats & Slovenes, 1921-1928: 43
Republic of Croatia, 1990 (Republika Hrvatska): 209
Socialist Rep. Croatia, 1945-1990: 181
Maria Theresa, Queen of Austria (1740-1780): 17, 18
Marie Louise (1791-1847): 19
Maribor (Marburg): 99, 100, 175
Marinković, Vojislav: 34
Maritsa (Evros) River: 29
Marković, Ante: 202, 212, 218, 229
Marković, Zvonimir: 275
Marshall, George (1880-1959): 147, 176
Martić, Milan: 275, 297
Marx, Karl (1818-1883): 140
Marxist-Leninist: 162
Mašin, Queen Draga (nee Lunjević): 26
Maslenica Bridge: 224, 257, 269, 270
Matesa, Zlatko: 305
Maun (Maon): 32
Maximian, Rom. Emp. (286-305): 4
Maximilian: 15
Mazowiecki, Tadeusz: 247, 252, 297
Mažuranić, Ivan (1814-1890): 23
Mbaye, Keba: 151
Međumurje: 17, 21
Meindl, Eugen: 114
Mein Kampf: 290
Memel (Lithuania): 68, 139
Merchant Ship "Sessa": 127
Mesić, Stjepan: 214, 218, 222, 224, 228, 276
Mesolithic Age: 1
Metaxas Line (Greece): 99, 103
Metković (Narona/Muicurum): 2, 7, 15
Metternich, Klemens von (1773-1859): 19
Mexico (México/Méjico): 62
Michael, King of Romania: 162
Midway Islands (Pacific Ocean): 144, 146
Mielec (Poland): 161
Mihajlović, Dragoljub (1893-1946): 112-113, 132, 142, 147, 151, 162-163, 170, 228, 231, 253
Mihanović, Antun (1796-1861): 20
Mihić: 142
Mikoyan, Anastas Ivanović: 76

Milan, King (1868-1889): 26
Milanovac (Serbija): 134
Milković, Josip: 6, 58
Military Frontier: (see Krajina)
Millon, Charles: 306, 310
Milošević, Slobodan: 200-205, 211-212, 214-217, 230-231, 239, 262, 269, 278, 289, 302, 305, 307-308, 310
Milošević, Marjana (Marković): 205, 217
Milutinovic, Ivan: 82
Mindszenty, Józef (1892-1975): 192
Mirgorod (Ukraine): 159, 160
Mirkovci: 221
Miroslav, King (945-949): 10
Mislav, Dalmatian Governor (835-845): 9
Mladenovac (Serbija): 175
Mladić, Ratko: 280, 281, 296, 297, 310
Mljet (Meleda Island): 32
Moasia: 5
Mock, Alois: 223, 232
Mohács (Hungary): 13
Mohammed II, Sultan (1451-1484): 13
Molotov, Mikhailovic V.: 96
Monfalcone, Italy: 109, 172
Monroe "Doctrine" (1823): 75
Monroe, James (1758-1831): 76
Montenegrins/Montenegro (Crno Gora): 24, 28-31, 38, 113, 118, 148, 153, 162, 169, 204, 206, 213, 225-226, 228-229, 234, 243, 250, 282, 284, 301, 308, 310
    League of Communists: 202
Moravia (Mähren): 40, 66, 68, 71, 139
Morgan, Frederick E.: 174
Mostar: 239, 279, 302
Most Favored Nation: 216
Mujaheddin (Islamic Holy Warriors):198
Mukden (Shenyang): 52
Munich (München): 66, 152, 286, 307
Murad I, Sultan (1359-1389): 12
Mur (Mura) River: 99
Mureck: 99
Muslims (see Bosnia)
Mussert, Anton Andrian (1894-1946): 76
Mussolini, Benito "Il Duce" (1883-1945): 52, 66, 69, 82-86, 88, 107, 109, 135, 151-152, 172, 176
Mutimir, Ban/Governor (892-910): 10
Mutiny of "Sankt Georg" in 1918: 37
Mystery of War: 155

N

Načertanije (Blueprint): 21
Nadinsko Blato (Mud): 167

Nagodba "Compromise" of 1868: 23
Nagy, Imre: 192
Nambiar, Satish: 237
Naples (Napoli, Italy): 161, 164
Napoleon (Bonaparte): 19
NATO: 186, 255, 261, 268, 272-273, 277-278, 280, 282-284, 291, 293-294, 297, 302, 304-306
    AWACS: 262
    Deliberate Force (DF): 302
    IFOR: 306, 308, 310
    RRF: 293, 296, 302
Nedić, Milan: 113, 122-123, 173, 228, 289
Neolithic/Stone Age: 1
Neretljani/Neretni (Pirates): 2, 9, 10
Neretva/Narenta/Naro River: 2, 9, 15
Netherlands(Holland): 17, 182, 266, 280, 291, 302
Neurath, Konstantin von (1873-1956): 64
New Order in Asia: 66
New Order in Europe: 86
New Zealand: 46, 71, 157, 182, 267
NGO (Non-Gov't Organization): 230, 264
Nicaragua: 138
Nicopolis (Nikopol): 13
Nikolas I, King of Montenegro: 33, 38, 118
Nikolas II (Czar, Russia): 27
Nimitz, Chester W.: 176
Nin/Nona/Aenona: 2, 9, 11
Ninčić, Momčilo: 34, 94, 142
Nišava River: 99
Niš (Nissa/Naissus): 99, 165
Normandy Peninsula D-Day: 160
Norway/Norwegian: 75, 76, 83, 167
Novak's "Blue Guard": 154
Novigrad (Channel/Sea): 14, 224, 270
Novi Sad (Vojvodina): 222
Novo Mesto: 101
Numerian, Roman Emperor (283-284):

O

Oak Ridge, TN (USA): 145
Obrenović, Aleksandar I: 25
Obrenović, Milan (1868-1889): 24
Obrovac: 259
Octavianus, Augustus (27 BC-14 AD): 3
Odacer: 6
Oeta Mountain: 106
Ogata, Sadako: 261, 294
O'Grady, Scott F.: 293
Ohrid Lake (Makedonija): 92
Okučani: 224, 288
Olib Island: 32

Omarska Prison (Bosnia): 273
Omiš (Oneum): 2
Opatija (Abbazia): 142
Operations (Code Names):
  Achse (Axle): 153
  Barbarossa: 84, 89, 116
  Case White: 71
  Desert Shield: 206
  Desert Storm: 206
  Dragoon: 164
  Enormous: 175
  Felix: 82
  Frantic: 159, 163
  Husky: 150, 151, 158
  Konstantin: 153
  Marita: 84, 89
  Merkur: 114
  Overlord: 150, 156, 158, 160
  Punishment: 99
  Rösselsprung (Knight's Move): 159, 162
  Ruebezahl: 162
  Sea Lion: 79
  Shingle: 157
  Tidalwave: 151
  Torch: 145
  Venona: 175
  Weser: 75
  Yellow: 76
Opsahl, Torkel: 251
Orahovac: 203
Oran (Algeria): 145
Orašje (Bosnia): 291
OSCE (see CSCE)
Osijek (Mursa): 3, 101, 222-224, 228-229
Osor Island: 8
Ostrogothic/Ostrogoths: 6
Ostroleka (Poland): 162
Oswald, Lee Harvey (1939-1963): 196
Otto I, "Otto the Great" (912-973): 10, 11
Ottoman/Ottoman Turks (see Turkey)
Owen, David Herold: 251, 258, 293
Ozren Mountain: 150

P

Pact (see Agreements/Treaties)
Padua/Padova (Italy): 172
Pag (Pago) Island: 15, 32
Pahlevi, Mohammad Riza: 123
Pahlevi, Riza Shah: 123
Pajacević, Theodore (Ban): 26
Pakistan: 198, 267
Pakrac: 212, 224
Palacol (Lalazzuoli): 32

Pale: 292, 293, 302
Paleolithic Age: 1
Palestine (Palaestina/Canaan): 69
Panama: 138
Panić, Milan: 243
Pannonia/Pannonian: 3, 4, 8, 9, 11
Papen, Franz von (1879-1969): 52
Paris (France): 162, 306
Pašić, Nikola P. (1845-1926): 34, 42
Paulist Missionary Society: 12, 15
Paulus, Aemilius: 3
Paulus, Friedrich (1890-1957): 91
Pavelić, Ante (1869-1959): 50, 59, 100, 109, 113, 116, 120, 122, 154, 228
Pearl Harbor: 137
Peć (Pech/Ipek): 167, 203
Pelagruža (Pelagosa) Island: 32
Pelješac (Sabbioncello) Peninsula: 163
Perelyakin, Aleksander: 287
Perić, Stjepo: 58
Pernar, Ivan: 46
Perović, Ivo: 57, 86
Perry, William J.: 276, 293, 296
Persecute: 14:
Perseus (King of Macedonia): 3
Persia/Persians (See Iran)
Peručka Dam (Nasip): 250, 258
Pešić, Petar: 86
Petacci, Clara (1912-1945): 172
Petain, Philippe H. (1856-1951): 79, 122
Petar I, King (1903-1921): 26, 33
Petersburg (Petrograd): 27, 37, 84, 157
Petrinja: 223
Philip V (King of Macedonia): 3
Philippines: 182
Piacenza (Italy): 296
Pindus Mountains (Pindhos Óros): 106
Pinheiro, Joao De Deus: 221
Pirot (Bulgaria): 99
Piryatin (Ukraine): 159, 160
Placenta Bay (Newfoundland): 120
Plitvice National Park (Croatia): 213
Ploče: 302
Ploesti (Romania): 94, 150, 151, 157, 161, 162
Plomin (Flamona): 2
Plotnikov, Viktor A.: 77
Podgorica: 38, 203
Pola (see Pula)
Polaca: 213
Poland/Poles (Polska):30, 38, 42, 46, 60, 66, 69-71, 73, 139, 150, 157, 162, 169
Polo, Marco (1254-1324): 12, 52, 63
Poltava (Ukraine): 159, 160, 161
Ponikve (near Varaždin): 1

Poos, Jacques: 218, 221
Pope Agatho (678-681): 8
Pope Benedict XIII (1724-1730): 17
Pope John Paul II: 280
Pope John IV (640-642): 8
Pope John X (914-928): 11
Pope Pius XI (1922-1939): 62
Pope Saint Caius (283-296): 4
Pope Sixtus V (1521-1590): 13
Popular Movement: 21
Poreć (Parentium): 2
Port Arthur/Lushan (China): 27
Portogruaro (Italy): 172
Portugal (Lusitania): 17, 31, 60
Posavski, Ljudevit: 8, 9
Potocari (Bosnia): 296
Potsdam Conference of 1945 (Germany):
169, 175, 176
Po Valley (Italy): 7
POW: 103-105
Pragmatic Sanction (1712): 17, 23
Prasca, Sebastino Visconti: 82, 83
Prekaja Mountains: 159
Premuda Island: 32
Prevlaka Peninsula (Poluotok): 250, 258
Pribičević, Adam: 38, 63, 66
Pribičević, Svetozar: 45
Princip, Gavrilo (1894-1918): 31
Priština (Kosova): 203, 204, 222
Probus, Rom. Emp. (276-282): 4
Protić, Stojan: 34, 38
Prozor (Bosnia): 254
Prussia/Prussian (Preussen): 19, 56, 104,
169
Pula (Pola/Pietas Julia): 2, 3, 153, 164, 166
Puppet (Quisling) Regimes: 75-76, 106,
142, 231

Q

Qemal, Ishmail (Albanian): 29
Quisling, Abraham Lauritz (1887-1945): 75

R

Rab (Arbe) Island: 8
Račić, Paniša: 46
Rademacher, Franz (1906-1973): 127,
134, 138
Radić, Ante (1868-1919): 25
Radić, Pavle: 44, 46
Radić, Stjepan (1871-1928): 25, 39, 42,
44-46
Ragusa (see Dubrovnik)

Radkersburg: 99
Ranković, Aleksandar: 82, 182, 197
Rape of Nanking (China): 63
Raša River: 3
Ravenna (Italy): 6, 7, 8
Ravna Gora: 112, 132
Ražnjatović, Zeljko "Arkan": 234
Reagan, Ronald Wilson: 199
Rechner, Patrick: 291
Recife (Pernan/Buco): 145
Redman, Charles: 275
Reichsrath (Vienna, Austria): 26, 30
Reichstag: 52
Reims (France): 174
Rendulic, Lothar (1887-1971): 159
Republic of St. Mark (see Venice)
Reynaud, Paul: 75
Rhineland (Germany): 61
Ribar, Ivan Lola: 159
Ribbentrop, Joachim von (1893-1946): 78,
83, 85, 91, 93-94, 97, 99, 109, 116, 119-
120, 122, 127, 131, 135, 138
Ricardi, Arturo: 84
Richthofen, Wolfram von (1895-1945): 99,
109
Ridgway, Andrew: 279
Rijeka/Tarsatica/Trsat/Fiume: 2-3, 17-18,
21-22, 26, 30, 40, 44, 153, 164-166
Rintelen, Emil von: 93, 116, 153
Ritter, Karl (1888-1977): 109, 128
Rizan River: 3
Robotti, Mario: 144
Robert, Karl (Anjou Dynasty): 12
Roman/Rome/Romanization: 2, 4, 9
    Eastern Empire: 5, 6
    Roman Catholics: 63
    Roman Law (Justinian Code): 5
    Roman Missionaries: 8
    Western Empire: 5, 6
Romania/Rumania (Walachians):29, 31,
38, 45-46, 53, 57, 60, 73, 78, 80, 82-83,
85, 91, 101, 127, 161-163, 167, 202, 273,
289
Rommel, Erwin (1891-1944): 152
Roosevelt, Franklin (1882-1945): 69, 73,
75, 91, 120, 127, 139, 143, 147-148, 156
Roosevelt, Theodore (1858-1919): 27
Rose, Michael: 271, 273, 276-277, 279,
280, 282
Royal Council of Austria: 18
Ruby, Jack (1911-1967): 196
Rudolph II, Holy Rom. Emp. (1576-1612):
15, 212
Ruhland (Germany): 161
Ruhr/Ruhrgebiet (Germany)): 42, 44

Ruhrort: 42
Rupnik's "White Guard": 154
Russia (see USSR)
Ruthenia: 66, 68, 298

S

Saarland/Saar (Germany): 60
Šabac: 127
Sabor (see Croatian Assembly)
Šaćirbey (Saćirbegović, Muhamed: 292
Sadova (Sadowa/Königgrä: 22
Saint Mark Church (Zagreb): 15
Saint Peter's Basilica (Rome): 14
Saint Pierre and Miquelon Islands: 140
Saint Simon (Sveti Simun): 201, 215
Sakhalin Island: 169
Salona/Salonae (see Solin)
Salonika (see Greece)
Sandalj (near Pula): 1
Sandžak: 128, 252, 308
San Francisco, CA (USA): 176
Saracens (Islamic nomadis): 9
Sarajevo: 31, 101, 120, 141, 238-242,
259, 261, 267, 270, 279-280, 282, 291,
293, 302
Šarinin, Hrvoje: 264
Sava River: 7
Savska Banovina (Croatia): 48
Scandinavian Peninsula: 76
Schools/Academies/Universities:
  Academy of Science at Zagreb: 15
  Academy of Science and Arts: 22
  School of Philosophy at Zagreb: 15
  University (Sveučiliste) of Zagreb: 16
  University (Sveučiliste) of Zadar: 18
Schwarze Korps (Black Corps): 80
Schwarzkopf, Norman H.: 206
Scodra (Shkoder): 3
Selassie, Haile: 60
Semmering Pass (Austria): 100
Senj (Senia/Zengg): 2
Serbia (Serbija) Serbian/Serbs: 25-33,
60, 123, 126, 128, 134, 142, 166-167, 201-
202, 205-206, 211, 213-215, 221-226, 228-
229, 231, 233-235, 237, 242- 243, 250,
256-259, 267, 269-270, 273, 279, 280,
284, 286-292, 298, 301, 304-305, 308, 310
  Black-Hand (Crna Ruka): 28, 31, 48
  Četnici (Četnik): 26, 29, 45, 57, 112-113,
  117-118, 120, 132, 146-148, 157-
  158, 163, 204, 213, 217, 221, 224, 230,
  233-234, 253, 257, 267, 278
  Chamber of Commerce: 202

Eastern Serb Orthodox: 21, 38, 63
Gendarmes: 45, 50, 57, 66
Karađorđević, Aleksandar I (1888-1934):
44-45, 47, 51, 57
Karađorđević, Pavle: 57, 61, 67, 78, 85-
88
Karađorđević, Petar I (1844-1921): 26
Karađorđević, Petar II (1923-1970): 57,
86, 88, 103, 112, 142, 147, 155, 162
Kingdom of Serbs, Croats, & Slovenes
(1921-1929): 42
Kingdom of Yugoslavia (1929): 48, 51
Law on Voters Lists: 52
League of Communists: 200
National Bank (Beograd): 211
National Parliament: 45-47, 61, 63-64
National Party: 60
Obrenović, Aleksandar I (1889-1903):
25, 26
Obrenović, King Milan (1868-1889): 26,
48
Pan-Slavic Empire: 27
Radical Party: 61, 276
Regency Council: 170
SANU: 63, 200
Serbiangate: 210
Serbobran: 25
Serb Orthodox Bishops: 63
Serboslavia: 27, 32, 39, 45, 213, 215,
230-231, 290, 302, 310
Socialist Party: 202, 203, 211
Socialist Republic of Serbia: 201
Varnara (Serbian Orthodox Patriarch):
63
Vidovdan Constitution: 42, 47
War of Aggression (1991-1995): 211,
217, 225, 231-232, 278, 283, 298,
308, 310
White Hand (Bela Ruka): 28
Zaklati ("Z"), Cutthroat: 253
Zbor Movement: 122
Živković, Petar: 48, 61
Serfdom/Serfs/Slaves: 13, 17, 21
Sernec, Dušan: 170
Sevez, Francois: 174
Seyss-Inquart, Arthur: 76
Shalikashvili, John: 296
Šibenik (Sebenico): 164, 167, 259, 302
Sicilia (Sicily) Island: 150, 151, 153
Sigismund of Hungary (1387-1437): 13
Silajdžić, Haris: 275, 286, 297
Silba Island: 32
Simeon of Bulgaria: 11
Šimić, Petar: 200
Simon, Gauleiter: 76

Šimović, Dušan: 88, 90, 93-94, 97, 101
Sinj: 15
Sirmium/Sremska Mitrovica: 307
Sisak (Sissek/Siscia): 3, 9, 11, 288
Skabrnje (Emergency Airport): 167
Skadar Lake: 92
Skopje (Skoplje): 99, 162, 167
Skorzeny, Otto (1908-1975): 152
Skradin (Scardona): 2, 7, 259
Škrda (Scherda) Island: 32
Škrip (Brač Island): 1
Skrlec, Baron Ivo (Ban): 30
Skutari/Shkoder (Albania): 6
Slatina: 92
Slave (see Serfdom)
Slavić, King Stjepan-Petar (1074-1075): 10
Slavonia/Slavonic: 11, 14, 16-17, 20, 30, 40, 199, 222, 226, 288, 307
Slovakia/Slovaks: 30, 66, 68, 71, 82, 139, 167
Slovenes/Slovenia (Slovenija): 19, 30, 38-39, 44, 52, 54, 101, 109, 126, 144, 148, 152-153, 202, 212, 214, 217-218, 220-221, 228, 232-233, 237-238, 281, 287
  Demos Party: 203
  Home Guards (Domobranci): 173
  League of Communists (SCL): 203
Slunj: 101
Smilčić (near Zadar): 1
Smith, Leighton W. Jr.: 310
Smith, Rupert: 282
Smith, Walter B. (1895-1961): 153, 174
Soddu, Ubaldo: 83
Sofia (Sophia/Sofiya): 99
Solana, Javier Madariaga: 306
Solin (Salona): 2, 3, 6, 7, 201
Šolta (Solta) Island: 32
Sombor: 165
Sonnleithner, Franz: 127
South Africa: 46
South Slav Committee of 1915: 32
Souvignet, Jośe: 306
Soviet Union (See USSR)
Spaatz, Carl: 174
Spain/Spanish (España/Hispania): 4, 17, 60-62, 291, 302
Sphere of Influence: 101
Split (Spalatum/Asphalathos/Spalato): 4, 6, 8, 11, 154, 164, 166, 213, 244, 293, 296, 301-302
Srebrenica (Bosnia): 238, 266-267, 276, 293, 296-298
Sremska Mitrovica (Sirmium/Mitrowitz): 7
Srijem (Syrmia/Srem/Szerém): 17, 22
Stalin, Josip (1879-1953): 56, 61-62, 69,

74, 148, 150, 156, 159, 162, 168-169, 174, 186, 197
Stanković, Radenko: 57, 86
Stanojević, Aca: 67
Starčević, Ante (1823-1896): 23
Starigrad (Dalmatia, Croatia): 15
Stari Trg Mine (Trepca): 203
Star of David: 129
Stepinac, Alojzije Victor (1898-1960): 184, 185, 192, 193
Stjepan I, King (1030-1058): 10
Stjepan II, King (1089-1091): 10, 12
Stobreć: 2
Stojadinović, Milan (1888-1961): 60, 61, 62, 63, 64, 78
Stojadinović, Nikola (1880-1964): 25
Stoltenberg, Thorvald: 269
Strossmayer, Josip Juraj (1815-1905): 21, 22, 23
Struga: 221
Struganik: 132
Stubica: 14
Styria/Steiermark (Austria): 99
Šubašić, Ivan (1892-1955): 71, 162, 166, 168-169
Subić, Pavle (Governor/Ban): 12
Subotica (Maria Theresiopel): 101, 165
Sudenten (Sudety/Sudeten): 66
Suessmann, Wilhelm: 114
Šufflay, Milan: 51
Suleiman (1520-1566): 14
Sumađa: 17
Suribachi Mount: 170
Suroj, Veton: 215
Sušac (Cazza) Island: 32
Susak, Gojko: 288
Sušić, Lovro: 110
Susjedgrad-Donja Subica: 14
Svačić, King Petar (1074-1075): 10
Sv. Andrija (St. Andrew): 32
Sveti Stefan's Church in Zagreb: 16, 22
Svetoslav, King (997-1000): 10
Syracuse (Siracusa): 51
Syria (Ash Shām/Aram): 4, 116
Sztojay, Dome: 87

T

Tadić, Dušan: 273
Tahi, Franjo: 14
Tassigny, Jean de Lattre de: 174
Tedder, Arthur: 174
Tehran (Teheran) Conference: 156
Tenja: 220

Teschen: 66, 139
Těšin/Český Těšin: 66, 139
Teuta (Queen of Illyria): 3
Theodoric, The Great (454-526): 6
Theodosius I, Rom. Emp. (379-395): 5
Thermopylae Pass (Greece): 106
Thornberry, Cedric: 237
Thrace/Thracians: 2, 7, 109
Tibbets, Paul W. Jr.: 177
Tiberius, Rom. Emp. (14-37 AD): 3
Tirana/Tiranë (Albania): 86
Tisza (Theiss/Tisa) River: 92, 101, 165
Tito, Josip Broz (1892-1980): 62, 82, 113, 132, 156, 162, 166-167, 169-171, 174, 176, 178, 192, 197, 199, 215, 228
  Communists/Partisans: 105, 132, 147, 151, 153, 156-159, 163, 174-175, 231, 284
  Tito-Šubašić Agreement: 166, 168-169
Tokyo War Crimes Trial: 182, 183
Tomaševic (King of Bosnia): 13
Tomislav, King (925-928): 10, 11
Train of Freedom (1995): 302
Transleithan (Budapest): 30
Transylvania (Transilvania/Erdély): 40, 80, 139, 163, 165
Travnik (Bosnia): 286
Treaty (see Agreements/Pacts)
Trentino (Italy): 32, 40
Treviso (Italy): 172
Trident (see Int'l. Trident Conference)
Trieste/Triest/Trst (Italy): 8, 17-18, 32, 40, 153, 164, 166, 172, 185
  Zone "A" (Italy): 188
  Zone "B" (Yugoslavia): 188
Trinitrotoluene-TNT: 177
Tripimir, Governor (845-864): 9
Tripimir II, King (928-935): 10
Tripimirović Dynasty: 12
Tripoli (Libya/Libia): 28
Trotski, Leon-Bronstein (1879-1940): 61
Trpanj: 163
Trogir (Trau/Tragurium): 2, 7, 8
Truman, Harry S. (1884-1972): 177
Trumbić, Ante (1864-1938): 32, 34
Trzebinia (Poland): 161
Tudjman, Franjo: 207, 213, 222-223, 228, 232, 242, 269, 275, 279-280, 285, 287, 295, 301, 305, 308
Tudjman, Miroslav: 295
Turkey/Turkish/Ottoman Turks: 13-18, 28-31, 57, 60, 266
Tuzla (Bosnia): 238, 267, 286-287, 291, 293, 296-297, 302
Tvrdalj (Hvar): 13

Tvrtko, Stjepan I (1376-1391): 12
Twardowski, Fritz von: 110
Tyrol (Tirol): 19, 32

U

Udbina: 283
Udine (Italy): 172
Ukraine/Ukrainians: 37, 232, 243, 279, 298
  Kiev: 84
Umag (Humagum): 2
Uniat (Uniyat): 41
Unije (Unie): 32
United Nations: 140, 147, 153, 176, 218, 224-226, 229-230, 234, 237, 240- 241, 244, 278, 283, 292, 295, 304-305
  Commission of Experts: 250, 252, 255, 259-261
  Comm. of Human Rights: 253, 255
  Conference on Yugoslavia (ICF): 236
  ICJ: 263, 264, 266, 270, 275
  Military Tribunal (IMT): 178
    German Defendants: 179, 180
    Japanese Defendants: 182, 183
  Peacekeepers Held Hostage: 291
  SCICY: 251, 257, 260-261, 264-265, 268-269
  Security Council Res. (see Appendix C)
  Special Rapporteur: 247, 252, 255
  UNCRO: 287
  UNICEF: 230, 233
  UNHCR: 230, 233, 235, 247, 253, 261, 264, 269
  UNPA: 235-237, 244, 252, 257-258, 260, 286
  UNPREDEP: 287
  UNPROFOR: 233, 236-238, 241-244, 249-250, 253, 258-262, 265-266, 268-269, 280-282, 286-287, 291-293, 310
  War Crimes Tribunal: 260, 291, 297
  WHO: 230, 233
Universities (See Schools)
Upper Silesia (Oberschlesien): 42
USA/United States: 31, 46, 56, 87, 104, 119, 121, 138, 142, 151, 153, 157- 158, 164, 168-169, 178, 182-183, 199, 232, 237-238, 272, 280, 287, 291, 298, 302
  Aleutian Islands: 143, 144
  Alien Registration Act of 1940: 78
  Civil Liberties Act of 1988: 143
  Civil War (1861-1865): 308
  Continental Congress (1776): 210
  Fourteen Points (Wilson's): 37

General Accounting Office (GAO): 140
Japanese Civilian Internment: 143
Manhattan Project: 144, 175
National Security Agency (NSA): 175
Neutrality Acts: 60, 73, 74, 134
Office of Strategic Services.: 158, 164
Pribilof Islands: 143
United Colonies (1776): 207, 210
U.S. Aircarrier "Theo. Roosevelt": 302
U.S. Assault Ship "Kearsarge": 293
U.S. Destroyer "Greer": 127
U.S. Destroyer "Reuben James": 134
U.S. Merchant "Steel Seafarer": 127
U.S.S. "Missouri" (1955): 177
War of Independence, (1775-1783): 207
War Power Act of 1941: 140
Washington, George (1732-1799): 210
USSR/Russia/Russian: 18-19, 27-28, 31,
37-38, 40, 56, 61-62, 69, 73-75, 78, 85,
101, 139, 142, 148, 160-161, 163, 168,
177-178, 182, 199, 267, 273, 278, 298
Bolsheviks Revolution of 1917: 113
Great Purge/Extermination: 167
Leningrad (See St. Petersburg)
Moscow: 84
Stalingrad (see Volgograd)

V

Val Canale: 126
Val di Gardena: 126
Valens, Rom. Emp. (364-378): 5
Valentić, Nikica: 264
Valentinian I, Rom. Emp. (364-375): 5
Valetta (Malta): 155
Valjevo: 116, 142
Valona/Vlorë (Albania): 29
Vance, Cyrus Robert: 226, 233-234, 238,
251, 258, 269
Varaždin (Warasdin/Varasd): 82, 92
Vardar (Axius/Vardares) River: 2
Vasiljević, Dušan: 34
Vatican (Vatican City): 63
Veesenmayer, Edmund: 93, 94, 96, 127
Velebit Mount: 15
Velika Kladusa (Bosnia): 280
Velika Plana: 163
Veliko Grašće (Brač Island): 1
Venezia Giulia (a.k.a. Istria): 174
Venezuela: 195, 267
Venice/Venetians (Republic of Venice): 6,
9-10, 12, 14-19, 172
Venizelos, Eleutherios (1868-1923): 32
Verudic (near Pula): 1

Veternica (near Zagreb): 1
Vichy French Government.: 77, 129
Vilnius (Lithuania): 68, 139
Vinkovci (Cibalae): 3, 167, 222-223, 228
Vinnitsa (Ukraine): 147
Višegrad: 141
Vis (Issa/Lissa) : 2, 18-19, 22, 32, 157,
159, 162
Višeslav (800-810): 9
Visigoths: 5, 6
Vistula River: 7
V-J Day (Victory over Japan): 177
Vlašić Mount: 286, 287
Vlorë (Valona/Aulon): 8
Vodice: 259
Vojna Kranjina: (see Kranjina)
Vojvodina: 16, 201, 204, 222, 252, 308
Volgograd (Stalingrad): 146, 148
Volksdeutsche (see Germany)
Vólos (Greece): 83
Vosnjak, Bogumil: 34
Vraniczany, Baron Ambrose: 22
Vrboska: 101
Vrgorac: 15
Vrlika: 15
Vukotić, Queen Milena: 118
Vukovar: 167, 222-224, 228-229, 252,
256, 261

W

Wagram (near Vienna): 19
Wahlgren, Lars-Eric: 237
Wake Island (Pacific Ocean): 137, 140
Walachians: 109
Walesa, Lech: 150
Wannsee (Germany): 141
Wars:
April War (1941):
Austro-Prussian War of 1866: 22
Austro-Turkish War (1716-1718): 17
Cretan War (1645-1665): 15
First Balkan War (1912-1913): 28
First World War (1914-1918): 30
German-Russian War (1941-1945): 116
Patriotic War of Croatia (1991-1995):
311
Persian Gulf: 206
Russo-Japanese War (1904-5): 27, 52
Russo-Turkish War (1877-1878): 23
Second Balkan War of 1913: 29
Second World War (1939-1945): 290
Casualties (Killed): 290
Serbian War of Aggression (1991-1995):

210-310
Sino-Japanese War (1937-1945): 63
Third Balkan War of 1914: 31
Tripolitan War (1911-1912): 28
Warlimont, Walter: 109
Warsaw/Warszawa (Poland): 255
Waterloo, Belgium (1815): 19
Webb, William: 182
Wedemeyer, Albert C.: 176
Weichs, Maximilian von (1881-1954): 100-101, 103, 151-152, 159, 165-166
Weizsäcker, Ernst von (1882-1951): 74, 78, 91, 118, 134
Welles, Sumner: 147
Western European Union (WEU): 222, 255, 282
Western Roman Empire: 6, 11
Weygand Line: 77
White Croatia/Bijela Hrvatska: 7
Wiener Neustadt (Austria): 16, 97, 100, 171
Wijnaendts, Henri: 223
Wilson, Maitland Henry: 103, 161, 164-166
Wilson, Woodrow T. (1856-1924): 34, 40
Woermann, Ernst: 107
Wörner, Manfred: 266
Wright-Patterson AFB, Dayton: 305

Y

Yalta Conference of 1945: 168
Yeltsin, Boris: 278
Yoshijiro, Umezu: 177
Yugoslav/Yugoslavia/Jugoslavija: 52, 54-55, 57, 60, 62, 82, 84, 93, 97, 99, 104, 146, 151, 153, 166, 174-175, 188, 218, 226, 230, 237-238, 248, 251, 281
   Agreement (Sporazum) of 1939: 71
   AVNOJ/ACNLY: 170, 177
   Axis Powers: 82, 85-87, 93, 94, 99, 104, 139-140, 149
   Central Committee of the CPY: 82, 116, 146, 200, 202
   Central Comm. of Nat'l. Liberation: 171
   Cominform: 185, 186
   Comintern: 116, 185
   Communist Party (CPY): 82, 116, 170, 198
   Constituent Assembly: 180
   Crown Council: 86, 87
   Federal Democratic Yugoslavia: 170, 176
   FPRY/FNRJ: 180, 183
   FRY/FRJ: 235, 238, 240, 243, 245, 252, 267-268, 271, 280, 304
   Killed during Second World War: 290
   League of Communists of Yugoslavia (LCY): 202-203, 205
   National Liberation Army (NLA): 146, 156, 162
   National Liberation Committee: 169, 171
   National Liberation Front: 178, 180
   OZN-a: 158, 169, 186
   SAWPY: 198
   SDB: 197
   SFRY/SFRJ: 168, 196, 198, 202-204, 212, 220, 238, 250, 272
   UDB-a: 186, 197
   Uzice/Uice: 132
Yugoslav Airlines (JAT): 239
Yugoslav Armed Forces: 92, 101
Yugoslav Falcon: 50
Yugoslav Gov't.-in-Exile: 146
Yugoslav National Bank: 111
Yugoslav National Party: 61
Yugoslav People's Army (YPA): 200, 204-205, 207, 211, 213-215, 217-218, 220-226, 228-229, 231-233, 237, 241, 252, 270, 291, 308
Yugoslav Politburo: 146
Yugoslav Radical Union: 66

Z

Zacharia/Zaharija: 11
Zadar(Zara/Jadera/Iadera): 2, 7-8, 12, 14, 18, 21, 26, 155, 164, 166-167, 201, 224, 226, 228, 257, 259, 270, 302
Zagorje: 14
Zagreb (Agram): 12, 15, 24, 100, 220, 224, 238, 245, 261, 288, 301
Zdeslav (Gov. of Dalmatia (878-879): 10
Zemun (Serbija): 138
Zemunik: 14, 257
Zepa: 238, 293
Zhukov, Gregori K.: 174
Zimbabwe: 250
Zimmermann, Warren: 214, 238-239, 249
Zmajevic, Vinko: 17
Zog, Ahmed Bey: 68
Zrinski, Petar (1621-1671): 16
Zrmanja River: 15
Zubak, Kresimir: 275, 279, 286
Županije: 7
Zvonimir, King Dmitar (1075-1089): 10, 11, 201
Zvornik (Bosnia): 33, 307
Zyklon "B" Gas: 141

A MOTTO FOR OUR READERS:

"TO ENSURE PEACE, TOIL FOR JUSTICE"

SIMON VLADOVICH
Author/Publisher

"CROATIA: THE MAKING OF A NATION"

This exclusive edition belongs in the library of:

MCMXCV

341